LAB WORKBOOK

Fourth Edition

MOTORCYCLES
FUNDAMENTALS, SERVICE, REPAIR

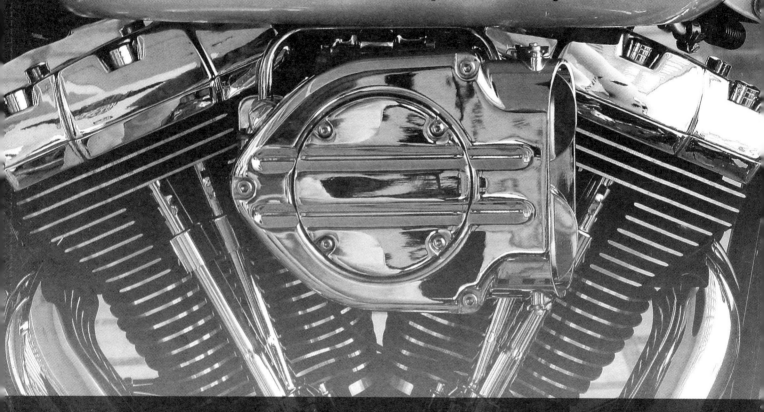

by
Matt Spitzer

Publisher
The Goodheart-Willcox Company, Inc.
Tinley Park, IL
www.g-w.com

Introduction

The *Lab Workbook for Motorcycles: Fundamentals, Service, Repair* is designed to be used with the *Motorcycles: Fundamentals, Service, Repair* textbook. The chapter quizzes and jobs in this lab workbook will help you master the subject matter presented in the text. The quizzes will help you remember important ideas and concepts, while the jobs will help you improve your hands-on service and repair techniques.

Each chapter in this lab workbook corresponds to a textbook chapter. After studying a chapter in the textbook, answer as many quiz questions as possible in the corresponding lab workbook chapter without looking at the textbook. Then, complete the remaining quiz questions by referring to the section of the textbook chapter where the topic is discussed. Finally, complete the jobs for the chapter you are studying. This will allow you to apply the information learned in the chapter.

After studying each chapter in the *Motorcycles: Fundamentals, Service, Repair* textbook and successfully completing the corresponding lab workbook quizzes and jobs, you will have developed a solid background in motorcycle service and repair. Further expertise can be gained through additional hands-on experience and by keeping current with trends and new technologies in the motorcycles field.

Table of Contents

Chapter 8

Engines

Chapter 9

Fuel Systems

Chapter 10

Ignition Systems

Chapter 11

Lubrication Systems

Chapter 12

Cooling Systems

Chapter 13

Exhaust Systems and Emissions Control

Chapter 14

Battery and Charging Systems

Chapter 15

Electrical Accessory Systems

CHAPTER 1

Introduction to Motorcycles, ATVs, UTVs, and Scooters

Chapter 1 Quiz

After studying Chapter 1 in the Motorcycles: Fundamentals, Service, Repair textbook, answer the following questions.

_____ 1. The chassis of a powersports vehicle includes the frame and _____ parts.

_____ 2. *True or False?* Regularly updating knowledge and skills is important for a qualified technician.

_____ 3. When additional work is required or recommended, the technician should advise the _____ or customer.

_____ 4. The owner of a motorcycle dealership signs a contract with a(n) _____ to sell and service a particular line of motorcycles.

_____ 5. *True or False?* Independent service shops employ a maximum of four people.

_____ 6. *True or False?* Vehicle manufacturers hire technicians to do a variety of jobs.

_____ 7. In most dealerships, a _____ greets customers.
    A. technician
    B. parts manager
    C. service manager
    D. service writer

_____ 8. Customer complaints are usually handled by the _____.
    A. parts manager
    B. service manager
    C. service advisor
    D. most experienced technician

For questions 9–15, match each type of vehicle with its description.

A. Scooter
B. Touring motorcycle
C. Trike

D. Motocross
E. ATV

F. Cruiser
G. Dirt bike

_____ 9. Street motorcycle with wide, low to the ground seats, big tanks, and wide tires.

_____ 10. Off-road motorcycle used for a competitive sport.

_____ 11. Street vehicle used for long-range travel.

_____ 12. Off-road machine useful for hunting, farming, and working.

_____ 13. Two-wheeled vehicle with a small displacement motor and limited speeds.

_____ 14. Light, powerful, rugged off-road motorcycle used for recreational riding.

_____ 15. Three-wheeled street motorcycle.

Name _____ Date _____ Class _____

Job 1-1

Interviewing an Industry Professional

Introduction

Making friends and contacts in any industry is important, as well as taking advice from positive people. This exercise is meant to get you, the student, out into the industry, looking at the stores and shops, meeting the people, and forming your own opinions about opportunities available in the industry.

Objective

After successful completion of this lab, the student will be able to share information about a position in the powersports industry with the class in either a written or oral presentation.

Materials and Equipment

To complete this job, you will need the following tools, equipment, and materials:

* This questionnaire
* Appropriate dress

Instructions

In this job, you will be setting up an appointment with a professional in the powersports industry. This person could be a mechanic, sales employee, manager, parts employee, machinist, corporate representative, or owner. They just need to be making their primary living from the powersports industry. Make an appointment in person but be prepared to conduct the interview immediately if the person to be interviewed is available. Present yourself with a good handshake, speak clearly, and make eye contact.

   Make sure to thank the interviewee for their time, obtain a business card, and send a thank you note or stop by to say thank you in person. This is good practice and will help you develop the courtesy needed when interacting with customers and fellow workers.

Business:

_____

Business Description:

_____

Date of Interview:

_____

Person Interviewed:

_____

Position:

_____

Interview Questions

Ask the interviewee the following questions.

1. How long have you worked in the powersports industry?

   _____

2. Where did you get your training in order to get into the industry?

   _____

   _____

   _____

3. Would you recommend to another person that they take the same path?

   _____

   _____

4. Would you do anything different now that you have experience?

   _____

   _____

5. What was your first job in the powersports industry?

   _____

   _____

6. What type of job would you expect someone without any training to be able to do in the powersports industry?

   _____

   _____

7. What type of job would someone who graduates from a two-year training program be able to obtain in the powersports industry?

   _____

   _____

8. What is the most important skill that someone can bring to your particular store or shop as an employee?

   _____

   _____

9. What do you like best about your job?

   _____

   _____

10. Would you recommend the powersports industry as a career?

   _____

   _____

Name _____

11. Do you have any questions for me, such as my course of study?

   _____

   _____

   _____

   _____

   _____

12. May I have one of your business cards?

   Card supplied _____ Card not supplied _____

> **NOTE** At the end of the interview, be sure to thank the person you are interviewing.

Final Assessment

1. What was the reaction of the workplace personnel when you introduced yourself and explained your purpose?

   _____

2. Was the person you interviewed interested in answering your questions?

   Yes _____ No _____ Explain:

   _____

   _____

3. Was this a positive experience for you?

   Yes _____ No _____ Why?

   _____

   _____

Final Instructor Approval: _____

Notes

CHAPTER 2 — Shop Safety and Environmental Protection

Chapter 2 Quiz

After studying Chapter 2 in the Motorcycles: Fundamentals, Service, Repair textbook, answer the following questions.

_____ 1. *True or False?* A technician's priority should be to work as quickly as possible.

_____ 2. *True or False?* Technicians should wear a watch at all times in order to track the amount of time taken to make repairs.

_____ 3. Which of the following should be worn for air filter oiling and oil draining?
  A. rubber disposable gloves
  B. thick insulated gloves
  C. leather gloves
  D. chemical-resistant gloves

_____ 4. All of the following statements are true, *except*:
  A. Fuel vapors are airborne contaminants.
  B. Hearing loss can occur gradually over a period of years.
  C. Prescription eyeglasses are shatterproof.
  D. Insulated gloves should be worn when working with exhaust pipes.

_____ 5. A helmet that is _____-approved should be worn when test riding.
  A. OSHA
  B. ASME
  C. EPA
  D. DOT

_____ 6. *True or False?* Keeping the shop organized promotes safety.

_____ 7. In the shop, a cleanup time should be set aside _____.
  A. at the end of each day
  B. at the beginning of each day
  C. at the end of each week
  D. three times per day

_____ 8. *True or False?* Oil-soaked rags should be placed on the floor in a far corner of the shop.

_____ 9. Devices for measuring engine power are called _____, or dynos.

_____ 10. *True or False?* A helmet is recommended PPE for doing a dyno test run.

_____ 11. *True or False?* When lifting a heavy motorcycle assembly, you should let your back do most of the work.

_____ 12. All of the following are good work habits, *except*:
A. When mounting an engine on a stand, work with another person.
B. A small hydraulic jack and a block of wood can be used to raise the chassis.
C. Discard and replace broken tools.
D. Open all tool chest drawers at once to do a thorough search for the right tool.

For questions 13–16, match the following fire types with their combustible materials.

A. Class A
B. Class B

C. Class C
D. Class D

_____ 13. Metal fragments and shavings.

_____ 14. Paper, wood, cloth, or trash.

_____ 15. Live electrical equipment.

_____ 16. Gasoline, oil, grease, or solvent.

_____ 17. Any fire extinguisher that has been used should be _____ immediately.
A. replaced
B. recharged
C. inspected
D. cleaned

_____ 18. *True or False?* When using a carbon dioxide extinguisher, you should start at the edge of the flames and gradually move forward and upward.

_____ 19. In the PASS acronym for fire extinguisher training, the P stands for _____.
A. pull
B. point
C. pressurize
D. None of the above.

_____ 20. Motorcycle shops should practice the three *R*s to protect the environment. The three *R*s are _____.
A. report, repair, and return
B. repair, reuse, and recycle
C. recover, repair, and recycle
D. regulate, repair, and recover

Name _____

_____ 21. Sheets that provide product composition and precautionary information for products that could present a health or safety hazard are called _____ sheets.
 A. chemical hazard
 B. safety data
 C. hazard information
 D. safety precaution

_____ 22. *True or False?* On a label, if the signal word *Warning* applies to one hazard and *Danger* applies to another, only *Warning* will appear on the label.

_____ 23. *True or False?* Many small parts washers use solvents that are considered hazardous materials.

_____ 24. *True or False?* Gloves are required when working with epoxies.

_____ 25. Hazardous waste to be disposed of must be handled according to _____ guidelines.
 A. DOT
 B. OSHA
 C. the supervisor's
 D. local

_____ 26. Right-to-Know laws are designed to protect _____.
 A. customers
 B. shop visitors
 C. shop owners
 D. employees

Notes

Name _____ Date _____ Class _____

Job 2-1

Creating a Shop Map

Introduction

Safety is the most important aspect of working in a shop. Being aware of your surroundings, understanding where tools and equipment are supposed to go, and knowing when these items are out of place are important aspects of shop safety. To help familiarize you with your new surroundings, you will be creating a shop map.

Objective

After successfully completing this job sheet, you will identify the location of all safety equipment and put those items on a map.

Materials and Equipment

To complete this job sheet, you will need the following tools, equipment, and materials:

- This job sheet
- Blank sheet of paper
- Access to the shop, classroom, and outside work areas

Instructions

On a separate sheet of paper, you will draw the outline of the shop, classroom, tool rooms, outside work areas, restrooms, and locker areas. You will then place abbreviations on the shop map according to the provided list. Have your instructor sign off when you have completed the task.

Procedures

1. Draw the map, include the following:
   a. Outline of shop area with work tables
   b. Outline of classroom
   c. Instructor office
   d. Restrooms and locker area if applicable
   e. Outside work areas with load/unload areas, storage areas, test tanks, or other features.

2. Locate and label the items in the following chart on the map. If there are more than one of a specific item on the map, label each item.

Item	Label to Be Put on Map
Exits	EXIT
Fire Escape Plan	ESC
Fire Extinguishers	FE
Pull Fire Alarm	FA
Emergency STOP Button/Pull	STOP
Eye Wash Station	EYE
First Aid Kit	AID
Flammable Material Cabinet	FLAM
Spill Cleanup Kit	SPILL
Safety Data Sheets	SDS
Hazardous Waste Disposal	HAZ
Scrap Metal Waste	MET
Dumpster	DUMP
Mop and Brooms	MOP
Compressor	COMP
Bathrooms	BATH
Lockers	LOCK
Fan or Exhaust Fan Switch	EXH
Ramps	RAMP
Hose	H_2O

Instructor Demonstration Signature: _____

Final Assessment

1. List the classes and locations of the fire extinguishers found in your shop.

   _____

   _____

   _____

2. Where is the gathering place in case of an evacuation?

   _____

3. Where is the Safety Data Sheet (SDS) for gasoline located in the shop?

   _____

4. Did you find any missing or damaged equipment that your instructor needs to know about?

   Yes _____ No _____ If Yes, explain.

   _____

   _____

Final Instructor Approval: _____

Name _____ Date _____ Class _____

Job 2-2

Understanding a Safety Data Sheet (SDS)

Introduction
Safety Data Sheets (SDS) are an important and integral part of your 'Right to Know' and indicate how to handle chemicals that you come in contact with in a shop environment.

Objective
After successfully completing this job sheet, you will be able to find needed and necessary information on SDS.

Materials and Equipment
To complete this job sheet, you will need the following tools, equipment, and materials:
- SDS binder

Instructions
In this job, you will find the SDS binder in your shop and locate information contained on the SDS sheets.

Procedures

1. Locate the SDS binder in your shop. Where is the SDS binder located?

   _____

2. How many tabs does the SDS binder have?

   _____

3. Find the SDS for brake fluid and fill in the following chart with the names of the 16 sections of the SDS:

> **NOTE**   Your instructor may provide you with an alternate SDS.
> If so, place the name of the substitute SDS here:
>
> _____

Number	Section Name
1	
2	
3	
4	
5	
6	
7	
8	

Continued

Number	Section Name
9	
10	
11	
12	
13	
14	
15	
16	

4. Find the SDS for gasoline. How many pages is the gasoline SDS?

_____

5. Which section of the gasoline SDS has instructions on what to do in case of skin contact?

_____

6. What is the SDS recommendation for eye contact with gasoline?

_____

_____

7. What SDS section gives you instructions on what to do in case of a fire?

_____

8. What type of fire extinguisher is unsuitable for a gasoline fire?

_____

9. What SDS section gives you information for disposal of gasoline?

_____

10. What is the general SDS recommendation for disposal of gasoline?

_____

11. What SDS section has the emergency telephone number of the chemical manufacturer?

_____

12. Give two instances when you would use an SDS.

_____

_____

13. Which SDS section has recommended uses for the product?

_____

14. If you do not have an SDS for a certain product in your shop, how can you obtain an SDS?

_____

_____

Final Instructor Approval: _____

CHAPTER 3

Tools and Shop Equipment

Chapter 3 Quiz

After studying Chapter 3 in the Motorcycles: Fundamentals, Service, Repair textbook, answer the following questions.

_____ 1. *True or False?* A manufacturer will fix or replace a broken tool at no cost if it is under warranty.

_____ 2. The three main parts to a typical tool box are the _____, the large roll-around cabinet, and the small carrying tray or tote.

_____ 3. Professional technicians will clean and put away their tools _____.
   A. once an hour
   B. after every job
   C. each day
   D. at the end of each week

_____ 4. Although this tool is the least desirable and is a fill-in tool, most technicians have a(n) _____ wrench in their tool box.
   A. open end wrench
   B. box end wrench
   C. adjustable wrench
   D. Allen wrench

_____ 5. Hex socket head screws are loosened and tightened with a(n) _____.
   A. Allen wrench
   B. adjustable wrench
   C. open-end wrench
   D. flare-nut wrench

_____ 6. *True or False?* An 11 mm wrench can be substituted for a 7/16″ wrench.

_____ 7. *True or False?* Whenever possible, a box-end wrench should be used rather than an open-end wrench.

_____ 8. The two general types of screwdriver most commonly used are _____ and _____.
   A. straight tip, Allen
   B. Phillips, Torx
   C. Torx, Allen
   D. straight tip, Phillips

_____   9. Which of the following tools provides the high torque and inward bit pressure that may be needed to loosen Phillips and other fasteners?
   A. Breaker bar.
   B. Phillips screwdriver.
   C. Impact driver.
   D. None of the above.

_____ 10. *True or False?* Torque is a twisting or turning force.

_____ 11. *True or False?* A 12-point socket is preferable to a 6-point socket because there is less chance of rounding off the fastener head.

_____ 12. Technicians use a variety of socket drivers. Which one is most commonly used?
   A. Ratchet.
   B. T-handle.
   C. Breaker bar.
   D. Speed handle

_____ 13. Which of the following would a technician use for loosening extremely tight fasteners?
   A. Ratchet.
   B. T-handle.
   C. Speed handle.
   D. Breaker bar.

_____ 14. A(n) _____ increases the distance between the drive tool and the socket.
   A. adapter
   B. extension
   C. socket
   D. torque multiplier

_____ 15. Which type of pliers has fine tips and should be used without a twisting action?
   A. Side cutters.
   B. Locking pliers.
   C. Needle-nose pliers.
   D. Slip joint pliers.

Name _____

16. Identify the types of hammers shown in the following illustration.

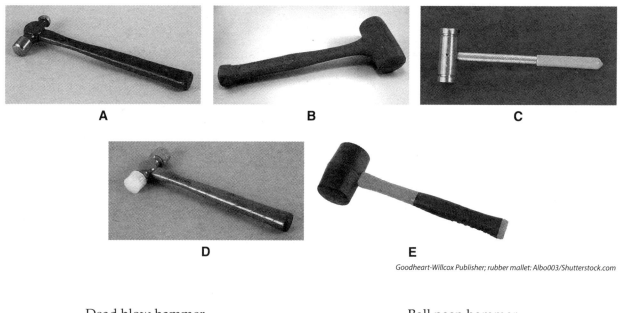

A   **B**   **C**

D   **E**

Goodheart-Willcox Publisher; rubber mallet: Albo003/Shutterstock.com

_____   Dead blow hammer   _____   Ball peen hammer

_____   Brass hammer   _____   Plastic hammer

_____   Rubber mallet

_____ 17. The _____ hammer is used for general-purpose hammering and striking.

_____ 18. *True or False?* To produce extra force, a hammer should be struck with another hammer.

_____ 19. All of the following statements about files are true, *except*:
   A. light pressure should be applied on the forward stroke.
   B. small file teeth are for soft materials.
   C. you should cut away from yourself.
   D. worn files should be replaced.

_____ 20. When repairing a chisel, use a chisel _____ to achieve proper angle and shape.

_____ 21. A(n) _____ is used to drive shafts and bolts out of parts.
   A. center punch
   B. alignment punch
   C. drift punch
   D. chisel

_____ 22. *True or False?* In order to use a hacksaw properly, the technician should release downward pressure on the backstroke.

_____ 23. *True or False?* The best tool to use for starting a bolt or nut is an impact tool.

_____ 24. *True or False?* Hand sockets should be used with an air wrench.

_____ 25. Which of the following should never be used for cleaning parts and tools?
A. Citrus-based cleaners.
B. Kerosene.
C. Solvents.
D. Degreasers.

_____ 26. When using a decarbonizing solvent, the technician should do all of the following, *except*:
A. soak the parts in the solvent for 15–30 minutes.
B. use protective gloves and safety glasses.
C. ensure that all plastic parts are soaked in the solvent.
D. rinse the parts in water after soaking them in the solvent.

_____ 27. *True or False?* A dry-blast cleaner is handy for cleaning difficult to reach areas.

_____ 28. When grinding small parts, the technician should hold small parts with _____ to prevent hand injuries.

_____ 29. In engine rebuilding, a hydraulic _____ is used for assembling and disassembling press-fit components.

_____ 30. What type of welding is becoming the preferred method in the motorcycle industry?
A. MIG.
B. TIG.
C. Arc welding.
D. Oxyacetylene welding.

_____ 31. How does brazing differ from oxyacetylene welding?
A. It uses an inert shielding gas.
B. It uses an electric arc.
C. It uses a filler rod that melts more slowly.
D. It uses less heat.

_____ 32. A _____ is used to machine worn engine cylinders to a larger diameter.
A. boring bar
B. lathe
C. vertical mill
D. hydraulic press

Name _____ Date _____ Class _____

Job 3-1

Tools and Shop Equipment

Introduction

Knowing which tool is the right tool for the job is the basis for being a good motorcycle technician. There are always several choices, but there is one correct choice that the professional makes, like using the box end of a wrench whenever possible. There are new tool inventions all the time, so be aware of the tools available to you and check out the tool truck. There are always new, more efficient ways to get the job done.

Objective

After successfully completing this job sheet, the student will recognize tools that are available to them in the shop.

Materials and Equipment

To complete this job sheet, you will need the following tools, equipment, and materials:

- Textbook
- Tool set
- Toolroom

Instructions

Follow the individual instructions in the job. When you reach a (STOP) sign, show your work to your instructor. Do not continue until you have instructor approval (instructor will initial job sheet).

Procedures

Answer the following questions and perform the following tasks. Use your textbook to answer the following questions.

1. Name the four wrenches shown in **Figure 3-1.1.**

   A. _____

   B. _____

   C. _____

   D. _____

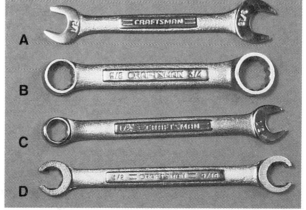

Goodheart-Willcox Publisher

_____   2. Which of the following wrench types is best for holding?

   A. Open end.

   B. Box end.

   C. Combination wrench.

   D. Flare nut wrench.

_____   3. Which of the following wrench types is best for turning?

   A. Open end.

   B. Box end.

   C. Combination wrench.

   D. Flare nut wrench.

_____   4. Which of the following wrench types is used for brake and fuel lines?

   A. Open end.

   B. Box end.

   C. Combination wrench.

   D. Flare nut wrench.

5. What are the two types of screwdrivers shown in **Figure 3-1.2**?

Goodheart-Willcox Publisher   *Goodheart-Willcox Publisher*

   A. _____

   B. _____

6. What tool does the following illustration show in **Figure 3-1.3**?

Goodheart-Willcox Publisher

_____

7. Would the tool identified in question 6 be used before or after using a regular screwdriver?

_____

8. Use the Internet to research JIS (Japanese Industrial Standard) screwdrivers.

9. Gather all the Phillips screwdrivers you have in your toolbox. Prepare to identify which are #1, #2, and #3 screwdrivers. Look at the tip ends to see which is closest to a JIS.

10. Procure an impact screwdriver and look up instructions for using it on the Internet. It is important to know how it works before you use it.

STOP 11. Demonstrate impact screwdriver use and show your instructor your screwdrivers.

Instructor's Initials: _____

Name _____

12. What types of pliers do you have in your toolbox?

_____

_____

13. What types of hammers do you have in your toolbox?

_____

_____

14. What types of punches and chisels do you have in your toolbox?

_____

_____

15. Clean and lubricate your vise, clean your air hose, and clean out any drain pans that you have.

🛑 16. Show your instructor that you have performed the tasks in step 15.

Instructor's Initials: _____

17. Which direction should a hacksaw blade cut?

_____

18. What types of brushes and scrapers do you have in your toolbox?

_____

_____

19. For what situation would you use a plastic parts brush?

_____

_____

20. Find the solvent tank in your shop. Read the instructions and locate the on/off button. Turn the solvent tank on. Does the solvent look dark and need changing?

_____

21. Find the ultrasonic cleaning tank in your shop. Read the instructions. Does your tank also have a heating element?

_____

22. Find the grinder in your shop.

Does it also have a wire wheel attachment? _____

Are the guards installed properly? _____

Are the guards the proper distance from the stone and the wire wheel? _____

Is the grinding stone straight? _____

23. While wearing the proper eye protection, turn the grinder on, and then turn the grinder off.

24. Find the press in your shop. Operate the press and release the pressure. Do not attempt to press anything. Find the operational controls.

25. Do you have welding equipment in your shop? _____
    If so, what kind of welder is in your shop?

    _____

    Is there a designated area for welding in your shop?

    _____

26. Where in your shop do you get gloves?

    _____

27. Where is a face shield kept in your shop?

    _____

28. What is the procedure for checking out special tools in your shop?

    _____

29. Is there a designated location to return tools in your shop?

    _____

(STOP) 30. Have your instructor look over your answers. Ask your instructor any questions you may have about checking out tools and returning tools.

Instructor's Initials: _____

Final Assessment

1. What is the procedure for replacing damaged tools in your shop?

    _____

    _____

2. What is the procedure for using consumable supplies in your shop?

    _____

    _____

3. Why are air-driven impact tools rarely used in motorcycle shops?

    _____

    _____

    _____

4. What are two advantages of modern cordless impact tools over air impact tools?

    _____

    _____

5. Why is a dial torque wrench preferred to a click-type wrench for low torque values?

    _____

    _____

Final Instructor Approval: _____

CHAPTER 4

Measurement and Measuring Tools

Chapter 4 Quiz

After studying Chapter 4 in the Motorcycles: Fundamentals, Service, Repair textbook, answer the following questions.

_____ 1. The measurement system used in the United States is called the _____.
A. International System of Units
B. SI system
C. US customary system
D. US metric system

_____ 2. In the metric system, the _____ is the standard unit of length.

_____ 3. In a decimal system such as the metric system, units can be converted by _____.
A. multiplying or dividing by multiples of 2
B. multiplying or dividing by multiples of 10
C. adding or subtracting multiples of 10
D. using random number indexes

_____ 4. A steel _____ is commonly used to verify chain adjustment.
A. yardstick
B. caliper
C. tape measure
D. None of the above.

_____ 5. *True or False?* A six-inch scale can be used as a straightedge.

For questions 6–14, identify the parts of the dial caliper indicated in the following illustration.

_____ 6. Depth gauge

_____ 7. Roll knob

_____ 8. Inside jaws

_____ 9. Lock screw

_____ 10. Body

_____ 11. Outside jaws

_____ 12. Dial lock

_____ 13. Bar scale

_____ 14. Dial scale

Goodheart-Willcox Publisher

_____ 15. *True or False?* On a conventional micrometer, the sleeve scale is marked off in increments of .025".

_____ 16. The first step in reading an outside micrometer is to _____.
   A. adjust the ratchet stop
   B. take the sleeve reading
   C. take the thimble edge reading
   D. count the thimble marks past the sleeve reference line

_____ 17. Which of the following instruments is commonly used to measure pistons, crank journals, valve shims, and valve stems?
   A. Inside micrometer.
   B. Vernier caliper.
   C. Outside micrometer.
   D. Digital caliper.

_____ 18. A telescoping gauge is used to measure _____.
   A. small clearances between parts
   B. the depth of a hole in a part
   C. a component's linear movement
   D. inside diameters

_____ 19. A dial bore gauge is a combination _____ and telescoping gauge.

_____ 20. Which of the following tools is commonly used in setting valve lash?
   A. Feeler gauge.
   B. Caliper.
   C. Wire gauge.
   D. Inside micrometer.

_____ 21. To make accurate throttle synchronization adjustments, _____ gauges are connected to intake ports.
   A. pressure
   B. vacuum
   C. feeler
   D. temperature

_____ 22. Liquid volume in cubic centimeters or millimeters is measured in a(n) _____ cylinder.

_____ 23. *True or False?* Precision measuring instruments should be cleaned with an air hose only.

_____ 24. A technician can check the accuracy of a micrometer by using a precisely machined block called a(n) _____.

Name _____ Date _____ Class _____

Job 4-1

Measurement and Measuring Tools

Introduction

Being able to measure accurately is an extremely important skill for a motorcycle technician to master. The difference between repairing an engine properly and having to redo a job can hinge on measuring and reading the measuring equipment. There are everyday measurements, like brake disc and pad thickness, valve adjustments, and cable free play. There are also very precise measurements, like clearances on the crankshaft of an engine. All of these measurements play an important role in making the correct fix the first time.

Objective

After successfully completing this job sheet, the student will be able to choose the correct measuring tool and use it.

Materials and Equipment

To complete this job sheet, you will need the following tools, equipment, and materials:

- Micrometer
- Dial indicator
- Dial caliper
- Pocket scale
- Ruler, yardstick, or tape measure

Instructions

Follow the individual instructions in the job. When you reach a (STOP) sign, show your work to your instructor. Do not continue until you have instructor approval (your instructor will initial job sheet).

Procedures

1. Use the appropriate service information to find the specification for chain stretching. Make the measurement on a motorcycle in your shop.

   Motorcycle make/model

   _____

   _____ Specification length for number of pins

   _____ Actual measurement

   _____ Tool used for measuring

2. Find the specification for clutch lever free play. Measure the free play using a motorcycle with a clutch cable adjustment.

   Motorcycle make/model

   _____

   _____ Specification distance for clutch lever free play

   _____ Actual measurement

   _____ Tool used for measuring

3. Using the dial caliper and a shim kit, measure the shims to make sure they match the size stamped on them. If there is no size stamped on them, write down the size. Your instructor will check your work.

   > **NOTE** Some shims are just slightly off, so it is always a good idea to measure them.

STOP 4. Have your instructor check your work on the shims, and the sizes of any shims that were not stamped or easily readable.

Instructor's Initials: _____

5. Review information on how to use a micrometer (pages 54–55 of the *Motorcycles: Fundamentals, Service, Repair* textbook). Then, use the micrometer to measure brake disc thickness. The brake rotor minimum thickness is usually stamped on the rotor. You will sometimes see the letters "MIN THK." If the rotor is not stamped, you will need to look up the minimum thickness for the brake rotor you are measuring.

   Motorcycle make/model

   _____

   _____ Rotor measuring

   _____ Minimum thickness specification

   _____ Actual measurement

   _____ Tool used for measuring

6. Fill in the following chart.

Tool	Location in Shop	Used to Measure
Bore gauge		
Leak-down tester		
Compression tester		
Vacuum gauges		
Fuel pressure tester		
Graduated cylinders		

7. Find the feeler gauges in your toolbox.

8. What is the lowest (thinnest) feeler gauge that you have?

   _____

Name _____

    9. Do you have bent feeler gauges?

_____

  10. What is the lowest (thinnest) bent feeler gauge that you have?

_____

  11. Do you have go/no go feeler gauges?

_____

(STOP) 12. Have your instructor demonstrate what feeler gauges should feel like at proper clearance.

Instructor's Initials: _____

Final Assessment

  1. Why is a micrometer a better tool for measuring brake rotors than a dial caliper?

_____

_____

  2. What tool is used to measure a telescoping gauge once the distance has been set on the gauge?

_____

  3. Why are some feeler gauges made of brass?

_____

_____

  4. What is the advantage of a liquid-filled air pressure gauge?

_____

_____

  5. How many liters is 678 cubic centimeters?

_____

Final Instructor Approval: _____

Notes

CHAPTER 5

Fasteners, Gaskets, Seals, and Sealers

Chapter 5 Quiz

After studying Chapter 5 in the Motorcycles: Fundamentals, Service, Repair textbook, answer the following questions.

_____ 1. Bolts, screws, and _____ are the most common types of threaded fasteners.

_____ 2. The thread pitch of USC bolts is the _____.
   A. distance from the bottom of the threads on one side to the bottom of the other
   B. number of threads in one inch of threaded bolt length
   C. distance between two adjacent threads in millimeters
   D. distance measured from the bottom of the head to the bolt tip

_____ 3. *True or False?* The metric system of measuring thread pitch determines the millimeters between two threads.

_____ 4. In the US customary system, radial lines on the bolt head indicate the bolt's _____.
   A. minor diameter
   B. major diameter
   C. metal type
   D. tensile strength

_____ 5. In the metric system, bolt tensile strength is identified by _____ on the bolt head.
   A. a property class number
   B. a letter from A through E
   C. grade marks
   D. radial lines

_____ 6. Nuts thread onto bolts and _____.
   A. studs
   B. washers
   C. screws
   D. All of the above.

_____ 7. *True or False?* Grade 8 nuts and bolts require the use of soft wrought washers.

_____ 8. *True or False?* Flat washers should be installed with the flat side down.

_____ 9. Some nuts are self-locking due to _____ or interference between the bolt or stud threads and the nut.

_____ 10. *True or False?* Studs are commonly used on intake manifold connections.

For questions 11–20, identify the machine screw head types indicated in the following illustration.

_____ 11. Slotted binding head

_____ 12. Slotted oval head

_____ 13. Slotted round head

_____ 14. Set screws

_____ 15. Slotted fillister head

_____ 16. Slotted flat head

_____ 17. Hex head

_____ 18. Hex head cap

_____ 19. Slotted pan head

_____ 20. Hex cap

Goodheart-Willcox Publisher

_____ 21. To prevent slotted and castle nuts from loosening, _____ pins are used.

_____ 22. *True or False?* A technician should use the thinnest cotter pin possible.

_____ 23. *True or False?* Keys and pins allow longitudinal movement while still causing parts to rotate together.

_____ 24. *True or False?* Snap rings should be installed with the chamfered edge facing away from the thrust of the mating part.

_____ 25. Tightening fasteners to a certain value in order to provide sufficient clamping force is called _____.

    A. torquing

    B. fastening

    C. preloading

    D. pinning

_____ 26. When installing bolts, a technician should torque them to service manual specifications using a(n) _____.

_____ 27. All of the following statements about using a torque wrench are true, except:

    A. place a steady pull on the torque wrench.

    B. lightly oil fastener threads.

    C. pull only on the torque wrench handle.

    D. begin by tightening one-half recommended torque.

_____ 28. *True or False?* Torque wrenches occasionally require recalibration.

_____ 29. *True or False?* When a bolt is removed and damage has been done to the hole left behind, a thread repair insert can be used.

_____ 30. Some fasteners are tightened using a torque wrench and a(n) _____, which allows the final tightening to be measured in degrees of rotation.

Name _____

31. Indicate the correct order of the following screw extractor procedures by numbering them.

_____ A. Use a hammer to tap in the screw extractor.

_____ B. Use a wrench to turn the screw extractor.

_____ C. Drill a hole in the center of the broken fastener.

32. Indicate the correct order of the following thread insert installation procedures by numbering the steps.

_____ A. Install the thread insert.

_____ B. Drill the damaged hole.

_____ C. Tap the hole, cleaning the tap as you work.

_____ 33. A flexible piece of material placed between two or more parts is called a(n) _____.

_____ 34. Which of the following statements about head gaskets are *true*?
A. They must withstand extreme temperatures created by combustion.
B. On liquid-cooled engines, the head gasket confines cooling system pressures.
C. O-rings are a type of head gasket used on two-stroke engines.
D. All of the above.

_____ 35. MLS gaskets _____.
A. are made of layers of different materials to control movement
B. are no longer used because they contain asbestos
C. require a large amount of sealer during installation
D. None of the above.

_____ 36. When servicing seals, all of the following are proper procedures, *except*:
A. inspect the seal for leakage before disassembly.
B. use a special puller if required to remove a seal.
C. tap directly on the seal to install it.
D. install the seal with the sealing lip facing inside the part.

_____ 37. *True or False?* An oil seal should be completely dry when installed.

_____ 38. *True or False?* Non-hardening sealers are used on hose connections.

_____ 39. *True or False?* RTV sealer cures in the absence of air.

_____ 40. When no gasket is used, _____ gasket is the required sealant for assembling engine cases and covers.

Notes

Name _____ Date _____ Class _____

Job 5-1

Gaskets and Sealers

Introduction

Gaskets play an important role in the proper function of many components. If gaskets are serviced improperly, mechanical failure can result. Properly applying sealer takes practice. Common form-in-place gasket sealers are Honda Bond, YamaBond, KawaBond, and 1-2-3 Bond. They must be applied in the correct amount and in the correct location. More is not better. Some applications are made entirely of form-in-place gaskets. In other applications, sealers are added at certain points to help seal another type of gasket, such as the corners of rubber gaskets.

Objective

After successfully completing this job sheet, you will be able to use form-in-place gaskets.

Materials and Equipment

To complete this job sheet, you will need the following tools, equipment, and materials:

- Core engine or other engine as assigned by your instructor
- Appropriate service manual or electronic service information
- Form-in-place gasket sealer

Instructions

In this job, you will clean old gasket material off the engine and prepare the engine for a new gasket. You will also practice applying form-in-place gasket. Often, paper gaskets cannot be replaced with form-in-place gasket because the paper gasket thickness provides clearance for a mechanism on the inside of the case. Some rubber valve cover gaskets that have half-moon cutouts where the cylinder head was machined need some form-in-place gasket sealer in the corners when applied.

   After you read the job procedures, perform the tasks and answer all the questions. As you work through these steps, you will be instructed to either list measurements or perform certain tasks. When you reach a sign in the job sheet, you will be told to show your instructor your work. Do not continue until you have the instructor initials to proceed.

 WARNING ⚠ Before performing this job, review all pertinent safety information in the text and discuss safety procedures with your instructor.

Procedures

Engine Gasket Removal

1. Obtain an engine to be used in this job.

2. Fill in the following chart as you remove the components listed. If your engine does not have one of the components listed, write NA in the chart.

Component	Type of Gasket
Valve Cover	
Clutch Cover	
Generator Cover	
Water Pump	
Oil Pan	

 3. Discuss your findings with your instructor and make sure to ask any questions that you have before continuing to the next section.

Instructor's Initials: _____

Cleaning Gasket Surfaces

4. Remove any dowel pins to make gasket removal easier.

5. Scrape off old gasket material. See **Figure 5-1**.

Goodheart-Willcox Publisher

Figure 5-1. Clean off debris from old gaskets carefully and inspect mating surfaces for damage.

Name _____

 NOTE Use a quality scraper that is sharp enough and strong enough for the job.

6. Use a wire brush to clean off the rest of the gasket.

 NOTE Repeat Steps 5 and 6 until all gasket material is removed.

7. Service the threaded components:
   A. Tap out all bolt holes.
   B. Blow out all holes after tapping.
   C. Inspect bolts for stretching by comparing them to each other.
   D. Blow off bolt threads.
8. Spray brake cleaner on a rag and wipe all the gasket surfaces. Do not spray cleaner directly on the engine. Turn or replace the rag so that you are always wiping with a clean rag.
 9. Discuss your findings with your instructor and have your instructor initial the cleaning section and approve the gasket installation steps before proceeding to the next section.

Instructor's Initials: _____

Installing the Form-in-Place Gaskets

 NOTE If this is a core engine, at your instructor's option you will be either practicing or actually replacing gaskets.

10. Ensure that the surfaces are totally clean and free of oil, holes are tapped and cleaned out, and the bolts are clean and ready to be installed. Do not forget to replace any removed dowels.
11. Apply a proper amount of form-in-place gasket.

 CAUTION The width of the applied gasket is usually only 2–3 mm. Check the repair manual to ensure that you apply the gasket in the proper places.

12. Secure the parts with the proper bolts and torque them to the proper value.
13. Allow the parts to dry overnight.
14. Disassemble the parts and check that you installed the correct amount of gasket material and that it is in the correct locations.
 15. Show your instructor the disassembled part and discuss the amount and location of the gasket material.

Instructor's Initials: _____

Job Wrap Up

16. Return all tools and materials to the proper storage areas and clean up your work area.

Final Assessment

_____   1. Two technicians are discussing applying gaskets. Technician A says that both surfaces must be clean and dry. Technician B says that paper gaskets don't need dry surfaces in order to seal. Who is correct?

   A. A only.

   B. B only.

   C. Both A and B.

   D. Neither A nor B.

_____   2. Two technicians are discussing gaskets. Technician A says that cork gaskets don't need additional sealer. Technician B says that cork gaskets usually need sealer to help hold them in place during assembly. Who is correct?

   A. A only.

   B. B only.

   C. Both A and B.

   D. Neither A nor B.

_____   3. Two technicians are discussing gaskets. Technician A says that if a clutch cover is leaking oil, you can apply a special sealer from the outside. Technician B says that you should never replace a paper gasket with just form-in-place gasket. Who is correct?

   A. A only.

   B. B only.

   C. Both A and B.

   D. Neither A nor B.

_____   4. Two technicians are discussing replacing gaskets. Technician A says to compare bolt threads to check for stretching. Technician B says to use a thread gauge to check for stretching. Who is correct?

   A. A only.

   B. B only.

   C. Both A and B.

   D. Neither A nor B.

_____   5. Two technicians are discussing gasket installation. Technician A says that over-torqueing cover gaskets can cause leaks. Technician B says that under-torqueing cover gaskets can cause leaks. Who is correct?

   A. A only.

   B. B only.

   C. Both A and B.

   D. Neither A nor B.

Final Instructor Approval: _____

CHAPTER 6

Troubleshooting and Service Information

Chapter 6 Quiz

After studying Chapter 6 in the Motorcycles: Fundamentals, Service, Repair textbook, answer the following questions.

_____ 1. The term _____ refers to identifying the problem and its cause.

_____ 2. The systematic, step-by-step analysis of a problem is called _____.

_____ 3. The most important factor in developing a troubleshooting system is to _____.

_____ 4. A written customer interview _____ is used to prepare a repair order.

_____ 5. *True or False?* A repair order is a legally binding document between the repair shop and the customer.

_____ 6. A complete repair order has the three Cs, which are complaint, _____, and correction.

_____ 7. Verifying the problem includes _____.
  A. asking the customer to imitate any sounds the vehicle is making
  B. consulting a system analysis chart
  C. installing a part that the technician thinks may solve the problem
  D. confirming that the problem exists as explained by the customer

_____ 8. A system analysis chart is helpful in _____.
  A. completing a customer interview checklist
  B. finding which system is most likely at fault
  C. repairing wiring in an electrical system
  D. finding information on systems in a service manual

_____ 9. *True or False?* The most important factor before and during the test-drive is safety.

_____ 10. Problems encountered by motorcycle technicians may be either permanent failures or _____ failures.

11. Indicate the correct order of the following troubleshooting steps by numbering them.

_____ A. Systematically eliminate potential problems.

_____ B. Verify the diagnosis.

_____ C. Repair the malfunction.

_____ D. Collect information.

_____ E. Isolate the cause of the problem.

_____ F. Confirm the repair.

_____ G. Visually inspect to identify symptoms.

_____ 12. *True or False?* When troubleshooting, the technician should overlook the obvious and seek out more complex causes of problems.

_____ 13. *True or False?* Each manufacturer's service manual covers motorcycles produced by a particular company.

_____ 14. *True or False?* Manufacturer's service manuals are written for use by do-it-yourselfers.

_____ 15. Which of the following covers one engine design over a period of years?
A. specialty repair manuals
B. factory manuals
C. technical service bulletins
D. general repair manuals

_____ 16. Information such as year produced and where the vehicle was built can be found using an alphanumeric code called a(n) _____.

_____ 17. The repair section of a service manual contains all of the following topics, *except*:
A. adjustments.
B. recommendations for oil.
C. testing/troubleshooting.
D. disassembly/assembly procedures.

_____ 18. *True or False?* Many diagrams in a service manual indicate the type of lubricant and location for application.

_____ 19. The purpose of a troubleshooting chart is to _____.
A. provide technicians with updates regarding recent technical changes
B. detail the steps involved in the troubleshooting process
C. guide technicians to the most common causes for a specific problem
D. All of the above.

_____ 20. *True or False?* Technical service bulletins are delivered to the shop manager.

_____ 21. New motorcycle owners should be encouraged to read their _____ manual.

Name _____   Date _____   Class _____

Job 6-1

Using Service Information

Introduction

Knowing where to find information is as important to repairing motorcycles as knowing how to use the tools on the actual bike. A technician can spend a lot of time looking up information that could be used fixing the motorcycle. Technicians who are really good at fixing motorcycles are also really good at finding information.

Objective

After successfully completing this job sheet, you will be able to find a wide variety of information that would be needed for motorcycle repair.

Materials and Equipment

To complete this job sheet, you will need the following tools, equipment, and materials:

- Factory (OEM) repair manuals (either electronic or paper) from two different manufacturers

Instructions

In this job, you will be finding information, sometimes a procedure and sometimes a specification. You should always try to remember in what section you found the information. Different manufacturers will put the information in different places. Sometimes a manufacturer will have a specification listed at the front of the book, sometimes at the beginning of the chapter and sometimes inside the chapter as part of the procedure you are working on.

Procedures

1. Obtain two repair manuals. List the manuals in the chart below.

	Make	Year	Model
Service Manual Number One			
Service Manual Number Two			

2. Using both repair manuals, locate the information requested. In the first column, indicate either the information requested or page number where the information was found. In the second column, indicate the section where the information was found.

Information Required	Manual One Information	Section Found	Manual Two Information	Section Found
Weight of Engine Oil				
Engine Oil Capacity				
Compression Ratio				
Compression Test Psi				
Original Tire Size				
Tire Pressure				
Gross Vehicle Weight				
Valve Clearance				
Valve Adjustment Procedure				
Brake Fluid Type				
Brake Bleeding Procedure				
Cylinder Head Bolt Torque				
Clutch Friction Disc Minimum Thickness				
Clutch Cable Routing Diagram Page				
Clutch Spring Bolt Torque				
Clutch Spring Height				
Front Brake Rotor Minimum Thickness				
Number of Transmission Gears				
Location of Cylinder #1				
Ignition Wiring Diagram				
Type of Ignition				
Fuel System Type: Carburetor or EFI				
EFI Code Chart				
Self Diagnostic Process (EFI)				
*Carburetor Float Level				
*Main Jet Size				
Idle RPM				

*If vehicle is carbureted

Job Wrap Up

3. Return the service manuals to the proper storage areas.

4. Ask your instructor to check your work and initial this task sheet.

Final Job Sheet Approval: _____

CHAPTER 7

Basic Electrical and Electronic Theory

Chapter 7 Quiz

After studying Chapter 7 in the Motorcycles: Fundamentals, Service, Repair textbook, answer the following questions.

_____ 1. Tiny particles of negatively charged matter are called _____.
  A. atoms
  B. electrons
  C. protons
  D. neutrons

_____ 2. The nucleus of an atom _____.
  A. contains neutrons and protons
  B. contains neutrons and electrons
  C. is negatively charged
  D. consists of bound electrons

_____ 3. *True or False?* Electricity is the movement of electrons from one atom to another.

_____ 4. The term _____ refers to the two sides of an electrical system.

_____ 5. Electrical systems on a motorcycle use both direct current and _____ current.

_____ 6. In most motorcycles, direct current is supplied by the _____.

_____ 7. A simple electrical circuit consists of a power source, conductors, and a _____.

_____ 8. Materials that do not conduct electricity are called _____.

9. Identify the types of electrical circuits shown in the following illustration.

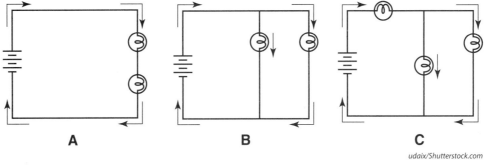

A   B   C

udaix/Shutterstock.com

_____ Parallel circuit

_____ Series-parallel circuit

_____ Series circuit

_____ 10. The term _amperage_ refers to the _____.

    A. pressure that forces free electrons to flow in a conductor

    B. opposition to current flow

    C. number of free electrons flowing in a conductor

    D. rate that electrical power is consumed

_____ 11. The pressure that forces free electrons to flow in a conductor is called _____.

    A. resistance

    B. voltage

    C. power

    D. amperage

_____ 12. Resistance is measured in units called _____.

    A. ohms

    B. watts

    C. amps

    D. volts

_____ 13. _True or False?_ Ohm's law states that current is inversely proportional to resistance.

_____ 14. Ohm's law states that _____.

    A. current = resistance × voltage

    B. voltage = current × resistance

    C. resistance = current ÷ voltage

    D. All of the above.

_____ 15. The equation for determining power consumption is expressed by _____ law.

_____ 16. A fuse protects a circuit against damage caused by a(n) _____.

_____ 17. _True or False?_ Fuses and circuit breakers perform different functions.

For questions 18–20, match each component with its description.

A. Relay   B. Solenoid   C. Switch

_____ 18. Turns a circuit on or off manually.

_____ 19. Consists of a control and a power circuit.

_____ 20. One or two coils around an iron core.

For questions 21–26, match each component with its description by placing the corresponding letter next to the description.

A. Diode   C. Transistor   E. Capacitor

B. Thyristor   D. Thermistor   F. Integrated circuit

_____ 21. Performs same function as a relay.

_____ 22. Contains miniaturized semiconductors.

_____ 23. Allow current to flow in one direction.

_____ 24. Also called silicone controlled rectifier.

_____ 25. Resistance value decreases as it gets hot.

_____ 26. Absorbs unwanted electrical pulses.

Name _____ Date _____ Class _____

_____ 27. *True or False?* A battery is made up of several 2-volt cells connected in series.

_____ 28. Magnetic lines of force can be used to produce movement or _____.

_____ 29. The insulation on primary wire is coded using _____.
   A. numbers
   B. bands of different thicknesses
   C. a series of letters and numbers
   D. different colors

_____ 30. *True or False?* Wire gage sizes are smaller on newer motorcycles than on older motorcycles.

_____ 31. *True or False?* When replacing a section of wire, the technician should use a wire of equal or larger size.

_____ 32. A wiring diagram is also called a(n) _____.

_____ 33. A(n) _____ is a tool that can function as an ohmmeter, an ammeter, and a voltmeter.

For questions 34–36, match each tool with the phrase that describes it.
A. Ohmmeter   B. Ammeter   C. Voltmeter

_____ 34. measures in parallel

_____ 35. measures resistance

_____ 36. measures in series

_____ 37. A(n) _____ must never be connected to a source of voltage.

_____ 38. A(n) _____ wire is handy for testing switches, wires, and other components.

_____ 39. *True or False?* A soldering gun can be used to permanently fasten wires.

_____ 40. Electrical solder joints are insulated with _____ tubing.

_____ 41. Technicians use _____ pliers to compress a connector or terminal around a wire.

_____ 42. Battery leads should not be disconnected while the _____ switch is on or the engine is running.

Notes

_____

_____

_____

_____

_____

_____

_____

_____

_____

_____

_____

_____

_____

_____

_____

_____

_____

_____

_____

_____

_____

_____

_____

_____

Name _____ Date _____ Class _____

Job 7-1

Multimeter Familiarization

Introduction

A multimeter is arguably the most valuable tool in a motorcycle technician's toolbox. A professional motorcycle technician will need to own a multimeter and become proficient at using it. In this job, you will become familiar with multimeters.

Objective

After successfully completing this job, you will be able to use a multimeter to make a variety of electrical tests.

Materials and Equipment

To complete this job, you will need the following tools, equipment, and materials:

- Multimeter (Fluke 88 or equivalent)

Instructions

In this job, you will be familiarizing yourself with a multimeter. It is not as important to understand the measurements as it is to understand the tool. You will be using multimeters many times as you complete other jobs in the lab workbook.

   After you read the job procedures, perform the tasks and answer all questions. As you complete steps you will be instructed to either fill in measurements or perform certain tasks. When you reach a sign show your work to your instructor. Do not continue until you have instructor approval (instructor will initial job sheet).

> **WARNING** ⚠️ Before performing this job, review all pertinent safety information in the text and discuss safety procedures with your instructor. Damage can be done to yourself and your multimeter if some of these measurements are done incorrectly.

Procedures

> **NOTE** The following procedures are based on the use of a Fluke 88 multimeter.

Install the Leads

1. Install meter leads to make voltage and resistance measurements as shown in **Figure 7-1.1**.

Goodheart-Willcox Publisher

Figure 7-1.1. Meter leads in proper position for measuring voltage and resistance.

You will be using **Figure 7-1** *for reference when answering the following questions.*

Selector Positions

2. Move the selector knob to ac volts (indicated by a V under a wavy line). If you have a different meter, what is the symbol for ac volts?

_____

3. What ac volts measurement range is displayed when the meter is first turned on?

_____

4. Press and hold down the RANGE button. What range does it change to? (Hint: It should appear in the upper-left corner.)

_____

5. Move the selector knob to the next position, which is dc volts (it has a V under a straight line).

6. What voltage range does the meter display when turned to dc volts?

_____

Name _____

7. Press and hold the range button. What word appears in the upper-left corner of the screen?

_____

8. Press the yellow SMOOTH button. What happens to the display screen?

_____

9. Press the MIN MAX button. What word appears at the top of the screen?

_____

10. Press the MIN MAX button again. What word appears at the top of the screen?

_____

11. Press the MIN MAX button again. What word appears at the top of the screen?

_____

12. Press the MIN MAX button again. What word appears at the top of the screen?

_____

13. Move the selector knob back to ac volts and press the MIN MAX button four more times. What happens?

_____

_____

STOP 14. Discuss the use of the MIN MAX button with your instructor.

Instructor's Initials: _____

> **NOTE** The MIN MAX button is useful when the voltage changes quickly or when the voltage changes when you are looking away from the meter. MIN MAX is also helpful when voltage drop testing a battery when cranking. Another use is checking stator ac output.

15. What other acronyms does the meter have at the dc volt position?

_____

_____

16. Move the selector to the millivolt position (position has V and mV indications). What voltage range comes up in this position?

_____

17. Move the selector to the resistance position (position has an omega symbol that looks like an upside down U). What letter comes up on the screen next to the omega? What does the letter mean?

_____

_____

18. While still in the resistance position, press the ALERT button. What did you hear? What was displayed on the screen?

_____

_____

19. Move the selector to the next position (position is for diode testing and has a picture of an arrow with a crossed line). What letters are displayed next to the measurement?

_____

_____

20. Move the selector to the next position (marked mA and A with a wavy line). This position is for measuring dc amperage in milliamps and amps. What numbers are displayed on the screen?

_____

NOTE	For amperage measurements taken in series, move the red testing lead into the jack port labeled with a capital A. In the picture below, a piece of tape has been put over the Jack port labeled mA. The internal fuse for this port has a low rating and the port is rarely used, so covering it reduces the chance of accidentally blowing the fuse.

21. With the leads in the position shown in **Figure 7-1.2**, move the selector knob back to dc volts. What does the meter do? Briefly explain why this happens.

Goodheart-Willcox Publisher

Figure 7-1.2. Meter leads in position for measuring voltage.

_____

_____

(STOP) 22. Discuss the meter and any questions you have with your instructor.

Instructor's Initials: _____

Name _____

23. Move the selector to dc volts and press the HOLD button. What is shown on the screen and what else does the meter do?

_____

_____

24. What is the purpose of the HOLD button as used in Step 23?

_____

_____

25. Reset the selector to dc volts and press the %DUTY button. What three symbols or letters appear on the screen?

_____

_____

> **NOTE** %DUTY is the same as duty cycle and is used in testing ignition-related circuits. The technician uses duty cycle to determine whether the ignition coils on transistorized ignition systems are being turned on and off.

26. Press the %DUTY button again (with the selector knob remaining on dc volts). What does the meter do? What does the screen now read?

_____

_____

> **NOTE** The ms means milliseconds and indicates the number of milliseconds the digital signal is on. This is a handy measurement when checking injector on time.

27. Press the %DUTY button again. What does the screen now display?

_____

_____

28. Move the selector knob to ac volts. A bar graph is displayed along the bottom of the screen. What numbers are shown on the bar graph?

_____

29. Move the selector knob to dc volts. Did the numbers on the bar graph change?

_____

> **NOTE** The bar graph is a helpful tool when looking at ac signals. The bar graph is used to check charging systems and ignition components.

(STOP) 30. Discuss your findings with your instructor.

Instructor's Initials: _____

Job Wrap Up

31. Return all tools and materials to the proper storage areas.

32. Clean up your work area.

Final Assessment

1. What position on the selector knob would you use to check battery voltage?

_____

2. What position would you use to check the position of a new switch before installation?

_____

3. What size internal battery does the Fluke 88 use?

_____

4. Where are the battery and fuses located on the Fluke 88?

_____

_____

5. How does the Fluke 88 indicate that internal battery is running low?

_____

_____

Final Instructor Approval: _____

Name _____ Date _____ Class _____

Job 7-2

Series Circuits—One Load

Introduction

You will use the electrical rules to predict measurements and then perform voltage and amperage testing to more fully understand how the circuit works. You must correlate your readings with the status of the load and determine whether the circuit is open or closed. Electrical rules all relate to understanding opens and loads and how voltage works with them.

Objective

After successfully completing this job, you will be able to make voltage and amperage measurements in a series circuit.

Materials and Equipment

To complete this job, you will need the following tools, equipment, and materials:
- Electrical board with components to build circuits
- Multimeter

Instructions

In this job you will be predicting voltages, then building a circuit and measuring voltage and amperage. You will use the electrical rules listed below. When you reach a (STOP) sign, show your work to your instructor. Do not continue until you have instructor approval (instructor will initial lab sheet).

Resources

Electrical Rules

Rule #1
With the circuit off or not working, voltage travels to an open.

Rule #2
Source voltage is measured before an open or before a working load.

Rule #3
Zero volts are measured after an open or after the last working load.

Rule #4
When available voltage is less than source and more than 0, the measurement is between two loads.

Electrical Tips

- Voltage drop and resistance are found together.
- Current takes its easiest or only path to ground.
- Current can only flow and be measured on a circuit that is operating.
- Current is the same throughout the series portion of a circuit.
- Loads use or share all of the source voltage.
- When checking electrical circuits, substitute electrical loads only with similar loads. Do not replace a load with a wire. A horn (for instance) is a load. If a horn is diagnosed as faulty, replace it with another load, such as a known good light and see if the light works. A switch can be bypassed with the correct size wire.

> **NOTE**   Remember that the *Electrical Rules* will help you predict circuit values and understand the measurements you will be making. The *Electrical Tips* will help you further understand certain measurements and how circuits work.

Procedures

Predicting Voltages

1. Using the circuit diagram shown in **Figure 7-2.1**, predict the voltages in the circuit with the switch open (circuit *off*) and the switch closed (circuit *on*). Record your predictions below. There are three possible answers:
   - S (source voltage)
   - LTS (less than source voltage, greater than zero)
   - 0 (zero)

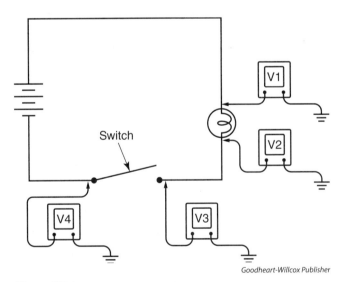

Goodheart-Willcox Publisher

Figure 7-2.1.

Predicted voltage with switch *open*

_____   Predicted voltage V1

_____   Predicted voltage V2

_____   Predicted voltage V3

_____   Predicted voltage V4

Name _____

Predicted voltage with switch *closed*

_____   Predicted voltage V1

_____   Predicted voltage V2

_____   Predicted voltage V3

_____   Predicted voltage V4

Build the Circuit

2. Build the series circuit shown in **Figure 7-2.1**.

3. With the switch *open*, make the measurements shown in **Figure 7-2.1**.

_____   Measured voltage V1

_____   Measured voltage V2

_____   Measured voltage V3

_____   Measured voltage V4

4. *Close* the switch and make the measurements shown in **Figure 7-2.1**.

_____   Measured voltage V1

_____   Measured voltage V2

_____   Measured voltage V3

_____   Measured voltage V4

5. Did you predict the voltage properly? If not, can you determine why not?

_____

_____

_____

_____

6. What rules were proven by your measurements in this circuit? Write the rules in their entirety here.

_____

_____

_____

_____

_____

_____

Measuring Amperage

7. Turn the circuit off (open the switch).

8. Set your ammeter to the 10A setting.

9. Install the ammeter in series as shown in **Figure 7-2.2A**. Note that the meter is part of the complete circuit and all current flows through the ammeter at the beginning of the circuit before to the load.

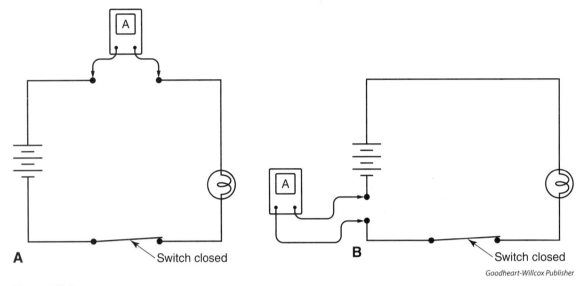

A

B

Switch closed

Switch closed

Figure 7-2.2.

10. Turn the circuit on (close the switch) and record the ammeter reading.

_____

11. Turn the circuit off and record the ammeter reading.

_____

12. Connect the ammeter at the end of the circuit (after the switch) as shown in **Figure 7-2.2B**.

13. Turn the circuit on and record the ammeter reading.

_____

14. Turn the circuit off and record the ammeter reading.

_____

15. Which electrical tips are proven with the ammeter measurements?

_____

_____

_____

 16. Discuss your findings with your instructor.

Instructor's Initials: _____

Job Wrap Up

17. Return all tools and materials to the proper storage areas and clean up your work area.

> **NOTE** If you are immediately continuing to the next Lab Sheet, you may leave your tools and materials out.

Name _____

Final Assessment

_____   1. A technician is diagnosing a faulty headlight. He or she makes a measurement of 12 volts at the fuse. What is this measurement called?

   A. Source voltage.

   B. Voltage drop.

   C. Available voltage.

   D. Resistance.

   E. Current draw.

_____   2. A technician is diagnosing a faulty headlight. He or she makes a measurement of 12 volts at the wire going into the bulb. What is this type of measurement called?

   A. Source voltage.

   B. Voltage drop.

   C. Available voltage.

   D. Resistance.

   E. Current draw.

_____   3. A technician is diagnosing a faulty headlight. He or she puts one lead on each wire going into and out of the bulb and makes a measurement of 12 volts .What is this type of measurement called?

   A. Source voltage.

   B. Voltage drop.

   C. Available voltage.

   D. Resistance.

   E. Current draw.

   4. A complete circuit needs four key components. Name the four components.

   _____

   _____

   5. Which part of a circuit is more important, the power supply or the ground path?

   _____

   _____

Final Instructor Approval: _____

Notes

Name _____ Date _____ Class _____

Job 7-3

Series Circuits—Two Loads

Introduction

You will be using the electrical rules to predict measurements and then make voltage and amperage tests to understand how the circuit works. You must correlate your readings with the status of the load and whether the circuit is open or closed. The Electrical rules all relate to understanding opens and loads and how voltage works with them.

Objective

After successfully completing this job, you will be able to make voltage and amperage measurements in a series circuit.

Materials and Equipment

To complete this job, you will need the following tools, equipment, and materials:
- Electrical board with components to build circuits
- Multimeter

Instructions

In this job you will be predicting voltages, and then building a circuit and measuring voltage and amperage. You will be asked to use the electrical rules listed below. When you reach a (STOP) sign, show your work to your instructor. Do not continue until you have instructor approval (instructor will initial job sheet).

Resources

Electrical Rules

Rule #1
With the circuit off or not working, voltage travels to an open.

Rule #2
Source voltage is measured before an open or before a working load.

Rule #3
Zero volts are measured after an open or after the last working load.

Rule #4
When available voltage is less than source and more than 0, the measurement is between two loads.

Electrical Tips

- Voltage drop and resistance are found together.
- Current takes its easiest or only path to ground.
- Current can only flow and be measured on a circuit that is operating.
- Current is the same throughout the series portion of a circuit.
- Loads use or share all of the source voltage.
- When checking electrical circuits, substitute electrical loads only with similar loads. Do not replace a load with a wire. A horn (for instance) is a load. If a horn is diagnosed as faulty, replace it with another load, such as a known good light and see if the light works. A switch can be bypassed with the correct size wire.

> **NOTE** Remember that the *Electrical Rules* will help you predict circuit values and understand the measurements you will be making. The *Electrical Tips* will help you further understand certain measurements and how circuits work.

Procedures

Predicting Voltages

1. Using the circuit diagram shown in **Figure 7-3.1**, predict the voltages in the circuit with the switch open (circuit *off*) and the switch closed (circuit *on*). Record your predictions below. There are three possible answers:
   - S (source voltage)
   - LTS (less than source voltage, greater than zero)
   - 0 (zero)

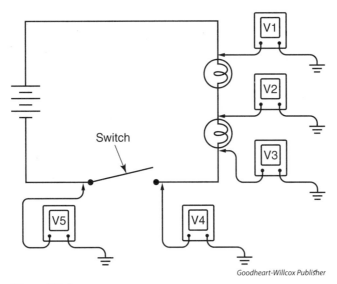

Goodheart-Willcox Publisher

Figure 7-3.1.

Predicted voltage with switch *open*:

_____ Predicted voltage V1

_____ Predicted voltage V2

_____ Predicted voltage V3

_____ Predicted voltage V4

_____ Predicted voltage V5

Name _____

Predicted voltage with switch *closed*:

_____   Predicted voltage V1

_____   Predicted voltage V2

_____   Predicted voltage V3

_____   Predicted voltage V4

_____   Predicted voltage V5

Build the Circuit

2. Build the circuit shown in **Figure 7-3.1**.

3. With the switch open, make the measurements shown in **Figure 7-3.1**.

_____   Measured voltage V1

_____   Measured voltage V2

_____   Measured voltage V3

_____   Measured voltage V4

_____   Measured voltage V5

4. Close the switch and make the measurements shown in **Figure 7-3.1**.

_____   Measured voltage V1

_____   Measured voltage V2

_____   Measured voltage V3

_____   Measured voltage V4

_____   Measured voltage V5

5. Did you predict the voltage properly? If not, can you determine why not?

_____

_____

_____

_____

6. What rules were proven by your measurements in this circuit? Write the rules in their entirety here.

_____

_____

_____

_____

_____

_____

Measuring Amperage

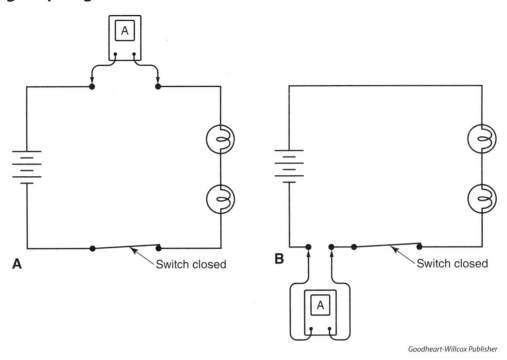

Goodheart-Willcox Publisher

Figure 7-3.2.

7. Open the switch and set the ammeter to the 10A setting.

8. With the circuit off (switch open), install the ammeter in series as shown in **Figure 7-3.2A**. The ammeter is part of the complete circuit and current must flow through the ammeter at the beginning of the circuit prior to the loads.

9. Close the switch and record the ammeter reading.

   _____

10. Open the switch and record the ammeter reading.

   _____

11. With the switch open, connect the ammeter at the end of the circuit after the switch as shown in **Figure 7-3.2B**.

12. Close the switch and record the ammeter reading.

   _____

13. Open the switch and record the ammeter reading.

   _____

14. Which electrical tips are proven with the ammeter measurements?

   _____

   _____

   _____

Name _____

15. With the circuit still intact and the ammeter in series after the switch, connect a jumper wire between the two loads to a good ground as shown in **Figure 7-3.3**.

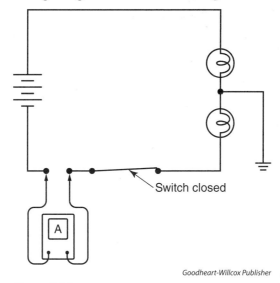

Switch closed

Figure 7-3.3.

16. Describe the bulb illumination.

_____
_____
_____

17. Explain the result in Step 14. (Hint: Use an electrical tip to answer the question.)

_____
_____
_____

STOP 18. Discuss your findings so far with your instructor.

Instructor's Initials: _____

Job Wrap Up

19. Return all tools and materials to the proper storage areas and clean up your work area.

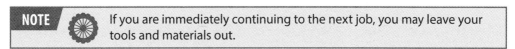

NOTE   If you are immediately continuing to the next job, you may leave your tools and materials out.

Final Assessment

_____ 1. Which symbol is used for volts?

     A. V

     B. mA

     C. mV

     D. A

_____ 2. Which symbol is used for amperage?

     A. V

     B. mA

     C. mV

     D. A

3. There are three possible dc voltage measurements when making an electrical diagnosis. What are they?

_____

_____

4. Give an example of a circuit protection device:

_____

5. If you were to replace a lightbulb with another component for diagnostic purposes, what do you need to make sure about the other component?

_____

_____

Final Instructor Approval: _____

Name _____ Date _____ Class _____

Job 7-4

Series Circuits—Three Loads

Introduction

You will use the electrical rules to predict measurements and make voltage and amperage tests to more fully understand how the circuit works. You must correlate your readings with the status of the load and determine whether the circuit is open or closed. The rules all relate to understanding opens and loads and how the voltage works with them.

Objective

After successfully completing this job, you will be able to make voltage and amperage measurements in a series circuit.

Materials and Equipment

To complete this job, you will need the following tools, equipment, and materials:

- Electrical board with components to build circuits
- Multimeter

Instructions

In this job you will be predicting voltages, then building a circuit and measuring voltage and amperage. You will be asked to use the electrical rules listed below. When you reach a (STOP) sign, show your work to your instructor. Do not continue until you have instructor approval (instructor will initial job sheet).

Resources

Electrical Rules

Rule #1
With the circuit off or not working, voltage travels to an open.

Rule #2
Source voltage is measured before an open or before a working load.

Rule #3
Zero volts is measured after an open or after the last working load.

Rule #4
When available voltage is less than source and more than 0, the measurement is between two loads.

Electrical Tips

- Voltage drop and resistance are found together.
- Current takes its easiest or only path to ground.
- Current can only flow and be measured on a circuit that is operating.
- Current is the same throughout the series portion of a circuit.
- Loads use or share all of the source voltage.
- When checking electrical circuits, substitute electrical loads only with similar loads. Do not replace a load with a wire. A horn (for instance) is a load. If a horn is diagnosed as faulty, replace it with another load, such as a known good light and see if the light works. A switch can be bypassed with the correct size wire.

> **NOTE** Remember that the *Electrical Rules* will help you predict circuit values and understand the measurements you will be making. The *Electrical Tips* will help you further understand certain measurements and how circuits work.

Procedures

Predicting Voltages

1. Using the circuit diagram shown in **Figure 7-4.1**, predict the voltages in the circuit with the switch open (circuit *off*) and the switch closed (circuit *on*). Record your predictions below. There are three possible answers:
   - S (source voltage)
   - LTS (less than source voltage, more than zero)
   - 0 (zero)

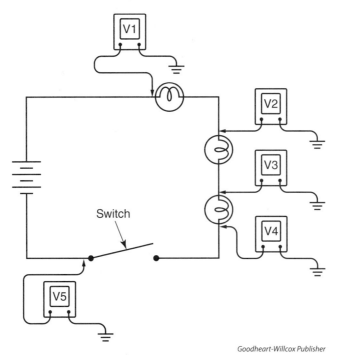

Goodheart-Willcox Publisher

Figure 7-4.1.

Name _____

Predicted voltage with switch *open*:

_____   Predicted voltage V1

_____   Predicted voltage V2

_____   Predicted voltage V3

_____   Predicted voltage V4

_____   Predicted voltage V5

Predicted voltage with switch *closed*:

_____   Predicted voltage V1

_____   Predicted voltage V2

_____   Predicted voltage V3

_____   Predicted voltage V4

_____   Predicted voltage V5

Build the Circuit

2. Build the circuit shown in **Figure 7-4.1**.

3. With the switch open, make the measurements shown in **Figure 7-4.1**.

_____   Measured voltage V1

_____   Measured voltage V2

_____   Measured voltage V3

_____   Measured voltage V4

_____   Measured voltage V5

4. Close the switch and make the measurements shown in **Figure 7-4.1**.

_____   Measured voltage V1

_____   Measured voltage V2

_____   Measured voltage V3

_____   Measured voltage V4

_____   Measured voltage V5

5. Did you predict the voltage properly? If not, can you determine why not?

_____

_____

_____

6. What rules were proven by your measurements in this circuit? Write the rules in their entirety here.

_____

_____

_____

_____

_____

7. Now move the switch so that it is before the loads as shown in **Figure 7-4.2**.

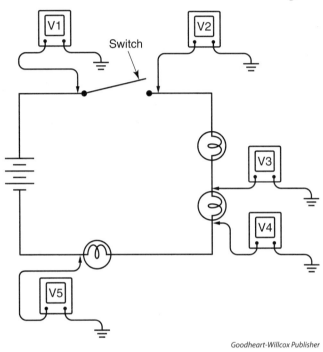

Goodheart-Willcox Publisher

Figure 7-4.2.

8. With the switch open, make the measurements shown in **Figure 7-4.2**.

_____ Measured voltage V1

_____ Measured voltage V2

_____ Measured voltage V3

_____ Measured voltage V4

_____ Measured voltage V5

9. Close the switch and make the measurements shown in **Figure 7-4.2**.

_____ Measured voltage V1

_____ Measured voltage V2

_____ Measured voltage V3

_____ Measured voltage V4

_____ Measured voltage V5

Name _____

10. What was the difference in readings when the switch was placed before and after the loads?

_____

_____

_____

_____

Voltage Drop

11. Voltage drop is the difference between the two points being measured. Using the circuit diagram shown in **Figure 7-4.3**, predict the measurements that you will read based upon the previous available voltage measurements that you have made.

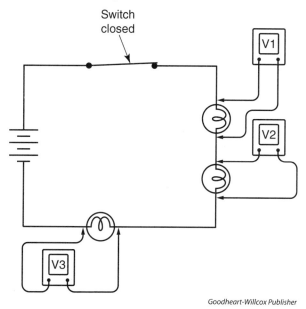

Goodheart-Willcox Publisher

Figure 7-4.3.

_____ Predicted voltage V1

_____ Predicted voltage V2

_____ Predicted voltage V3

12. Now build the circuit shown in **Figure 7-4.3** and make the actual measurements.

_____ Measured voltage V1

_____ Measured voltage V2

_____ Measured voltage V3

13. What do you notice about the voltage drop measurements?

_____

_____

14. Add the three voltage drop measurements up. What do they total?

_____

_____

 15. Discuss your findings so far with your instructor.

Instructor's Initials: _____

Measuring Amperage

16. Turn the circuit off (switch open) and make sure that the ammeter is set to the 10A setting.

17. Install the ammeter in series as shown in **Figure 7-4.4A**. The ammeter is part of the complete circuit and current must flow through the ammeter at the beginning of the circuit prior to the loads.

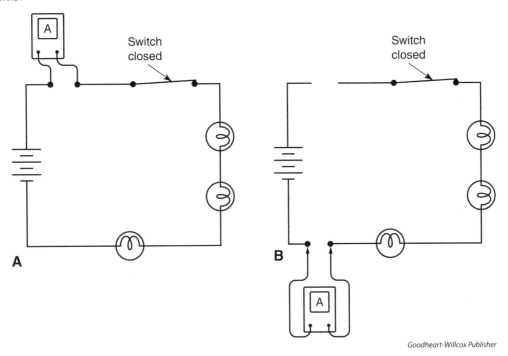

Goodheart-Willcox Publisher

Figure 7-4.4.

18. Turn the circuit on and record the ammeter reading.

_____

19. Turn the circuit off and record the ammeter reading.

_____

20. Connect the ammeter at the end of the circuit after the switch as shown in **Figure 7-4.2B**.

21. Turn the circuit on and record the ammeter reading.

_____

22. Turn the circuit off and record the ammeter reading.

_____

Name _____

23. Which electrical tips are proven with the ammeter measurements?

_____

_____

_____

24. Compare the amperage reading from the series circuit in Job 7-2, with the amperage reading from this job.

Job 7-2—ammeter reading (one bulb): _____

Job 7-4—ammeter reading (three bulbs): _____

25. Explain why there is a difference in amperage readings.

_____

_____

26. What happened to the bulbs?

_____

_____

27. Explain why this happened. (Hint: Use an electrical tip to answer the question.)

_____

_____

🛑 28. Discuss your findings so far with your instructor.

Instructor's Initials: _____

Job Wrap Up

29. Return all tools and materials to the proper storage areas and clean up your work area.

> **NOTE** ⚙ If you are immediately continuing to the next job, you may leave your tools and materials out.

Final Assessment

1. Source voltage is measured in a circuit with the load activated or on. Is the measurement being made before or after the load?

_____

2. A voltage drop measurement of 0 volts is made in a circuit where the load is not activated or inoperative. Is the fault before the load or after the load?

_____

_____ 3. With the switch closed on a circuit with one load, a voltage drop measurement across the load is equal to source voltage. The load is inoperative. Technician A says to replace the switch. Technician B says to replace the load. Who is correct?

    A. A only.

    B. B only.

    C. Both A and B.

    D. Neither A nor B.

4. One bulb in a parallel circuit is inoperative, and the available voltage is source voltage before and after the bulb. Is the fault before the bulb or after the bulb?

_____

_____ 5. Technician A says that all of the current paths in a parallel circuit add up to the total current of the circuit. Technician B says the different paths of a parallel circuit can have the same voltage drop but different current flow. Who is correct?

    A. A only.

    B. B only.

    C. Both A and B.

    D. Neither A nor B.

Final Instructor Approval: _____

Name _____ Date _____ Class _____

Job 7-5

Series Circuit Voltage Drop Testing

Introduction

You will be using the electrical rules to predict measurements and then perform voltage and amperage testing to more fully understand how the circuit works. You must correlate your readings with the status of the load and determine whether the circuit is open or closed. The electrical rules all relate to understanding opens and loads and how voltage works with them.

Objective

After successfully completing this job, you will be able to make voltage and resistance measurements in a series circuit.

Materials and Equipment

To complete this job, you will need the following tools, equipment, and materials:

- Electrical board with components to build circuits
- Two different bulbs
- 8 or 10 gauge wire
- Multimeter

Instructions

In this job you will be measuring resistance of loads, and then measuring voltage of those loads when current is flowing. You will be asked to identify the correlation between resistance and voltage drop and when each can be used for diagnosis. You will be asked to use the electrical rules explained below. When you reach a (STOP) sign, show your work to your instructor. Do not continue until you have instructor approval (instructor will initial job sheet).

Resources

Electrical Rules

Rule #1
With the circuit off or not working, voltage travels to an open.

Rule #2
Source voltage is measured before an open or before a working load.

Rule #3
Zero volts is measured after an open or after the last working load.

Rule #4
When available voltage is less than source and more than 0, the measurement is between two loads.

Electrical Tips

- Voltage drop and resistance are found together.
- Current takes its easiest or only path to ground.
- Current only flows and can only be measured on a circuit that is operating.
- Current is the same throughout the series portion of a circuit.
- Loads use or share all of the source voltage.
- When checking electrical circuits, substitute electrical loads only with similar loads. Do not replace a load with a wire. A horn (for instance) is a load. If a horn is diagnosed as faulty, replace it with another load, such as a known good light, and see if the light works. A switch can be bypassed with the correct size wire.

Procedures

Measuring Resistance

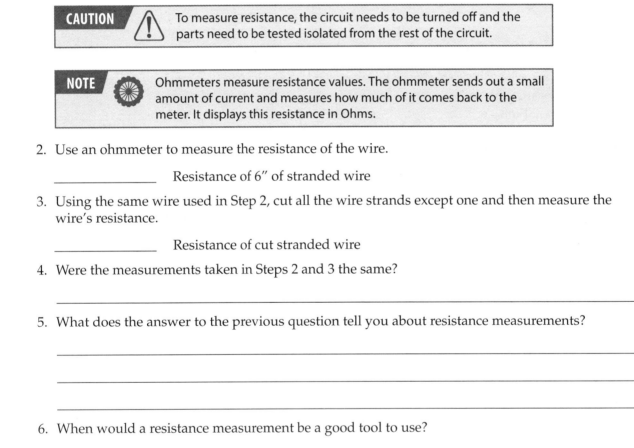

1. Obtain a piece of 8 or 10 gauge stranded wire.

   CAUTION To measure resistance, the circuit needs to be turned off and the parts need to be tested isolated from the rest of the circuit.

   NOTE Ohmmeters measure resistance values. The ohmmeter sends out a small amount of current and measures how much of it comes back to the meter. It displays this resistance in Ohms.

2. Use an ohmmeter to measure the resistance of the wire.

   _____   Resistance of 6″ of stranded wire

3. Using the same wire used in Step 2, cut all the wire strands except one and then measure the wire's resistance.

   _____   Resistance of cut stranded wire

4. Were the measurements taken in Steps 2 and 3 the same?

   _____

5. What does the answer to the previous question tell you about resistance measurements?

   _____

   _____

   _____

6. When would a resistance measurement be a good tool to use?

   _____

   _____

   _____

Name _____

7. Measure the resistance of components to be used in building a circuit shown in **Figure 7-5.1**, and fill in the Resistance Value column following chart. Be sure to use two different-sized bulbs. The results will be compared to voltage drop measurements.

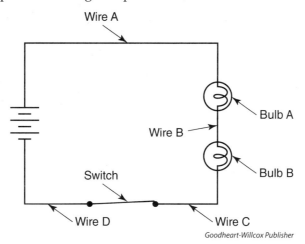

Goodheart-Willcox Publisher

Figure 7-5.1.

Component	Resistance Value	Voltage Drop
Wire A		
Bulb A		
Wire B		
Bulb B		
Wire C		
Switch		
Wire D		
Total		

Build the Circuit

8. Build the circuit shown in **Figure 7-5.1**.

9. Disconnect the power and ground from your power source and measure resistance of the entire circuit as shown in **Figure 7-5.2**.

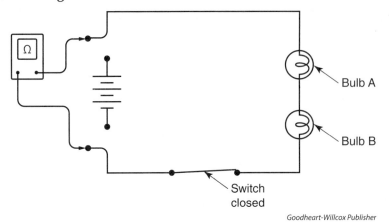

Goodheart-Willcox Publisher

Figure 7-5.2.

_____ Total Circuit Resistance

10. Was the measurement the same as the total resistance value calculated in Step 6?

_____

_____

11. Measure voltage drops at the locations shown in **Figure 7-5.3** and record your measurements. Also, record your voltage drop measurements next to the resistance values of each component in the chart in Step 6.

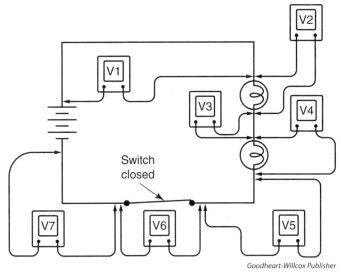

Goodheart-Willcox Publisher

Figure 7-5.3.

Name ____

_______________ Voltage drop V1 (Wire A)

_______________ Voltage drop V2 (Bulb A)

_______________ Voltage drop V3 (Wire B)

_______________ Voltage drop V4 (Bulb B)

_______________ Voltage drop V5 (Wire C)

_______________ Voltage drop V6 (Switch)

_______________ Voltage drop V7 (Wire D)

12. Describe the correlation that can be made between resistance values and voltage drop in a working circuit.

____

____

____

13. List the electrical tips that were proven with these tests.

____

____

____

14. Switch the bulb locations. Measure and record the voltage drop of each bulb as shown in **Figure 7-5.4**.

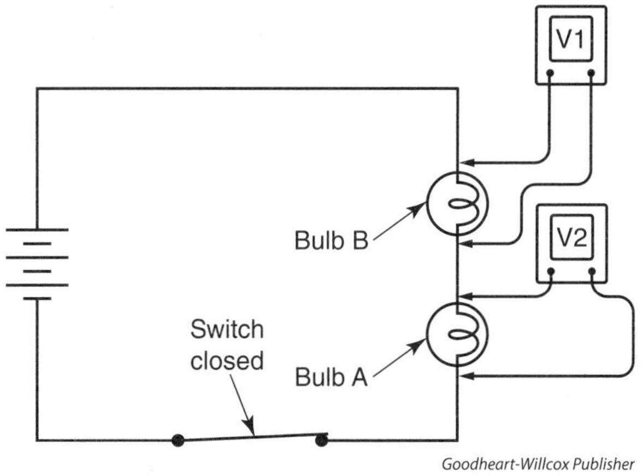
V1
V2
Bulb B
Bulb A
Switch closed
Goodheart-Willcox Publisher

Figure 7-5.4.

_______________ Measured voltage V1

_______________ Measured voltage V2

15. Describe the conclusions that can be made by these measurements.

____

____

____

16. Make available voltage measurements of the same circuit as shown in **Figure 7-5.5** and record your answers.

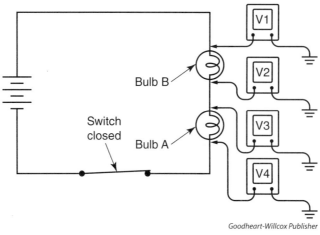

Goodheart-Willcox Publisher

Figure 7-5.5.

_____ Measured voltage V1

_____ Measured voltage V2

_____ Measured voltage V3

_____ Measured voltage V4

17. Describe the relationship between voltage drop and available voltage. What conclusions can be made? (Keep your answer simple.)

_____

_____

18. Are the four electrical rules based on available voltage or voltage drop?

_____

19. When is voltage drop a good measurement to use?

_____

_____

_____

STOP 20. Discuss your findings so far with your instructor.

Instructor's Initials: _____

Job Wrap Up

21. Return all tools and materials to the proper storage areas and clean up your work area.

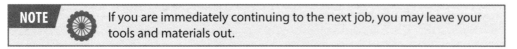

NOTE If you are immediately continuing to the next job, you may leave your tools and materials out.

Name _____

Final Assessment

_____   1.   A voltage drop measurement of a bulb is being taken. The measurement indicates source voltage and the bulb does not work. Technician A says that the fault is after the bulb in the circuit. Technician B says the fault is the bulb itself. Who is correct?

A.   A only.

B.   B only.

C.   Both A and B.

D.   Neither A nor B.

_____   2.   An available voltage measurement is taken before a load that is not working. Full source voltage is available. Technician A says the fault is before the load. Technician B says the fault is in the load or after the load. Who is correct?

A.   A only.

B.   B only.

C.   Both A and B.

D.   Neither A nor B.

_____   3.   A voltage drop measurement of 0 volts is made at a bulb that is not working. Technician A says that you cannot tell if the fault is before or after the bulb. Technician B says the fault is the bulb. Who is correct?

A.   A only.

B.   B only.

C.   Both A and B.

D.   Neither A nor B.

_____   4.   A voltage drop measurement is made at a bulb that is not working. The measurement indicates source voltage. Technician A says that you cannot tell if the fault is before or after the bulb. Technician B says the fault is the bulb. Who is correct?

A.   A only.

B.   B only.

C.   Both A and B.

D.   Neither A nor B.

_____   5.   An available voltage measurement is taken after a load that is not working. The reading indicates source voltage. Technician A says the fault is before the load. Technician B says the fault is after the load. Who is correct?

A.   A only.

B.   B only.

C.   Both A and B.

D.   Neither A nor B.

Final Instructor Approval: _____

Name _____ Date _____ Class _____

Job 7-6

Parallel Circuits

Introduction

You will be using the electrical rules to predict measurements and then perform voltage and amperage tests to more fully understand how circuits work. You must correlate your readings with the status of the load and determine whether the circuit is open or closed. The rules all relate to understanding opens and loads and how voltage works with them.

Objective

After successfully completing this job, you will be able to make voltage and amperage measurements in a parallel circuit.

Materials and Equipment

To complete this job, you will need the following tools, equipment, and materials:

- Electrical board with components to build circuits
- Two different wattage bulbs for building circuits
- Multimeter

Instructions

In this job you will be predicting voltages, then building a circuit and measuring voltage and amperage. You will be asked to use the electrical rules explained below. When you reach a (STOP) sign, show your work to your instructor. Do not continue until you have instructor approval (instructor will initial job sheet).

Resources

Electrical Rules

Rule #1
With the circuit off or not working, voltage travels to an open.

Rule #2
Source voltage is measured before an open or before a working load.

Rule #3
Zero volts is measured after an open or after the last working load.

Rule #4
When available voltage is less than source and more than 0, the measurement is between two loads.

Electrical Tips

- Voltage drop and resistance are found together.
- Current takes its easiest or only path to ground.
- Current only flows and can be measured on a circuit that is operating.
- Current is the same throughout the series portion of a circuit.
- Loads use or share all of the source voltage.
- When checking electrical circuits, substitute electrical loads only with similar loads. Do not replace a load with a wire. A horn (for instance) is a load. If a horn is diagnosed as faulty, replace it with another load, such as a known good light, and see if the light works. A switch can be bypassed with the correct size wire.

 NOTE Remember that the *Electrical Rules* will help you predict circuit values and understand the measurements you will be making. The *Electrical Tips* will help you further understand certain measurements and how circuits work.

Procedures

Predicting Voltages

1. Using the circuit shown in **Figure 7-6.1**, predict the voltages in the circuit with the switch open (circuit *off*) and the switch closed (circuit *on*). Record your predictions below. There are three possible answers:
   - S (source voltage)
   - LTS (less than source voltage, more than zero)
   - 0 (zero)

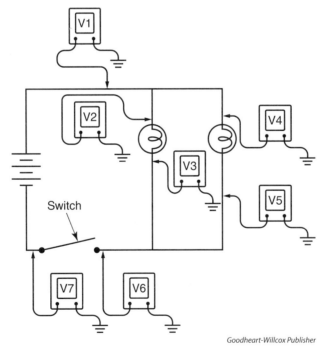

Goodheart-Willcox Publisher

Figure 7-6.1.

Predicted voltage with switch *open*:

_____ Predicted voltage V1

_____ Predicted voltage V2

Name _____

_____   Predicted voltage V3

_____   Predicted voltage V4

_____   Predicted voltage V5

_____   Predicted voltage V6

_____   Predicted voltage V7

Predicted voltage with switch *closed*:

_____   Predicted voltage V1

_____   Predicted voltage V2

_____   Predicted voltage V3

_____   Predicted voltage V4

_____   Predicted voltage V5

_____   Predicted voltage V6

_____   Predicted voltage V7

Build the Circuit

2. Build the parallel circuit shown in **Figure 7-6.1** with two different loads (such as bulbs of different wattages).

3. With the switch open, make the measurements shown in **Figure 7-6.1**.

_____   Measured voltage V1

_____   Measured voltage V2

_____   Measured voltage V3

_____   Measured voltage V4

_____   Measured voltage V5

_____   Measured voltage V6

_____   Measured voltage V7

4. Close the switch and make the measurements shown in **Figure 7-6.1**.

_____   Measured voltage V1

_____   Measured voltage V2

_____   Measured voltage V3

_____   Measured voltage V4

_____   Measured voltage V5

_____   Measured voltage V6

_____   Measured voltage V7

5. Did you predict the voltage properly? Yes _____ No _____ If no, why?

_____

_____

_____

6. What rules were proven by your measurements in this circuit? Write the rules in their entirety here.

_____

_____

_____

_____

Measuring Amperage

7. Make the amperage measurements shown in **Figure 7-6.2** and record them below. Make each measurement separately and in the order shown. Be sure to turn the circuit off (switch open) when moving the ammeter to a new location. Continue until all four ammeter measurements are made.

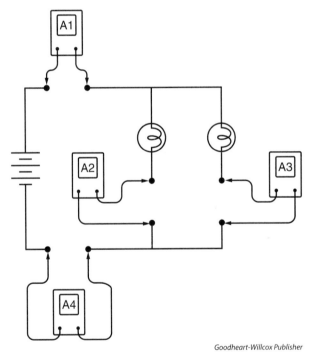

Goodheart-Willcox Publisher

Figure 7-6.2.

_____ Measured amperage A1

_____ Measured amperage A2

_____ Measured amperage A3

_____ Measured amperage A4

8. Add the amperage readings of #1 and #4. Write your conclusions about amperage total measurements of #1 and #4.

_____

Name _____

9. Add up amperage readings of #2 and #3. Write your conclusions about the total amperage of #2 and #3, in relation to the total amperage of #1 and #4.

_____

_____

10. Add another load in parallel and make the measurements shown in **Figure 7-6.3**.

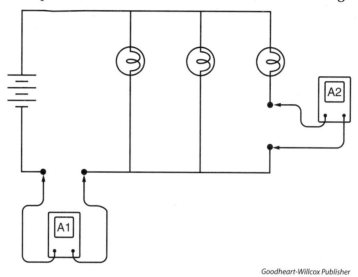

Goodheart-Willcox Publisher

Figure 7-6.3.

11. Write your conclusions about what happened to the amperage reading for the whole circuit as compared with two bulbs in parallel.

_____

12. Briefly describe the conclusion that can be drawn from this.

_____

_____

_____

_____

13. List the electrical tips that are proven with your ammeter measurements.

_____

_____

_____

STOP 14. Discuss your findings so far with your instructor.

Instructor's Initials: _____

Job Wrap Up

15. Return all tools and materials to the proper storage areas and clean up your work area.

> **NOTE** If you are immediately continuing to the next job, you may leave your tools and materials out.

Final Assessment

_____ 1. Only one load in a parallel circuit is working. Technician A says that the switch is probably defective. Technician B says to start with the faulty load when making measurements. Who is correct?

A. A only.

B. B only.

C. Both A and B.

D. Neither A nor B.

_____ 2. Neither of the loads work in a parallel circuit. Source voltage is found to be available before each load. Technician A says both loads could be faulty. Technician B says the switch after the loads could be faulty. Who is correct?

A. A only.

B. B only.

C. Both A and B.

D. Neither A nor B.

_____ 3. Neither of the loads in a parallel circuit work. Zero volts is measured before each load. Technician A says both loads could be faulty. Technician B says the switch after the loads could be faulty. Who is correct?

A. A only.

B. B only.

C. Both A and B.

D. Neither A nor B.

_____ 4. Neither of the loads in a parallel circuit work. Source voltage is measured after each load. Technician A says both loads could be faulty. Technician B says the switch after the loads could be faulty. Who is correct?

A. A only.

B. B only.

C. Both A and B.

D. Neither A nor B.

_____ 5. Only one load in a parallel circuit is working. Source voltage is measured after the faulty load. Technician A says that the switch after the loads should be tested. Technician B says to replace the faulty load with a known good load. Who is correct?

A. A only.

B. B only.

C. Both A and B.

D. Neither A nor B.

Final Instructor Approval: _____

Name _____ Date _____ Class _____

Job 7-7

Parallel Circuits with Faults

Introduction

You will be using the electrical rules to predict measurements and then make voltage measurements to understand how to find faults in parallel circuits. You must correlate your readings with the status of the load and determine whether the circuit is open or closed. The rules all relate to understanding opens and loads and how voltage works with them.

Objective

After successfully completing this job, you will be able to make voltage measurements and find faults in a parallel circuit.

Materials and Equipment

To complete this job, you will need the following tools, equipment, and materials:
- Electrical board with components to build circuits
- Multimeter

Instructions

In this job you will be predicting voltages, then building a circuit and measuring voltage. You will be asked to use the electrical rules explained below. When you reach a **STOP** sign, show your work to your instructor. Do not continue until you have instructor approval (instructor will initial job sheet).

Resources

Electrical Rules

Rule #1
With the circuit off or not working, voltage travels to an open.

Rule #2
Source voltage is measured before an open or before a working load.

Rule #3
Zero volts is measured after an open or after the last working load.

Rule #4
When available voltage is less than source and more than 0, the measurement is between two loads.

Electrical Tips
- Voltage drop and resistance are found together.
- Current takes its easiest or only path to ground.
- Current only flows and can be measured on a circuit that is operating.

- Current is the same throughout the series portion of a circuit.
- Loads use or share all of the source voltage.
- When checking electrical circuits, substitute electrical loads only with similar loads. Do not replace a load with a wire. A horn (for instance) is a load. If a horn is diagnosed as faulty, replace it with another load, such as a known good light, and see if the light works. A switch can be bypassed with the correct size wire.

| NOTE | | Remember that the *Electrical Rules* will help you predict circuit values and understand the measurements you will be making. The *Electrical Tips* will help you further understand certain measurements and how circuits work. |

Procedures

Predicting Voltages

1. Using the circuit shown in **Figure 7-7.1**, predict the voltages in the circuit with the switch open (circuit *off*) and the switch closed (circuit *on*). Record your predictions below. There are three possible answers:
   - S (source voltage)
   - LTS (less than source voltage, greater than zero)
   - 0 (zero)

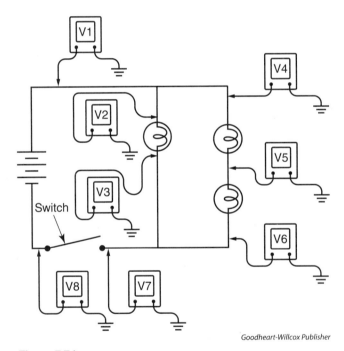

Goodheart-Willcox Publisher

Figure 7-7.1.

Predicted voltage with switch *open*:

_____ Predicted voltage V1

_____ Predicted voltage V2

_____ Predicted voltage V3

_____ Predicted voltage V4

_____ Predicted voltage V5

Name _____

_____   Predicted voltage V6

_____   Predicted voltage V7

_____   Predicted voltage V8

Predicted voltage with switch *closed*:

_____   Predicted voltage V1

_____   Predicted voltage V2

_____   Predicted voltage V3

_____   Predicted voltage V4

_____   Predicted voltage V5

_____   Predicted voltage V6

_____   Predicted voltage V7

_____   Predicted voltage V8

Build the Circuit

2. Build the series circuit shown in **Figure 7-7.1**.

3. With the switch open, make the measurements shown in **Figure 7-7.1**.

_____   Measured voltage V1

_____   Measured voltage V2

_____   Measured voltage V3

_____   Measured voltage V4

_____   Measured voltage V5

_____   Measured voltage V6

_____   Measured voltage V7

_____   Measured voltage V8

4. Close the switch and make the measurements shown in **Figure 7-7.1**.

_____   Measured voltage V1

_____   Measured voltage V2

_____   Measured voltage V3

_____   Measured voltage V4

_____   Measured voltage V5

_____   Measured voltage V6

_____   Measured voltage V7

_____   Measured voltage V8

5. Did you predict the voltage properly? Yes _____ No _____ If no, why?

_____

_____

_____

6. What rules were proven by your measurements in this circuit? Write the rules in their entirety here.

_____

_____

_____

_____

_____

STOP 7. Discuss your findings so far with your instructor and receive permission to move forward in the Job if you are working independently.

Instructor's Initials: _____

Diagnosing Faults

In this section, you will create faults by installing an additional load to the circuit. You will then predict and measure voltages to diagnose faults in a parallel circuit.

8. Using the circuit shown in **Figure 7-7.2**, predict the voltages in the circuit with the switch closed (circuit on). Record your predictions below. There are three possible answers:
   - S (source voltage)
   - LTS (less than source voltage, greater than zero)
   - 0 (zero)

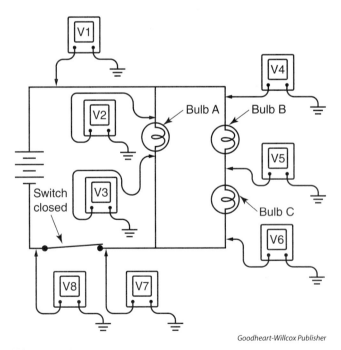

Goodheart-Willcox Publisher

Figure 7-7.2

Name _____

Predicted voltage with switch *closed*:

_____ Predicted voltage V1

_____ Predicted voltage V2

_____ Predicted voltage V3

_____ Predicted voltage V4

_____ Predicted voltage V5

_____ Predicted voltage V6

_____ Predicted voltage V7

_____ Predicted voltage V8

9. Build the circuit shown in **Figure 7-7.2**.

10. With the switch closed, make the measurements shown and record your measurements below.

_____ Measured voltage V1

_____ Measured voltage V2

_____ Measured voltage V3

_____ Measured voltage V4

_____ Measured voltage V5

_____ Measured voltage V6

_____ Measured voltage V7

_____ Measured voltage V8

11. Did you predict the voltage properly? Yes _____ No _____ If no, why?

_____

_____

_____

12. Determine which rules were proven by measured voltage V5. Write the rules in their entirety here.

_____

_____

_____

13. Cover bulb B in **Figure 7-7.2** as if it were the fault. Do not move the voltmeter.

14. Describe how you can use the voltage measurement to diagnose a fault at bulb B.

_____

_____

_____

_____

15. Using the circuit shown in **Figure 7-7.3**, which has a jumper wire installed between bulb B and bulb C, predict the voltages in the circuit when the switch is closed. Record the value that you predict below. There are three possible answers:
    - S (source voltage)
    - LTS (less than source voltage, greater than zero)
    - 0 (zero)

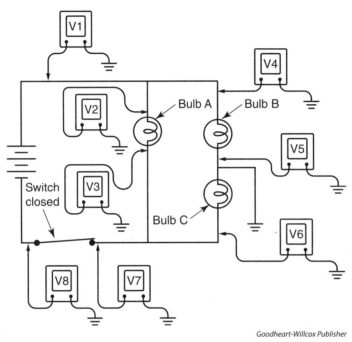

Goodheart-Willcox Publisher

Figure 7-7.3

Predicted voltage with switch *closed*:

_____ Predicted voltage V1

_____ Predicted voltage V2

_____ Predicted voltage V3

_____ Predicted voltage V4

_____ Predicted voltage V5

_____ Predicted voltage V6

_____ Predicted voltage V7

_____ Predicted voltage V8

16. Build the circuit shown in **Figure 7-7.3**.

Name _____

17. With the switch closed, make the measurements shown.

_____ Measured voltage V1

_____ Measured voltage V2

_____ Measured voltage V3

_____ Measured voltage V4

_____ Measured voltage V5

_____ Measured voltage V6

_____ Measured voltage V7

_____ Measured voltage V8

18. Explain your measurements and what happened in the circuit with one or more of the rules or tips.

_____

_____

_____

_____

Job Wrap Up

19. Return all tools and materials to the proper storage areas and clean up your work area.

> **NOTE**   If you are immediately continuing to the next job, you may leave your tools and materials out.

Final Assessment

_____ 1. Voltage drop measurement on a load is 0 volts. This reading would mean that _____.
A. zero volts available before and after the load
B. six volts available before and after the load
C. source voltage available before and after the load
D. Any of the above.

_____ 2. An available voltage measurement is being taken between two loads, neither of which is working. The measurement is 0 volts. Technician A says the fault is before the measurement. Technician B says the fault is after the measurement. Who is correct?
A. A only.
B. B only.
C. Both A and B.
D. Neither A nor B.

_____ 3. An available voltage measurement is being taken between two loads, neither of which is working. The measurement is source voltage. Technician A says the fault is before the measurement. Technician B says the fault is after the measurement. Who is correct?

A. A only.

B. B only.

C. Both A and B.

D. Neither A nor B.

_____ 4. A voltage drop measurement across a load of 0 voltage would mean which of the following?

A. Source voltage available before the load and 0 volts after the load.

B. Six volts available before and after the load.

C. Source voltage available before and after the load.

D. Any of the above.

_____ 5. An available voltage measurement of two volts is measured before a dim bulb and after a closed switch. Technician A says the fault is before the measurement point. Technician B says the fault is after the measurement point. Who is correct?

A. A only.

B. B only.

C. Both A and B.

D. Neither A nor B.

Final Instructor Approval: _____

Name _____   Date _____   Class _____

Job 7-8

Series-Parallel Circuits

Introduction

You will be using the electrical rules to predict measurements and perform voltage and amperage tests to more fully understand how the circuit works. You must correlate your readings with the status of the load and determine whether the circuit is open or closed. The electrical rules all relate to understanding opens and loads and how voltage works with them.

Objective

After successfully completing this job, you will be able to make voltage measurements in a series-parallel circuit.

Materials and Equipment

To complete this job, you will need the following tools, equipment, and materials:

- Electrical board with components to build circuits
- Two different wattage bulbs for building circuits
- Bimetal flasher
- Rheostat (variable resistor)
- Multimeter

Instructions

In this job you will be predicting voltages, then building a circuit and measuring voltage and amperage. You will be asked to use the electrical rules explained below. When you reach a (STOP) sign, show your work to your instructor. Do not continue until you have instructor approval (instructor will initial job sheet).

Resources

Electrical Rules

Rule #1
With the circuit off or not working, voltage travels to an open.

Rule #2
Source voltage is measured before an open or before a working load.

Rule #3
Zero volts is measured after an open or after the last working load.

Rule #4
When available voltage is less than source and more than 0, the measurement is between two loads.

Electrical Tips

- Voltage drop and resistance are found together.
- Current takes its easiest or only path to ground.
- Current only flows and can be measured on a circuit that is operating.
- Current is the same throughout the series portion of a circuit.
- Loads use or share all of the source voltage.
- When checking electrical circuits, substitute electrical loads only with similar loads. Do not replace a load with a wire. A horn (for instance) is a load. If a horn is diagnosed as faulty, replace it with another load, such as a known good light, and see if the light works. A switch can be bypassed with the correct size wire.

> **NOTE** Remember that the *Electrical Rules* will help you predict circuit values and understand the measurements you will be making. The *Electrical Tips* will help you further understand certain measurements and how circuits work.

Procedures

Predicting Voltages

1. Using the circuit shown in **Figure 7-8.1**, predict the voltages in the circuit with the switch open (circuit *off*) and the switch closed (circuit *on*). Record your predictions below. There are three possible answers:
   - S (source voltage)
   - LTS (less than source voltage, greater than zero)
   - 0 (zero)

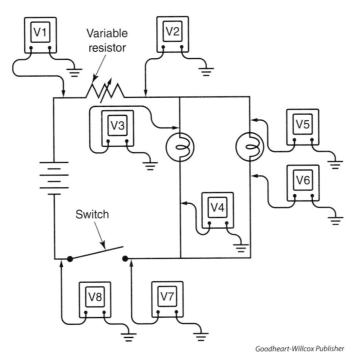

Goodheart-Willcox Publisher

Figure 7-8.1

Name _____

Predicted voltage with switch *open*:

_____ Predicted voltage V1

_____ Predicted voltage V2

_____ Predicted voltage V3

_____ Predicted voltage V4

_____ Predicted voltage V5

_____ Predicted voltage V6

_____ Predicted voltage V7

_____ Predicted voltage V8

Predicted voltage with switch *closed*:

_____ Predicted voltage V1

_____ Predicted voltage V2

_____ Predicted voltage V3

_____ Predicted voltage V4

_____ Predicted voltage V5

_____ Predicted voltage V6

_____ Predicted voltage V7

_____ Predicted voltage V8

Build the Circuit

2. Build the circuit shown in **Figure 7-8.1** using different loads (different wattage bulbs).

3. With the switch open, make the measurements shown in **Figure 7-8.1** and record your measurements below.

_____ Measured voltage V1

_____ Measured voltage V2

_____ Measured voltage V3

_____ Measured voltage V4

_____ Measured voltage V5

_____ Measured voltage V6

_____ Measured voltage V7

_____ Measured voltage V8

4. Close the switch and make the measurements shown in **Figure 7-8.1**. Record your measurements below.

_____   Measured voltage V1

_____   Measured voltage V2

_____   Measured voltage V3

_____   Measured voltage V4

_____   Measured voltage V5

_____   Measured voltage V6

_____   Measured voltage V7

_____   Measured voltage V8

5. Did you predict the voltage properly? Yes _____ No _____ If no, why?

_____

_____

_____

6. Determine which rules were proven by your measurements in this circuit and write them in their entirety here.

_____

_____

_____

_____

_____

7. Explain why this circuit is called a series-parallel circuit.

_____

_____

_____

8. Discuss your findings so far with your instructor and receive permission to move forward in the job if you are working independently.

Instructor's Initials: _____

Name _____

Full Bright

9. Build the circuit shown in **Figure 7-8.2**. Adjust the rheostat (variable resistor) to make the bulbs glow brightly. Take the voltage measurements shown in **Figure 7-8.2** and record your measurements below.

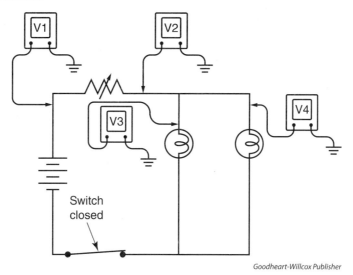

Goodheart-Willcox Publisher

Figure 7-8.2

_____   Measured voltage V1

_____   Measured voltage V2

_____   Measured voltage V3

_____   Measured voltage V4

10. Describe the correlation between the rheostat voltage drop to the brightness of the bulbs.

_____

_____

_____

11. Using knowledge learned in a prior job about resistance and voltage drop, describe the level of rheostat resistance when the bulbs are brightest.

_____

_____

_____

Full Dim

12. Next, adjust the rheostat (variable resistor) to make the bulbs dim (stop just before they are completely off). Again, take the voltage measurements shown in **Figure 7-8.2** and record your measurements below.

    _______________ Measured voltage V1

    _______________ Measured voltage V2

    _______________ Measured voltage V3

    _______________ Measured voltage V4

13. Describe how this proves what you learned with the bulbs in Step 8.

    ____

    ____

    ____

STOP 14. Discuss your findings so far with your instructor and receive permission to move forward in the job if you are working independently.

Instructor's Initials: ____

Flasher

15. Build the circuit shown in **Figure 7-8.3**, replacing the rheostat with a bimetal flasher. Observe the rate at which the bulbs flash.

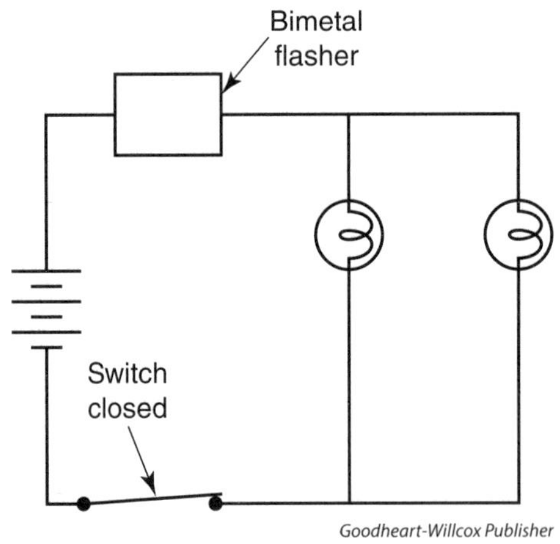
Bimetal
flasher
Switch
closed
Goodheart-Willcox Publisher

Figure 7-8.3

16. Explain how a bimetal flasher works.

    ____

    ____

    ____

Name _____

17. Add more bulbs to the circuit in parallel with the flasher as shown in **Figure 7-8.4**. Describe what happens to the bulb flash rate.

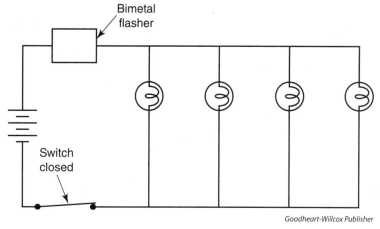

Figure 7-8.4

_____

_____

_____

18. Explain why the bulbs are doing what they are doing.

_____

_____

_____

Job Wrap Up

19. Return all tools and materials to the proper storage areas and clean up your work area.

 NOTE   If you are immediately continuing to the next job, you may leave your tools and materials out.

Final Assessment

_____ 1. Source voltage is 12 volts, a rheostat is set to a voltage drop of 5 volts. How many volts are available to the bulbs after the rheostat?

   A. 3.

   B. 5.

   C. 7.

   D. 12.

_____ 2. Source voltage is 12 volts, and a rheostat is installed in the circuit. Five volts is available after the rheostat. How many volts are available to the bulbs?

   A. 3.

   B. 5.

   C. 7.

   D. 12.

_____ 3. Bulbs that are in parallel in a series-parallel circuit are using 1 volt (voltage drop). How many volts is the rheostat using if the source voltage is 12 volts?

   A. 5.

   B. 7.

   C. 9.

   D. 11.

_____ 4. Neither of the loads in a series-parallel circuit are working. Source voltage is measured after the rheostat and before each load. Technician A says both loads could be faulty. Technician B says the rheostat could be faulty. Who is correct?

   A. A only.

   B. B only.

   C. Both A and B.

   D. Neither A nor B.

_____ 5. One load in a series-parallel circuit is working, and source voltage is found to be available before and after the faulty load. Technician A says that the rheostat should be tested. Technician B says to test the ground path for the faulty load.

   A. A only.

   B. B only.

   C. Both A and B.

   D. Neither A nor B.

Final Instructor Approval: _____

Name _____ Date _____ Class _____

Job 7-9

Normally Open Relay Circuits

Introduction

Relays are becoming more and more common on motorcycles, and the technician must learn how to diagnose a relay circuit. Relays use a small amount of current in a control circuit to regulate a large amount of current in a load circuit. An example is a fuel pump relay. The computer can control the magnet in the relay with a very small amount of current, and when the magnet closes the switch in the relay, a large amount of current flows to the fuel pump. There are three common types of relays, based on what position the switch is in when the relay is off. There is a normally open (NO) relay, a normally closed (NC) relay and a five-pin relay. The most common is the NO relay. In this relay, when the magnet is energized, the switch closes.

Objective

After successfully completing this job, you will be able to make voltage measurements in a NO relay controlled circuit.

Materials and Equipment

To complete this job, you will need the following tools, equipment, and materials:

- Electrical board with components to build circuits
- NO relay
- Multimeter

Instructions

In this job you will be predicting voltages, then building a circuit and measuring voltage and amperage. You will be asked to use the electrical rules explained below. When you reach a 🛑 sign, show your work to your instructor. Do not continue until you have instructor approval (instructor will initial job sheet).

Resources

Electrical Rules

Rule #1
With the circuit off or not working, voltage travels to an open.

Rule #2
Source voltage is measured before an open or before a working load.

Rule #3
Zero volts is measured after an open or after the last working load.

Rule #4
When available voltage is less than source and more than 0, the measurement is between two loads.

Electrical Tips

- Voltage drop and resistance are found together.
- Current takes its easiest or only path to ground.
- Current only flows and can be measured on a circuit that is operating.
- Current is the same throughout the series portion of a circuit.
- Loads use or share all of the source voltage.
- When checking electrical circuits, substitute electrical loads only with similar loads. Do not replace a load with a wire. A horn (for instance) is a load. If a horn is diagnosed as faulty, replace it with another load, such as a known good light, and see if the light works. A switch can be bypassed with the correct size wire.

> **NOTE** Remember that the *Electrical Rules* will help you predict circuit values and understand the measurements you will be making. The *Electrical Tips* will help you further understand certain measurements and how circuits work.

Procedures

Relay Familiarization

Wiring diagrams are available for most motorcycles, but many times a technician will come across an aftermarket accessory and will need to identify the electrical contacts on a relay.

1. Using a NO relay and a multimeter, measure the resistance between different pins on the relay to locate the magnet and the switch.

> **NOTE** Find the magnet first (it is usually 75-150 ohms), and then check the switch. The switch has no continuity when it is off/open and will have continuity when it is on/closed.

Once the magnet and the switch are located, energize the magnet by giving it power and ground from the electrical board power source. Retest the switch, making sure that it is now closed. Fill out the following chart.

Component	Resistance	Pins/Names/Colors	Working?
Magnet			
Switch			

2. Using the pin numbers shown in **Figure 7-9.1**, identify which pins connect to the control side (magnet) and which pins connect to the load side (switch).

_____ Control side pins

_____ Load side pins

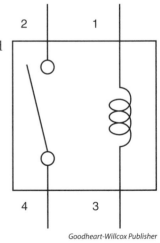

Goodheart-Willcox Publisher

Figure 7-9.1

Name _____

Relay Circuit

3. Study the circuit shown in **Figure 7-9.2** and predict the voltages in the circuit with the switch open (circuit *off*) and the switch closed (circuit *on*). Record your predictions below. There are three possible answers:
   - S (source voltage)
   - LTS (less than source voltage, greater than zero)
   - 0 (zero)

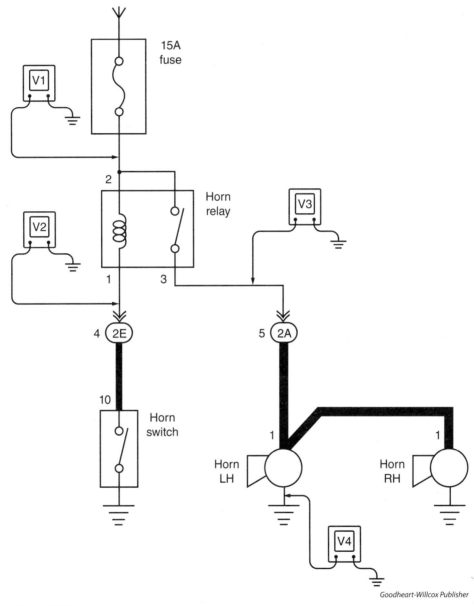

Goodheart-Willcox Publisher

Figure 7-9.2

Predicted voltage with switch *open*:

_____ Predicted voltage V1

_____ Predicted voltage V2

_____ Predicted voltage V3

_____ Predicted voltage V4

Predicted voltage with switch *closed*:

_____ Predicted voltage V1

_____ Predicted voltage V2

_____ Predicted voltage V3

_____ Predicted voltage V4

4. Build the circuit shown in **Figure 7-9.2**.

5. With the switch open, make the measurements shown in **Figure 7-9.2**.

_____ Measured voltage V1

_____ Measured voltage V2

_____ Measured voltage V3

_____ Measured voltage V4

6. Close the switch and make the measurements shown in **Figure 7-9.2**.

_____ Measured voltage V1

_____ Measured voltage V2

_____ Measured voltage V3

_____ Measured voltage V4

7. Did you predict the voltage properly? Yes _____ No _____ If no, why?

_____

_____

_____

8. Determine the rules that were proven by your measurements in this circuit. Write the rules in their entirety here.

_____

_____

_____

_____

STOP 9. Discuss your findings so far with your instructor.

Instructor's Initials: _____

Name _____

Job Wrap Up

10. Return all tools and materials to the proper storage areas and clean up your work area.

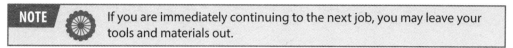

NOTE   If you are immediately continuing to the next job, you may leave your tools and materials out.

Final Assessment

1. Based on the readings in **Figure 7-9.3**, what complaint would the customer have?

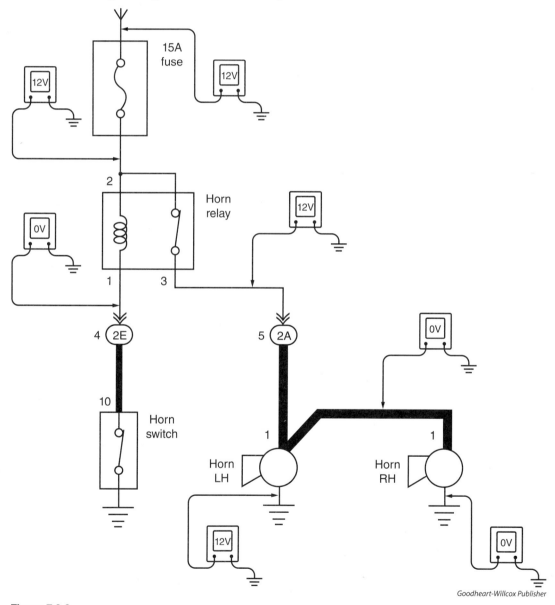

Figure 7-9.3

Goodheart-Willcox Publisher

_____

_____

2. Can you tell whether the fuse is intact (not blown)? Explain your answer.

_____

_____

3. Can you tell from the measurements if the horn switch works? Explain your answer.

_____

_____

_____

4. Can you tell if the relay works? Explain your answer.

_____

_____

_____

5. Are both loads operating properly? Explain your answer.

_____

_____

_____

_____

Final Instructor Approval: _____

CHAPTER
8   Engines

Chapter 8 Quiz

After studying Chapter 8 in the Motorcycles: Fundamentals, Service, Repair textbook, answer the following questions.

_____ 1. *True or False?* Powersports vehicles use both two-stroke and four-stroke engines.

_____ 2. An engine changes the energy of burning fuel into useful _____ energy.
   A. chemical
   B. heat
   C. mechanical
   D. All of the above.

_____ 3. In a four-stroke engine, the piston moves down on the _____ strokes.
   A. intake and exhaust
   B. intake and power
   C. compression and exhaust
   D. intake and compression

_____ 4. *True or False?* During the compression stroke, a spark plug fires and ignites the compressed air-fuel mixture.

_____ 5. *True or False?* The exhaust valve remains partially open during the start of the intake stroke.

_____ 6. The period of time when the intake and exhaust valves are open at the same time is called valve _____.

_____ 7. The camshaft rotates at _____ the speed of the crankshaft.
   A. twice
   B. one-half
   C. one-third
   D. one-quarter

_____ 8. *True or False?* Increased camshaft lift and duration reduce engine power at low to medium speeds.

_____ 9. A(n) _____ drive is the most commonly used mechanism to drive the camshaft.

_____ 10. Camshaft-in-crankcase engines are also known as _____ engines.

_____ 11. *True or False?* Pushrods and lifters are used in the SOHC camshaft design.

_____ 12. *True or False?* In a shim-and-bucket DOHC configuration, the camshaft must be removed when valve clearance is out of specification.

_____ 13. A DOHC configuration with rocker arms _____.

    A. can be used in engines with five valves per cylinder

    B. can be used in engines with three valves per cylinder

    C. reduces the likelihood of valve float

    D. All of the above.

_____ 14. Valve _____ are often used to close the valves.

_____ 15. When the valve springs fail to close the valves completely at high engine speeds, valve _____ occurs.

For questions 16–21, identify the valve parts indicated in the following illustration.

A. Valve stem tip   C. Stem   E. Margin

B. Keeper groove   D. Face   F. Head

_____ 16. Forms a portion of the combustion chamber.

_____ 17. Protects the face from high temperature.

_____ 18. The part that slides in and out of the valve guide.

_____ 19. The part that comes in contact with valve opener.

_____ 20. Retains the valve springs.

_____ 21. The part that matches the seat.

Exhaust Valve   **Intake Valve**

Goodheart-Willcox Publisher

_____ 22. A(n) _____ combustion chamber has three intake valves and two exhaust valves.

_____ 23. Cylinder _____ is the volume of air displaced by the piston as it travels from BDC to TDC.

_____ 24. The diameter of the cylinder is called the _____.

    A. bore

    B. taper

    C. stroke

    D. dead center

_____ 25. In a(n) _____ twin-cylinder engine, the cylinders lie horizontally at right angles to the motorcycle frame.

Name _____

_____ 26. Pistons move up and down together in a _____ crankshaft.
A. 90°
B. 180°
C. 270°
D. 360°

_____ 27. Pistons move up and down alternately in a _____ crankshaft.
A. 90°
B. 180°
C. 270°
D. 360°

_____ 28. *True or False?* On most V twin-cylinder engines, the crankshafts have a common journal for both connecting rods.

_____ 29. All of the following statements about a pressed-in sleeve are true, *except*:
A. it is rarely used in two-stroke engines.
B. the sleeve is a liner made of aluminum.
C. it has a high manufacturing cost.
D. it can be bored when worn.

_____ 30. Four-stroke engine pistons are either cast or _____.

_____ 31. All of the following statements about forged pistons are true, *except*:
A. they are made by pouring molten metal into a mold.
B. they are more expensive to produce than cast pistons.
C. they are often used in high-performance applications.
D. they require more cylinder-to-piston clearance than a cast piston.

For questions 32–38, match each piston-related term with its description.

A. Piston ring   D. Offset pin   F. Ring land
B. Piston taper   E. Piston crown   G. Ring groove
C. Cam ground

_____ 32. Compensates for uneven enlargement of the piston.

_____ 33. Connects the piston to the small end of the connecting rod.

_____ 34. The top of the piston exposed to the heat and pressure of combustion.

_____ 35. Reduces piston clearance when the piston is cold.

_____ 36. Seals the space between the piston and the cylinder wall.

_____ 37. Machined below the piston crown to accept the piston rings.

_____ 38. Supporting area between ring grooves.

_____ 39. A piston ring that acts as a compression ring and also helps remove excess oil from the cylinder wall is a(n) _____ ring.

_____ 40. The piston ring is forced against the cylinder wall by _____ pressure.

_____ 41. An engine bearing allows movement between parts and reduces _____.

For questions 42–44, identify the types of bearings indicated in the following illustration.

_____ 42. Roller bearing

_____ 43. Plain bearing

_____ 44. Ball bearing

Goodheart-Willcox Publisher

_____ 45. *True or False?* Most motorcycle engines with two or more cylinders have vertically split crankcases.

_____ 46. *True or False?* A two-stroke engine produces power twice during each crankshaft revolution.

_____ 47. *True or False?* In a two-stroke engine, the air-fuel mixture enters the crankcase below the piston.

_____ 48. In a two-stroke engine, the _____ port connects the crankcase to the upper part of the cylinder.

_____ 49. *True or False?* Radical timing allows a larger amount of air-fuel mixture to enter the crankcase.

_____ 50. The _____ valve is located between the carburetor and the engine on two-stroke engines.

_____ 51. The rotary valve opens and closes the _____ port.

_____ 52. Single-cylinder crankshafts are made of several pieces _____ together.

_____ 53. Three-cylinder crankshafts consist of three sets of _____ assemblies connected together.

_____ 54. *True or False?* A transfer cutout matches the transfer opening in the cylinder wall and crankcase when the piston is at TDC.

_____ 55. In a two-stroke engine, piston rings are required to seal compression, _____, and combustion pressures.

_____ 56. To locate ring end gaps away from ports in the cylinder, _____ pins are positioned so the piston rings move past the ports.

_____ 57. Most engines are rated in the amount of _____ they can produce.

    A. horsepower

    B. speed

    C. revolutions per minute

    D. energy

Name _____ Date _____ Class _____

Understanding Four-Stroke Engines

Introduction

An understanding of the operation of a four-stroke engine is very important when assembling and timing an engine, diagnosing engine-related concerns, and performing engine diagnosis steps, such as cylinder leak-down tests. This job will help you understand not only the order of the engine strokes but the other actions happening during the strokes.

Objective

After successfully completing this job, you will understand the four strokes of a four-stroke engine.

Materials and Equipment

To complete this job, you will need the following tools, equipment, and materials:

- Textbook
- Cutaway engine on a stand (helpful but not required)
- Instructional video provided by instructor (if available)

Instructions

In this job, you will be answering some questions and filling out some charts to help you understand what happens during the strokes of a four-stroke internal combustion engine. You will need to use your textbook and it would be helpful to have a cutaway engine in order to watch four-stroke operation. Your instructor may also have a video that you can watch to help facilitate this job. When you reach a (STOP) sign, show your work to your instructor. Do not continue until you have instructor approval (instructor will initial job sheet).

Procedures

Using the information in the textbook, answer the questions.

1. Fill in the chart by naming the four engine strokes in order, starting with the intake stroke.

Stroke
1.
2.
3.
4.

2. How many times does the crankshaft turn to complete all four strokes?

_____

3. How many times does the crankshaft turn during one revolution of the camshaft?

_____

4. How many times does the camshaft turn for one revolution of the crankshaft?

_____

5. What is overlap in relation to valves?

_____

_____

6. Between what two strokes does overlap occur?

_____

> **NOTE** ⚙ Overlap on variable valve intake engines varies from none at startup and low engine speed loads, to a large amount at heavy engine loads and engine speeds.

7. Fill in the chart with the appropriate stroke for the condition given in the piston direction box and the valve open box (valves can open and close on different strokes).

Piston Direction	Intake or Exhaust Valve Open	Stroke
Down	Yes	1.
Up	No	2.
Down	No	3.
Up	Yes	4.

8. Fill in the chart by indicating whether the valve is opening or closing. Also indicate whether or not overlap is involved. Overlap can be built into the camshaft or performed by a variable valve timing mechanism.

Valve	Opening	Closing	Overlap?
Intake	1.	2.	Yes/No
Exhaust	3.	4.	Yes/No
Intake	5.	6.	Yes/No
Exhaust	7.	8.	Yes/No

9. On which stroke is the intake valve closed (disregard overlap)?

_____

10. On which stroke is the exhaust valve open (disregard overlap)?

_____

Name _____

NOTE It is very important to understand that the intake valve closes on the compression stroke and has a direct impact on engine performance. Opening the intake valve adjustment to the widest specification is a common tactic used in the industry to gain performance. Many engines will suffer from a hard start and low compression if the valve clearance has tightened or there is no clearance. Lack of clearance keeps the intake valve open longer on the compression stroke. This shortens the length of the compression stroke. Understanding this concept is a major requirement for diagnosing hard starts and run-ability, especially on carbureted vehicles.

STOP 11. Discuss with your instructor the four strokes and especially how the compression stroke is affected by where the intake valve closes.

Instructor's Initials: _____

12. On what stroke does the spark plug fire?

_____

13. On what stroke does maximum combustion pressure occur?

_____

14. On what stroke does a compression release occur?

_____

15. Which valve is held open for compression release?

_____

16. On what stroke is fuel and air drawn in on both carbureted or fuel-injected engines?

_____

17. What is the job of the camshaft?

_____

_____

18. What does TDC stand for?

_____

19. What does BDC stand for?

_____

20. Fill in the following chart to demonstrate your knowledge of four-stroke operation in engines with more than one cylinder. There are many cylinder configurations, but we will be using a two-cylinder 360 degree engine shown in Figure 8-1.1 for this example because the pistons travel together.

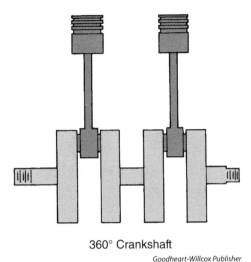

360° Crankshaft

Goodheart-Willcox Publisher

Figure 8-1.1. Pistons in an inline twin-cylinder engine with a 360° crankshaft move up and down together.

Fill in which stroke just finished. Indicate whether the piston is at BDC or TDC. Use the first row as a starting point and fill in the strokes in the correct order.

Piston Direction	Cylinder 1	Cylinder 2
Up	TDC Compression	TDC Exhaust
Down	1.	2.
Up	3.	4.
Down	5.	6.

21. Discuss with your instructor the above chart and your progress so far.

Instructor's Initials: _____

Final Assessment

1. What is the firing order for the four-cylinder engine used in the last exercise?

_____

2. An engine is running at 1000 rpm. At how many rpm is the camshaft turning?

_____

3. What is the purpose of a compression release mechanism?

_____

_____

Name _____

4. Intake valve clearance is too tight. What effect does that have on the length of the compression stroke?

_____

_____

_____

_____

5. At what piston position would both valves be closed for adjustment?

_____

Final Instructor Approval: _____

Notes

Name _____ Date _____ Class _____

Job 8-2

Four-Stroke Engine Operation

Introduction

There is a lot more to the operation of a four-stroke engine than the piston going up and down and the valves opening. They are, however, the basis of engine operation.

Objective

After successfully completing this job, you will be able to demonstrate the four strokes of an engine and what is happening during those four strokes.

Materials and Equipment

To complete this job, you will need the following tools, equipment, and materials:

- Cutaway engine (can be motorcycle or core engine)
- Appropriate service manual or electronic service information
- Hand tools

Instructions

In this job, you will be turning an engine and showing your instructor how the camshafts and valves open and close as the engine moves through the four strokes. You will need to be able to tell your instructor about other engine operations during the four strokes, such as spark plug firing and compression release.

As you complete steps, you will either fill in measurements or perform certain tasks. When you reach a sign, show your work to your instructor. Do not continue until you have instructor approval (instructor will initial job sheet).

> **WARNING** ⚠️ Before performing this job, review all pertinent safety information in the text and discuss safety procedures with your instructor.

Procedures

Check Engine Mechanical Timing

1. Safely secure the vehicle or engine for disassembly.

2. Using the service manual, find the procedure for setting the mechanical timing. This information is usually in the valve adjustment or camshaft installation sections.

3. If the appropriate covers are not already removed, remove them.

 4. Demonstrate to your instructor that the engine is timed properly. If it is not timed properly, discuss how to correct the problem before proceeding with the job.

Instructor's Initials: _____

Demonstrate the Four Strokes

5. Figure out in which direction the engine rotates.

 NOTE There are a couple of ways to determine this. Sometimes there are arrows that show the direction of rotation. If there are no arrows, bump the starter (either electric or kick) and note the turning direction. If you turn the crankshaft and it drives the starter, then you are going backward!

6. Turn the engine and memorize the four strokes.

7. Show your instructor when the following happens:

_____   Intake valve opens and closes

_____   Exhaust valve opens and closes

_____   Compression releases

_____   Spark plug fires

 NOTE It may be helpful to remove the spark plug(s) and put a rod, stick, or screwdriver into the spark plug hole so that you can determine piston position. Some engines have a very short stroke.

8. Demonstrate to your instructor:

_____   Intake valve opening

_____   Intake valve closing

_____   Compression releasing (which valve?)

_____   Spark occurring

_____   TDC compression occurring

_____   Maximum pressure occurring

_____   Power stroke occurring

_____   Exhaust valve opening

_____   Exhaust stroke occurring

_____   TDC exhaust occurring

Instructor's Initials: _____

Job Wrap Up

9. Return all tools and materials to the proper storage areas and clean up the work area.

10. Ask your instructor to check your work and initial this job sheet.

Name _____

Final Assessment

1. Define engine compression ratio.

   _____

   _____

2. Define engine displacement.

   _____

   _____

3. Define piston stroke.

   _____

4. Define engine bore.

   _____

5. If the cylinder is bored over by 0.050″, which would this increase, torque or horsepower?

   _____

Final Instructor Approval: _____

Notes

Name _____ Date _____ Class _____

Job 8-3

Two-Stroke Engine Operation

Introduction

To diagnose and repair a two-stroke engine, the technician must understand how it works. This includes a solid grasp of where the piston is during the up and down strokes, when the transfer ports are open, and how and when the reed valves open and close.

Objective

After successfully completing this job, you will be able to demonstrate what is happening during both strokes of the two-stroke engine.

Materials and Equipment

To complete this job, you will need the following tools, equipment, and materials:

- Textbook
- Appropriate service manual or electronic service information
- Two-stroke engine with the top of the cylinder removed to observe piston movement

Instructions

In this job, you will be answering questions and performing tasks with a two-stroke engine. You will need your textbook to answer some questions. You will also need to demonstrate to your instructor the two strokes and explain what is happening during those two strokes. When you reach a sign, show your work to your instructor. Do not continue until you have instructor approval (instructor will initial job sheet).

> **WARNING** ⚠️ Before performing this job, review all pertinent safety information in the text and discuss safety procedures with your instructor.

Procedures

Two-Stroke Operation

1. During what stroke is the air-fuel mixture drawn into the engine? Is the piston moving up or down?

   _____

2. How does the air-fuel mixture get drawn into the engine?

   _____

   _____

   _____

3. Does the air-fuel mixture enter the cylinder above or below the piston?

_____

4. Where is compression developed in a two-cycle engine when the piston is moving down in the cylinder?

_____

_____

_____

5. Where is compression developed in a two-cycle engine when the piston is moving up in the cylinder?

_____

_____

6. How does the air-fuel charge get from below the piston to above the piston?

_____

_____

_____

7. When does the spark plug fire?

_____

8. How are the exhaust gases removed from the cylinder?

_____

_____

_____

9. How is the crankshaft lubricated?

_____

_____

10. What parts of the engine make up the top end?

_____

11. What closes the reed valves?

_____

_____

🛑 12. Have your instructor check your answers and assign an engine in order to demonstrate what is happening during the two strokes.

Instructor's Initials: _____

Name _____

Demonstrate Two-Stroke Operation

13. Using the assigned two-stroke engine, practice filling out the checklist below.

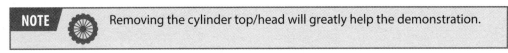

NOTE   Removing the cylinder top/head will greatly help the demonstration.

14. After practicing, demonstrate to your instructor that you understand what is happening as the piston moves from TDC to BDC and then back to TDC.

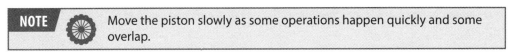

NOTE   Move the piston slowly as some operations happen quickly and some overlap.

Start with the piston at TDC

Operation	Instructor Check
Finish of intake	
Power	
Transfer	
Exhaust	
Crankcase compression	
Intake to crankcase	
Finish transfer	
Finish exhaust	
Compression above piston	
Ignition	
TDC	

Instructor's Initials: _____

Job Wrap Up

15. Return all tools and materials to the proper storage areas and clean up your work area.

16. Ask your instructor to check your work and initial the job sheet.

Final Assessment

1. How many times does the crankshaft go around (rotate) for every power stroke?

   _____

2. What is a typical fuel-to-oil ratio for a two-stroke motorcycle?

   _____

3. Why are two-stroke rings pinned to the piston so they cannot rotate?

   _____

4. On some two-cycle engines, oil is not mixed with fuel in the fuel tank. How does oil get into the fuel on these engines?

   _____

   _____

5. Why must the crankcase of a two-cycle engine be tightly sealed?

   _____

Final Instructor Approval: _____

CHAPTER 9 — Fuel Systems

Chapter 9 Quiz

After studying Chapter 9 in the Motorcycles: Fundamentals, Service, Repair textbook, answer the following questions.

_____ 1. A fuel petcock _____.
   A. holds the fuel supply
   B. carries fuel to the fuel pump
   C. is a valve that turns fuel flow on and off
   D. removes foreign matter from fuel

_____ 2. *True or False?* Vacuum is required to provide the fuel flow when a petcock is in the prime position.

_____ 3. *True or False?* The best source for replacement fuel tubing is the original equipment manufacturer.

_____ 4. A fuel _____ is required on carbureted vehicles where the tank is too low for gravity to feed fuel to the carburetor.

_____ 5. Fuel injection fuel pumps require pressures in the range of _____.
   A. 4 psi–8 psi (28 kPa–55 kPa)
   B. 20 psi–25 psi (138 kPa–172 kPa)
   C. 45 psi–50 psi (310 kPa–350 kPa)
   D. 50 psi–66 psi (350 kPa–455 kPa)

_____ 6. The three types of air filters commonly used are paper, foam, and _____.

_____ 7. Off-road air filters are most commonly made of _____.

_____ 8. The throttle cable connects the _____ to the throttle linkage.

_____ 9. *True or False?* Ethanol is an additive used to oxygenate gasoline.

_____ 10. Long-term storage can cause _____ of chemicals in fuel, which can result in a clogged system.

_____ 11. The ideal air-fuel ratio that would result in complete combustion is _____.
   A. 15:1
   B. 14.7:1
   C. 14:1
   D. 1.7:14

_____ 12. A carburetor relies on _____ to draw fuel into the airstream.
- A. vacuum
- B. high pressure
- C. pressure difference
- D. fuel pressure

_____ 13. The three types of carburetors are _____, vacuum, and butterfly.

For questions 14–21, identify the parts of a float system indicated in the following illustration.

_____ 14. Reservoir

_____ 15. Float seat

_____ 16. Vent

_____ 17. Float pivot pin

_____ 19. Overflow tube

_____ 19. Float tang

_____ 20. Float assembly

_____ 21. Float needle

Fuel from petcock

Atmospheric pressure

Fuel level

H

G

F

E

A

B

C

D

Goodheart-Willcox Publisher

For questions 22–28, match each of the circuits with the phrase that describes it.

- A. Float circuit
- B. Starter circuit
- C. Pilot circuit
- D. Accelerator pump circuit
- E. Off-idle circuit
- F. Needle circuit
- G. Main fuel circuit

_____ 22. Meters air and fuel at and above idle.

_____ 23. Provides an enriched 3:1 mixture.

_____ 24. Prevents hesitation during sudden throttle opening.

_____ 25. Also called the high-speed circuit.

_____ 26. Maintains fuel in the carburetor.

_____ 27. Meters fuel from one-eighth to one-quarter throttle in a slide carburetor.

_____ 28. Also called the midrange circuit.

_____ 29. _True or False?_ Needle circuits operate from one-half to three-quarter throttle opening.

_____ 30. _True or False?_ A vacuum-controlled carburetor is also called a constant velocity (CV) carburetor.

_____ 31. On a vacuum controlled carburetor, the vacuum piston position is determined by _____ vacuum.

Name _____

_____ 32. The three systems that meter fuel in a(n) _____-controlled carburetor are the pilot circuit, main circuit, and accelerator pump circuit.

_____ 33. *True or False?* Turning a pilot air adjustment screw counterclockwise richens the low speed mixture.

_____ 34. *True or False?* To make a low speed mixture leaner, the pilot fuel adjustment screw should be turned in.

_____ 35. *True or False?* Idle speed is adjusted with a throttle stop screw.

_____ 36. *True or False?* Change in float level affects the air-fuel mixture.

_____ 37. The float level is adjusted by _____.
   A. changing the float weight
   B. installing a new float jet
   C. bending a tang on the float
   D. using a longer float needle

_____ 38. Motorcycle carburetors require cleaning to remove _____ and other deposits.

_____ 39. *True or False?* The carburetor should be only partially disassembled when it is cleaned.

_____ 40. *True or False?* When a carburetor is reassembled, new O-rings should be used.

_____ 41. During final synchronization, small changes in throttle openings change the _____ gauge reading.

_____ 42. *True or False?* During final synchronization, if one gauge reads higher than the others, its carburetor's slide is closed more than the others and must be opened.

_____ 43. *True or False?* To perform final pilot adjustment with the engine running, the pilot screw is first turned out until the engine rpm begins to drop.

_____ 44. The on-board computer that performs fuel injection control, ignition system control, and self-diagnostics is called a(n) _____.
   A. electronic control module
   B. power supply circuit
   C. central processing unit
   D. EFI regulator

_____ 45. Most ECMs have fuel _____ functions that operate with the side stand switch, clutch switch, and neutral switch.

_____ 46. In a(n) _____/throttle opening system, the ECM monitors input from various sensors and calculates the amount of air entering the engine.

_____ 47. A fuel injector is a fuel valve controlled by an electronic _____.

_____ 48. The throttle body performs the same task as the throttle valve and _____ in a carburetor.

_____ 49. *True or False?* A fuel pump mounted inside the fuel tank prevents vapor lock.

_____ 50. An ECT sensor converts the engine's coolant temperature to electrical _____.

_____ 51. An oxygen sensor generates _____ because of the difference in oxygen concentrations in the exhaust gas and the atmosphere.

A. resistance

B. current

C. voltage

D. electromagnetism

_____ 52. *True or False?* When an FI warning light blinks every .5–1 second, it is sending a fault code.

Name _____ Date _____ Class _____

Job 9-1

Fuel Petcock Testing on Carbureted Vehicles

Introduction

It is important to understand fuel delivery systems when diagnosing fuel issues. The carburetor must have enough fuel at all throttle openings. Gas tanks, petcocks, and fuel pumps (if used) can all cause fuel delivery issues. The technician must also have a good understanding of what atmospheric pressure and engine vacuum do to help deliver fuel. In this job you will be checking the operation of the fuel petcock.

Objective

After successfully completing this job, you will be able to test petcocks on carbureted vehicles.

Materials and Equipment

To complete this job, you will need the following tools, equipment, and materials:

- At least one vehicle with a manually operated petcock
- At least one vehicle with a vacuum-controlled petcock
- Appropriate service manual or electronic service information
- Hand tools
- Handheld vacuum pump
- Gasoline
- Cylinder to catch fuel
- Bench petcocks or petcocks that can be taken apart

Instructions

In this job, you will be familiarizing yourself with and testing fuel petcocks. You will need to take extra precautions when working around fuel. Make sure that:

- There is adequate ventilation in the shop.
- There is no source of open flame or spark that could ignite the fuel.

Read the job procedures, perform the tasks, and answer all questions. As you complete the steps, you will be given instructions to either fill in measurements or perform certain tasks. When you reach a (STOP) sign, show your work to your instructor. Do not continue until you receive instructor approval (instructor will initial job sheet).

> **WARNING** ⚠ Before performing this job, review all pertinent safety information in the text and discuss safety procedures with your instructor.

Procedures

1. Identify the type of petcock.

2. Look at five different bikes in your shop that are carbureted (if possible, look at different manufacturers' bikes). Write down the brand of bike in the first column, the labeled positions of each petcock (in correct order), and indicate whether or not the petcock is vacuum actuated. You need at least one manually operated petcock and one vacuum operated petcock to complete this job.

Bike	Positions on Petcock	Vacuum Operated?

 3. Discuss with your instructor the different positions on the petcock and what they mean.

Instructor's Initials: _____

Testing a Manual Petcock

> **CAUTION** ⚠ Use all appropriate safety measures when working with gasoline.

4. Using the instructions in the service manual, remove the gas tank from the motorcycle.

5. Test the petcock by observing whether fuel flows from the petcock.

6. Fill in the chart by filling in the positions on the petcock and then putting an "X" in the appropriate box based on your observations:

Positions on the Petcock	Fuel is Flowing	Fuel is Not Flowing

7. Ask your instructor if you have permission to remove the petcock. Removing a petcock can tear the gasket between the petcock and the tank.

 8. Discuss your findings from testing the manual petcock.

Instructor's Initials: _____

Name _____

Testing a Vacuum Petcock

> **CAUTION** ⚠ Use all appropriate safety measures when working with gasoline.

9. Using the instructions in the service manual, remove the gas tank from the motorcycle.

> **NOTE** ⚙ Pay attention to which hose is the vacuum supply hose from the intake side of the carburetor.

10. Test the petcock by observing at which positions fuel flows from the petcock. Do not apply vacuum at this time.

Positions on the Petcock	Fuel is Flowing	Fuel is Not Flowing

11. After taking the above readings, apply vacuum to the vacuum port of the petcock and observe whether it holds vacuum.

    Holds vacuum? Yes _____ No _____ If no, explain.

    _____

    _____

12. Leaving vacuum applied, fill in the chart by filling in the positions on the petcock and then putting an "X" in the appropriate box based on your observations.

Positions on the Petcock	Fuel is Flowing	Fuel is Not Flowing

13. Take apart a petcock that your instructor has supplied and determine the amount of fuel in the reserve portion of the petcock.

    _____ Amount of fuel

🛑 14. Discuss your findings of testing the petcocks and explain the petcock that you took apart to your instructor.

Instructor's Initials: _____

Job Wrap Up

15. Return all tools and materials to the proper storage areas and clean up your work area.

Final Assessment

1. What could happen if a manual petcock does not shut off the fuel?

   _____

   _____

2. What type of symptoms would a plugged tank vent cause? Why?

   _____

   _____

   _____

   _____

3. What symptoms could a rider experience if the vacuum diaphragm in a vacuum petcock leaks?

   _____

   _____

   _____

4. What should the technician check if fuel flows when the petcock is in the on position but does not flow from the reserve?

   _____

   _____

5. What is the purpose of having a vacuum petcock?

   _____

   _____

Final Instructor Approval: _____

Name _____ Date _____ Class _____

Job 9-2

Checking Compression Prior to Carburetor Service

Introduction

When tuning carbureted vehicles, it is important to understand that the engine drives the carburetor and not the other way around. The cylinders must have proper compression and a quality spark. Without those two factors, tuning carburetors will not yield the results that you want. This job will cover compression checking.

Objective

After successfully completing this job, you will be able to check an engine for sufficient compression.

Materials and Equipment

To complete this job, you will need the following tools, equipment, and materials:

- Motorcycle
- Appropriate service manual or electronic service information
- Compression tester
- Standard tools
- Feeler gauges

Instructions

In this job, you will be performing a compression test on an engine. You cannot properly tune a carbureted engine without good compression, equal across all cylinders. Compression needs to be within specifications for the engine to properly control the carburetors. If compression is low, you will perform a leak down test. If there is no leak down, you will then adjust the valves and re-check compression. As you complete the steps, you will be given instructions to either fill in measurements or perform certain tasks. When you reach a sign, show your work to your instructor. Do not continue until you receive instructor approval (instructor will initial job sheet).

> **WARNING** ⚠ Before performing this job, review all pertinent safety information in the text and discuss safety procedures with your instructor.

Procedures

Checking for Compression

1. Secure the vehicle properly.

2. Check the repair manual for compression specification.

   Compression spec: _____

3. Make sure that the battery is charged or is connected to a charger. The starter must be able to crank the engine at the proper speed for testing.

4. Remove all spark plugs and disable the ignition. The ignition can be disabled by disconnecting wires to the primary side of the coil or by using a spark tester that will accommodate all the ignition wires.

   > **CAUTION** ⚠️ Make sure that there are no flammable fluids or vapors nearby in case of sparks.

5. Install the compression tester in the first cylinder to be tested.

6. Hold the throttle open and crank the engine until the compression reading stops rising. The service manual may state how many compression strokes should be recorded during cranking. As a general rule, four strokes is considered the minimum. Record your findings below in the *Cranking Compression* column.

7. Perform wet compression tests as directed by your instructor and record your results in the *Wet Compression* column.

8. Perform leak down tests as directed by your instructor and record your results in the *Leak Down Test* column.

Cylinder	Cranking Compression	Wet Compression	Leak Down Test
Cylinder 1			
Cylinder 2			
Cylinder 3			
Cylinder 4			

> **NOTE** It is very important to understand that compression specification numbers are based on how the test in the service manual is performed. In most cases, the engine should be warm, with all spark plugs removed, and the throttle wide open. All of these conditions contribute to compression specifications. If these conditions are not met, the actual number may be artificially low.

 9. Discuss your results in the chart above with your instructor. You will need permission to perform carburetor or valve adjustments or perform further engine testing.

Instructor's Initials: _____

Name _____

Valve Adjustment

> **NOTE** For the purpose of this job, we will focus on just doing a valve adjustment. Internal engine repairs will be addressed in a later job.

10. Look up the valve specifications in the service manual and record them below.

    Valve Clearance Intake Specification: _____

    Valve Clearance Exhaust Specification: _____

11. Use the service manual instructions to perform a valve adjustment.

Cylinder	Valve Clearance Intake	Valve Clearance Exhaust	Compression after Valve Adjustment
Cylinder 1			
Cylinder 2			
Cylinder 3			
Cylinder 4			

(STOP) 12. Discuss your results in the chart above with your instructor.

Instructor's Initials: _____

Job Wrap Up

13. Return all tools and materials to the proper storage areas and clean up your work area.

14. Ask your instructor to check your work and initial this job sheet.

Final Assessment

1. If an engine has very low compression, what test should be performed next?

   _____

2. Loosening the intake valve to the maximum clearance (or even slightly beyond) increased the compression. Why?

   _____

   _____

   _____

3. Why should the throttle valve be wide open during a compression test?

   _____

   _____

   _____

4. Why should all of the spark plugs be removed during a compression test?

_____

_____

_____

5. Once the engine is confirmed to have good spark and compression, what is the next step in carburetor tuning?

_____

_____

Final Instructor Approval: _____

Name _____ Date _____ Class _____

Job 9-3

CV Carburetor Complete Service

Introduction

This job covers CV carburetor teardown, cleaning, assembly, and tuning. It is meant to be done on a live motorcycle.

Objective

After successfully completing this job, you will be able to fully service CV carburetors on a running motorcycle.

Materials and Equipment

To complete this job, you will need the following tools, equipment, and materials:

- Motorcycle with CV carburetor(s)
- Appropriate service manual or electronic service information
- Float level gauge
- Various screwdrivers
- Pocket scale
- Balancing gauges
- Carburetor cleaner

Instructions

In this job, you will be performing all types of service on CV carburetors, from removing and taking them apart to making final tuning adjustments.

 WARNING Take precautions when working with gasoline. Wear protective gloves, wipe up spills immediately, and properly dispose of rags soaked with gasoline.

Read the job procedures, perform the tasks, and answer all questions. As you complete steps, you will be given instructions to either fill in measurements or perform certain tasks. When you reach a 🛑 sign, show your work to your instructor. Do not continue until you have instructor approval (instructor will initial job sheet).

 NOTE There are many makes and types of carburetors and many do not use the same circuits and parts. For this reason, this job should be used as a general guide only. Always consult the service manual for the specific carburetor being serviced.

 WARNING Before performing this job, review all pertinent safety information in the text and discuss safety procedures with your instructor.

Procedures

Carburetor Removal

1. Secure the motorcycle properly.
2. Use the repair manual to remove the carburetors without bending linkages and cables.

Carburetor Measurements Prior to Teardown

3. Before disassembly, take and record the following measurements:
   Throttle opening:

   _____

   Idle (pilot) mixture screw:

   _____

4. Check the operation of the vacuum piston. It should move through its full range of motion and make a smooth sucking sound.
5. Discuss the measurements that you have made and the operation of the vacuum piston with your instructor.

Instructor's Initials: _____

Carburetor Teardown

> **NOTE** ⚙ Ensure that you have an exploded view of the internal parts of the carburetor for use with this job.

6. Remove the carburetor components and record their condition.

Component	Dirty	Clean	Damaged	Spec/Actual
Diaphragm				
Spring				
Jet Needle				
Float Bowl				
Float Needle				
Filter				
Accelerator Pump Diaphragm				
Leak Jet				
Coasting Enricher (Air Cut)				
Cold Start Enricher				
Starter Jet				

(Continued)

Name _____

Component	Dirty	Clean	Damaged	Spec/Actual
Pilot Jet				
Main Jet				
Emulsion Tube				
Needle Jet				

 7. Discuss your findings with your instructor and get permission to move to the cleaning section.

Instructor's Initials: _____

Carburetor Cleaning

8. Spray carburetor cleaner through the passages or jets listed in the chart and indicate whether they are clean, plugged, or partly plugged. If you have questions about how passages should spray, ask your instructor.

> **WARNING** Use eye protection and gloves with these steps. Plugged holes can spray cleaner back at your face.

> **NOTE** In order to check/clean the transfer ports properly, gently reinstall the idle mixture screw without the spring, washer, and O-ring. Plug off the pilot air bleed/jet and spray through where the pilot fuel jet is located to force cleaner through the transfer ports.

Component	Clean	Plugged	Partly Plugged
Accelerator Pump Orifices			
Leak Jet			
Cold Start Enricher Air Passage			
Cold Start Enricher Air-Fuel Passage			
Starter Jet			
Pilot Jet Air Bleed			
Pilot Jet			
Pilot Jet Fuel Passage			
Air-Fuel Mixture Passage			
Transfer Ports (see Note above)			
Main Jet Air Bleed			
Main Jet			

Sonic Tank Cleaning

9. Make sure that you understand how to operate the sonic cleaner. Maintain the proper mix and mix level to protect the heating elements. Ask your instructor for help if you have questions. The length of time in the sonic cleaner depends on how dirty the carburetors are.

10. Perform a final check of each component using carburetor cleaner and compressed air. Check off as each component is cleaned.

Component	Clean
Accelerator Pump Orifices	
Leak Jet	
Cold Start Enricher Air Passage	
Cold Start Enricher Air-Fuel Passage	
Starter Jet	
Pilot Jet Air Bleed	
Pilot Jet	
Pilot Jet Fuel Passage	
Air-Fuel Mixture Passage	
Main Jet Air Bleed	
Main Jet	

Record Carburetor Information

11. Record the following information from earlier sections of this job. You will want this information in case you need to re-jet the carburetor during tuning.

Air-Fuel Mixture Screw Turns Out	
Float Level	
Starter Jet (if applicable)	
Pilot Jet	
Pilot Air Jet (if applicable)	
Main Jet	
Main Air Jet (if applicable)	
Needle Size (if labeled)	

Name _____

Carburetor Assembly

12. Use the checklist to install applicable components in reverse order of removal. Once the float is *Installed*, keep the carburetor upright as much as possible.

13. Put a check mark in the *Installed* column once complete. Put a N/A in the *Installed* column if that part is not used on your carburetor.

Component	Installed
Any Throttle Hardware Removed	
Cold Start Enricher Plunger	
Accelerator Pump	
Leak Jet	
Starter Jet	
Pilot Air Jet	
Pilot Jet	
Air-Fuel Mixture Screw with Spring, Washer, and O-Ring	
Needle Jet	
Emulsion Tube	
Main Jet	
Air Cut Diaphragm	
Vacuum Piston and Diaphragm with Jet Needle	
Float System with Float to Proper Height	

Bench Sync Throttle Plates

14. Use the information from Step 3 to reset the throttle speed and mixture screws in their original positions; then use the service manual to find the throttle adjustment screws and adjust the throttle openings so they are equal to each other.

Carburetor Installation and Tuning

15. Using the service manual, properly install the carburetor(s), cables, enricher controls, vacuum lines, and drain hoses. Make sure everything is routed properly.

 16. Once the carburetor is installed, fill the tank with fuel and start the engine.

> **NOTE** ⚙ If the engine will not start or has problems starting, check with your instructor.

Instructor's Initials: _____

17. Check for vacuum leaks.

   With the engine idling, check for vacuum leaks. Correct any vacuum leaks before attempting any tuning. Some vacuum leaks can be difficult to find. If there are any vacuum lines that connect to other components like vacuum petcocks and vacuum-driven emission controls, make sure the diaphragms in those components are not leaking.

18. Halfway mixture adjustment method.

   A. Attach a tachometer and a vacuum gauge to help manage "stumble."

   B. Set the idle speed to specification.

   C. Turn the air-fuel mixture screw in until the engine begins to stumble. Count the turns in quarter-turn increments.

   _____ Number of turns in

   D. Turn the air-fuel mixture screw out, counting in quarter-turn increments until the engine stumbles rich (approximately the same amount of stumble as at lean).

   _____ Number of turns out

   E. Turn the air-fuel mixture screw back in half the number of turns recorded in Step D. At this point, the vacuum gauge should be at or close to its best reading (highest vacuum).

   F. Reset the idle speed.

19. Multiple cylinder engine balance. Balance the carburetors by adjusting the throttle openings. The vacuum gauges should read between 25–30 inches of vacuum.

> **NOTE** On four-carburetor systems, there will be three screws to balance the carburetors. One screw balances the left two carbs and another screw balances the right two carbs. Once the two pairs of carburetors are balanced, use the middle screw to balance them to each other. Ask your instructor for help, if necessary.

 20. Show your instructor that the cylinders are balanced and that the idle speed is correct. If your shop has a dynamometer, ask your instructor about running the motorcycle on the dyno so that you can best judge throttle response and performance through the needle and main circuits. If a dyno is not available, test-drive the motorcycle.

Instructor's Initials: _____

Job Wrap Up

21. Return all tools and materials to the proper storage areas and clean up your work area.

Final Assessment

1. A motorcycle will not start unless starting fluid is sprayed into the airbox, and then will not stay running. What circuits in the carburetor could cause this problem?

   _____

2. A motorcycle starts and idles okay, but will not accelerate. What circuits in the carburetor could cause this problem?

   _____

   _____

Name _____

3. If a pilot jet remains plugged after sonic cleaning and spraying, what other steps can the technician try?

_____

_____

_____

4. A bowl screw is damaged and the technician wants to replace it. Should the technician replace it with a stock Phillips head or an Allen head?

_____

_____

_____

5. The vacuum piston diaphragm seems old. Should the technician lubricate it?

_____

_____

_____

Final Instructor Approval: _____

Notes

Name _____ Date _____ Class _____

Job 9-4

Throttle Slide Carburetor Complete Service

Introduction

This job covers throttle slide carburetor teardown, cleaning, assembly, and tuning. It is meant to be done on a live motorcycle, not on core carburetors.

Objective

After successfully completing this job, you will be able to service throttle slide carburetors on an operating motorcycle.

Materials and Equipment

To complete this job, you will need the following tools, equipment, and materials:

- Motorcycle with throttle slide carburetor(s)
- Appropriate service manual or electronic service information
- Float level gauge
- Various screwdrivers
- Pocket scale
- Carburetor cleaner
- Sonic tank
- Balancing gauges

Instructions

In this job, you will be completely servicing throttle slide carburetors from removal and teardown to final tuning on a running engine.

 WARNING Take precautions when working with gasoline. Wear protective gloves, wipe up spills immediately, and properly dispose of rags soaked with gasoline.

Read the job procedures, perform the tasks, and answer all questions. As you complete steps, you will be given instructions to either fill in measurements or perform certain tasks. When you reach a 🛑 sign, show your work to your instructor. Do not continue until you have instructor approval (instructor will initial job sheet).

 NOTE There are many makes and types of carburetors and many will not use the same circuits and parts. For this reason, this job should be used as a general guide to disassembly. Always consult the service manual for the specific carburetor being serviced.

 WARNING Before performing this job, review all pertinent safety information in the text and discuss safety procedures with your instructor.

Procedures

Carburetor Removal

1. Secure the motorcycle properly for service.

2. Use the service manual to remove the carburetor(s), being careful with linkages and cables.

Carburetor Measurements Prior to Teardown

3. Take the following measurements and record them in the space below:

   _____   Throttle opening

   _____   Idle (pilot) mixture screw

4. Check the operation of the piston. It should move through its full range of motion and not bind or get stuck.

STOP 5. Discuss the measurements that you have made and the operation of the piston with your instructor.

Instructor's Initials: _____

Carburetor Teardown

> **NOTE**   Ensure that you have an exploded view of the internal parts of the carburetor and make a copy for use with this job. Keep your workbench clean and organized as you take the carburetor apart.

6. Remove the carburetor components and record their condition.

Component	Dirty	Clean	Damaged	Spec/Actual
Piston				
Needle Size				
Needle Clip				
Float Bowl				
Float Needle				
Filter				
Accelerator Pump Diaphragm				
Leak Jet				
Coasting Enricher (Air Cut)				
Cold Start Enricher				
Starter Jet				
Pilot Jet				
Main Jet				
Emulsion Tube				
Needle Jet				

Name _____

🛑 7. Discuss your findings so far with your instructor and get permission to move to the cleaning steps.

Instructor's Initials: _____

Carburetor Cleaning

8. Spray carb cleaner through the passages or jets listed in the chart and indicate whether it is clean, plugged, or partly plugged in the chart. If you have questions about how the passages should spray, ask your instructor.

> **WARNING** ⚠️ Use eye protection and gloves with these steps. Plugged holes can spray cleaner back at your face.

Component	Clean	Plugged	Partly Plugged
Accelerator Pump Orifices			
Leak Jet			
Cold Start Enricher Air Passage			
Cold Start Enricher Air-Fuel Passage			
Starter Jet			
Pilot Jet Air Bleed			
Pilot Jet			
Pilot Jet Fuel Passage			
Air-Fuel Mixture Passage			
Main Jet Air Bleed			
Main Jet			

Sonic Tank Cleaning

Make sure that you understand how to operate the sonic cleaner properly. The proper mix and mix level should be used to prevent damage to the heating elements. Ask your instructor for help if you have questions. The length of time in the sonic cleaner depends on how dirty the carburetors are.

9. Perform a final check of each component using carburetor cleaner and compressed air and check off as each component is cleaned.

Component	Clean
Accelerator Pump Orifices	
Leak Jet	
Cold Start Enricher Air Passage	
Cold Start Enricher Air-Fuel Passage	
Starter Jet	
Pilot Jet Air Bleed	

(Continued)

Component	Clean
Pilot Jet	
Pilot Jet Fuel Passage	
Air-Fuel Mixture Passage	
Main Jet Air Bleed	
Main Jet	

Throttle Slide Carburetor Information

10. Record the following information.

Air-Fuel Mixture Screw Turns Out	
Float Level	
Starter Jet (if applicable)	
Pilot Jet	
Pilot Air Jet (if applicable)	
Main Jet	
Main Air Jet (if applicable)	
Needle Size (if labeled)	

Throttle Slide Carburetor Reassembly

11. Use the checklist to install all the applicable components in reverse order of disassembly. Once the float is installed, keep the carburetor upright as much as possible.

12. Put a check mark in the *Installed* column once complete. Put a N/A in the *Installed* column if that part is not part of your carburetor.

Component	Installed
Any Throttle Hardware Removed	
Cold Start Enricher Plunger	
Accelerator Pump	
Leak Jet	
Starter Jet	
Pilot Air Jet	
Pilot Jet	
Air-Fuel Mix Screw with Spring, Washer, and O-Ring	
Needle Jet	
Emulsion Tube	
Main Jet	
Air Cut Diaphragm	

(Continued)

Name _____

Component	Installed
Piston and Needle (if a live bike, this will go on last)	
Float System with Float Adjusted to Proper Height	

Bench Synchronizing Multiple Carburetor Throttle Plates

13. Use the information from Step 3 to reset the throttle speed and mixture screws in their original positions. Use the service manual to find the screws needed to adjust all throttle openings an equal amount, then adjust the plates.

Throttle Slide Carburetor Installation and Tuning

14. Use the service manual to properly install the carburetor(s), cables, enricher controls, vacuum lines, and drain hoses. Make sure everything is routed properly.

15. Once the carburetor is installed, fill the tank with fuel and start the engine.

16. Check for vacuum leaks. With the engine idling, check for vacuum leaks. Correct any vacuum leaks before attempting any tuning. Some vacuum leaks can be difficult to find. If there are any vacuum lines that connect to other components, like vacuum petcocks and vacuum-driven emission controls, make sure the diaphragms in those components are not leaking.

17. Halfway mixture adjustment method.
    A. Attach a tachometer and a vacuum gauge to help manage "stumble."
    B. Set the idle speed to specification.
    C. Turn the air-fuel mixture screw in until the engine begins to stumble. Count the turns in quarter-turn increments.

    _____   Number of turns in

    D. Turn the air-fuel mixture screw out, counting in quarter-turn increments until the engine stumbles rich (approximately the same amount of stumble as at lean).

    _____   Number of turns out

    E. Turn the air-fuel mixture screw back in one-half the number of turns out as recorded in Step D. At this point the vacuum gauge should be at or close to best reading (highest vacuum).
    F. Reset the idle speed.

18. Multiple cylinder engine balance. Balance the carburetors by adjusting the throttle openings. The vacuum gauges should read between 25–30 inches of vacuum.

> **NOTE** On four-carburetor systems, there will be three screws to balance the carburetors. One screw balances the left two carbs and another screw balances the right two carbs. Once the two pairs of carburetors are balanced, use the middle screw to balance them to each other. Ask your instructor for help, if necessary.

 19. Show your instructor that the cylinders are balanced and that the idle speed is correct. If your shop has a dynamometer, ask your instructor about running the motorcycle on the dyno so that you can best judge throttle response and performance through the needle and main circuits. If a dyno is not available, test-drive the motorcycle.

Instructor's Initials: _____

Job Wrap Up

20. Return all tools and materials to the proper storage areas and clean up your work area.

Final Assessment

1. If the clip on the needle is moved down, what effect will this have on performance?

_____

_____

_____

2. How is the piston moved on this carburetor compared to a CV carburetor?

_____

_____

_____

3. List the circuits in order from idle to wide open throttle that overlap with each other.

_____

_____

4. How is the idle speed adjusted on a throttle slide carburetor?

_____

_____

_____

5. The idle air mix screw is on the air filter side of the carburetor rather than on the engine side of the carburetor. What does this indicate?

_____

_____

_____

_____

Final Instructor Approval: _____

Name _____ Date _____ Class _____

Job 9-5

Butterfly Carburetor Complete Service

Introduction

This job covers butterfly carburetor service, including teardown, cleaning, assembly, and tuning. It is meant to be done on a live motorcycle, not on core carburetors.

Objective

After successfully completing this job, you will be able to fully service butterfly carburetors on an operating motorcycle.

Materials and Equipment

To complete this job, you will need the following tools, equipment, and materials:

- Motorcycle with butterfly carburetor(s)
- Appropriate service manual or electronic service information
- Float level gauge
- Various screwdrivers
- Pocket scale
- Carburetor cleaner
- Vacuum balance gauges

Instructions

In this job, you will completely service butterfly carburetors.

 WARNING Take precautions when working with gasoline. Wear protective gloves, wipe up spills immediately, and properly dispose of rags soaked with gasoline.

Read the job procedures, perform the tasks, and answer all questions. As you complete steps, you will be given instructions to either fill in measurements or perform certain tasks. When you reach a 🛑 sign, show your work to your instructor. Do not continue until you have instructor approval (instructor will initial job sheet).

NOTE There are many makes and types of carburetors, and many will not use the same circuits and parts. For this reason, this job should be used as a general guide to disassembly. Always consult the service manual for the specific carburetor being serviced.

WARNING Before performing this job, review all pertinent safety information in the text and discuss safety procedures with your instructor.

Procedures

Carburetor Removal

1. Secure the motorcycle properly for service.

2. Use the service manual to remove the carburetor(s), being careful with linkages and cables.

Carburetor Measurements Prior to Teardown

3. Make sure you identify the difference between throttle opening adjustment (idle speed) and idle (pilot) mixture screw (idle mixture) adjustment prior to taking anything apart.

4. Note and record the throttle opening screw adjustment. Count how many quarter turns it takes to back the throttle off to where the adjustment just finishes touching the throttle.

_____ Throttle opening

_____ Idle mixture screw turns from bottom

5. Discuss your findings so far with your instructor and receive permission to move to the next section.

Instructor's Initials: _____

Carburetor Teardown

6. In the service manual, find an exploded view of the internal parts of the carburetor and make a copy for use in this job.

7. Remove the carburetor components and record their condition.

Component	Dirty	Clean	Damaged	Spec/Actual
Float Bowl				
Float Needle				
Filter				
Leak Jet				
Cold Start Enricher				
Starter Jet				
Pilot Jet				
Main Jet				
Emulsion Tube				
Needle Jet				

8. Discuss your findings with your instructor.

Instructor's Initials: _____

Name _____

Carburetor Cleaning

9. Spray carburetor cleaner through the passages or jets listed in the chart and indicate whether the passage is clean, plugged, or partly plugged in the chart.

 WARNING Use eye protection and gloves with these steps. Plugged holes can spray cleaner back in your face.

 NOTE In order to check/clean the transfer ports properly, gently reinstall the idle mixture screw without the spring, washer, and O-ring. Plug off the pilot air bleed/jet and spray to force cleaner through the transfer ports.

Component	Clean	Plugged	Partly Plugged
Accelerator Pump Orifices			
Leak Jet			
Cold Start Enricher Air Passage			
Cold Start Enricher Air-Fuel Passage			
Starter Jet			
Pilot Jet Air Bleed			
Pilot Jet			
Pilot Jet Fuel Passage			
Air-Fuel Mixture Passage			
Transfer Ports (see Note above)			
Main Jet Air Bleed			
Main Jet			

 10. Discuss your findings so far with your instructor and get permission to continue with the cleaning steps.

 NOTE Make sure your work area is clean and organized, spills are cleaned up, and chart is filled in.

Instructor's Initials: _____

Sonic Tank Cleaning

Make sure that you understand how to operate the sonic cleaner properly. The proper mix and mix level should be used to avoid damaging the heating elements. Ask your instructor for help if you have questions.

Final Carburetor Cleaning

11. Repeat the previous procedures for cleaning with carburetor cleaner, although this time you have to clean until all passages are completely clean and all jets spray with a good pattern, not just a straight stream. Observe all safety precautions for handling flammable materials and wear eye and hand protection.

Component	Clean
Accelerator Pump Orifices	
Leak Jet	
Cold Start Enricher Air Passage	
Cold Start Enricher Air-Fuel Passage	
Starter Jet	
Pilot Jet Air Bleed	
Pilot Jet	
Pilot Jet Fuel Passage	
Air-Fuel Mixture Passage	
Transfer Ports (see Note above)	
Main Jet Air Bleed	
Main Jet	

🛑 12. Discuss your findings so far with your instructor and get permission to move to the carburetor reassembly steps.

Instructor's Initials: _____

Carburetor Reassembly

13. Use the checklist to install all of the applicable components in reverse order of disassembly. Once the float is installed, keep the carburetor upright as much as possible.

14. Put a check mark in the *Installed* column once complete. Put a N/A in the *Installed* column if that part is not used on this carburetor.

Component	Installed
Any Throttle Hardware Removed	
Cold Start Enricher Plunger	
Accelerator Pump	
Leak Jet	
Starter Jet	
Pilot air Jet	

(Continued)

Name _____

Component	Installed
Pilot jet	
Air-fuel Mix Screw with Spring, Washer, and O-ring	
Emulsion Tube	
Main Jet	
Float System with Float to Proper Height	

 15. Discuss reassembly with your instructor and any special instructions needed for installing and tuning the carburetor(s).

Instructor's Initials: _____

Install the Carburetor(s)

16. Use the service manual to properly install the carburetors, cables, enricher controls, vacuum lines, and drain hoses. Ensure that all parts are routed properly.

> **NOTE** If the carburetor does not have an accelerator pump, do not turn the throttle before starting. If the motorcycle does have an accelerator pump, make one or two pumps before starting.

 17. If the engine will not start or has problems starting, have your instructor approve a method for checking for vacuum leaks.

Instructor Initials: _____

Butterfly Carburetor Tuning

18. Check for vacuum leaks. With the engine idling, check for vacuum leaks. Correct any vacuum leaks before attempting any tuning. Some vacuum leaks can be difficult to find. If there are any vacuum lines that connect to other components, like vacuum petcocks and vacuum-driven emission controls, make sure the diaphragms in those components are not leaking.

19. Halfway mixture adjustment method.
   A. Attach a tachometer and a vacuum gauge to help manage "stumble."
   B. Set the idle speed to specification.
   C. Turn the air-fuel mixture screw in until the engine begins to stumble. Count the turns in quarter-turn increments.

   _____ Number of turns in

   D. Turn the air-fuel mixture screw out, counting in quarter-turn increments until the engine stumbles rich (approximately the same amount of stumble as at lean).

   _____ Number of turns out

   E. Turn the air-fuel mixture screw back in one-half the number of turns out as recorded in Step D. At this point the vacuum gauge should be at or close to best reading (highest vacuum).
   F. Reset the idle speed.

20. Multiple cylinder engine balance. Balance the carburetors by adjusting the throttle openings. The vacuum gauges should read between 25–30 inches of vacuum.

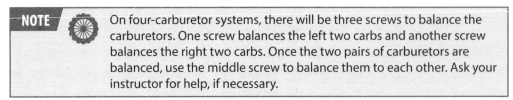

> **NOTE** On four-carburetor systems, there will be three screws to balance the carburetors. One screw balances the left two carbs and another screw balances the right two carbs. Once the two pairs of carburetors are balanced, use the middle screw to balance them to each other. Ask your instructor for help, if necessary.

 21. Show your instructor that the cylinders are balanced and that the idle speed is correct. If your shop has a dynamometer, ask your instructor about running the motorcycle on the dyno so that you can best judge throttle response and performance through the needle and main circuits. If a dyno is not available, test-drive motorcycle.

Job Wrap Up

22. Return all tools and materials to the proper storage areas and clean up your work area.

Final Assessment

1. What type of pressure is present on top of the fuel in the bowl?

_____

2. What type of pressure is present on the engine side of the throttle with the engine running?

_____

3. What type of pressure is present on the air filter side of the throttle?

_____

4. When is pressure in the venturi at its lowest (vacuum strongest)?

_____

_____

5. On what side of the venturi is the choke located, assuming that it is an actual choke?

_____

_____

Final Instructor Approval: _____

Name _____ Date _____ Class _____

Job 9-6

Carburetor Troubleshooting

Introduction

If a motorcycle is not running correctly, the carburetor often gets the blame. It is your job to determine whether the carburetor is at fault, and then perform the proper repair. This job is designed to help you understand that the engine drives the carburetor and that faults in compression and ignition must be repaired first. It also gives some tips to decide if the engine is running lean or rich. Not all tests are conclusive, but you will get better at troubleshooting with more experience.

Objective

After successfully completing this job, you will be able to troubleshoot a carbureted motorcycle engine and classify the faults.

Materials and Equipment

To complete this job, you will need the following tools, equipment, and materials:

- Carbureted motorcycle with a drivability or no-start problem
- Appropriate service manual or electronic service information
- Vacuum balancers
- Compression tester
- Spark tester
- Aerosol can of brake cleaner

Instructions

In this job, you will troubleshoot a carbureted motorcycle, classify the problem, and decide what circuits in the carburetor may be causing the problem. You will practice strategies to make the carburetor leaner or richer to decide if the engine is getting too little or too much fuel.

> **WARNING** Use all proper precautions when working with gasoline and flammable fluids. Spraying flammable fluids on a running engine can be dangerous, especially on a hot engine.

Read the job procedures, perform the tasks, and answer all questions. As you complete steps, you will be given instructions to either fill in measurements or perform certain tasks. When you reach a 🛑 sign, show your work to your instructor. Do not continue until you have instructor approval (instructor will initial job sheet).

> **WARNING** Before performing this job, review all pertinent safety information in the text and discuss safety procedures with your instructor.

Procedures

Trying to Start the Engine

> **NOTE** Take a minute to decide what the engine needs to start and run. Compression and ignition are just as important as fuel. A well-tuned engine should need very little fuel to start.

1. Crank the engine to start.

Operation	How well does the engine do this operation?
Does the engine start?	
Does the engine idle?	

 2. Discuss with your instructor how well the engine started or if it did not start and what your next steps will be.

Instructor's Initials: _____

If the Engine Does Not Start

3. If the engine does not start with the enricher or choke on, make the following checks and fill out the chart below. Professional technicians know that even when one defect is found, the proper repair may involve more than one service operation.

4. If more information is needed, write your notes in the boxes.

Test/Inspection	Okay		No Good	
Air Filter				
Spark through Spark Plug				
Compression				
Compression Spec				

5. If the compression is low or the spark is weak or absent, discuss what your next move should be. The real fix may be adjusting valves, other engine work, or diagnosing the ignition system.

 6. Discuss the results of your tests with your instructor. There are choices of what to do next, depending on your above results.

Instructor's Initials: _____

Name _____

If the Engine Does Not Start, but Spark and Compression Are Good

7. Spray starting fluid (discuss the type with your instructor and how much and where to spray) into the intake with the air filter not installed. Then crank the engine and see if the engine starts.

> **NOTE**   If the engine starts, it will likely only run for a few seconds.

8. If the engine starts and continues to run, concentrate on cleaning the carburetor, paying special attention to both the starting and pilot circuits.

STOP 9. Discuss the results of your tests with your instructor. There are choices of what to do next, depending on your above results.

Instructor's Initials: _____

If the Engine Runs, but Does Not Run Well or Stay Running

10. Classify what the engine is doing at various speeds. Operate the engine with clear tubes attached to the bowl drain (bowl drain open) to observe the fuel level in the bowl as the engine operates. Use tubes that are long enough to run well above the carburetor. Ask your instructor to help you with line positioning.

Operation	Working	Not Working/Hesitation	Fuel Level in Bowl
Idle			
Throttle Response			
Quarter Throttle			
Half Throttle			
Three-Quarter Throttle			

11. Run the engine and spray carburetor cleaner around the intake boots and on the engine side of the carburetor. Pinch off or cap any vacuum lines going to other devices.

> **NOTE** This procedure is used to locate vacuum leaks.

Test	Better	Worse	Notes
Vacuum Leaks			
Plugging Vacuum Lines			

12. Run the engine with a cloth restricting the air filter opening. This test will help you determine if the engine is running rich or lean.

Cloth Restriction Test	Ran Better	Ran Worse

13. Find a vacuum port on the engine side of the carburetor or intake manifold and attach a vacuum gauge.

14. Start the engine and measure vacuum at idle.

15. Remove the gauge and create a vacuum leak, using your finger to control vacuum leak size.

16. Spray carburetor cleaner into the vacuum port (richen mixture) and record the effect on engine operation in the chart below.

17. Operate the engine at half throttle, repeat Steps 15 and 16, and record the results in the chart below.

18. Check the ignition firing using a timing light.

> **NOTE** The timing light should flash steadily every time the spark fires. Using a timing light determines whether the spark plug is firing or if there is a misfire. This helps to determine whether the fault is fuel- or ignition-related.

Test	Idle	3,000 rpm	Notes
Vacuum Gauge Reading			
Vacuum Leak Idle			
Vacuum Leak 3,000 rpm			
Extra Fuel Idle			
Extra Fuel 3,000 rpm			
Timing Light Spark Test Idle			
Timing Light Test 3,000 rpm			

19. Review the tests above and decide on a plan of action. If the engine runs either lean or rich at all throttle openings, make sure the float level is correct. If the engine only has a fault in one throttle opening range, think about what circuit that could be. Be prepared to discuss your findings with your instructor.

(STOP) 20. Discuss the tests with your instructor and decide if more tests are needed or whether the carburetor is faulty.

Instructor's Initials: _____

Name _____

Job Wrap Up

21. Return all tools and materials to the proper storage areas and clean up your work area.

Final Assessment

1. If the engine runs better when a cloth is put over the air filter, what does this indicate?

    _____

    _____

2. If the timing light flickers or does not flash at half throttle, what checks should be made next?

    _____

    _____

3. The engine is misfiring at one-half throttle and runs better when fuel is sprayed into the intake at half throttle. What circuits could be at fault?

    _____

    _____

4. The engine runs lean at all throttle openings. What circuit(s) could be at fault?

    _____

5. The engine hesitates badly when throttle is opened quickly. What circuit(s) could be at fault?

    _____

    _____

Final Instructor Approval: _____

Notes

Name _____ Date _____ Class _____

Job 9-7

Locate Fuel Injection Components

Introduction

Fuel injection systems are complex and can have different components, depending on the motorcycle. For example, not all fuel injection systems use an O_2 sensor. Several components are used on all fuel-injected systems, but their locations may be different. For example, most fuel pumps will be in the tank, but some are outside the tank. Locating components can take valuable time. This job is intended to help you locate the components and understand their location.

Objective

After successfully completing this job, you will be able to locate fuel injection components on a motorcycle.

Materials and Equipment

To complete this job, you will need the following tools, equipment, and materials:
- Street bike with fuel injection
- Dirt bike with fuel injection
- Appropriate service manual or electronic service information
- Hand tools as needed

Instructions

In this job, you will be locating fuel injection system components, but not removing them. You may have to remove pieces of the motorcycle to access locations where components are installed. Removing seats, tanks, and plastic components is a common task that must be done to prepare for other work on a motorcycle. As you complete steps you will be given instructions to fill in measurements or perform certain tasks. When you reach a sign, show your work to your instructor. Do not continue until you have instructor approval (instructor will initial job sheet).

> **WARNING** ⚠ Before performing this job, review all pertinent safety information in the text and discuss safety procedures with your instructor. Protect the painted surfaces of the motorcycle from any possible damage due to contact during disassembly.

Procedures

Removing Tank, Seats, and other Components

1. Secure the motorcycle for service.

2. Using service manual instructions, remove the seat, fuel tank, and plastic components as necessary. Check with your instructor on exactly what pieces to remove. Keep pieces in order and protect them from damage.

> **CAUTION** ⚠ Follow service manual procedures for relieving fuel pressure. Most fuel injection systems have fuel pressure of 40–60 psi.

Fuel Injection Component Location

3. Find the components on the chart and fill in a basic location, for example, "top of intake manifold."

4. Note and record the number of wires attached to each component.

Motorcycle #1

 NOTE If a component is not on the motorcycle, write N/A in the column. You will have to use the service manual to decide whether some components are used on the motorcycle.

Motorcycle (Year/Make/Model)

Component	General Location	# of Wires
Ignition Coil		
Air Cleaner Case		
Fuel Filter		
Intake Air Temp Sensor		
Fuel Supply Delivery Hose		
Fuel Return Hose		
Fuel Tank		
Fuel Pump		
Fuel Pressure Regulator		
Manifold Pressure Sensor (MAP)		
Atmospheric Pressure Sensor		
Throttle Position Sensor (TPS)		
Sub-Throttle Position Sensor		
Idle Air Control Valve (IAC)		
Fuel Injector(s)		
O_2 Sensor(s)		
Catalytic Converter		
Crankshaft Position Sensor (CKP)		
Engine Coolant Temperature Sensor (ECT)		
Camshaft Sensor		
Electronic Control Module (ECM)		
Electronic Fuel Injection (EFI) Main Relay		
Fall Detection Sensor		

Name _____

5. Prior to putting the plastic components, tank, and seat back on the motorcycle, have your instructor check your work.

6. Return the motorcycle to proper operating condition by correctly reinstalling all parts that were removed.

🛑 7. Have your instructor check your work.

Instructor's Initials: _____

Motorcycle #2

8. Fill in the chart below. If the listed component is not on your motorcycle, write N/A in the column. Use a service manual if needed to decide if some of these components are on the motorcycle.

Motorcycle (Year/Make/Model) _____

Component	General Location	# of Wires
Ignition Coil		
Air Cleaner Case		
Fuel Filter		
Intake Air Temp Sensor		
Fuel Supply Delivery Hose		
Fuel Return Hose		
Fuel Tank		
Fuel Pump		
Fuel Pressure Regulator		
Manifold Pressure Sensor (MAP)		
Atmospheric Pressure Sensor		
Throttle Position Sensor (TPS)		
Sub-Throttle Position Sensor		
Idle Air Control Valve (IAC)		
Fuel Injector(s)		
O_2 Sensor(s)		
Catalytic Converter		
Crankshaft Position Sensor (CKP)		
Engine Coolant Temperature Sensor (ECT)		
Camshaft Sensor		

(Continued)

Component	General Location	# of Wires
Electronic Control Module (ECM)		
Electronic Fuel Injection (EFI) Main Relay		
Fall Detection Sensor		

9. Have your instructor check that you have accurately located the fuel injection components.

10. Return the motorcycle to proper operating condition by correctly reinstalling all parts that were removed.

(STOP) 11. Have your instructor check your work.

Instructor's Initials: _____

Job Wrap Up

12. Return all tools and materials to the proper storage areas and clean up your work area.

Final Assessment

1. What types of problems can be overcome by using electronic fuel injection (EFI) rather than a carburetor?

_____

_____

_____

_____

2. List seven engine functions monitored by sensors in EFI systems.

_____

_____

_____

_____

3. What is the function of the EFI pressure regulator?

_____

_____

_____

_____

_____ 4. *True or False?* Most powersports vehicles with electronic fuel injection have the injector(s) mounted in the cylinder head.

_____ 5. *True or False?* Closed-loop EFI systems do not use oxygen sensors.

Final Instructor Approval: _____

Name _____ Date _____ Class _____

Job 9-8

Testing Computer Power Supply and Grounds

Introduction

Before deciding that a motorcycle computer is not working properly, always begin diagnosis by testing the computer power supply and ground. If a desktop computer is not working, the first thing to do is to check and see if the computer is plugged in. Motorcycle computer checking is similar, but there are usually two or three power wires and sometimes more than one ground.

Another test is to check whether voltage is being delivered to the sensors by the computer. This power is called sensor voltage, voltage control (VC), or reference voltage. This sensor voltage is almost always 5 volts. Its presence is a good sign that the computer has power and ground and is able to convert voltage from 12 volts to 5 volts. The proper tool for making these measurements is a high-impedance multimeter such as a Fluke 88. Do not use a test light or self-powered test light on computerized circuits, as they can be destroyed by too much voltage or amperage.

> **NOTE** There are many names for motorcycle computers, such as ECM (electronic control module), ECU (electronic control unit), and microprocessor. In this job we will refer to all units as computers.

Objective

After successfully completing this job, you will be able to test motorcycle computer power and grounds.

Materials and Equipment

To complete this job, you will need the following tools, equipment, and materials:
- Motorcycle with electronic fuel injection
- Appropriate service manual or electronic service information
- Fluke 88 or comparable multimeter

Instructions

In this job, you will need to use the service manual and wiring diagram to find the proper wires and process for checking power and ground. On some motorcycles, the service manual will give a process for testing power and ground, which may include using a scan tool.

Read the job procedures, perform the tasks, and answer all questions. As you complete steps you will be given instructions to either fill in measurements or perform certain tasks. When you reach a sign, show your work to your instructor. Do not continue until you have instructor approval (instructor will initial job).

> **WARNING** ⚠ Before performing this job, review all pertinent safety information in the text and discuss safety procedures with your instructor.

Procedures

Why You Would Be Testing for Computer Power and Ground

1. What are three reasons why you would want to test a fuel-injected computer for power and ground?

_____

_____

_____

Pre-Checks

2. Fill in the chart below by checking the appropriate box.

Check	Yes	No
Check engine light or FI light illuminates		
Fuel pump cycles on		
Motorcycle cranks and starts		

Use Wiring Diagram to Locate Ground

3. Using the wiring diagram, locate the circuit for the check engine light and for the fuel pump.

> **NOTE** 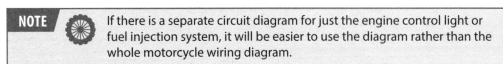 If there is a separate circuit diagram for just the engine control light or fuel injection system, it will be easier to use the diagram rather than the whole motorcycle wiring diagram.

4. Using the wiring diagram(s), answer the following questions:

    A. Is the check engine light grounded by the computer?

       Yes _____ No _____

    B. Is the fuel pump controlled by the computer (usually the fuel pump is energized by a relay control coil ground that is controlled by the computer)?

       Yes _____ No _____

Test for Power

If the check engine light does not come on with the key cycle or the fuel pump does not cycle when the key is turned on, one of the possible causes is that the computer does not have power.

5. Test for power at the computer or closest connector to the computer and record the readings in the chart on the next page.

> **NOTE** Follow all service manual precautions when using back-probes to read voltages. Ask your instructor for advice on what type of back-probe to use. If possible, ground the multimeter at computer ground to test for power to ensure that the ground is good.

Name _____

Name of Wire, Acronym, or Where It Comes from	Wire Color	Voltage Reading with the Key On

 6. Discuss your measurements with your instructor.

Instructor's Initials: _____

Testing for Voltage Sensor Power

NOTE The computer takes 12-volt power from the battery and turns it into output voltage for some sensors. This output voltage is 5 volts. If the voltage as tested is not 5 volts, there is a fault inside the computer or a faulty computer ground.

7. Find the easiest sensor to access having 5-volt sensor voltage. Common sensors using 5 volts are: MAP (manifold air pressure), BARO (barometric) pressure, and TPS (throttle position sensor) pressures.

8. Back probe the sensor wire or disconnect the wire and test voltage. Repeat the test with other sensors as your instructor directs.

9. Fill in the chart with the voltages. Check that your ground is good by testing to a known good power supply.

Component	Power Wire Color	Voltage
MAP		
BARO		
TPS		

 10. Discuss your findings with your instructor.

Instructor's Initials: _____

Job Wrap Up

11. Return all tools and materials to the proper storage areas and clean up your work area.

12. Ask your instructor to check your work and initial this job sheet.

Final Assessment

_____ 1. *True or False?* A fully charged battery is necessary for a fuel injection computer to work properly.

_____ 2. *True or False?* A computer will turn the battery power into 5 volts to operate the sensors.

_____ 3. *True or False?* Most computers have more than one power supply and more than one ground.

4. A computer is unable to communicate with a scan tool. What would be one of the first checks that the technician should make?

_____

_____

_____

5. An FI or check engine light does not turn on when the key is turned on. What would be one of the first checks that the technician should make?

_____

_____

Final Instructor Approval: _____

Name _____ Date _____ Class _____

Job 9-9

Checking Codes

Introduction

Any electronic fuel injection diagnosis should begin with checking codes and related scan tool data. Even when the check engine or FI light is not illuminated, there may be active fault codes. There are also prior or historical codes which can be accessed, depending on the design of the computer and scan tool. The motorcycle industry is moving more toward OBDII requirements that are standardized on cars, such as the diagnostic connector plug. As of 2018, all motorcycles sold in Europe are required to have the OBDII plug, but not yet in the United States.

Not all fuel-injected motorcycles will have all of the same components. Even motorcycles with the bare minimum of sensors, like dirt bikes, will have a way to access codes and data. A scan tool is best for retrieving data, but the system usually has a way to retrieve codes by flashing a light in a specific sequence or by displaying codes on a screen.

A wide variety of tools connect to a motorcycle computer for codes and data. Some tools will connect through Bluetooth to a smartphone.

Objective

After successfully completing this job, you will be able to retrieve codes and data from a fuel-injected motorcycle.

Materials and Equipment

To complete this job, you will need the following tools, equipment, and materials:

- Motorcycle with electronic fuel injection
- Appropriate service manual or electronic service information
- Compatible scan tool for retrieving codes

Instructions

Use the correct service manual to find the procedure for retrieving codes with or without a scan tool. (Most motorcycle systems will allow you to retrieve codes without a scan tool but you will need a scan tool for retrieving data.)

Read the job procedures, perform the tasks, and answer all questions. As you complete steps, you will be given instructions to either fill in measurements or perform certain tasks. When you reach a sign, show your work to your instructor. Do not continue until you have instructor approval (instructor will initial job sheet).

> **WARNING** ⚠ Before performing this job, review all pertinent safety information in the text and discuss safety procedures with your instructor.

Procedures

Make Key On Preliminary Tests

1. Obtain the procedure for checking codes and retrieving data from the service manual.

2. Where is the connector located for connecting a scan tool to the motorcycle?

    _____

3. Turn the key on, making sure the run switch is on (if used), and observe the FI light or check engine light while listening for fuel pump operation. Record results in the chart.

Process	Yes	No
Fuel pump cycles on for 3–5 seconds?		
FI illuminates and then turns off?		

Perform Code Check without Scan Tool

4. Use the service manual to obtain the information to put the motorcycle into self-diagnostic mode for displaying codes.

5. Record the process here in your own words:

    _____

    _____

    _____

    _____

    _____

    _____

    _____

    _____

    _____

    _____

    _____

    _____

6. Perform the process and record your results here:

    _____

    _____

    _____

7. Unplug a sensor that is easy to access. Check the service manual for a sensor that is monitored for codes.

8. What sensor did you unplug?

    _____

Name _____

9. Repeat the process in Step 6 with the sensor unplugged. What code(s) are now present?

_____

_____

10. Now reattach the sensor and cycle the key off and back on again. Did the code clear itself?

Yes _____ No _____

11. If the code did not clear itself, perform the procedure for clearing codes.

12. Was the procedure for clearing codes successful?

Yes _____ No _____

🛑 13. Discuss your findings with your instructor. Be prepared to show the code description page to your instructor.

Instructor's Initials: _____

Perform Scan Tool Code Check

14. Obtain a scan tool from your instructor and, using the service manual procedure, connect it to the motorcycle and retrieve any codes. If it is necessary to obtain a code, unplug the sensor that you used on the self-test procedure above.

Codes:

_____

15. Look up any fail-safes or backups that the computer will use for this code (for example, some computers will set the BARO pressure at atmospheric pressure at sea level as a fail-safe in case of a BARO code).

Fail-safe or backup, if used:

_____

16. Reattach the sensor that you unplugged and cycle the key off and back on again. Did the code clear itself?

Yes _____ No _____

Clear Codes with Scan Tool

17. If the code did not clear itself, perform the code clearing procedure on the scan tool. Briefly describe the code clearing procedure below.

_____

_____

_____

_____

18. Was the code clearing procedure successful?

Yes _____ No _____

Retrieve Data with Scan Tool

For fuel injection diagnosis, it is vital to obtain actual engine data and compare it to normal data readings. Some of the most difficult diagnoses occur when there is a problem, but no codes. Sometimes data analysis can really help.

Example: An engine is hard to start, but runs well once warmed up, and has no codes. A technician would want to look at both engine coolant temperature and intake manifold temperature to ensure that they are both changing as the engine warms up. If the coolant temperature indicates that the engine is hot when the engine is actually cold, it is likely that the coolant temperature sensor needs additional testing.

19. Find the data for the following, starting with the engine cold.

Parameter	Key On	Engine Idle	3000 rpm
Manifold Air Pressure (MAP)			
Barometric (BARO) pressure			
Engine Coolant Temp (ECT)			
Intake Air Temp (IAT)			
Engine Speed			
Throttle Position % or V			

20. Discuss your findings with your instructor. Be prepared to show the code description page to your instructor.

Instructor's Initials: _____

Job Wrap Up

21. Return all tools and materials to the proper storage areas and clean up your work area.

Final Assessment

_____ 1. Under what condition would BARO and MAP readings be the same?
   A. Engine idle.
   B. WOT (wide open throttle).
   C. Deceleration.
   D. Key on, engine off.

_____ 2. Under what condition would engine coolant temperature and intake air temperature be the same or close to each other?
   A. Engine idle.
   B. WOT (wide open throttle).
   C. Cold start.
   D. Hot start.

_____ 3. An engine is hard to start and, once started, runs rough. The check engine light is on. What should the first step in diagnosis be?
   A. Check oil level.
   B. Check battery charge.
   C. Check codes.
   D. Test ride.

Name _____

_____ 4. An engine is hard to start and runs rough but the check engine light is off. What check should the technician perform first?

A. Check oil level.

B. Check battery charge.

C. Check codes.

D. Test ride.

_____ 5. Two technicians are discussing data analysis. Technician A says to check the data with the engine cold and watch the data as it warms up. Technician B says to check the data at different engine rpm. Who is correct?

A. A only.

B. B only.

C. Both A and B.

D. Neither A nor B.

Final Instructor Approval: _____

Notes

Name _____ Date _____ Class _____

Job 9-10

EFI Fuel Pump Testing

Introduction

Fuel delivery is one of the main systems on a motorcycle, especially on fuel-injected motorcycles. A technician must have a solid understanding of how fuel delivery systems work and the volume and pressure that they must deliver under all driving conditions.

There are two different kinds of fuel injection systems, the return system with a return line back to the tank, and the returnless system, with no return line.

Some systems will have test ports that can be accessed easily for pressure and volume tests. Other systems require special tools to access the fuel system for testing purposes.

Objective

After successfully completing this job, you will be able to test fuel pressure and volume on a fuel-injected motorcycle.

Materials and Equipment

To complete this job, you will need the following tools, equipment, and materials:

- Motorcycle with electronic fuel injection
- Appropriate service manual or electronic service information
- Fuel pressure tester, preferably with a drain for checking volume
- Graduated cylinder

Instructions

The fact that fuel sprays or the pump works is not enough to know that the pump is able to deliver the pressure and volume needed. In this job, you will use service manual information concerning proper procedures and precautions for testing and working with fuel. You will also need to refer to the service manual for the proper specifications.

> **WARNING** ⚠ Pay close attention to precautions for handling gasoline and releasing pressure in the lines properly. Clean up spills promptly and properly dispose of gasoline-soaked rags.

Read the job procedures, perform the tasks, and answer all questions. As you complete steps, you will be given instructions to either fill in measurements or perform certain tasks. When you reach a sign, show your work to your instructor. Do not continue until you have instructor approval (instructor will initial job sheet).

> **WARNING** ⚠ Before performing this job, review all pertinent safety information in the text and discuss safety procedures with your instructor.

Procedures

Identify Fuel System

1. Determine whether the motorcycle has a return or returnless fuel delivery system. Locate any filters, regulators, or dampers outside the tank. Use the service manual to answer the questions using a parts location page in the fuel injection chapter and then locate the components on actual motorcycles. In the chart below, write the information as it applies to one or more motorcycles.

Motorcycle #1	Answer
Return or returnless	
Filter location	
Regulator location	
Service port on fuel rail	

Motorcycle #2	Answer
Return or returnless	
Filter location	
Regulator location	
Service port on fuel rail	

Motorcycle #3	Answer
Return or returnless	
Filter location	
Regulator location	
Service port on fuel rail	

Motorcycle #4	Answer
Return or returnless	
Filter location	
Regulator location	
Service port on fuel rail	

 2. Discuss your findings with your instructor. Ask any questions that you may have before continuing.

Instructor's Initials: _____

Name _____

Check Fuel Pump Pressure and Volume

Motorcycle (Year/Make/Model)

_____

3. Is this a returnless or return system?

_____

4. Can you locate the pressure regulator? Where is it?

_____

_____

5. If it is a return system, answer the following:

   Does the regulator have a vacuum line?

   Yes _____   No _____

   Where does the vacuum line originate and where is the other end located?

   _____

   _____

   (Hint: If the vacuum line is used and it originates in the intake manifold, this will be different than if the line originates in the airbox.)

6. Release the fuel pressure according to the service manual procedure and record the steps below.

   _____

   _____

   _____

   _____

   _____

   _____

   _____

   _____

   _____

   _____

   _____

   _____

   _____

   _____

   _____

7. Install the fuel pressure tester.

8. Perform pressure testing and fill in the chart below.

	What Component Is Being Tested?	Pressure
Key on		
Cranking		
Idle		
3,000 rpm		
Pinched return line		
Key off residual pressure after 5 minutes		

9. With fuel pressure still in the lines (showing a gauge reading), remove the fuel cap and observe the fuel pressure. Did removing the cap lower the pressure in the lines?

_____

10. Using the fuel pressure tester and a graduated cylinder, fill the cylinder during the key on cycle (3–5 seconds when ignition is turned on) and measure the volume.

   A. Key on volume:

   _____

   B. Five second volume, if applicable:

   _____

 When diagnosing engines that will run but lack power, hesitate, or stall, fuel pressure and volume are critical tests to make and be familiar with.

 11. Discuss your findings with your instructor.

Instructor's Initials: _____

Remove and Replace Fuel Pump

Motorcycle (Year/Make/Model)

_____

12. Relieve fuel pressure.

 Follow all precautions with relieving fuel pressure and handling and storing gasoline.

13. Follow the instructions in the service manual and remove the fuel pump. Carefully note all of the components that were removed along with the fuel pump (sending unit, regulator, filter, damper) and the wires to each component.

 14. Discuss your findings with your instructor.

Instructor's Initials: _____

Name _____

Job Wrap Up

15. Return all tools and materials to the proper storage areas and clean up your work area.

Final Assessment

_____ 1. A motorcycle with a return fuel system cranks for a long time before starting and then runs normally. The motorcycle starts normally when the return line is pinched off. Technician A says that the fuel pump check valve is defective. Technician B says that the fuel pressure regulator is leaking. Who is correct?

   A. A only.

   B. B only.

   C. Both A and B.

   D. Neither A nor B.

_____ 2. A motorcycle is towed in with a crank, no-start condition. The switch side of the fuel pump relay is bypassed with a jumper wire and the motorcycle starts. Technician A says that the fuel pump relay should be replaced. Technician B says the problem could be on the control side of the relay. Who is correct?

   A. A only.

   B. B only.

   C. Both A and B.

   D. Neither A nor B.

_____ 3. Two technicians are discussing an inoperative fuel pump. Technician A says that the fuel pump should be disconnected and battery voltage to the pump measured. Technician B says that a voltage drop test should be made at the pump connector. Who is correct?

   A. A only.

   B. B only.

   C. Both A and B.

   D. Neither A nor B.

_____ 4. Technician A says that a fuel pump is usually controlled by the computer. Technician B says that if the fuel pump has a relay, the computer will control the ground of the relay coil. Who is correct?

   A. A only.

   B. B only.

   C. Both A and B.

   D. Neither A nor B.

_____ 5. Two technicians are discussing a motorcycle that stumbles and dies with a full tank of gas. Technician A says that the fuel pump filter could be partially plugged. Technician B says that the fuel could be contaminated. Who is correct?

   A. A only.

   B. B only.

   C. Both A and B.

   D. Neither A nor B.

Final Instructor Approval: _____

Notes

Name _____ Date _____ Class _____

Job 9-11

Fuel Injector Testing

Introduction

Testing fuel injectors requires special attention to detail. Remove injectors carefully to ensure that injectors and O-rings are not damaged. Defective injectors may set a misfire code. Some systems set a code that identifies the defective injector.

Make sure that you understand that an injector is a solenoid operated by an electromagnet. Electromagnet operation can be measured as electrical activity. Testing this electrical activity may be used to isolate a cylinder that has a slight misfire and is hard to locate. If all injectors have the same peak voltage, the electromagnets are all acting alike and are probably in good shape. Swapping injectors is also a good strategy for isolating slight misfires.

Objective

After successfully completing this job, you will be able to test and service fuel injectors.

Materials and Equipment

To complete this job, you will need the following tools, equipment, and materials:

- Motorcycle with electronic fuel injection
- Appropriate service manual or electronic service information
- Fluke 88 or comparable multimeter
- Peak voltage adapter
- Noid light
- Stethoscope

Instructions

In this job, you will use the service manual and wiring diagram to find the proper connections and procedures to check power and ground. You will also locate procedures for removing and replacing injectors.

> **WARNING** Pay special attention to precautions for releasing fuel pressure and handling gasoline. Wipe up spilled gasoline and properly dispose of gasoline-soaked rags.

Read the job procedures, perform the tasks, and answer all questions. As you complete steps, you will be given instructions to either fill in measurements or perform certain tasks. When you reach a 🛑 sign, show your work to your instructor. Do not continue until you have instructor approval (instructor will initial job sheet).

> **WARNING** Before performing this job, review all pertinent safety information in the text and discuss safety procedures with your instructor.

Procedures

Find Fuel Injector Wiring Power Flow on Wiring Diagram

1. Find the fuel injector(s) on a wiring diagram and discuss the power flow with your instructor.

2. What source voltage would you expect the fuel injector to have based on the electrical wiring diagram?

_____

3. Unplug a fuel injector and test the voltage on each wire.

| _____ Wire color | _____ Wire color |
| _____ Voltage | _____ Voltage |

Use Noid Light

4. Using a noid light, test whether or not the injector is receiving voltage. If it is, what can you conclude about the injector circuit?

_____

_____

5. When would you use the test in Step 4?

_____

Make Peak Voltage Test

6. Test an injector for peak voltage on the injector ground wire. Write your findings in the chart below.

Cylinder	Peak Voltage Idle	Peak Voltage 2,500 rpm
1		
2		
3		
4		

7. When would you test for peak voltage?

_____

_____

STOP 8. Discuss your findings with your instructor.

Instructor's Initials: _____

Name _____

Stethoscope

9. Obtain a stethoscope and place it against each injector of a running engine. Listen to all of the injectors to see if they are making a similar sound.

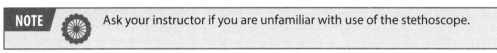

> **NOTE** Ask your instructor if you are unfamiliar with use of the stethoscope.

10. If the engine will run with one injector unplugged, do so, but run it only for a short time. You will likely hear the injector(s) that are still working through the injector that is not working. (The sound travels through the nonworking injector, but it is not as loud.)

 11. Discuss your findings with your instructor.

Instructor's Initials: _____

Remove and Replace Fuel Injector #1

Motorcycle (Year/Make/Model)

_____

12. After releasing fuel pressure, use service manual procedures to remove a fuel injector and measure the following:

A. Fuel injector resistance

_____

B. Fuel injector specifications

_____

 13. Show the injector(s) to your instructor and discuss precautions for storing a motorcycle without injectors installed.

Instructor's Initials: _____

14. Make sure to lubricate the injector O-ring with silicone. Follow your instructor's advice to install the injector.

15. Check the motorcycle for fuel leaks by turning the key on to pressurize the system.

16. Check the motorcycle for vacuum leaks at the base of the injector. Ask your instructor for the approved method in your shop.

17. Make sure all hoses and wires are routed properly and the motorcycle is returned to normal operation.

 18. Show your instructor the motorcycle running without:

A. Fuel leaks between the injector and fuel rail

B. Vacuum leaks between the injector and intake manifold

Instructor's Initials: _____

Remove and Replace Fuel Injector #2

Motorcycle (Year/Make/Model)
(Must be different from first motorcycle that you removed an injector from.)

_____

19. After releasing fuel pressure, use service manual procedures to remove a fuel injector and measure the following:

    A. Fuel injector resistance

    _____

    B. Fuel injector specifications

    _____

(STOP) 20. Show the injector(s) to your instructor and discuss precautions of storing a motorcycle without injectors installed.

Instructor's Initials: _____

21. Make sure to lubricate the injector O-ring with silicone. Follow your instructor's advice to install the injector.

22. Check the motorcycle for fuel leaks by turning the key on to pressurize the system.

23. Check the motorcycle for vacuum leaks at the base of the injector. Ask your instructor for the approved method in your shop.

24. Make sure all hoses and wires are routed properly and the motorcycle is returned to normal operation.

(STOP) 25. Show your instructor the motorcycle running without:

    A. Fuel leaks between the injector and fuel rail
    B. Vacuum leaks between the injector and intake manifold

Instructor's Initials: _____

Job Wrap Up

26. Return all tools and materials to the proper storage areas and clean up your work area.

Name _____

Final Assessment

_____ 1. Technician A says that faulty fuel injectors always create a code. Technician B says that swapping injectors is a valuable skill for diagnosing injectors. Who is correct?

A. A only.

B. B only.

C. Both A and B.

D. Neither A nor B.

_____ 2. Technician A says if a faulty injector is diagnosed, all injectors should be replaced. Technician B says that if a faulty injector is diagnosed, the other injectors should at least be cleaned. Who is correct?

A. A only.

B. B only.

C. Both A and B.

D. Neither A nor B.

_____ 3. Technician A says that a noid light test is performed to check whether the injector is working. Technician B says a noid light test is performed to check whether the computer is trying to turn the injector on and off. Who is correct?

A. A only.

B. B only.

C. Both A and B.

D. Neither A nor B.

_____ 4. Technician A says a resistance test of OL means that the injector should work. Technician B says a resistance test of OL means that the coil portion of the injector has failed. Who is correct?

A. A only.

B. B only.

C. Both A and B.

D. Neither A nor B.

_____ 5. Technician A says that a peak voltage test can tell whether one injector is working harder than another. Technician B says that a dirty injector may have to work harder than a clean injector to open. Who is correct?

A. A only.

B. B only.

C. Both A and B.

D. Neither A nor B.

Final Instructor Approval: _____

Notes

Name _____ Date _____ Class _____

Job 9-12

Intake Pressure Sensor Testing

Introduction

The intake pressure sensor is also commonly known as a MAP (manifold absolute pressure) sensor. This sensor measures the pressure inside the intake manifold and sends a voltage signal to the computer in order to adjust fuel injection duration. The sensor is an IC (integrated circuit) sensor with three wires: power, ground, and a signal wire. The sensor has a flexible silicone chip that will alter voltage based on how much it flexes from being exposed to air pressure. The sensor receives a 5-volt output from the computer and the ground wire typically goes back through the computer to ground.

When the key is turned on and the engine is not running, there is atmospheric pressure inside the intake manifold. The pressure reading will be high, and so will the output voltage. When the engine starts, the pistons pulling air into the cylinders will cause low pressure (a vacuum) in the intake manifold and the voltage will drop.

MAP sensors work the same on all motorcycles. They can also be used as barometric (BARO) pressure sensors and to measure air pressure in the gas tank or turbocharger pressure.

Objective

After successfully completing this job, you will be able to test an intake manifold pressure sensor.

Materials and Equipment

To complete this job, you will need the following tools, equipment, and materials:

- Motorcycle with electronic fuel injection
- Appropriate service manual or electronic service information
- Fluke 88 or comparable multimeter
- Scan tool
- Air pressure gauge/pump

Instructions

In this job, you will need to use the service manual and wiring diagram to find the proper wires and procedures for checking power, ground, and signal from the MAP sensor to the engine computer. You will need to back probe wires, either at the sensor or at the computer, to make your measurements, unless you have a breakout box or test harness.

Read the job procedures, perform the tasks, and answer all questions. As you complete steps, you will be given instructions to either fill in measurements or perform certain tasks. When you reach a sign, show your work to your instructor. Do not continue until you have instructor approval (instructor will initial job sheet).

> **WARNING** ⚠ Before performing this job, review all pertinent safety information in the text and discuss safety procedures with your instructor.

Procedures

Test Intake Pressure/MAP Sensor

Motorcycle (Year/Make/Model)

_____

1. Look up the code for the intake pressure sensor/MAP sensor on this particular motorcycle. What is the code number?

_____

2. What is the fail-safe setting for this code? (What value will the computer use if there is a code for the MAP?)

_____

3. How many wires go to the sensor?

_____

4. What are the wires used for?

_____

5. Does the power wire read 5 volts? If yes, what does this mean?

_____

_____

6. Back probe the wires, taking appropriate precautions, and make sure that the multimeter is set to display the proper voltage. Connect a vacuum T into the MAP sensor vacuum line.
   A. Fill in the first column of the chart below.
   B. Start the engine and fill in the second column of the chart below.
   C. Accelerate the engine to 2,500 rpm and fill in the third column of the chart below.

Wire	Key On Voltage	Voltage Idle	Voltage 2,500 rpm
Power			
Signal			
Ground			
Pressure			

7. What relationship can you determine between voltage and manifold pressure? Write your conclusions in the space below.

_____

_____

STOP 8. Discuss your findings with your instructor.

Instructor's Initials: _____

Name _____

Make Dynamic Test of Intake Pressure/MAP Sensor

9. Connect the scan tool to the motorcycle and set it to display the intake pressure/MAP data.

10. Turn the ignition switch on without starting the engine and unplug the sensor.

    A. Are any codes present?

    Yes _____ No _____ If yes, write them in the space below.

    _____

    _____

    B. What sensor data is displayed?

    _____

    _____

11. Turn the motorcycle off and try to restart it. Did it start easily?

    Yes _____ No _____

12. Does the engine rev up?

    Yes _____ No _____

13. Are any codes present?

    Yes _____ No _____ If yes, write them in the space below.

    _____

    _____

14. Plug the sensor back in and clear the code using the procedure outlined in the scan tool instructions.

🛑 15. Discuss your tests with your instructor and be prepared to discuss what the engine did while the intake pressure sensor/MAP was unplugged.

Instructor's Initials: _____

Job Wrap Up

16. Return all tools and materials to the proper storage areas and clean up your work area.

Final Assessment

_____ 1. A MAP sensor code is found on a fuel-injected engine. Technician A says to check the voltages at the sensor. Technician B says to swap the sensor with a known good sensor. Who is correct?

    A. A only.

    B. B only.

    C. Both A and B.

    D. Neither A nor B.

_____ 2. A MAP sensor code is found on a fuel-injected engine. Technician A says that the engine will not run with a MAP code. Technician B says that the MAP sensor can cause the engine to run rough. Who is correct?

    A. A only.

    B. B only.

    C. Both A and B.

    D. Neither A nor B.

_____ 3. Technician A says that a BARO sensor can be swapped with a MAP sensor to help diagnosis. Technician B says that with the engine off both the BARO and MAP should read the same pressure. Who is correct?

    A. A only.

    B. B only.

    C. Both A and B.

    D. Neither A nor B.

_____ 4. _True or False?_ MAP sensors are used on carbureted engines.

_____ 5. _True or False?_ Some engines will use the throttle position sensor and the crank sensor signals when a MAP sensor code is present.

Final Instructor Approval: _____

Name _____ Date _____ Class _____

Job 9-13

Throttle Position Sensor Testing

Introduction

The throttle position sensor (TPS) measures throttle position during engine operation. The TPS sends a voltage signal to the computer. The computer uses the TPS signal to alter ignition timing and fuel injection duration based on the throttle opening. The TPS that you will be testing is used on a cable-driven throttle system. Newer drive-by-wire systems can only be diagnosed by scan tool.

Most throttle position sensors fail because they have internal contacts that slide on a fixed resistor. Eventually, the contacts and resistor wear.

The TPS can cause a variety of problems based on how it fails. Typical problems are hard start, rough running, stalling, and misfiring. A thorough diagnosis of the TPS is critical to proper fuel injection diagnosis.

Objective

After successfully completing this job, you will be able to test and diagnose throttle position sensors.

Materials and Equipment

To complete this job, you will need the following tools, equipment, and materials:

- Motorcycle with electronic fuel injection with cable-operated throttle and TPS
- Appropriate service manual or electronic service information
- Fluke 88 or comparable multimeter
- Scan tool

Instructions

In this job, you will use the service manual and wiring diagram to find the proper wires, connectors, and procedures for checking power, ground, and signal between the throttle position sensor and the engine computer. You will need to back probe wires, either at the TPS or at the computer, to make your measurements unless you have a breakout box or test harness.

Read the job procedures, perform the tasks, and answer all questions. As you complete steps, you will be given instructions to either fill in measurements or perform certain tasks. When you reach a sign, show your work to your instructor. Do not continue until you have instructor approval (instructor will initial job sheet).

> **WARNING** ⚠ Before performing this job, review all pertinent safety information in the text and discuss safety procedures with your instructor.

Procedures

Test Throttle Position Sensor (TPS)

Motorcycle (Year/Make/Model)

_____

1. Use the service manual and the electrical wiring diagram for the motorcycle being worked on. The throttle position sensor has three wires. List the color of the wires and what they are used for:

Wire Color	Used For

2. Make KOEO (Key On Engine Off) voltage measurements with the throttle closed:
   A. Power

   _____

   B. Signal

   _____

   C. Ground

   _____

3. Open the throttle and sweep the throttle position sensor from closed (idle) through WOT (wide open throttle). Test for voltage on each wire. Move the throttle slowly enough to watch each tenth of a volt. Write the voltage measurements for the following:
   A. Power

   _____

   B. Signal

   _____

   C. Ground

   _____

4. Locate the service information for the above sensor and the procedure for testing it.

🛑 5. Show the instructor the information you found and explain how it varies from the above testing procedure. Discuss all your findings with your instructor.

Instructor's Initials: _____

Name _____

Dynamic Testing

6. With the key off, disconnect the TPS. Turn the key on and check for codes.

   A. Codes present:

   Yes _____ No _____ If yes, list the codes in the space below.

   _____

   _____

   B. Fail-safe or backup setting for this code:

   _____

   _____

7. Try to start the motorcycle engine. Does the engine start?

   Yes _____ No _____ If the engine starts, what sensors allow it to start?

   _____

   _____

8. Try and increase engine speed. Does the engine speed up?

   Yes _____ No _____ If the engine speeds up, what sensors allow it to do so?

   _____

   _____

Throttle Position Sensor Adjustment

 NOTE TPS adjustment is simple but critical. If the TPS is adjustable, then it must be adjusted properly. If the TPS is not adjustable, skip this procedure.

9. Find the procedure in the service manual for setting up the TPS.

10. If the procedure asks for resistance measurements to be made, what other measurement could replace the resistance measurements?

    _____

    _____

11. Do not remove the TPS, but check the setup and show your instructor the test.

 12. Discuss your findings with your instructor.

Instructor's Initials: _____

Job Wrap Up

13. Return all tools and materials to the proper storage areas and clean up your work area.

Final Assessment

_____ 1. *True or False?* The throttle position sensor is one of the main fuel injection system inputs to the computer.

_____ 2. *True or False?* Some throttle position sensors have three wires and some have four.

_____ 3. *True or False?* Some sensors can share the 5-volt source and the ground in parallel, but cannot share the signal wire.

_____ 4. *True or False?* A faulty throttle position sensor can cause the engine to run rough or stall.

_____ 5. *True or False?* Some engines can have more than one throttle position sensor.

Final Instructor Approval: _____

Name _____ Date _____ Class _____

Job 9-14

Temperature Sensor Testing

Introduction

The engine coolant temperature sensor is one of the critical inputs of a fuel injection system. The sensor is a thermistor that changes resistance, and therefore voltage drop, across the sensor as the temperature changes. Codes for this sensor are usually for opens or shorts, but on some late model vehicles the temperature reading is monitored. On vehicles where the temperature is monitored there will be additional codes to indicate incorrect engine temperature. This is important to know, since a sensor can get stuck on one resistance value and not create a code. In that instance the engine can be hard to start, misfire, and run rich.

Knowledge of how to use a scan tool and digital multimeter and an understanding of how the circuit works are critical for diagnosis. Other temperature sensors work in the same way, including intake air, exhaust, and ambient air temperature sensors.

Objective

After successfully completing this job, you will be able to diagnose a temperature sensor.

Materials and Equipment

To complete this job, you will need the following tools, equipment, and materials:

- Motorcycle with electronic fuel injection and temperature sensor
- Appropriate service manual or electronic service information
- Fluke 88 or comparable multimeter
- Scan tool

Instructions

In this job, you will use the repair manual and wiring diagram to find the proper connections and procedures for checking power, ground, and signal from the coolant temperature sensor to the engine computer. You will need to back-probe wires between the sensor and computer to make your measurements unless you have a breakout box or test harness.

Read the job procedures, perform the tasks, and answer all questions. As you complete steps you will be given instructions to either fill in measurements or perform certain tasks. When you reach a sign, show your work to your instructor. Do not continue until you have instructor approval (instructor will initial job sheet).

> **WARNING** ⚠ Before performing this job, review all pertinent safety information in the text and discuss safety procedures with your instructor.

Procedures

Motorcycle (Year/Make/Model)

_____

Basic Information

Use the repair manual and wiring diagram to answer the following questions.

1. Are the codes on this particular engine just for shorts and opens, or are there others that monitor temperature?

_____

_____

2. How many wires go to the sensor?

_____

3. What are the wires used for?

_____

_____

4. Is the power wire a 5-volt source? What does this mean?

_____

_____

_____

Testing

5. Connect the scan tool.

6. Back probe the power/signal wire.

Sensor Wire Voltage	Coolant Temperature	Intake Air Temperature

7. If the two temperatures above are the same, what information does the engine computer have?

_____

_____

8. Start the motorcycle and allow it to warm up. What happens to the voltage reading as the engine warms up?

_____

_____

9. Can you determine the relationship between the voltage reading and engine temperature?

_____

_____

Name _____

10. Unplug the temperature sensor.

11. Look up the code(s) for a defective coolant temperature sensor circuit. List the code(s) below.

_____

12. What is the fail-safe/backup setting for this code?

_____

_____

_____

13. What engine temperature is shown on the scan tool?

_____

14. What is the voltage reading on the sensor wire with the sensor unplugged?

_____

15. Try to start the motorcycle with the sensor unplugged. Did it start easily?

Yes _____ No _____ Can you explain why?

_____

_____

16. After checking with your instructor, create a short between the two wires with a fused jumper wire.

A. Did the code change when the circuit went from open to short?

Yes _____ No _____ If yes, can you determine the reason?

_____

B. What is the temperature reading on the scan tool?

_____

C. What is the voltage reading on the sensor wire?

_____

17. What conclusion can you make from these measurements?

_____

_____

_____

(STOP) 18. Discuss your findings with your instructor.

Instructor's Initials: _____

Intake Air Temperature

Motorcycle (Year/Make/Model)

_____

Basic Information

Use the repair manual and wiring diagram to answer the following questions.

19. Are the codes on this particular engine just for shorts and opens or are there others that monitor temperature?

_____

_____

20. How many wires go to the sensor?

_____

21. What are the wires used for?

_____

_____

22. Is the power wire a 5-volt source? What does that mean if it is?

_____

_____

Testing

23. Connect the scan tool.

24. Back probe the power/signal wire.

Sensor Wire Voltage	Coolant Temperature	Intake Air Temperature

25. If the two temperatures above are the same, what does the engine computer know?

_____

_____

26. Start the motorcycle and allow it to warm up. What happens to the voltage reading as the engine warms up?

_____

_____

27. What relationship can you determine between the voltage reading and engine temperature?

_____

_____

28. Unplug the temperature sensor.

Name _____

29. Look up the code(s) for a defective intake air temperature sensor circuit. List the code(s) below.

_____

30. What is the fail-safe/backup setting for this code?

_____

_____

31. What air intake temperature is shown on the scan tool?

_____

32. What is the voltage reading on the sensor wire with the sensor unplugged?

_____

33. After checking with your instructor, create a short between the two wires with a fused jumper wire.

34. Did the code change when the circuit went from open to short?

Yes _____ No _____

A. If yes, can you determine the reason?

_____

_____

B. What is the temperature reading on the scan tool?

_____

C. What is the voltage reading on the sensor wire?

_____

35. What conclusion can you make from these measurements?

_____

_____

_____

STOP 36. Discuss your findings with your instructor.

Instructor's Initials: _____

Job Wrap Up

37. Return all tools and materials to the proper storage areas and clean up your work area.

38. Ask your instructor to check your work and sign this job sheet.

Final Assessment

_____ 1. Two technicians are discussing coolant temperature sensors. Technician A says that an opening in the sensor will cause a code. Technician B says that the sensor being stuck on a temperature will always set a code. Who is correct?

A. A only.

B. B only.

C. Both A and B.

D. Neither A nor B.

_____ 2. Two technicians are discussing coolant temperature sensor diagnosis. Technician A says that the coolant sensor voltage drop changes as the temperature changes. Technician B says the sensor changes resistance as the temperature changes. Who is correct?

A. A only.

B. B only.

C. Both A and B.

D. Neither A nor B.

_____ 3. Technician A says that a coolant temperature sensor code will also cause an intake air temperature sensor code. Technician B says the two sensors are on two separate circuits. Who is correct?

A. A only.

B. B only.

C. Both A and B.

D. Neither A nor B.

_____ 4. Technician A says a faulty coolant temperature sensor can cause hard start or rough running. Technician B says a faulty coolant temperature sensor can cause fluctuating idle or stalling. Who is correct?

A. A only.

B. B only.

C. Both A and B.

D. Neither A nor B.

_____ 5. Two technicians are discussing temperature sensors. Technician A says the oil temperature sensor uses the same basic operation as the coolant temperature sensor. Technician B says an exhaust gas temperature sensor is the same basic operation as an air intake temperature sensor. Who is correct?

A. A only.

B. B only.

C. Both A and B.

D. Neither A nor B.

Final Instructor Approval: _____

CHAPTER 10 Ignition Systems

Chapter 10 Quiz

After studying Chapter 10 in the Motorcycles: Fundamentals, Service, Repair textbook, answer the following questions.

_____ 1. Ignition systems are powered by either a battery or a(n) _____.

_____ 2. High _____ is needed to fire the spark plug.

_____ 3. The amount of voltage and spark duration at the spark plug gap is referred to as spark _____.

_____ 4. The ignition _____ circuit consists of components that use low voltage.

_____ 5. When the ignition switch is turned on, power is provided to the ignition primary circuit by the _____.

_____ 6. *True or False?* In all ignition systems, the spark is triggered by a switching device.

For questions 7–11, match each of the ignition system components with the circuit that contains it. Answers will be used more than once.

A. Primary circuit   B. Secondary circuit

_____ 7. Spark plug

_____ 8. Ignition switch

_____ 9. Spark plug wire

_____ 10. Switching device

_____ 11. Condenser (on some systems)

_____ 12. An ignition _____ is made up of a primary winding and a secondary winding.

_____ 13. *True or False?* Ignition occurs after TDC.

_____ 14. The spark fires on the _____ stroke.
   A. intake
   B. compression
   C. power
   D. exhaust

_____ 15. As engine speed increases, ignition timing must be _____ because there is less time for the air-fuel mixture to burn.

_____ 16. In a(n) _____ advance unit, spring-loaded weights attached to the point cam or rotor are thrown outward.

_____ 17. *True or False?* A waste spark system fires two spark plugs at one time.

_____ 18. The capacity of a spark plug to dissipate combustion heat is called _____.
A. spark buildup
B. operating range
C. heat value
D. heat range

_____ 19. Plug reach that is too long results in _____ buildup on the exposed spark plug threads.

_____ 20. Spark plug _____ transfer high secondary voltage to the plugs.

_____ 21. Electronic ignition has all of the following components, *except*:
A. trigger wheel.
B. contact points.
C. magnetic pick up.
D. control module.

_____ 22. In a flywheel magneto ignition system, _____ current powers the ignition system.

_____ 23. In a digitally controlled transistorized ignition system, the _____ unit contains a(n) _____ that controls ignition timing.

_____ 24. In a CDI system, the capacitor _____.
A. stores primary voltage
B. releases voltage to the ignition coil
C. opens and closes the contact points
D. All of the above.

_____ 25. The charging coil in a magneto-supported CDI is also called a(n) _____ coil.

_____ 26. Discharge of the capacitor in a magneto-supported CDI is controlled by the _____.
A. diode
B. trigger coil voltage
C. SCR
D. None of the above.

_____ 27. As engine speed increases, trigger coil voltage rises. This principle is used to _____ timing.

_____ 28. In a DC/CDI system, the _____ is used as a power source.

Name _____ Date _____ Class _____

Job 10-1

Checking for Spark

Introduction

Checking for spark is one of the most basic technician skills. You must have a solid understanding of how to check for spark and what a quality spark looks like. Knowing what to check based on spark condition or no spark is also a fundamental skill of a motorcycle technician.

Objective

After successfully completing this job, you will be able to check an engine for the presence of quality spark.

Materials and Equipment

To complete this job, you will need the following tools, equipment, and materials:

- Motorcycle
- Appropriate service manual or electronic service information
- Spark tester
- Hand tools to include wrenches with box end
- Timing light

Instructions

In this job, you will observe spark while cranking and then use a timing light to check for a consistent spark as the engine runs. If the timing light fails to light up at the same time that a misfire occurs, further ignition system testing is needed.

Read the job procedures, perform the tasks, and answer all questions. As you complete steps you will be given instructions to either fill in measurements or perform certain tasks. When you reach a (STOP) sign, show your work to your instructor. Do not continue until you have instructor approval (instructor will initial job sheet).

 **WARNING** ⚠ Before performing this job, review all pertinent safety information in the text and discuss safety procedures with your instructor.

Procedures

Checking for Spark

1. Secure the vehicle properly.

2. Make sure that the battery stays charged or has a booster and is able to crank the engine at the proper speed for all testing.

3. Remove all of the spark plug wires and install them into a spark tester. The best type of tester to use can check all cylinders at the same time. If a spark tester for multiple cylinders is not available, test the cylinders individually.

4. Crank the engine and observe the spark. Write down your observations in the *From Tester* column in the chart below. If the engine has fewer than four cylinders, write N/A in the unused columns.

> **NOTE** If you are unsure about what constitutes a good spark, consult your instructor.

5. Remove the spark plugs from the engine. Reinstall the spark plug wire on one of the plugs and ground the plug to the engine case. Crank the engine and observe the spark. Repeat this test for each spark plug and record your findings below in the *From Spark Plug* column.

> **WARNING** ⚠ Remove all sources of flammable fluid, such as gasoline, and make sure that spark does not travel to sensitive equipment on the motorcycle.

6. Perform the next test as if there were no spark or a weak spark in Steps 4 and 5.

> **NOTE** If the system uses a stick coil or igniter on coil, skip this step.

Remove the spark plug wire from the plug and remove the cap (boot) from the end of the wire (it will usually twist off). Hold the wire approximately 1/4″ from the engine case and crank the engine. Repeat this test for each wire and record your findings in the *From Plug Wire* column below.

Cylinder	From Tester	From Spark Plug	From Plug Wire
1			
2			
3			
4			

🛑 7. Discuss your results in the chart with your instructor.

Instructor's Initials: _____

> **NOTE** If there was no spark in any of the tests, more ignition system testing is needed. These tests are covered in another chapter and other jobs.

Checking Spark with Engine Running

The timing light will flash when spark occurs. This test can reveal whether spark is completed each time spark should occur. This test should not be used alone unless it concludes that spark is okay and not the issue. If the light does not flash or flashes intermittently, further ignition testing is required.

> **NOTE** If this test cannot be done on an engine with stick coils or igniters, only on an engine with a spark plug wire that is accessible to a timing light clamp.

8. Attach the timing light according to instructions. The clip may need to face a certain direction. Usually an arrow on the clip will point toward the spark plug.

9. Start the engine.

10. Observe the timing light flash by pointing it at a dark surface or into your cupped hand. Observe the flash at cranking, idling, and 3000 rpm. Fill out the chart with your findings. If the engine has fewer than four cylinders, write N/A in the unused columns.

Name _____

Record whether the flashing is steady, intermittent, or none at all.

Cylinder	While Cranking	Idle	3,000 RPM
1			
2			
3			
4			

STOP 11. Discuss your results in the chart above with your instructor.

Instructor's Initials: _____

Job Wrap Up

12. Return all tools and materials to the proper storage areas and clean up your work area.

Final Assessment

1. The spark is blue and sharp from the spark tester, but weak and orange from the spark plug. What is the proper procedure to correct the problem?

   _____

   _____

2. The spark is blue and sharp from the coil wire, but weak and orange from the spark tester. What is the proper procedure to correct the problem?

   _____

   _____

3. There is no spark from the spark plug, but there is spark from the spark tester. What is the proper procedure to correct the problem?

   _____

   _____

4. There is no spark from the spark tester or plug, but there is spark from the coil wire. What is the proper procedure to correct the problem?

   _____

   _____

5. The spark is intermittent when observed by the timing light. What does this mean? What further diagnostic steps can be taken?

   _____

   _____

Final Instructor Approval: _____

Notes

Name _____ Date _____ Class _____

Job 10-2

Ignition System Identification

Introduction

Prior to diagnosing an ignition system the technician must identify the type of ignition system. Components, wiring, and diagnosis and repair procedures can change with different ignition systems. There are three basic ignition systems in use today. The ignition system most widely used on street bikes is the transistorized system. This system is also the system used in modern cars and trucks. The most widely used on dirt bikes, quads, and off-road equipment is the capacitor discharge ignition (CDI). The magneto system is used on small pit bikes and some scooters.

> **NOTE** Point ignitions have not been used for over 30 years. They are only found on vintage motorcycles and will not be covered here. If you need to service a vintage motorcycle with point ignition, consult older service literature for information.

Objective

After successfully completing this job, you will be able to identify the type of ignition system prior to troubleshooting.

Materials and Equipment

To complete this job, you will need the following tools, equipment, and materials:

- Appropriate service manual or electronic service information
- List of motorcycles and other vehicles to be looked up (should be a variety, to include street, off-road, snowmobile, quad, and side-by-side)

Instructions

In this job you will be looking at wiring diagrams and actual motorcycles to identify the three types of ignition systems used.

Read the job procedures, perform the tasks, and answer all questions. As you complete steps you will be given instructions to either fill in measurements or perform certain tasks. When you reach a (STOP) sign, show your work to your instructor. Do not continue until you have instructor approval (instructor will initial job).

> **WARNING** Before performing this job, review all pertinent safety information in the text and discuss safety procedures with your instructor. Be careful making any electrical measurements. Use only the proper test equipment.

Procedures

Wiring Diagram Review

All ignition systems have an electrical power source and a switching device. Both CDI and transistorized ignition systems can have batteries, so the presence of a battery cannot be used to determine the type of ignition system.

The best method of identifying an ignition system is by obtaining a wiring diagram of the system. Transistorized ignitions will have battery power to the primary side of the ignition coil, usually through the ignition or run switch. Other systems will not have battery power at the coil.

Direct current CDI systems (DC/CDI systems) receive power from the battery and are called battery-supported ignition systems. Some dirt bikes have batteries but the battery is not always used for the ignition system. These are alternating current CDI systems (AC/CDI systems) with the power coming from the charging system. In the system shown in the figure, the CDI is charged from the battery. On both types of CDI systems, the ignition coil receives peak voltage from the CDI and not from the battery.

An AC/CDI system will receive CDI power from a stator or magneto. On these systems the ignition coil will have a wire going straight to ground.

Classify the Ignition

1. Obtain electronic service information and wiring diagrams for several motorcycles and other vehicles. Choose dirt bikes, street bikes, side-by-sides, snowmobiles, and quads.

> **NOTE** The type of ignition system may be listed in the general information and specifications at the beginning of the service manual.

2. Fill in the charts below with information from five different motorcycles or other vehicles.

Vehicle 1	
Year	
Make	
Model	
Type of ignition	
How did you determine the type of ignition system?	
Name of switching device? (e.g., trigger, crank sensor, pickup)	
How many spark plugs does the coil control?	
How does the kill switch disable the ignition? (e.g., cuts off power to the coil, grounds power from the exciter)	

 3. Before proceeding to the next vehicle, check with your instructor to ensure that you are filling out the information correctly. Ask any questions you may have at this time.

Instructor's Initials: _____

Name _____

Vehicle 2	
Year	
Make	
Model	
Type of ignition	
How did you determine the type of ignition system?	
Name of switching device? (e.g., trigger, crank sensor, pickup)	
How many spark plugs does the coil control?	
How does the kill switch disable the ignition? (e.g., cuts off power to the coil, grounds power from the exciter)	

Vehicle 3	
Year	
Make	
Model	
Type of ignition	
How did you determine the type of ignition system?	
Name of switching device? (e.g., trigger, crank sensor, pickup)	
How many spark plugs does the coil control?	
How does the kill switch disable the ignition? (e.g., cuts off power to the coil, grounds power from the exciter)	

Vehicle 4	
Year	
Make	
Model	
Type of ignition	
How did you determine the type of ignition system?	
Name of switching device? (e.g., trigger, crank sensor, pickup)	
How many spark plugs does the coil control?	
How does the kill switch disable the ignition? (e.g., cuts off power to the coil, grounds power from the exciter)	

Vehicle 5	
Year	
Make	
Model	
Type of ignition	
How did you determine the type of ignition system?	
Name of switching device? (e.g., trigger, crank sensor, pickup)	
How many spark plugs does the coil control?	
How does the kill switch disable the ignition? (e.g., cuts off power to the coil, grounds power from the exciter)	

STOP   4. Discuss your results with your instructor.

Instructor's Initials: _____

Job Wrap Up

5. Return all tools and materials to the proper storage areas and clean up your work area.

Name _____

Final Assessment

1. Battery power is coming straight to the primary side of the coil and the ground of the primary goes through the igniter. What type of ignition system is it?

   _____

2. The trigger/switching device is located next to the stator for charging. Can you identify the type of ignition system?

   _____

   _____

3. List different names for the switching devices you have found in this job.

   _____

   _____

4. What are different names for the AC/CDI power sources that you have found in this job?

   _____

   _____

5. A motorcycle has a transistorized ignition system. How much voltage would you expect to have on both the primary wires with the key on, in run, but the engine not running?

   _____

   _____

   _____

Final Instructor Approval: _____

Notes

Name _____ Date _____ Class _____

Job 10-3

AC Capacitive-Discharge Ignition (CDI) Testing

Introduction

A motorcycle technician must know how to accurately diagnose CDI systems. CDI systems are found on motorcycles, quads, snowmobiles, side-by-sides, outboard engines, and small power equipment. CDI systems create a magnetic field by sending voltage from the CDI capacitor to the primary winding of the ignition coil. Creation of a magnetic field in the primary winding induces high voltage in the secondary winding. This high voltage fires the plug.

When testing CDI systems, keep in mind that active voltage tests are always better than resistance tests. There are active tests for all components.

> **NOTE** A technician using a Fluke 88 or equivalent meter will need an adapter to measure high voltage from the CDI to the ignition coil. A Fluke 88 or equivalent can make all other measurements without a peak voltage adapter.

Objective

After successfully completing this job, you will be able to test components of an ac-powered CDI system.

Materials and Equipment

To complete this job, you will need the following tools, equipment, and materials:

- Motorcycle or other vehicle with an AC/CDI system
- Appropriate service manual or electronic service information
- Fluke 88 multimeter or equivalent
- Spark tester
- Peak voltage adapter

Instructions

In this job, you will be testing a CDI system and its components to determine if they are functioning properly. If you are testing a vehicle that has a good spark, use this opportunity to observe and understand good spark measurements. If you have good spark and your measurement shows a defect, you should check your meter setup and range. When you reach a (**STOP**) sign, show your work to your instructor. Do not continue until you have instructor approval (instructor will initial job sheet).

> **WARNING** Before performing this job, review all pertinent safety information in the text and discuss safety procedures with your instructor. Be careful and use all precautions when making electrical measurements with sensitive equipment.

Procedures

Determine the Type of Ignition System

1. Using the service manual, determine what type of ignition system is being diagnosed.

   A. Type of ignition system:

   _____

   B. How did you determine this?

   _____

   _____

2. Make a photocopy of the ignition wiring diagram. (A separate diagram of the ignition system is preferred.)

3. Have your instructor confirm that you have the proper information and tools to continue.

Instructor's Initials: _____

Visually Check for Spark

4. Check for spark and record your readings in the chart below.

Test	Result
Confirm spark from the spark plug	
Confirm spark from the spark plug wire cap	
Confirm spark from the wire (cap removed)	

Check Peak Voltage to the Coil

> **NOTE** Even though checking spark was the first test, you would ordinarily perform this test only if there was no spark or a poor spark.

5. Test the voltage to the coil with a multimeter (set to proper scale) and a direct (peak) voltage adapter. On some engines, you will need to reverse the polarity/bias of the peak voltage adapter leads.

   A. Record your observations:

   _____

   B. If the tester indicates low voltage, what do you think would be your next logical step?

   _____

   _____

   _____

Name _____

> **NOTE** If the vehicle is misfiring, this voltage reading can be correct, or close to correct, but the exciter coil or trigger can still be intermittently faulty.

6. Mark tested connections on the wiring diagram photocopy.

Test the Kill Switch

> **NOTE** Kill switches commonly fail, especially the ones that use a button on the handle bar.

7. Test the kill switch of the CDI system. Explain the test you made and where the kill switch was located. (Note that this test can be inconclusive.)

_____

_____

_____

_____

8. Label the tested connections as Step 2 on the wiring diagram photocopy.

Test for Power to the CDI

(Used when there is no voltage, low voltage, or intermittent voltage to the coil.)

> **NOTE** Even if the vehicle has a battery for starting and charging, the power for the CDI may still be provided by an exciter or stator. A wiring diagram or tracing wires will help to distinguish which system is being worked on.

9. Test the ac voltage output of the exciter coil/stator as follows:

> **NOTE** Use the Min/Max function on a Fluke 88. If another multimeter is used, make the appropriate setting.

A. Obtain the specification or minimum value in the service manual.
B. Follow the output test procedure given in the service manual. Usually this test is done with the exciter unplugged and leads on both wires.
C. Describe test results and why any tests could not be performed or gave inconclusive results.

_____

_____

_____

🛑 10. After completing this test, label the tested connections on the wiring diagram photocopy.

Instructor's Initials: _____

Test Pulse Generator/Trigger Coil Testing

11. Test the ac voltage output of the pulse coil:

    A. Set the multimeter to its lowest voltage range, usually 4 or 6 volts.

    B. Ground the multimeter and test each wire (there should be two wires).

    C. Observe the analog scale as it fluctuates. Ask your instructor for help if you are not getting the desired readings. Record readings in the chart below.

12. Test the ac voltage output of the pulse coil by unplugging the sensor and connecting the sensor wires to the multimeter leads. Record your readings in the chart below.

> **NOTE** Use the Min/Max function on your Fluke 88. If another multimeter is used, make the appropriate setting.

	Wire Color	Voltage Reading	Specification
1			
2			

13. Record the tested connections as Step 4 on your wiring diagram photocopy.

Test the CDI Module Ground

14. Test the ground of the CDI module, and explain how it was done. (Remember that resistance tests can be inconclusive and that the best test for a wire is to use a comparable load through it.)

    _____

    _____

    _____

> **NOTE** This would be a good opportunity to experiment with using a test light on a positive terminal of the battery to perform an active test. If the bulb lights up, the ground is good. Ask your instructor to help you make this active test.

 15. Be prepared to discuss all of your measurements and to show your instructor any that are inconclusive.

16. When you have finished labeling your diagram, show it to your instructor. (You can use this diagram as a cheat sheet in the future.)

Instructor's Initials: _____

Job Wrap Up

17. Return all tools and materials to the proper storage areas and clean up your work area.

Name _____

Final Assessment

_____   1. Two technicians are discussing CDI diagnosis. Technician A says a faulty coil would receive correct peak voltage from the capacitor. Technician B says a faulty coil would have low peak voltage from the capacitor. Who is correct?

   A. A only.

   B. B only.

   C. Both A and B.

   D. Neither A nor B.

_____   2. Two technicians are discussing CDI diagnosis. Technician A says the kill switch on some CDI systems should be opened and then closed to kill the engine. Technician B says the kill switch on some CDI systems should be closed and then opened to kill the engine. Who is correct?

   A. A only.

   B. B only.

   C. Both A and B.

   D. Neither A nor B.

_____   3. Two technicians are discussing CDI diagnosis. Technician A says that a trigger voltage should go up and down consistently. Technician B says a trigger voltage just needs to rise above a certain number one time. Who is correct?

   A. A only.

   B. B only.

   C. Both A and B.

   D. Neither A nor B.

_____   4. Two technicians are discussing CDI diagnosis. Technician A says that if there is no spark from the plug, but there is spark from the coil, replace the plug and recheck for spark. Technician B says that if there is no spark from the coil, try testing for peak voltage to the coil. Who is correct?

   A. A only.

   B. B only.

   C. Both A and B.

   D. Neither A nor B.

_____   5. Two technicians are discussing CDI diagnosis. Technician A says that if the ground for the CDI is faulty, a new CDI will need to be ordered. Technician B says to run a jumper wire between the CDI and ground and test again. Who is correct?

   A. A only.

   B. B only.

   C. Both A and B.

   D. Neither A nor B.

Final Instructor Approval: _____

Notes

Name _____ Date _____ Class _____

Job 10-4

DC Capacitive Discharge Ignition (CDI) Testing

Introduction

A motorcycle technician must know how to accurately diagnose CDI systems. CDI systems are found on motorcycles, quads, snowmobiles, side-by-sides, outboard engines, and small power equipment. CDI systems create a magnetic field by sending voltage from the CDI capacitor to the primary winding of the ignition coil. Creation of a magnetic field in the primary winding induces high voltage in the secondary winding. This high voltage fires the plug.

When testing CDI systems, keep in mind that active voltage tests are always better than resistance tests. There are active tests for all components.

> **NOTE** A technician using a Fluke 88 or equivalent meter will need an adapter to measure high voltage from the CDI to the ignition coil. A Fluke 88 or equivalent can make all other measurements without a peak voltage adapter.

Objective

After successfully completing this job, you will be able to test components of a dc-powered CDI system.

Materials and Equipment

To complete this job, you will need the following tools, equipment, and materials:

- Motorcycle or other vehicle with DC/CDI
- Appropriate service manual or electronic service information
- Fluke 88 multimeter or equivalent
- Spark tester
- Peak voltage adapter

Instructions

In this job, you will be testing a CDI system and its components to determine if they are functioning properly. If you are testing a vehicle that has a good spark, use this opportunity to observe and understand good spark measurements. If you have good spark and your measurement shows a defect, you should check your meter setup and range. When you reach a sign, show your work to your instructor. Do not continue until you have instructor approval (instructor will initial job sheet).

> **WARNING** ⚠ Before performing this job, review all pertinent safety information in the text and discuss safety procedures with your instructor. Be careful and use all precautions when making electrical measurements with sensitive equipment.

Procedures

Determine the Type of Ignition System

1. Using the service manual, determine the type of ignition system.

   A. Type of ignition system:

   _____

   B. How did you determine this?

   _____

   _____

2. Make a photocopy of the ignition wiring diagram. (A separate diagram of just the ignition system is preferred.)

🛑 3. Have your instructor confirm that you have the proper information and tools to continue.

Instructor's Initials: _____

Checking for Spark

4. Check for spark and record your readings in the chart below.

Test	Result
Confirm spark from the spark plug	
Confirm spark from the spark plug wire cap	
Confirm spark from the wire (cap removed)	

Check Peak Voltage to the Coil

5. Test the voltage to the coil with a multimeter set to the proper scale and a direct (peak) voltage adapter.

   > **NOTE** ⚙ On some multimeters, you will need to reverse polarity/bias of the peak voltage adapter leads.

   A. Record your observations:

   _____

   B. If the tester indicates low voltage, what would be the next logical step?

   _____

6. Mark tested connections on your wiring diagram photocopy as Step 1.

   > **NOTE** ⚙ Even though checking spark was the first job test, you would ordinarily perform this test only if there was no spark or a poor spark.

Name _____

 NOTE If the vehicle is misfiring, this voltage reading may be correct, or close to correct, but the exciter coil or trigger can still be intermittently faulty.

Test the Kill Switch

 NOTE Kill switches commonly fail, especially those that are just a button on the handle bar.

7. Test the kill switch of the CDI system. Explain the test you made and where the kill switch was located. (Note that this test can be inconclusive.)

_____

_____

_____

_____

8. Label tested connections on the wiring diagram photocopy as Step 2.

Test for Power to the CDI

9. All DC/CDI systems get power from a battery rather than the exciter coil, so you will need to test battery source voltage. There may be more than one wire that provides power to the CDI module. Test all power wires.

Voltage to CDI Module

	Wire Color	Voltage Cranking	Voltage Key On
1			
2			
3			

 NOTE One of the voltage readings may be lower than battery voltage. This is because some powersports vehicles use a resistor in the ignition switch to drop voltage. This is a security device and, if the ignition switch is bypassed, the CDI system will not create spark.

10. Write tested connections on your wiring diagram photocopy as Step 3.

Test Pulse Generator/Trigger Coil

11. Test the ac voltage output of the pulse coil by the following procedure:
    A. Set the meter on its lowest voltage range, usually 4 or 6 volts.
    B. Ground the multimeter and test each wire (there should be two wires).
    C. Observe the analog scale as it fluctuates. Ask your instructor for help if you are not getting desired readings. Record the readings in the chart on the next page.

12. Test the ac voltage output of the pulse coil by unplugging the sensor and connecting the wires to the multimeter (similar to testing a stator). Record your readings in the chart below.

> **NOTE** Use the Min/Max function on the Fluke 88. If another multimeter is used, make the appropriate setting.

	Wire Color	Voltage Reading	Specification
1			
2			

13. Record tested connections on your wiring diagram photocopy as Step 4.

Test CDI Ground

14. Test the ground of the CDI module and explain how it was done. Remember that resistance tests can be inconclusive and the best test for a wire is to replace the module with a comparable load.

> **NOTE** This is a good opportunity to place a test light on a positive terminal of the battery and perform an active test. If the bulb lights up, then the ground is good. Ask your instructor for help to make this an active test. Describe what you did below.

_____

_____

_____

_____

 15. Be prepared to discuss all of your measurements and to show your instructor any inconsistent measurements.

16. Show the instructor your wiring diagram photocopy with the steps written on it. (You can use this sheet as a cheat sheet in the future.)

Instructor's Initials: _____

Job Wrap Up

17. Return all tools and materials to the proper storage areas and clean up your work area.

Name _____

Final Assessment

_____ 1. Two technicians are discussing DC/CDI diagnosis. Technician A says the CDI must get proper voltage from the battery. Technician B says that a charging problem could cause ignition problems. Who is correct?

   A. A only.

   B. B only.

   C. Both A and B.

   D. Neither A nor B.

_____ 2. Two technicians are discussing DC/CDI diagnosis. Technician A says the kill switch could also be called the run switch. Technician B says the kill switch can ground the power going from the capacitor to the coil on some systems. Who is correct?

   A. A only.

   B. B only.

   C. Both A and B.

   D. Neither A nor B.

_____ 3. Two technicians are discussing CDI diagnosis. Technician A says that the trigger voltage is very low. Technician B says the trigger voltage must fluctuate to prove it is working. Who is correct?

   A. A only.

   B. B only.

   C. Both A and B.

   D. Neither A nor B.

_____ 4. Two technicians are discussing CDI diagnosis. Technician A says that a critical step is checking spark without the spark plug cap on the coil wire. Technician B says that with no spark from a known good plug, the coil must be faulty. Who is correct?

   A. A only.

   B. B only.

   C. Both A and B.

   D. Neither A nor B.

_____ 5. Two technicians are discussing CDI diagnosis. Technician A says that of all CDI components, only a capacitor can be intermittently faulty. Technician B says that any of the components of a CDI system can be intermittently faulty. Who is correct?

   A. A only.

   B. B only.

   C. Both A and B.

   D. Neither A nor B.

Final Instructor Approval: _____

Notes

Name _____ Date _____ Class _____

Job 10-5

Transistorized Ignition

Introduction

Diagnosing transistorized ignition systems is a critical skill for a motorcycle technician. Transistorized ignition systems are common, especially on street bikes. This is the same kind of ignition system found on modern cars, trucks, and SUVs.

Having a good grasp of the different tests is imperative. Follow the service manual tests, keeping in mind that active voltage tests are always better than resistance tests. There are active tests for all components.

The peak voltage test on a transistorized ignition coil is very informative. The test measures the voltage spike of the primary side of the coil after the magnetic field has collapsed. This tells the technician that the primary side is working and, if there are spark issues, they are on the system's secondary side.

Objective

After successfully completing this job, you will be able to test components of a transistorized ignition system.

Materials and Equipment

To complete this job, you will need the following tools, equipment, and materials:

- Motorcycle or other vehicle with dc-powered transistorized ignition system
- Appropriate service manual or electronic service information
- Fluke 88 multimeter or equivalent
- Spark tester
- Peak voltage adapter

Instructions

In this job, you will be testing a transistorized ignition system and its components to determine whether they are functioning properly. If you are testing a vehicle that has a good spark, use this opportunity to observe and understand good spark measurements. If you have good spark and your measurement reads faulty, then you have not made a good measurement and should check your multimeter setup and range. When you reach a (STOP) sign, show your work to your instructor. Do not continue until you have instructor approval (instructor will initial job sheet).

NOTE   Many of the steps in this job consist of answering questions about spark diagnosis. Answer all questions briefly but completely.

WARNING   Before performing this job, review all pertinent safety information in the text and discuss safety procedures with your instructor. Be careful and use all precautions when making electrical measurements with sensitive equipment.

Procedures

Vehicle (Year/Make/Model): _____

_____

Determine the Type of Ignition System

1. Using the service manual, determine the type of ignition system.

   A. Type of ignition system:

   _____

   B. How did you determine this?

   _____

   _____

   C. How many cylinders does the engine have?

   _____

2. How many ignition coils does the engine have?

   _____

3. If an ignition coil has two spark plug leads (fires two cylinders), what is this type of system called?

   _____

4. Does the coil fire for both cylinders at the same time?

   _____

5. Make a photocopy of the ignition wiring diagram. (A separate diagram of just the ignition system is preferable.)

🛑 6. Have your instructor confirm that you have the proper information and tools to continue.

Instructor's Initials: _____

Check for Spark

7. Check for spark and record your readings in the chart below.

Test	Result
Confirm spark from the spark plug	
Confirm spark from the spark plug wire cap	
Confirm spark from the wire (cap removed)	

Name _____

Test the Ignition Coil

NOTE For the purposes of this job, you will be making the following tests even if your engine has spark.

	Wire Color	Voltage Key On
Wire from power to coil (positive)		
Wire from coil to igniter (negative)		

8. What do the above test results tell you about the condition of the primary side?

_____

_____

_____

9. Use the wiring diagram to determine which wire is the ground side wire of the coil. (The ground wire runs from the coil to the igniter.)

10. Test the ground side wire for peak voltage and compare to the service manual specification. Peak voltage on this wire occurs when the primary side winding turns off, collapsing through the secondary winding. This test determines whether the primary winding is working and whether the igniter is controlling the coil.

	Ignition Coil Ground Side Wire Color	Peak Voltage While Cranking
Coil 1		
Coil 2		
Coil 3		
Coil 4		

11. There is no spark from the coil and the peak voltage is correct. What would your next step be?

_____

_____

12. There is no spark from the coil and the peak voltage is low. What would your next step be?

_____

_____

13. There is no spark from the coil and the peak voltage is zero. What would your next step be?

_____

_____

14. Test for ground side switching. Use the multimeter to check for duty cycle (percent of time that current is flowing). This test determines whether the igniter is trying to turn the coil on and off. There is usually not a switching specification, but fuel-injected bikes typically show single-digit readings.

> **NOTE** Ask your instructor to explain duty cycle if not done previously.

	Ignition Coil Ground Side Wire Color	**Duty Cycle**
Coil 1		
Coil 2		
Coil 3		
Coil 4		

15. Peak voltage reads zero and a duty cycle is observed. What would your next step be?

_____

_____

_____

16. Peak voltage reads zero and no duty cycle is observed. What would your next step be?

_____

_____

17. Does the ignition coil in a transistorized ignition fire when the coil primary winding is turned on or when the winding is turned off?

_____

_____

🛑 18. Be prepared to discuss all of your measurements and to show your instructor any inconsistent measurements.

Instructor's Initials: _____

Test Power and Ground to the Igniter

19. Use the wiring diagram to locate the igniter power and ground wires. (The igniter can be located inside other components, such as onboard computers.)

20. Test for voltage to the igniter and determine whether voltage is present with the key on or key off.

Name _____

21. Obtain a high impedance multimeter (like the Fluke 88) to make the following tests. Record the readings in the chart below.

> **CAUTION** ⚠ Do not use a test light! This will damage module circuits.

Source of Power Wire (e.g., Ignition Switch or Main Relay)	Wire Color	Voltage Reading

> **NOTE** Remember when checking for ground to hook the multimeter to a power source. Service information usually recommends using igniter power to test the igniter ground.

Location of Igniter Ground Wire	Wire Color	Voltage Reading

22. The igniter did not create a duty cycle and there is no power or ground. What would your next step be?

_____

_____

23. The igniter did not create a duty cycle and there was power and ground. What would your next step be?

_____

Test Inputs to the Igniter

Kill/Run Switch

24. Use the wiring diagram to determine where the kill switch is located. (On street bikes, it is typically called the run switch.)The kill switch has to be closed in order for the starter to crank. Study the wiring diagram. If the engine cranks with the run switch closed, the run switch is working.

🛑 25. Be prepared to discuss all of your measurements and to discuss the next steps in testing crank and cam sensors.

Instructor's Initials: _____

Test Crankshaft Position Sensor-Trigger-Pulse Generator

Transistorized ignition engines will not create spark without a crankshaft position sensor. If using an EFI vehicle, check to determine whether crank sensor codes are present. Some vehicles will start without a cam position sensor signal, but will store a code. Carbureted vehicles usually do not have cam and crank sensors.

There are some differences between carbureted and fuel-injected engine crank sensors. The carbureted engine service manual will usually state a voltage output. On fuel-injected engines, the computer reads sensor patterns. A loose or damaged sensor or tone wheel can create a faulty pattern that can create a code, but at the same time, produce the proper voltage.

26. Make measurements of the crank sensors and record them in the chart below. Use the service manual for procedures and specifications.

	Wire Colors to Crank Sensor	AC Voltage	Specification
1			
2			

27. Make measurements of the cam sensor and record them in the chart below. Not all vehicles will have cam sensors.

>   **NOTE** Some cam sensors convert ac to dc inside the sensor and the output will be a dc signal. Use the service manual to check procedures and specifications.

	Wire Colors to Cam Sensor	AC Voltage	Specification
1			
2			

28. Be prepared to discuss all of your measurements and to discuss your next steps in testing other possible inputs to the igniter.

Instructor's Initials: _____

Test other Igniter Inputs

Throttle Position Sensor

29. Test the throttle position sensor for both resistance and voltage when possible. Use the service manual for procedures and specifications. Both resistance and voltage should rise smoothly as the throttle is opened.

Purpose	Wire Color	Resistance	Specification
Power			
Signal			
Ground			

Name _____

Purpose	Wire Color	Voltage	Specification
Power			
Signal			
Ground			

30. What conclusion can you make from comparing the voltage and resistance values?

_____

Side Stand Switch

 NOTE If the engine is in gear and the side stand is down, the igniter will kill the spark as a safety precaution. If, however, the switch fails with the side stand up, this will cause a no spark condition.

31. Use the service manual to test the side stand switch. If the repair manual uses resistance values, try to calculate the voltages using Ohm's law.

Purpose	Wire Color	Resistance	Specification

Oil Level Sensor

 NOTE The ignition system may be disabled if the engine has an oil level sensor and it is faulty or the engine is actually low on oil. This is done to save the engine. This system is typical on generators, power equipment, and outboards, but not unheard of on motorcycles.

32. Use the wiring diagram to determine if this system is used on your vehicle and, if so, write the wire information in the chart.

Purpose	Wire Color	Resistance	Specification
Power			
Signal			
Ground			

33. All of the inputs to the igniter are correct, but the igniter does not produce a duty cycle to turn the ignition coil on and off. What would your next step be?

_____

STOP 34. Be prepared to discuss all of your measurements with your instructor.

Instructor's Initials: _____

Job Wrap Up

35. Return all tools and materials to the proper storage areas and clean up your work area.

Final Assessment

Use Figure 10-5.1 to answer the following questions.

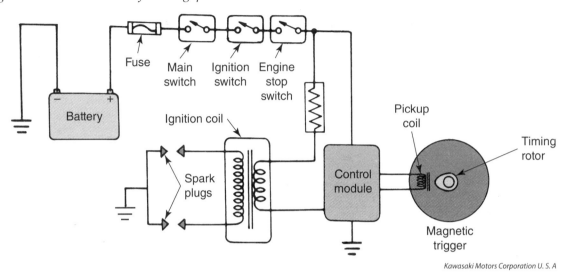

Kawasaki Motors Corporation U. S. A

Figure 10-5.1.

1. Where in Figure 10-5.1 would you test peak voltage of the ignition coil?

_____

2. Where in Figure 10-5.1 would you test power to the igniter?

_____

3. What type of voltage would you expect to find at the pickup coil?

_____

4. How many spark plugs does this coil fire at the same time?

_____

5. There is no spark from the coil and the peak voltage reading is correct. What would be the next step?

_____

_____

Final Instructor Approval: _____

CHAPTER 11 Lubrication Systems

Chapter 11 Quiz

After studying Chapter 11 in the Motorcycles: Fundamentals, Service, Repair textbook, answer the following questions.

_____ 1. Lubricants are needed to reduce _____ and the heat it produces in order to prevent part wear and damage.

_____ 2. *True or False?* Lubricants help to dissipate heat.

_____ 3. A thin film of oil between the piston rings and cylinder wall _____ combustion pressure.
  A. seals
  B. reduces
  C. increases
  D. eliminates

_____ 4. A function of oil is to dissolve _____ formed during the combustion process.
  A. acids
  B. varnish
  C. rust
  D. gases

_____ 5. *True or False?* Synthetic four-stroke engine oil is derived from mineral oils.

_____ 6. The term *film strength* refers to the ability of an oil to _____.
  A. saturate with air bubbles
  B. flow under controlled conditions
  C. combine with oxygen
  D. remain between two lubricated parts

_____ 7. Foaming reduces the ability of oil to lubricate and _____.

_____ 8. _____ additives keep unwanted particles suspended until caught in the filter.
  A. Lubricant
  B. Detergent
  C. Viscosity
  D. Temperature

_____ 9. The Society of Automotive Engineers classifies oils according to their intended use and _____.
  A. price
  B. oxidation action
  C. resistance to foaming
  D. viscosity

_____ 10. The ideal oils for motorcycles are classified by JASO standards and have the _____ designation.
   A. SN
   B. M1
   C. MA
   D. EC-II

_____ 11. *True or False?* A 20 weight oil will pour more slowly than a 30 weight oil.

_____ 12. In a premixed two-stroke engine lubrication system, oil is combined with _____ before it reaches the carburetor.

_____ 13. *True or False?* Almost all scooters and street motorcycles use a pump-operated system to lubricate two-stroke engine components.

_____ 14. *True or False?* Direct bearing injection provides undiluted oil to engine main bearings.

_____ 15. *True or False?* A plunger oil pump produces high volume but low pressure.

_____ 16. *True or False?* Oil consumption is controlled by engine speed and load.

_____ 17. The output of a two-stroke oil injection pump is controlled by engine speed and _____ position.

_____ 18. *True or False?* Adjusting the throttle cable to compensate for normal wear is an important maintenance procedure.

_____ 19. *True or False?* To bleed most oil injection pumps, the oil line must be loosened at the pump to purge the air.

_____ 20. Oil tank venting methods include a vent hole in the tank cap and a vent _____ attached to the top of the oil tank.

_____ 21. *True or False?* A sticking check valve can cause oil to flow into the engine when it is not running.

_____ 22. The term *sump* refers to the _____.
   A. lowest part of the crankcase cavity
   B. pressure side of a two-sided oil pump
   C. scavenging side of an oil pump
   D. oil reservoir

_____ 23. *True or False?* A spray system can be used in wet and dry sump systems.

_____ 24. *True or False?* A gear oil pump produces high volume and high pressure.

_____ 25. The most common oil pump design on four-stroke engines is the _____ oil pump.

_____ 26. *True or False?* In a rotor oil pump, oil is squeezed between two rotors to produce pressure.

_____ 27. *True or False?* A check valve is used to control maximum oil pressure.

Name _____

_____ 28. All of the following statements about oil filters are true, *except*:
A. a bypass valve allows oil to flow around a clogged element oil filter.
B. in a centrifugal oil filter, oil slingers are attached to the crankshaft.
C. element filters are easier to service than centrifugal filters.
D. a centrifugal filter removes particles that are lighter than oil.

_____ 29. Bent or collapsed fins on oil-to-air coolers should be _____.
A. cleaned
B. straightened
C. replaced
D. removed

_____ 30. *True or False?* Oil should be checked after the engine is started and oil has been allowed to circulate thoroughly.

_____ 31. If possible, a dirty oil filter screen should be removed and cleaned in _____ if deposits are found.

_____ 32. Which of the following is a possible cause of high oil pressure?
A. Clogged oil filter.
B. Damaged oil seal.
C. Clogged oil passage.
D. All of the above.

_____ 33. *True or False?* In a four-stroke engine lubricating system, a low oil level can be caused by incorrect piston ring installation.

Notes

Name _____ Date _____ Class _____

Job 11-1

Types of Oil, Lubricants, and Sealants

Introduction

To properly service a motorcycle, the technician must be familiar with many different chemicals and fluids. There are lubricants for motorcycle engines, transmissions, and final drives, as well as lubricants for cables, pivots, and handles. Sealants are also used in many places on a motorcycle. Being able to find the proper lubricant is critical to proper service.

Objective

After successfully completing this job, you will be able to locate proper lubricants to use on and in a motorcycle.

Materials and Equipment

To complete this job, you will need the following tools, equipment, and materials:
- Appropriate service manual or electronic service information
- Variety of oils and lubricants

Instructions

In this job, you will be identifying a variety of oils, lubricants, and sealants used to service motorcycles. You will then locate those items in the specific locations in the shop. You will also find out from your instructor how these items are billed to customers.

 After you read the job procedures, perform the tasks and answer all questions. As you complete steps, you will be given instructions to either fill in measurements or perform certain tasks. When you reach a sign, show your work to your instructor. Do not continue until you have instructor approval (instructor will initial job sheet).

> **WARNING** ⚠ Before performing this job, review all pertinent safety information in the text and discuss safety procedures with your instructor.

Procedures

Vehicle (Year/Make/Model)

_____

1. Using the information that you have, either electronic or a service manual, find the type of lubricant and fill in the following chart.

Application	Weight or Type	Capacity	Location in Shop	Proper Disposal in Your Shop
Engine oil				
Transmission oil				
Final drive oil				
Engine coolant				
Brake fluid				
Clutch hydraulic fluid				

2. Interview your instructor to determine how to confirm that fluids are billed to customers and what paperwork is necessary.

 3. Discuss your findings with your instructor and make sure to ask any questions that you may have before continuing.

Instructor's Initials: _____

4. The following are lubricants or sealants commonly used while repairing a motorcycle. Look up the proper chemical for the application.

Application	Type Product Used	Location in Your Shop	Brand in Your Shop
Brake and clutch cables			
Spark plugs			
Brake rotor bolts			
Brake pedal pivot			
Brake caliper slides			
Drive chain			
Engine case sealant			

5. Discuss your findings with your instructor from the fuel pressure and volume tests.

Instructor's Initials: _____

Job Wrap Up

6. Return all tools and materials to the proper storage areas and clean up your work area.

Name _____

Final Assessment

_____ 1. Two technicians are discussing engine oil. Technician A says as long as the weight is correct any oil will be fine to use in any engine. Technician B says that motorcycle engine oil will protect wet clutches. Who is correct?

A. A only.

B. B only.

C. Both A and B.

D. Neither A nor B.

_____ 2. Two technicians are discussing engine oil. Technician A says that synthetic oil is better than petroleum-based oil. Technician B says that petroleum-based oil is better than synthetic. Who is correct?

A. A only.

B. B only.

C. Both A and B.

D. Neither A nor B.

_____ 3. Two technicians are discussing final drive oil. Technician A says that hypoid gear oil is typically used in a final drive. Technician B says that GL-5 oil is typically used in a final drive. Who is correct?

A. A only.

B. B only.

C. Both A and B.

D. Neither A nor B.

_____ 4. Two technicians are discussing brake fluid. Technician A says that DOT 3 is compatible with DOT 4 but has a lower boiling point. Technician B says DOT 4 and DOT 5 are not compatible. Who is correct?

A. A only.

B. B only.

C. Both A and B.

D. Neither A nor B.

_____ 5. Two technicians are discussing what to put on threads of a spark plug. Technician A says that engine oil is acceptable for spark plug threads. Technician B says that anti-seize is the best for spark plug threads. Who is correct?

A. A only.

B. B only.

C. Both A and B.

D. Neither A nor B.

Final Instructor Approval: _____

Notes

Name _____ Date _____ Class _____

Job 11-2

Change Engine Oil and Filter

Introduction

The most common engine service performed on a motorcycle is changing oil. You must become proficient at changing oil because it will likely be the first job that you do at a motorcycle repair shop. Engine oil changes are also done on just about every job that comes into the shop.

Some engines require running the vehicle to determine the proper oil level. Most engines have a window and the engine must be off and held level to properly check oil level. Other engines have a dipstick. You must become familiar with the procedure for the engines that you work on. Do not assume that you know what the procedure is.

Objective

After successfully completing this job, you will be able to change the engine oil and filter on a motorcycle.

Materials and Equipment

To complete this job, you will need the following tools, equipment, and materials:

- Motorcycle with four-stroke engine
- Appropriate service manual or electronic service information
- Engine oil
- Filter
- Oil filter O-rings and drain plug gasket
- Funnel, drain pan, and towels
- Graduated cylinder large enough to measure amount of oil drained

Instructions

In this job, you will be changing engine oil. You will need to locate the process in the repair manual and pay attention to all procedures. Most manufacturers want you to warm the engine up first, but be sure there is engine oil in the engine prior to starting it.

After you read the job procedures, perform the tasks and answer all questions. As you complete steps, you will be given instructions to either fill in measurements or perform certain tasks. When you reach a sign, show your work to your instructor. Do not continue until you have instructor approval (instructor will initial job sheet).

> **WARNING** ⚠ Before performing this job, review all pertinent safety information in the text and discuss safety procedures with your instructor.

Procedures

Vehicle (Year/Make/Model)

_____

1. Record the following information as indicated in the chart below.

How to check oil	
Any oil leaks visible	
Current crankcase oil level	
Current oil condition	

 2. Discuss your findings with your instructor and make sure to ask any questions that you may have before continuing.

Instructor's Initials: _____

3. After confirming there is oil in the engine, warm up the engine. If you cannot confirm there is oil in the engine, do not start the engine and continue to Step 4.

4. Perform the oil change tasks and record the appropriate information below.
   A. Drain the oil.

   _____ Were there other fluids in the oil?

   _____ How much oil was drained from the engine?

   B. Remove the oil filter.

   _____ Was the proper gasket installed on the filter?

   C. Replace the drain plug gasket and install the drain plug. Torque the plug to specifications.
   D. Install a new filter and O-ring. Lubricate the O-ring before installing the filter.
   E. Fill the engine with oil.

   _____ What type of oil was used (weight)?

   _____ How much oil was added?

   F. Start the engine and check for leaks.

   _____ Did the oil light go out after the engine was started?

5. Describe the place in your shop for disposing of waste engine oil, oil filters, and oily rags.

   _____

   _____

   _____

 6. Discuss your findings with your instructor and have your instructor check your work.

Instructor's Initials: _____

Job Wrap Up

7. Return all tools and materials to the proper storage areas and clean up your work area.

Name _____

Final Assessment

_____ 1. Two technicians are discussing engine oil change. Technician A says that 10w30 and 10w40 are basically the same oil and can replace each other. Technician B says that the incorrect weight of oil can have an effect on engine performance. Who is correct?

A. A only.

B. B only.

C. Both A and B.

D. Neither A nor B.

_____ 2. Two technicians are discussing engine oil changes. Technician A says fuel in the engine oil indicates a problem in the fuel system. Technician B says that coolant in the oil can be a normal condition. Who is correct?

A. A only.

B. B only.

C. Both A and B.

D. Neither A nor B.

_____ 3. Two technicians are discussing engine oil changes. Technician A says that if the engine has a window to look through, the bike needs to be upright to check properly. Technician B says that if the engine has a window to look through, the rider should be on the bike to check the level correctly. Who is correct?

A. A only.

B. B only.

C. Both A and B.

D. Neither A nor B.

_____ 4. Two technicians are discussing oil filters. Technician A says that spin-on oil filters should have the O-ring lubricated before installing. Technician B says that spin-on oil filters are sometimes supposed to be filled prior to installation. Who is correct?

A. A only.

B. B only.

C. Both A and B.

D. Neither A nor B.

_____ 5. Two technicians are discussing oil changes. Technician A says that measuring how much oil came out is used to determine the amount of oil to be added. Technician B says that measuring how much oil came out is used to see if the engine might be burning or leaking oil. Who is correct?

A. A only.

B. B only.

C. Both A and B.

D. Neither A nor B.

Final Instructor Approval: _____

Notes

Name _____   Date _____   Class _____

Job 11-3

Oil Pressure Testing

Introduction

The oil pressure test is usually performed for one of two reasons—the oil light stays on or the engine is making noises. Proper oil pressure is critical for engine life. The oil pump moves enough oil to provide lubrication to the entire engine. The pressure relief valve in the oil pump opens to prevent excessive oil pressure. Common causes of low oil pressure are worn pump gears and/or body, the pressure regulator is stuck open, and excessive bearing clearances.

If the oil light is on but the engine is running quietly, the oil pressure sensor may be faulty. The oil pressure sensor is usually a switch that closes and turns on the oil light when the oil pressure is low. Oil light illumination is normal when the key is turned on but the engine is not running. Understanding this circuit is very important to avoid diagnosing an internal engine problem that is actually an electrical problem.

Objective

After successfully completing this job, you will be able to diagnose engine oil pressure problems.

Materials and Equipment

To complete this job, you will need the following tools, equipment, and materials:

- Four-stroke engine
- Appropriate service manual or electronic service information
- Oil pressure tester

Instructions

In this job, you will first be diagnosing an oil pressure light electrical circuit. You will then install an oil pressure gauge in place of the oil pressure sending unit.

> **WARNING** Be very careful when removing the sending unit and when installing the pressure gauge, as the threads are easy to cross thread or to break if you are not careful.

Read the job procedures, perform the tasks, and answer all questions. As you complete steps, you will be given instructions to either fill in measurements or perform certain tasks. When you reach a 🛑 sign, show your work to your instructor. Do not continue until you have instructor approval (instructor will initial job sheet).

> **WARNING** Before performing this job, review all pertinent safety information in the text and discuss safety procedures with your instructor.

Procedures

Checking the Oil Light Operation

Vehicle (Year/Make/Model)

_____

1. Locate the wiring diagram for the oil pressure light.

   A. Does the oil light come on when the switch is closed or when the switch is open?

   _____

   B. How many wires are going to the oil pressure sending unit?

   _____

2. Where does the engine oil pressure sending unit find ground?

   _____

3. Locate the oil pressure sending unit on the motorcycle. (It is usually near the oil filter, or you can use the parts location of the engine section in the repair manual.)

4. Unplug the wire from the oil pressure sending unit and turn the key on. Is the oil light on or off?

   _____

5. Run a jumper wire from the oil pressure sending unit wire to a known good ground and turn the key on, but do not start the engine. What does the light do now?

   _____

 6. Discuss your findings with your instructor and make sure to ask any questions that you may have before continuing.

Instructor's Initials: _____

Testing Oil Pressure

7. Remove the oil pressure sending unit.

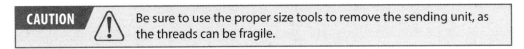

CAUTION ⚠ Be sure to use the proper size tools to remove the sending unit, as the threads can be fragile.

8. Install the oil pressure gauge in the pressure switch opening.

9. Double-check that the oil level is correct.

10. Be prepared to turn the engine off, start the engine, and read the oil pressure. Fill in the chart below.

Condition	Oil Pressure	Oil Light On/Off	Specification
Key On			
Idle			
3,000 rpm			

Name _____

11. Does the repair manual indicate at what pressure the oil light will turn on?

_____

(STOP) 12. Discuss your findings with your instructor and have your instructor check your work on the oil change.

Instructor's Initials: _____

Job Wrap Up

13. Return all tools and materials to the proper storage areas and clean up your work area.

Final Assessment

_____ 1. Two technicians are discussing engine oil pressure. Technician A says the light flickering on and off when the engine is running is normal. Technician B says if the oil light is on any time the engine is running, it should be diagnosed immediately. Who is correct?

A. A only.

B. B only.

C. Both A and B.

D. Neither A nor B.

_____ 2. Two technicians are discussing engine oil pressure. Technician A says that a failed pressure relief valve can cause low oil pressure. Technician B says that a failed pressure relief valve can cause high oil pressure. Who is correct?

A. A only.

B. B only.

C. Both A and B.

D. Neither A nor B.

_____ 3. Two technicians are discussing engine oil pressure. Technician A says that the oil goes through the oil pickup screen before the oil pump. Technician B says that oil goes through the filter before the oil pump. Who is correct?

A. A only.

B. B only.

C. Both A and B.

D. Neither A nor B.

_____ 4. Two technicians are discussing oil pressures. Technician A says that the oil goes through the pressure relief valve before the pump. Technician B says that the oil goes through the pump before the relief valve. Who is correct?

A. A only.

B. B only.

C. Both A and B.

D. Neither A nor B.

_____ 5. Two technicians are discussing oil pressure. Technician A says that low oil pressure will cause engine damage very quickly. Technician B says that an engine can be full of oil and have low oil pressure. Who is correct?

A. A only.

B. B only.

C. Both A and B.

D. Neither A nor B.

Final Instructor Approval: _____

CHAPTER 12 — Cooling Systems

Chapter 12 Quiz

After studying Chapter 12 in the Motorcycles: Fundamentals, Service, Repair textbook, answer the following questions.

_____ 1. Cylinders on _____-cooled engines have fins to increase the outside surface area of the engine.

_____ 2. In order to maintain optimal operating temperature, a liquid-cooled engine requires airflow through a(n) _____.

_____ 3. *True or False?* A liquid-cooled engine maintains a more consistent operating temperature than an air-cooled engine.

For questions 4–13, identify the components of the four-stroke liquid cooling system shown in the following illustration.

_____ 4. Cooling fan

_____ 5. Lower hose

_____ 6. Radiator cap

_____ 7. Water pump

_____ 8. Upper hose

_____ 9. Switch

_____ 10. Radiator

_____ 11. Thermostat

_____ 12. Water pipe

_____ 13. Water pipe

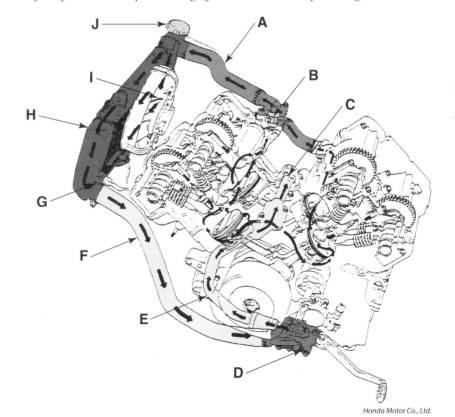

Honda Motor Co., Ltd.

For questions 14–19, identify the components of the two-stroke liquid cooling system shown in the following illustration.

_____ 14. Radiator

_____ 15. Cylinder

_____ 16. Coolant recovery

_____ 17. Radiator cap

_____ 18. Water pump

_____ 19. Thermostat

Honda Motor Co., Ltd.

_____ 20. An antifreeze mixture that contains more than 60% antifreeze _____.
  A. reduces the coolant's ability to inhibit rust
  B. is acceptable in warm climates
  C. reduces the coolant's efficiency
  D. is the ideal mixture

_____ 21. The best type of water to mix with coolant is _____ water.
  A. carbonated
  B. tap
  C. distilled
  D. artesian

_____ 22. *True or False?* The most common type of coolant is based on propylene glycol.

_____ 23. The _____ is basically a heat exchanger.
  A. radiator
  B. thermostat
  C. water pump
  D. radiator cap

_____ 24. The recovery tank works in conjunction with the _____ to allow coolant back into the system when cooling down.

_____ 25. The radiator cap increases _____ in the radiator, which raises the coolant's boiling point.

Name _____

_____ 26. The main purpose of the thermostat is to _____.
A. help seal the coolant
B. turn the radiator fan on
C. turn the radiator fan off
D. provide quicker warm-up of a cold engine

_____ 27. *True or False?* When the engine is cold, the thermostat is closed.

_____ 28. The water pump has a(n) _____ that keeps coolant from passing by the pump shaft and into the oil.

_____ 29. At low speeds and idle, a cooling _____ pulls air through the radiator in liquid-cooling systems.

_____ 30. *True or False?* The fan switch on a typical motorcycle automatically turns the fan on or off based on coolant temperature.

_____ 31. In order to determine a cooling system's freezing point, the technician will use a(n) _____ to check the specific gravity of the coolant.

_____ 32. Vehicles with a long distance between the radiator and engine will usually need _____.
A. more frequent flushing of the radiator
B. more expensive coolant
C. a special procedure for bleeding the cooling system
D. oil coolers in addition to radiators

_____ 33. If the cooling system is filled with rust, scale, or lime, then a(n) _____ compound should be used to clean out the system.

_____ 34. *True or False?* The first test for a thermostat is to suspend it in a small container of boiling water.

_____ 35. *True or False?* The weep hole on a water pump indicates if an internal leak has occurred.

Notes

Name _____ Date _____ Class _____

Job 12-1

Cooling System Pressure Testing

Introduction

Cooling system pressure testing is a standard test made by technicians after cooling system service, when diagnosing overheating, or when diagnosing coolant leaks. Understanding where coolant is located inside the engine is necessary for diagnosing overheating and leaking.

When pressure testing a coolant leak caused by a blown head gasket, coolant will leak into the cylinder if the head gasket is blown internally. Sometimes you may need to warm the engine up before testing, as some head gaskets only leak when they are hot. This is often the same for other coolant leaks. You have to be patient when checking for leaks.

Objective

After successfully completing this job, you will be able to pressure test a cooling system.

Materials and Equipment

To complete this job, you will need the following tools, equipment, and materials:
- Vehicle with liquid cooling system
- Appropriate service manual or electronic service information
- Cooling system pressure tester

Instructions

Use the service manual to find instructions for pressure testing the cooling system and the maximum pressure that can safely be applied to the cooling system. Then pressure test the system and inspect for leaks.

Read the job procedures, perform the tasks, and answer all questions. As you complete steps you will be given instructions to either fill in measurements or perform certain tasks. When you reach a sign, show your work to your instructor. Do not continue until you have instructor approval (instructor will initial job sheet).

> **WARNING** ⚠ Before performing this job, review all pertinent safety information in the text and discuss safety procedures with your instructor.

Procedures

Inspect Cooling System

1. Ensure that the engine is cool, then remove the radiator cap and check that the cooling system is full. Fill in the chart. Write N/A if the column does not apply to your machine.

> **NOTE** Some engines do not have an overflow tank (common with dirt bikes). Systems without overflow tanks will lose some coolant and the radiator caps on those systems are rated to higher pressures than systems with overflow tanks. Write N/A if the column does not apply to your machine.

	Condition	Tool Used
Coolant Level		
Coolant Condition		
Overflow Tank Level		

2. If the cooling system is low, top off the coolant with a mixture of 50/50 coolant before proceeding to the pressure test. A pressure test will not be accurate if the coolant level is low.

3. Discuss your findings with your instructor.

Instructor's Initials: _____

Test System Pressure

4. Install the pressure cap on the pressure tester, then pressurize the cap and determine its condition. Record your findings below.

_____

5. Install the pressure tester on the radiator and pressurize the system to the maximum specified pressure. Record your findings below.

Radiator cap pressure test:

_____ Pass

_____ Fail

_____ At what psi does cap pressure release?

System radiator pressure test:

_____ Pass

_____ Fail

_____ To what psi does the system pressurize?

6. With the system still pressurized, inspect the entire vehicle.

Name _____

    A. Inspect the weep hole of the water pump and water pump seals.

       Result:

       _____

    B. Inspect the hoses and clamps to and from the radiator (use your hands, not just your eyes).

       Result:

       _____

    C. Remove the spark plugs and crank the engine to look for coolant coming from the blown head gasket.

       Result:

       _____

STOP 7. Discuss your findings with your instructor.

Instructor's Initials: _____

Job Wrap Up

    8. Return all tools and materials to the proper storage areas and clean up your work area.

Final Assessment

_____ 1. Two technicians are discussing cooling system pressure tests. Technician A says that a slow pressure drop indicates a leak. Technician B says that a slow pressure drop could be from the cooling system not being full of coolant. Who is correct?

    A. A only.

    B. B only.

    C. Both A and B.

    D. Neither A nor B.

_____ 2. Two technicians are discussing cooling system pressure tests. Technician A says that a cooling system pressure test will determine whether a thermostat is working properly. Technician B says that a cooling system pressure test does not test thermostat condition. Who is correct?

    A. A only.

    B. B only.

    C. Both A and B.

    D. Neither A nor B.

_____   3. Two technicians are discussing cooling system pressure tests. Technician A says that a radiator cap should release pressure and then allow coolant back into the system as the engine cools off. Technician B says that a radiator cap should not release pressure under any circumstances. Who is correct?

A. A only.

B. B only.

C. Both A and B.

D. Neither A nor B.

_____   4. Two technicians are discussing cooling system operation. Technician A says that the radiator cap increases the coolant boiling point temperature. Technician B says that the radiator cap decreases the boiling point temperature. Who is correct?

A. A only.

B. B only.

C. Both A and B.

D. Neither A nor B.

_____   5. Two technicians are discussing diagnosing coolant entering an engine cylinder. Technician A says that coolant in the cylinder is evidence of a blown head gasket. Technician B says that coolant in the cylinder is evidence of a cracked head. Who is correct?

A. A only.

B. B only.

C. Both A and B.

D. Neither A nor B.

Final Instructor Approval: _____

Name _____   Date _____   Class _____

Job 12-2

Changing Coolant and Inspecting Thermostats

Introduction

Changing the coolant and inspecting the thermostat is a regular service on liquid-cooled motorcycles. The cooling system is critical for proper engine operation. Damage can occur quickly when an engine overheats. Draining and filling the cooling system is fairly easy, but "burping" the system to remove air pockets can be difficult.

In order to bleed air from the system, some engines will have an air bleed fitting at the top of the cooling system. Once all the air has been removed and the system is full, operating the engine and checking for leaks is very important before test riding.

Objective

After successfully completing this job, you will be able to properly change coolant and inspect thermostats.

Materials and Equipment

To complete this job, you will need the following tools, equipment, and materials:

- Motorcycle or other vehicle with liquid cooling (electric cooling fan preferred)
- Appropriate service manual or electronic service information
- Coolant
- Thermostat gasket
- Refilling funnel

Instructions

Use the service manual and read the procedure for draining the cooling system. There may be a drain bolt on the bottom of the water pump, but some engines can only be drained by removing a lower radiator hose to completely drain the system. Once you have changed the coolant, you will be running the engine and inspecting the thermostat opening and the cooling fan for proper operation.

Read the job procedures, perform the tasks, and answer all questions. As you complete steps, you will be given instructions to either fill in measurements or perform certain tasks. When you reach a sign, show your work to your instructor. Do not continue until you have instructor approval (instructor will initial job sheet).

> **WARNING** ⚠️ Before performing this job, review all pertinent safety information in the text and discuss safety procedures with your instructor.

Procedures

Check Fan Operation

> **NOTE**   You must ensure that the fan works and know how to make it come on in case the engine is overheating and you need to cool it off.

1. Check the wiring diagram for the cooling fan to determine how it operates. Usually the temperature switch on the radiator is open when the cooling system is cold. When the engine warms up, the switch closes and the fan turns on. Some engines will be wired differently and the temperature switch will be closed until the engine heats up.

2. Unplug the fan temperature sensor (usually a thermal switch).

3. Turn the key on and note whether the fan comes on.
   Result:

   _____

4. If the fan did not come on, after checking with your instructor, put a jumper wire in place of the thermal switch and note whether the fan comes on.
   Result:

   _____

5. Make sure that the radiator is free of dirt, debris, and damage.

 6. Discuss your findings with your instructor.

Instructor's Initials: _____

Drain Cooling System

7. If necessary, safely release cooling system pressure.

8. Using a drain pan that will hold enough volume, drain the coolant according to manufacturer directions.

Volume of coolant drained:

_____

> **NOTE**   Do not discard coolant. You may be reusing the coolant if this is a school-owned vehicle.

9. Remove the thermostat.

10. Boil the thermostat in a pot of water and note the temperature at which it opens. The repair manual will have an opening temperature specification.

> **NOTE**   This step is not usually done in a shop when just draining and filling, but is helpful to visualize how a thermostat works and to confirm if the thermostat is opening properly.

Name _____

11. Compare the thermostat opening temperature with the specification.

A. Thermostat opening temperature as observed:

_____

B. Opening temperature specification:

_____

(STOP) 12. Discuss your findings with your instructor.

Instructor's Initials: _____

Fill the Cooling System

13. Reinstall the thermostat with a new gasket.

14. If the engine has a bleed valve, open it.

15. Reinstall drain plugs and hoses as necessary.

16. Fill the system with a 50/50 mix of the correct coolant. Typically, you will be using premixed coolant.

17. If the engine has a bleeder valve, fill until the coolant comes out of the valve, then close the valve.

> **NOTE** ⚙ Since you will be running the engine without the radiator cap installed, it helps to use a special funnel that fits on top of the radiator to keep from spilling coolant when you remove air.

(STOP) 18. Discuss your findings with your instructor.

Instructor's Initials: _____

Remove Air from the System (or "Burp" the System)

> **WARNING** ⚠ Never leave a running engine unattended.

19. Run the engine and monitor coolant level. (This process is critical and may take a while.)

20. Monitor upper and lower radiator hose temperatures with your hands until both hoses are the same temperature. This indicates that the thermostat has opened.

> **WARNING** ⚠ Be careful when touching the hoses or any other engine part, as they can become very hot in a short time.

Thermostat open:

Yes _____ No _____

If yes, proceed to the next step. If no, continue to monitor the radiator hoses.

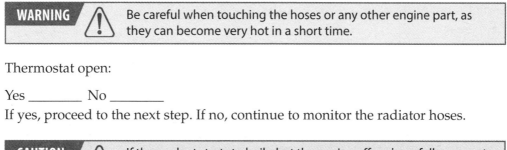

> **CAUTION** ⚠ If the coolant starts to boil, shut the engine off and carefully connect a jumper wire between the electric fan and a power source. This will allow the fan to cool the engine. Do not spray the engine down with cold water, since that can do engine damage. Let it cool down slowly.

21. Wait until the fan turns on; then install the radiator cap.

Fan turns on:

Yes _____ No _____
If yes, proceed to the next step. If no, continue to monitor the cooling system.

22. Shut the engine off and:
   A. top off the radiator.
   B. reinstall the radiator cap.
   C. fill the overflow bottle (if used) halfway.

23. Restart the engine and inspect for leaks.

(STOP) 24. Discuss your findings with your instructor.

Instructor's Initials: _____

Job Wrap Up

25. Return all tools and materials to the proper storage areas and clean up your work area.

Final Assessment

_____ 1. Two technicians are discussing cooling system service. Technician A says that a thermostat should be replaced every time the coolant is serviced. Technician B says thermostat replacement is not part of regular coolant service. Who is correct?
   A. A only.
   B. B only.
   C. Both A and B.
   D. Neither A nor B.

_____ 2. Two technicians are discussing cooling system service. Technician A says that burping is not necessary with a bleed valve. Technician B says that burping is much easier with a bleed valve. Who is correct?
   A. A only.
   B. B only.
   C. Both A and B.
   D. Neither A nor B.

_____ 3. Two technicians are discussing cooling system service. Technician A says that the proper mixture of coolant and water is 50/50. Technician B says to mix coolant with distilled water if not using premix. Who is correct?
   A. A only.
   B. B only.
   C. Both A and B.
   D. Neither A nor B.

Name _____

_____   4. Two technicians are discussing cooling system operation. Technician A says that if the fan runs all the time, the engine will take a long time to warm up. Technician B says that if the fan never turns on, the engine will overheat. Who is correct?
   A. A only.
   B. B only.
   C. Both A and B.
   D. Neither A nor B.

_____   5. Two technicians are discussing cooling system service. Technician A says if the thermostat sticks open, the engine will overheat. Technician B says if the thermostat sticks shut, the engine will overheat. Who is correct?
   A. A only.
   B. B only.
   C. Both A and B.
   D. Neither A nor B.

Final Instructor Approval: _____

Notes

Name _____ Date _____ Class _____

Job 12-3

Replacing Water Pumps

Introduction

The water pump (sometimes called a coolant pump) is a critical part of any liquid-cooled system. Replacing the water pump is a normal service procedure that must be carried out with special attention.

The water pump is shaft-driven by the crankshaft through meshing gears. An inside seal is used to keep the oil inside the engine, while an outside seal is used to keep coolant from entering the engine. A weep hole keeps coolant out of the engine oiling system and indicates water pump leakage.

Objective

After successfully completing this job, you will be able to properly service a water pump.

Materials and Equipment

To complete this job, you will need the following tools, equipment, and materials:

- Vehicle with liquid cooling system (preferably with an electric cooling fan or a core liquid-cooled engine)
- Appropriate service manual or electronic service information
- Cooling system pressure tester
- Coolant
- Water pump gasket and seals
- Hand tools as necessary

Instructions

Read the instructions first so that you completely understand water pump replacement procedures. Do not simply begin disassembling parts.

Perform the tasks and answer all questions. As you complete steps, you will be given instructions to either fill in measurements or perform certain tasks. When you reach a sign, show your work to your instructor. Do not continue until you have instructor approval (instructor will initial job sheet).

> **WARNING** ⚠ Before performing this job, review all pertinent safety information in the text and discuss safety procedures with your instructor.

Procedures

Drain Cooling System

1. Using the appropriate pan that will hold the entire cooling system volume, follow the service manual instructions to depressurize the system and drain the coolant.

   Approximate volume of coolant drained:

   _____

NOTE	Do not discard coolant. You may be reusing the coolant if this is a school-owned vehicle.

Remove and Replace Water Pump

2. Remove the water pump according to the service manual instructions.

3. Remove seals as necessary.

 **CAUTION**	Do not remove all of the seals until approved by your instructor.

4. Remove the old water pump gasket material from the engine and from the water pump if you are reusing the pump.

 **CAUTION**	Use scrapers carefully to avoid damaging the sealing surfaces.

5. Install the water pump using new gaskets and seals as necessary. Torque all pump fasteners to their proper values.

 6. Discuss your findings with your instructor and discuss seal removal and replacement.

Instructor's Initials: _____

Fill Cooling System

7. If the vehicle has a bleed valve, open the valve.

8. Ensure the drain plugs and hoses are reinstalled and properly tightened.

9. Fill the system with the proper 50/50 mix of coolant.

NOTE	Premixed coolant is usually used in the power sports industry.

10. If the engine has a bleed valve, fill until the coolant comes out of the valve and then close the bleeder.

Name _____

11. Start and run the engine without the radiator cap installed.

 **NOTE** Use a special funnel that fits on top of the radiator, if available. This funnel keeps the system from spilling as it "burps" air.

 12. Discuss your findings with your instructor.

Instructor's Initials: _____

Remove Air From System (Burp)

WARNING Never leave a running engine unattended.

13. Run the engine and make sure it stays full of coolant. This process is critical and may take some time.

14. Check the upper and lower radiator hose temperatures with your hands. When both hoses are the same temperature, the thermostat is open.

    Temperature at which the thermostat opens:

    _____

 CAUTION The engine parts become hot quickly. Be careful when feeling the radiator hoses. Also, stay clear of the filler neck. When the thermostat opens, it can expel coolant violently.

 WARNING If the coolant starts to boil, shut the engine off and, if possible, use a jumper to operate the electric fan to cool the engine. Do not spray the engine with cold water, as this can cause engine damage. Let the engine cool down slowly.

15. Wait until the fan turns on before installing the radiator cap.

    Temperature at which the fan turns on:

    _____

16. Stop the engine, top off the radiator, and reinstall the radiator cap. If there is an overflow bottle, fill the bottle to the half-full mark.

17. Run the engine until pressure builds up in the cooling system and inspect for leaks.

 18. Discuss your findings with your instructor.

Instructor's Initials: _____

Job Wrap Up

19. Return all tools and materials to the proper storage areas and clean up your work area. Be sure to properly dispose of coolant.

Final Assessment

_____ 1. Two technicians are discussing water pumps. Technician A says that the water pump moves coolant directly around the cylinder and head passages after it has been cooled in the radiator. Technician B says that the water pump moves coolant to the radiator after it has been heated by the engine. Who is correct?

A. A only.

B. B only.

C. Both A and B.

D. Neither A nor B.

_____ 2. Two technicians are discussing water pump service. Technician A says that a faulty water pump can cause the engine to overheat. Technician B says that a faulty water pump can be noisy. Who is correct?

A. A only.

B. B only.

C. Both A and B.

D. Neither A nor B.

_____ 3. Two technicians are discussing water pump service. Technician A says that when replacing a water pump, the thermostat should also be replaced. Technician B says that when replacing the thermostat, the water pump should also be replaced. Who is correct?

A. A only.

B. B only.

C. Both A and B.

D. Neither A nor B.

_____ 4. Two technicians are discussing cooling system service. Technician A says that the radiator cap should also be replaced when a faulty water pump is replaced. Technician B says that the radiator cap should be replaced only when it fails. Who is correct?

A. A only.

B. B only.

C. Both A and B.

D. Neither A nor B.

_____ 5. Two technicians are discussing cooling system service. Technician A says if the engine overheats, the water pump, thermostat, and radiator cap should be checked. Technician B says that if the engine overheats, the technician must ensure that the head gasket has not failed before replacing other cooling system parts. Who is correct?

A. A only.

B. B only.

C. Both A and B.

D. Neither A nor B.

Final Instructor Approval: _____

CHAPTER 13
Exhaust Systems and Emissions Control

Chapter 13 Quiz

After studying Chapter 13 in the Motorcycles: Fundamentals, Service, Repair textbook, answer the following questions.

_____ 1. Exhaust systems perform all of the following functions, *except*:
   A. route burned exhaust gases to the rear of the vehicle
   B. change the elements of waste exhaust gases
   C. aid in engine emission control
   D. reduce engine exhaust noise

For questions 2–7, identify the parts of an exhaust system indicated in the following illustration.

_____ 2. Muffler assembly

_____ 3. Heat shield

_____ 4. Header pipes

_____ 5. Heat diffuser

_____ 6. Gasket

_____ 7. Exhaust chamber

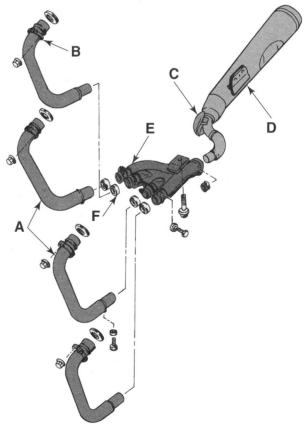

Goodheart-Willcox Publisher

_____ 8. *True or False?* The exhaust system on an off-road motorcycle is mounted closer to the ground than the exhaust system on a street motorcycle.

_____ 9. A heat _____ helps dissipate exhaust gas heat and prevent the header pipe from overheating.

_____ 10. Exhaust _____ prevent leakage between exhaust system connections.
   A. gaskets
   B. seals
   C. clamps
   D. collectors

_____ 11. *True or False?* Scavenging is affected by the length and diameter of exhaust system components.

_____ 12. A(n) _____ chamber is used in a two-stroke exhaust system to help exhaust scavenging and to increase engine power.

_____ 13. In an exhaust power valve system, a computer varies the diameter of the exhaust tube based on engine _____.
   A. breathing characteristics
   B. operating temperature
   C. rpm
   D. Both B and C.

_____ 14. In order to help prevent wildfires, power sports vehicles made in the United States and Canada are required to be equipped with _____.
   A. oversized mufflers
   B. multiple stingers
   C. spark arresters
   D. Both B and C.

_____ 15. A frequently needed service of both two-stroke and four-stroke off-road vehicles is _____ of the silencer.

_____ 16. *True or False?* In a turbocharger, a compressor wheel is spun by exhaust gases blowing through the turbo.

_____ 17. *True or False?* Many current motorcycle designs incorporate a turbocharger.

_____ 18. Excessively high hydrocarbons can indicate that the engine is _____.
   A. running lean
   B. running rich
   C. misfiring
   D. Both B and C.

_____ 19. Carbon monoxide is produced by an engine when _____.
   A. the air-fuel mixture is too lean
   B. insufficient combustion has taken place
   C. the fuel filter is partially blocked
   D. All of the above.

Name _____

_____ 20. Oxides of nitrogen (NO_x) are an undesirable compound found in exhaust gases when the
_____.
   A. engine idles too long
   B. engine combustion temperature is too high
   C. engine is burning oil
   D. engine is started when hot

_____ 21. In a crankcase emission control system, crankcase emissions are routed into
the _____ and into the combustion chamber to be reburned.

_____ 22. An exhaust emission control system converts hydrocarbons and carbon monoxide to
carbon dioxide and water by _____.
   A. rerouting exhaust emissions
   B. adding oxygen to the exhaust gases
   C. drawing fresh air into the exhaust port
   D. None of the above.

_____ 23. *True or False?* A catalytic converter converts undesirable elements in exhaust
gases into carbon dioxide, oxygen, and water vapor.

_____ 24. A three-way catalytic conversion system works in conjunction with the _____
system and oxygen sensor.

_____ 25. An exhaust _____ analyzer measures how well an engine converts air and
fuel into power.

_____ 26. *True or False?* A technician can use an exhaust gas analyzer to diagnose and
locate a problem by comparing the carbon monoxide readings to engine
factory specification.

_____ 27. A modification to the intake system that results in increased noise is an
example of _____, which is prohibited by federal, state, and local laws.

Notes

Name _____ Date _____ Class _____

Job 13-1

Removing and Replacing Exhaust Systems

Introduction

Damaged or rusted exhaust systems must be replaced. Exhaust systems are also frequently replaced for improved sound, performance, and sometimes for aesthetic reasons.

Objective

After successfully completing this job, you will be able to remove and replace exhaust systems.

Materials and Equipment

To complete this job, you will need the following tools, equipment, and materials:

- Motorcycle or other vehicle (preferably with slip-on exhaust muffler)
- Appropriate service manual or electronic service information
- Anti-seize compound
- Hand tools as needed

Instructions

In this job, you will be removing the exhaust system and separating the pieces of the exhaust. Check for any special precautions in the service manual. Nuts and bolts used with the exhaust should get a coating of anti-seize compound. Use a small amount of anti-seize compound. If anti-seize compound can be seen after assembly, too much was used.

Read the job procedures, perform the tasks, and answer all questions. As you complete steps, you will be given instructions to either fill in measurements or perform certain tasks. When you reach a sign, show your work to your instructor. Do not continue until you have instructor approval (instructor will initial job sheet).

> **WARNING** ⚠ Before performing this job, review all pertinent safety information in the text and discuss safety procedures with your instructor.

Procedures

Vehicle (Year/Make/Model)

_____

Remove Exhaust Components

1. Ensure that the engine and exhaust have cooled completely.

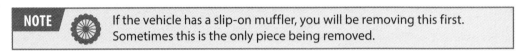

NOTE If the vehicle has a slip-on muffler, you will be removing this first. Sometimes this is the only piece being removed.

2. Protect any nearby chrome from being scratched.

3. Loosen all fasteners before removing exhaust system components.

4. Remove all exhaust system components.

5. **STOP** Discuss with your instructor any challenges you had with removing the exhaust.

Instructor's Initials: _____

Install Exhaust Components

6. Lightly coat threads of all fasteners with anti-seize compound.

7. Loosely install exhaust system components and start all bolts and nuts, without fully tightening any of them.

NOTE Do not install the slip-on muffler at this time.

8. Tighten the bolts and/or nuts at the cylinder head and torque them properly.

9. Torque the cylinder head bolts or nuts to the exhaust.
   Torque value:

   _____

10. Loosely install the slip-on muffler and related nuts and bolts.

11. Tighten the nuts and bolts from front to rear.

12. Recheck the tightness of all connections and ensure that the exhaust system parts do not contact any other components.

13. Start the engine and check the exhaust system for leaks by using your hands to feel for leaks.

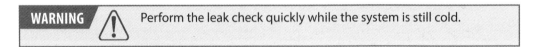

WARNING Perform the leak check quickly while the system is still cold.

14. Rev the engine a few times while cold and listen for leaks.

15. **STOP** Discuss with your instructor the exhaust removal and installation.

Instructor's Initials: _____

Name _____

Job Wrap Up

16. Return all tools and materials to the proper storage areas and clean up your work area.

Final Assessment

_____ 1. Two technicians are discussing exhaust system service. Technician A says that exhaust systems can be changed for performance. Technician B says that exhaust systems can be changed for better sound. Who is correct?

A. A only.

B. B only.

C. Both A and B.

D. Neither A nor B.

_____ 2. Two technicians are discussing exhaust system service. Technician A says that anti-seize is used to help seal exhaust leaks. Technician B says that anti-seize is used to make fasteners easier to loosen. Who is correct?

A. A only.

B. B only.

C. Both A and B.

D. Neither A nor B.

_____ 3. Two technicians are discussing exhaust upgrades. Technician A says that the engine may need to be retuned after an exhaust installation. Technician B says most exhaust modifications that are just for sound will not need engine tuning. Who is correct?

A. A only.

B. B only.

C. Both A and B.

D. Neither A nor B.

_____ 4. Two technicians are discussing exhaust installation. Technician A says that exhaust gaskets should be replaced each time the exhaust is taken apart. Technician B says that exhaust gaskets need to be replaced only when they leak. Who is correct?

A. A only.

B. B only.

C. Both A and B.

D. Neither A nor B.

_____ 5. Two technicians are discussing exhaust leaks. Technician A says that an exhaust leak may cause an oxygen sensor to read too much oxygen. Technician B says back pressure is affected by an exhaust leak. Who is correct?

A. A only.

B. B only.

C. Both A and B.

D. Neither A nor B.

Final Instructor Approval: _____

Notes

Name _____ Date _____ Class _____

Job 13-2

Identifying Emission Components

Introduction

Emission requirements have changed over time, so different motorcycles will have different emission systems. If a motorcycle is licensed in California, it will have more systems than those motorcycles in other states. Different components are used to eliminate different emissions.

Catalytic converters (sometimes called three-way converters [TWC]) need as much oxygen as possible to chemically convert unburned hydrocarbons (HC), carbon monoxide (CO), and oxides of nitrogen (NO_x) into oxygen (O_2), water (H_2O), and carbon dioxide (CO_2). O_2 sensors work with other parts of the control system to maximize oxygen entering the TWC.

Positive crankcase ventilation (PCV) systems are used on all four-stroke engines to reduce HC emissions by recirculating crankcase blowby gases. Air injection systems inject air into the exhaust system to burn more HC and CO before they exit the tailpipe. Air injection systems can also be used to add more oxygen to the TWC. Evaporative emission systems are used to keep HC from evaporating and entering the atmosphere. Exhaust gas recirculation (EGR) systems recirculate a small amount of inert exhaust gas back into the cylinder to reduce NO_x by lowering combustion temperatures. EGR systems are rare on motorcycles. Variable valve timing (VVT) engines have a built-in EGR effect when the valves are in the overlap position.

Objective

After successfully completing this job, you will be able to identify what emission components are on a vehicle and the purpose of that emission component.

Materials and Equipment

To complete this job, you will need the following tools, equipment, and materials:

- Several modern motorcycles or other vehicles (preferably at least one California vehicle)
- Appropriate service manual or electronic service information

Instructions

Use the service manual to determine which emission components are used on the vehicle(s) that you are working on. Then use the service manual parts location diagrams and wiring diagrams to locate the components on the schematics and on the vehicle. As you complete steps, you will be given instructions to either fill in measurements or perform certain tasks. When you reach a sign, show your work to your instructor. Do not continue until you have the instructor initials to proceed.

 WARNING ⚠ Before performing this job, review all pertinent safety information in the text and discuss safety procedures with your instructor.

Procedures

First Vehicle

1. Fill in the chart with the type(s) of emission components used on this vehicle, the type of gas reduced by the emission component, the component's general location, the number and color of any wires that help locate the component, and whether or not you were able to physically locate the component.

   Vehicle (Year/Make/Model)

   _____

   Is this a California vehicle? Yes _____ No _____

Component	Type of gas reduced	Location on vehicle	How many wires? Wire colors	Could you find it? Yes/No
Catalytic Converter (TWC)				
Oxygen (O_2) Sensor				
Positive Crankcase Ventilation (PCV)				
Air Injection System				
Evaporative Emission System				
Variable Valve Timing (VVT)				
Exhaust Gas Recirculation (EGR)				

(STOP)   2. Discuss your findings with your instructor.

Instructor's Initials: _____

Name _____

Second Vehicle

3. Fill in the chart with the type(s) of emission components used on this vehicle, the type of gas reduced by the emission component, the component's general location, the number and color of any wires that help locate the component, and whether or not you were able to physically locate the component.

Vehicle (Year/Make/Model)

_____

Is this a California vehicle? Yes _____ No _____

Component	Type of gas reduced	Location on vehicle	How many wires? Wire colors	Could you find it? Yes/No
Catalytic Converter (TWC)				
Oxygen (O_2) Sensor				
Positive Crankcase Ventilation (PCV)				
Air Injection System				
Evaporative Emission System				
Variable Valve Timing (VVT)				
Exhaust Gas Recirculation (EGR)				

(STOP) 4. Discuss your findings with your instructor.

Instructor's Initials: _____

Third Vehicle

5. Fill in the chart with the type(s) of emission components used on this vehicle, the type of gas reduced by the emission component, the component's general location, the number and color of any wires that help locate the component, and whether or not you were able to physically locate the component.

Vehicle (Year/Make/Model)

_____

Is this a California vehicle? Yes _____ No _____

Component	Type of gas reduced	Location on vehicle	How many wires? Wire colors	Could you find it? Yes/No
Catalytic Converter (TWC)				
Oxygen (O_2) Sensor				
Positive Crankcase Ventilation (PCV)				
Air Injection System				
Evaporative Emission System				
Variable Valve Timing (VVT)				
Exhaust Gas Recirculation (EGR)				

STOP 6. Discuss your findings with your instructor.

Instructor's Initials: _____

Job Wrap Up

7. Return all tools and materials to the proper storage areas and clean up your work area.

Name _____

Final Assessment

_____   1. Two technicians are discussing catalytic converters. Technician A says that a catalytic converter is used to both clean up emissions and make the engine run better. Technician B says that catalytic converters are for emissions reduction only. Who is correct?

A. A only.

B. B only.

C. Both A and B.

D. Neither A nor B.

_____   2. Two technicians are discussing PCV valves. Technician A says the PCV recirculates fumes from the crankcase and sends them back to the air filter housing. Technician B says if the PCV gets plugged up it can cause oil leaks from pressure buildup in the engine. Who is correct?

A. A only.

B. B only.

C. Both A and B.

D. Neither A nor B.

_____   3. Two technicians are discussing electronic fuel injection systems. Technician A says that when the system is in open loop, it uses information from the O_2 sensor. Technician B says that when the system is in closed loop, it uses information from the O_2 sensor. Who is correct?

A. A only.

B. B only.

C. Both A and B.

D. Neither A nor B.

_____   4. Two technicians are discussing evaporative emission systems. Technician A says that the gas tank is part of the evaporative emission system. Technician B says that the gas cap is part of the evaporative emission system. Who is correct?

A. A only.

B. B only.

C. Both A and B.

D. Neither A nor B.

_____   5. Two technicians are discussing evaporative emission systems. Technician A says that the charcoal canister holds fumes from the gas tank. Technician B says the purge valve will allow fumes stored in the charcoal canister to be burned in the engine. Who is correct?

A. A only.

B. B only.

C. Both A and B.

D. Neither A nor B.

Final Instructor Approval: _____

Notes

Name _____ Date _____ Class _____

Job 13-3

Testing Oxygen Sensors

Introduction

Oxygen (O_2) sensors can be either narrow range or wide range types. Most power sports oxygen sensors are narrow range, since their O_2 heater circuits require less amperage than those on wide range sensors. Both types of sensors are physically similar, but test quite differently. The best way to tell what type of sensor is on the vehicle is to consult the service manual. Whenever possible, use a scan tool to test oxygen sensors. If the scan tool has an active test, you can add fuel or air to the engine and watch oxygen sensor voltage to determine whether it responds.

Objective

After successfully completing this job, you will be able to test oxygen sensor operation.

Materials and Equipment

To complete this job, you will need the following tools, equipment, and materials:

- Vehicle with an oxygen sensor
- Appropriate service manual or electronic service information
- Scan tool capable of checking oxygen sensors (preferably with active test provisions)
- Voltmeter (Fluke 88 or comparable multimeter)

Instructions

In this job, you will need to use the service manual oxygen sensor testing procedures. Oxygen sensors have two circuits, the heater circuit that can be tested with a voltmeter and the sensor circuit that can be tested with a voltmeter or a scan tool.

Read the job procedures, perform the tasks, and answer all questions. As you complete steps, you will be given instructions to either fill in measurements or perform certain tasks. When you reach a sign, show your work to your instructor. Do not continue until you have instructor approval (instructor will initial job sheet).

> **WARNING** ⚠ Before performing this job, review all pertinent safety information in the text and discuss safety procedures with your instructor.

Procedures

Classify Sensor

Vehicle (Year/Make/Model)

_____

1. Read the service manual to determine the type of oxygen sensor used.

> **NOTE** Narrow range O_2 sensor voltage varies from 0–1 volt, with actual measurements from 0.1 to 0.9 volt. Wide range O_2 sensor voltage varies from 0–5 volts, but voltage can only be read on a scan tool. Wide range sensors react so quickly that they are usually near their optimal voltage of 3.3 volts.

Type of sensor:

_____

2. Use the wiring diagram and the service manual to determine the purpose of the wires.

Color of Wire	Purpose of Wire

 3. Discuss your findings with your instructor.

Instructor's Initials: _____

Test Heater Circuit

4. Ensure that the engine and exhaust system are below operating temperature.

5. Test for power to the sensor heater circuit with the key on.

_____

6. Test for sensor heater circuit ground.

> **NOTE** The computer may provide ground only with the sensor plugged in and the engine started. Unplugging the sensor with the key on may create a code and cause the computer to turn off the sensor ground. Consult the service manual for the correct procedure.

7. Test the heater coil resistance with the sensor unplugged and key off.
   Resistance reading:

_____

Resistance specification:

_____

Name _____

 8. Discuss your sensor heating circuit findings with your instructor.

Instructor's Initials: _____

Test Sensor with Voltmeter

> **NOTE** Narrow range sensors must be tested while trying to work. The engine must be running and held above 1,500 rpm for testing. To operate properly, the sensor needs both heat and exhaust flow. Sensor tests at idle will be inconclusive.
> You will be testing for two parameters:
> First—Voltage varies from low to high at least eight times in 10 seconds.
> Second—Average voltage is close to 0.450 volts.

Voltmeter Setup

9. Set voltmeter on dc volts.

10. Set voltmeter range to 4- or 6-volt range.

11. Set up the meter:
    A. Press the MIN/MAX button. The meter will start recording.
    B. Let the meter record, then press the MIN/MAX button again while the meter is still backprobing.

> **CAUTION** Unplugging the meter before pressing the MIN/MAX button will cause the average to default to 0 volts.

12. Backprobe the sensor wire according to your instructor's directions.

13. Start the engine.

14. Raise engine speed to at least 1,500 rpm and allow the engine to warm up. Hold this rpm during this entire test.

15. Watch the analog portion of the meter, just below the digital numbers, and count the numbers of deflections in a 10-second interval.

    Number of deflections in 10 seconds: _____

> **NOTE** If the sensor produces fewer than eight deflections in 10 seconds, the sensor is working, but considered lazy and will need to be replaced no matter the voltage readings.

16. If the sensor is switching at least eight times (or more) in 10 seconds, measure voltage:

    A. Press the MIN/MAX button.

    B. Record for at least 20 seconds.

> **CAUTION** Keep the engine at the same rpm while reading MIN, MAX, and AVG.

    C. Press the MIN/MAX button and record the numbers. Do not let engine rpm drop to idle and do not remove the meter connections.

    Record MIN (should be about 0.2 volts on a normal running):

    _____

    Record MAX (should be about 0.8 volts on a normal running):

    _____

    Record AVG:

    _____

> **NOTE** The average voltage indicates engine and sensor condition. The sensor must first switch enough times so that the computer can get enough samples. The average should be 0.450 volts or close to it.
> Above 0.450 volts indicates either a defective sensor or an engine running rich.
> Below 0.450 volts indicates either a defective sensor or an engine running lean.
> If the sensor does not reach the maximum high and low readings, replace the sensor.

(STOP) 17. Discuss your findings with your instructor.

Instructor's Initials: _____

Test the Sensor Reaction to Mixture Changes

18. Backprobe the sensor wires and watch the voltages just as you have previously.

> **NOTE** Remember to keep the engine running at 1,500 rpm or higher.

19. Cause the engine to run leaner by either:

    A. Creating a vacuum leak.

    B. Using the scan tool to cause the injector(s) to run lean.

20. Note whether the sensor picked up the lean mixture (voltage dropping).

    Yes _____ No _____

21. Cause the engine to run richer by either:

    A. Adding fuel to the intake system (spray carburetor cleaner can be used).

    B. Using the scan tool to cause the injector(s) to run rich.

Name _____

22. Note whether the sensor picked up the lean mixture (voltage rising).

     Yes _____ No _____

(STOP) 23. Discuss your findings with your instructor.

Instructor's Initials: _____

Job Wrap Up

24. Return all tools and materials to the proper storage areas and clean up your work area.

Final Assessment

_____ 1. Two technicians are discussing oxygen sensors. Technician A says that a heater sensor code will not allow the sensor to operate. Technician B says that with a heater sensor code, the sensor circuit will still operate but will take longer to heat up and begin working. Who is correct?

    A. A only.

    B. B only.

    C. Both A and B.

    D. Neither A nor B.

_____ 2. Two technicians are discussing O_2 sensor diagnosis. Technician A says that an average sensor voltage of 0.7 volts could be caused by a plugged air filter. Technician B says an average sensor voltage of 0.7 volts could be caused by a leaking injector. Who is correct?

    A. A only.

    B. B only.

    C. Both A and B.

    D. Neither A nor B.

_____ 3. An engine is running lean with an O_2 sensor average voltage of 0.3 volt. Technician A says that dirty injectors can cause this condition. Technician B says an exhaust leak can cause this condition. Who is correct?

    A. A only.

    B. B only.

    C. Both A and B.

    D. Neither A nor B.

_____ 4. Two technicians are discussing O_2 sensor diagnosis. Technician A says an open heater sensor will read OL when tested for resistance. Technician B says a sensor heater can intermittently fail. Who is correct?

    A. A only.

    B. B only.

    C. Both A and B.

    D. Neither A nor B.

_____   5. Two technicians are discussing O_2 sensors. Technician A says that O_2 sensors can be contaminated by oil leaking on them. Technician B says O_2 sensors can get contaminated from oil burning in the engine. Who is correct?

A. A only.

B. B only.

C. Both A and B.

D. Neither A nor B.

Final Instructor Approval: _____

CHAPTER 14 | Battery and Charging Systems

Chapter 14 Quiz

After studying Chapter 14 in the Motorcycles: Fundamentals, Service, Repair textbook, answer the following questions.

_____ 1. The battery is the main source of power for the ignition circuit, accessory circuits, and _____ circuit.

_____ 2. Battery electrolyte is a combination of water and _____ acid.

_____ 3. All electrolyte spills should be immediately neutralized with _____ and then cleaned.

_____ 4. *True or False?* The hydrogen gas produced during charging can explode if flames or sparks are brought near the battery.

_____ 5. *True or False?* A 12-volt battery has three 2-volt cells connected in series.

_____ 6. *True or False?* The battery charging and discharging cycles cause the water in the electrolyte to boil off.

_____ 7. Maintenance-free batteries have a safety valve that opens when _____.
   A. electrolyte level is low
   B. excessive gas is produced
   C. the battery is exposed to a flame
   D. internal pressures are normal

_____ 8. *True or False?* Gel batteries must be mounted in an upright position.

_____ 9. The amp-hour rating system determines the battery's ability to _____.
   A. perform in high temperatures
   B. discharge current for an extended period of time
   C. perform in high-demand applications
   D. charge in a shorter period of time

_____ 10. All of the following statements about a battery's cold start rating are true, *except*:
   A. it indicates how well the battery is expected to perform in low temperature.
   B. it is also called the cold start rating.
   C. the rating is based on plate material.
   D. it is determined by measuring the discharge with a voltmeter.

_____ 11. *True or False?* Special charging procedures may be needed for lithium batteries.

_____ 12. *True or False?* When a battery is removed, the negative cable should be disconnected first.

_____ 13. If a conventional battery is low on electrolyte, the technician should top off the battery with _____.

    A. electrolyte

    B. sulfuric acid

    C. distilled water

    D. tap water

_____ 14. Excessive vibration from improper mounting can cause _____ buildup in the battery case.

_____ 15. The two types of battery tests are the unloaded test and the _____ test.

_____ 16. When checked with a hydrometer, each cell must have a specific gravity of at least _____.

_____ 17. A battery electrolyte specific gravity will change based on the _____.

    A. battery location

    B. humidity reading

    C. battery temperature

    D. None of the above.

_____ 18. _True or False?_ Before a conventional battery is being charged, the filler plugs should be tightened.

_____ 19. When a battery is overcharged, the _____.

    A. plates emit volatile gas

    B. electrolyte temperature rises

    C. battery experiences rapid water loss

    D. All of the above.

_____ 20. When a conventional battery is activated, the battery should be placed on charge for _____ hours.

    A. one to two

    B. one to three

    C. three to four

    D. three to five

_____ 21. When installing a battery, the technician should be careful to avoid bending or pinching the _____ tube.

_____ 22. A(n) _____ changes mechanical energy, such as rotating motion, into electrical energy.

_____ 23. The alternator consists of a(n) _____ and a stator.

_____ 24. The rotor is typically a crankshaft-driven flywheel with _____ attached.

_____ 25. The _____ of an alternator is a winding of wire coils wound around soft iron poles.

_____ 26. _True or False?_ Current is induced into the wire coils as the magnets rotate around the wire coils.

Name _____

_____ 27. The most common type of alternator is the _____ alternator.

A. electromagnet

B. magneto

C. permanent magnet

D. ac/dc

_____ 28. An electromagnet alternator uses _____ to create magnetism.

A. electric current

B. permanent magnets

C. high voltage

D. stationary field coils with brushes

_____ 29. *True or False?* An electromagnet alternator requires battery voltage for initial alternator output.

_____ 30. The process of converting ac into dc is called _____.

A. polarization

B. rectification

C. regulation

D. induction

_____ 31. An electronic regulator in a permanent magnet charging system limits the voltage delivered to the _____.

_____ 32. In a permanent magnet charging system, the regulator shunts excess electricity to _____.

_____ 33. During charging system inspection and testing, a technician should do all of the following, *except*:

A. reconnect the battery ground cable after all wiring connections have been made.

B. make sure the battery is fully charged before testing.

C. start the engine with the battery disconnected.

D. disconnect the battery ground cable before charging the battery.

_____ 34. A(n) _____ test determines if components are operating unnecessarily, causing the battery to drain.

_____ 35. A voltage output test includes all of the following, *except*:

A. removing the battery from the vehicle.

B. running the engine to 2,000 rpm.

C. turning the headlights and taillights on.

D. measure voltage at the battery.

_____ 36. In a current output test, a high capacity _____ is required to handle starter motor draws.

_____ 37. The second part of a stator continuity test _____.

A. measures stator coil resistance

B. measures stator coil continuity

C. checks for shorted or grounded stator coils

D. tests the load capacity of the stator

_____   38. In a charging coil test for single-phase coils with grounded ends, the resistance is measured between the _____ line and ground.

_____   39. If the stator is determined to be faulty, it is recommended to also replace the _____.

   A. rotor

   B. regulator/rectifier

   C. battery

   D. starter

_____   40. _True or False?_ High rpm riding tends to discharge the battery.

Name _____ Date _____ Class _____

Job 14-1

Testing Batteries

Introduction

Battery testing is considered a foundational skill. Motorcycle batteries are relatively small, but can have large demands put on them. The job that the battery must perform is to provide enough amperage for the starter while maintaining enough voltage to operate the ignition system and/or the injectors.

The most important battery test is the loaded test. Automatic battery testers/chargers like the BatteryMate are standard equipment in motorcycle repair shops.

There are several types of batteries on the market today. Lead-acid and AGM (absorbed glass mat) are two of the most common batteries and both need to be tested and charged. Newer lithium batteries are lighter and more powerful, but do not work as well as older batteries in cold weather. Lithium batteries require a special charger and are not yet widely used.

Objective

After successfully completing this job, you will be able to test a battery.

Materials and Equipment

To complete this job, you will need the following tools, equipment, and materials:

- Lead-acid battery
- Automatic battery tester
- Voltmeter (Fluke 88 or comparable multimeter)

Instructions

In this job, you will be making measurements of a battery with both a voltmeter and an automatic battery charger. You should consult the service manual for precautions and special instructions for the vehicle being tested.

Read the job procedures, perform the tasks, and answer all questions. As you complete steps, you will be given instructions to either fill in measurements or perform certain tasks. When you reach a sign, show your work to your instructor. Do not continue until you have instructor approval (instructor will initial job sheet).

| **WARNING** | ⚠ | Before performing this job, review all pertinent safety information in the text and discuss safety procedures with your instructor. |

Procedures

Voltage Test Battery

1. Obtain a battery for testing from your instructor.

2. Check for open circuit voltage of battery.
   Voltage reading:

   _____

3. Check for surface charge on battery case (highest reading).
   Voltage reading:

   _____

4. Remove the battery cap(s) and check each cell to see whether the electrolyte level is correct. If necessary, top off low cells with distilled water and charge the battery before testing. Charging a battery with low electrolyte will not be effective. Record levels for each cell in the chart.

Cell	1	2	3	4	5	6
Level						

Battery Load Test

5. Follow automatic battery tester instructions to make the battery load test.

> **NOTE** 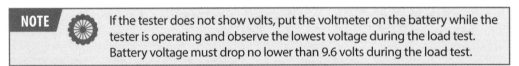 If the tester does not show volts, put the voltmeter on the battery while the tester is operating and observe the lowest voltage during the load test. Battery voltage must drop no lower than 9.6 volts during the load test.

> **NOTE** If the automatic tester will not perform the test, the measured voltage is too low and you will need to charge the battery first.

6. Perform a voltage drop test of each cell. Put the leads of your voltmeter in each accompanying cell. Each cell should show at least a 2.1 volt drop. Record the voltage drop for each cell in the chart.

Cell	1	2	3	4	5	6
Level						

> **CAUTION** ⚠ Thoroughly clean acid off the voltmeter and leads when the test is complete.

 7. Discuss your findings with your instructor.

Instructor's Initials: _____

Job Wrap Up

8. Return all tools and materials to the proper storage areas and clean up your work area.

Name _____

Final Assessment

_____   1. What component places the largest electrical load on a vehicle battery?
A. Starter.
B. Lights.
C. Ignition.
D. Charging field winding.

_____   2. What vehicle condition does load testing a battery simulate?
A. Charging system.
B. Lights being turned on.
C. Parasitic draw.
D. Starter cranking.

_____   3. What type of acid is used in a lead-acid battery?
A. Parasitic.
B. Absorbed.
C. Lead.
D. Sulfuric.

_____   4. What type of gas is given off during charging of a lead-acid battery?
A. Nitrogen.
B. Hydrogen.
C. Sulfuric.
D. Acetylene.

_____   5. Define *amp hour rating*.
A. How long a battery can provide voltage at a certain amperage.
B. How long a battery can provide amperage at a certain voltage.
C. How many amps the battery can hold for one hour.
D. How many amps the battery can be charged in one hour.

Final Instructor Approval: _____ _____

Notes

Name _____ Date _____ Class _____

Job 14-2

Charging Batteries

Introduction

Battery charging is an everyday operation in a motorcycle repair shop. Performing this skill with accuracy and in a safe manner is mandatory. Batteries that are not charged properly or should not be charged can pose a risk.

Objective

After successfully completing this job, you will be able to properly charge a battery.

Materials and Equipment

To complete this job, you will need the following tools, equipment, and materials:

- Lead-acid battery
- Specific gravity tester
- Automatic battery tester
- Automatic battery charger
- Voltmeter (Fluke 88 or comparable multimeter)

Instructions

In this job, you will be charging a battery and making battery measurements with a voltmeter and an automatic battery charger. Consult the service manual for any precautions and special instructions for the vehicle battery that you are charging and testing.

Read the job procedures, perform the tasks, and answer all questions. As you complete steps, you will be given instructions to either fill in measurements or perform certain tasks. When you reach a sign, show your work to your instructor. Do not continue until you have instructor approval (instructor will initial job sheet).

> **WARNING** ⚠ Before performing this job, review all pertinent safety information in the text and discuss safety procedures with your instructor.

Procedures

Test Voltage

1. Obtain a battery for charging and testing from your instructor.

2. Check for open circuit voltage of battery.
   Voltage:

   _____

3. Check for surface charge on battery case (highest reading).
   Surface charge:

   _____

4. Clean the battery with approved battery cleaner.

5. Remove the battery cap(s) and check each cell to see if the electrolyte level is correct. If not, top off low cells with distilled water and charge the battery.

Charge Battery

6. Follow the instructions on the automatic battery charger to charge the battery.

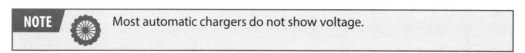

   NOTE   Most automatic chargers do not show voltage.

7. Attach the voltmeter to the battery while charging to observe the voltage cycling on and off. Ask your instructor whether you should remove the caps from the battery during charging.
   Charging voltage applied to battery by automatic charger:

   _____

8. Allow the battery charger to operate until it indicates that the battery is fully charged.

Retest Battery

9. Check open circuit voltage of battery.
   Voltage:

   _____

10. Load test the battery with an automatic battery tester. Have your voltmeter on the battery while it is being load tested.
    Voltage during load test:

    _____

    Load test results:

    _____

11. Discuss your findings with your instructor.

Instructor's Initials: _____

Name _____

Job Wrap Up

12. Return all tools and materials to the proper storage areas and clean up your work area.

Final Assessment

_____   1. Two technicians are discussing batteries. Technician A says that a trickle charger is a good device for customers to own. Technician B says that, if a battery needs to be repeatedly charged, it should be replaced. Who is correct?

A. A only.

B. B only.

C. Both A and B.

D. Neither A nor B.

_____   2. Two technicians are discussing battery chargers. Technician A says to test a battery only before charging. Technician B says to always test a battery after charging. Who is correct?

A. A only.

B. B only.

C. Both A and B.

D. Neither A nor B.

_____   3. Two technicians are discussing batteries. Technician A says dirty battery connections will shorten battery life. Technician B says vibration and bouncing can shorten battery life. Who is correct?

A. A only.

B. B only.

C. Both A and B.

D. Neither A nor B.

_____   4. Two technicians are discussing battery replacement. Technician A says that a lead-acid battery can be replaced only with another lead-acid battery. Technician B says that a lead-acid battery can also be replaced by an AGM battery. Who is correct?

A. A only.

B. B only.

C. Both A and B.

D. Neither A nor B.

_____   5. Two technicians are discussing cleaning a battery. Technician A says to clean a battery while it is in the vehicle. Technician B says to clean a battery with the fill caps removed. Who is correct?

A. A only.

B. B only.

C. Both A and B.

D. Neither A nor B.

Final Instructor Approval: _____

Notes

Name _____ Date _____ Class _____

Job 14-3

Testing Permanent Magnet Charging Systems

Introduction

The two main types of charging systems are excited field (alternator) and permanent magnet (PM). The PM charging system is common on motorcycles and has been used for a long time. Its components are basically the same on all motorcycles, but may be in different locations. Some motorcycles may have two PM systems for higher output.

Having a solid understanding of how to diagnose these systems is a basic motorcycle technician skill. Diagnosing these systems gives the technician an opportunity to practice and understand ac electricity, which will be used in many other applications.

Objective

After successfully completing this job, you will be able to test a permanent magnet charging system.

Materials and Equipment

To complete this job, you will need the following tools, equipment, and materials:

- Motorcycle or other vehicle with permanent magnet charging system
- Appropriate service manual or electronic service information
- Fluke 88 or comparable multimeter
- Load tester

Instructions

In this job, you will need to use the service manual and wiring diagrams to confirm the type of charging system and determine the proper test tools and procedures. Many of the tests in the service manual will be resistance tests, but it is always better to make a voltage output test instead. Voltage drop increases when there is excessive resistance. However, the resistance test uses such low current that if any part of the wire is intact, the system will pass a resistance test.

Read the job procedures, perform the tasks, and answer all questions. As you complete steps, you will be given instructions to either fill in measurements or perform certain tasks. When you reach a 🛑 sign, show your work to your instructor. Do not continue until you have instructor approval (instructor will initial job sheet).

> **WARNING** ⚠️ Before performing this job, review all pertinent safety information in the text and discuss safety procedures with your instructor.

Procedures

Test Charging System — Permanent Magnet #1

Vehicle (Year/Make/Model)

_____

1. Make tests and complete the following table for output voltage and amperage at the battery. The ac ripple test detects any ac voltage at the battery. If you cannot find a specification for ac ripple, as a general rule, there should be no more than 0.5 volts ac at the battery.

CAUTION ⚠ Do not perform a loaded idle test.

	Charging Voltage	Charging Amperage	AC Ripple
Idle No Load			
3,000 rpm			
3,000 rpm Loaded to 12 Volts			

2. If the tests above indicate overcharging, what should be the next component to be diagnosed? (Refer to the service manual as necessary.)

_____

3. If the tests above indicate undercharging, what components should be tested further?

A. _____

B. _____

C. _____

4. Unplug the stator wire and test for ac voltage output by pairing two of the three wires coming from the stator. (Since there are three wires, there are three possible combinations.)

WARNING ⚠ Be careful. The wires are electrically live. Do not ground the wires.

Pair 1 (idle):

_____

Pair 1 (3,000 rpm):

_____

Pair 2 (idle):

_____

Pair 2 (3,000 rpm):

_____

Pair 3 (idle):

_____

Pair 3 (3,000 rpm):

_____

5. Compare your numbers with service manual specifications.

Name _____

6. What do the results of the above tests indicate?

_____

_____

7. If the test outputs were low, what parts could be faulty?

_____

_____

8. Test the stator resistance.

Wire	Resistance to Each Other	Wire	Resistance to Ground
1-2		1	
2-3		2	
3-1		3	

9. Test the dc output of the regulator.

Regulator Wire	Idle	3,000 rpm Loaded
DC into the Regulator (If a separate wire is used)		
DC out of Regulator		
Regulator Ground Voltage Drop		

(STOP) 10. Discuss your findings with your instructor.

Instructor's Initials: _____

Test Charging System — Permanent Magnet #2

Vehicle (Year/Make/Model)

_____

11. Make tests and complete the following table for output voltage and amperage at the battery. The ac ripple test detects any ac voltage at the battery. If you cannot find a specification for ac ripple, as a general rule, there should be no more than .5 volts ac at the battery.

CAUTION ⚠ Do not perform a loaded idle test.

	Charging Voltage	Charging Amperage	AC Ripple
Idle No Load			
3,000 rpm			
3,000 rpm Loaded to 12 Volts			

12. If the tests above indicate overcharging, where does diagnosis take you next? (Refer to the service manual as necessary.)

_____

13. If the tests above indicate undercharging, what components need to be tested further?

A. _____

B. _____

C. _____

14. Unplug the stator wire and test for ac voltage output by paring two of the three wires coming from the stator. (Since there are three wires, there are three possible combinations.)

> **WARNING** ⚠ Be careful. The wires are electrically live. Do not ground the wires.

Pair 1 (idle):

_____

Pair 1 (3,000 rpm):

_____

Pair 2 (idle):

_____

Pair 2 (3,000 rpm):

_____

Pair 3 (idle):

_____

Pair 3 (3,000 rpm):

_____

15. Compare your numbers with service manual specifications.

16. What do the results of the above test indicate?

_____

_____

17. If the test outputs were low, what parts could be faulty?

_____

_____

18. Test the stator resistance.

Wire	Resistance to Each Other	Wire	Resistance to Ground
1-2		1	
2-3		2	
3-1		3	

Name _____

19. Test the dc output of the regulator.

Regulator Wire	Idle	3,000 rpm Loaded
DC into the Regulator (If a separate wire is used)		
DC out of Regulator		
Regulator Ground Voltage Drop		

STOP 20. Discuss your findings with your instructor.

Instructor's Initials: _____

Job Wrap Up

21. Return all tools and materials to the proper storage areas and clean up your work area.

Final Assessment

_____ 1. If the voltage output of the stator is correct, but the voltage output of the regulator rectifier is low, which part is at fault?

A. Stator.

B. Battery.

C. Regulator/rectifier.

D. Connectors.

_____ 2. If the ac voltage output of the stator is correct at idle but incorrect at 3,000 rpm, what component would be at fault?

A. Stator.

B. Battery.

C. Regulator/rectifier.

D. Connectors.

_____ 3. Two technicians are discussing intermittent charging faults. Technician A says that connectors with high resistance can cause intermittent charging. Technician B says a faulty regulator/rectifier can cause intermittent charging. Who is correct?

A. A only.

B. B only.

C. Both A and B.

D. Neither A nor B.

_____ 4. Two technicians are discussing charging system repair. Technician A says if the stator is faulty, it is best to also replace the regulator/rectifier. Technician B says if the regulator/rectifier is faulty, it is best practice to also replace the stator. Who is correct?

A. A only.

B. B only.

C. Both A and B.

D. Neither A nor B.

_____   5. Two technicians are discussing charging system diagnosis. Technician A says if the battery dies overnight, the charging system should be tested. Technician B says if the battery dies overnight, the vehicle should be tested for parasitic draw. Who is correct?

A. A only.

B. B only.

C. Both A and B.

D. Neither A nor B.

Final Instructor Approval: _____

Name _____   Date _____   Class _____

Job 14-4

Testing Excited Field (Alternator) Charging Systems

Introduction

The two main types of charging systems are excited field and permanent magnet. The excited field system is identical to the charging system used in car and truck alternators. The magnetic field is controlled by the voltage regulator. The more output needed, the stronger the voltage regulator makes the magnetic field. The excited field charging system has much higher output capability than the permanent magnet system.

In this job, we will focus on modern excited field charging systems with the components combined into a single unit. Older system components were separated and today are only found on vintage motorcycles.

Objective

After successfully completing this job, you will be able to test an excited field charging system.

Materials and Equipment

To complete this job, you will need the following tools, equipment, and materials:

- Vehicle with excited field charging system
- Appropriate service manual or electronic service information
- Fluke 88 or comparable multimeter
- Load tester

Instructions

In this job, you will need to use the service manual and wiring diagrams to confirm the type of charging system and determine the proper test tools and procedures. Many of the tests in the service manual will be resistance tests. Voltage drop is increased when there is excessive resistance. However, the test uses such low current that if any part of the wire is intact, it will pass a resistance test. For this reason, it is always better to make a voltage output test rather than a resistance test.

Read the job procedures, perform the tasks, and answer all questions. As you complete steps, you will be given instructions to either fill in measurements or perform certain tasks. When you reach a sign, show your work to your instructor. Do not continue until you have instructor approval (instructor will initial job sheet).

> **WARNING** ⚠️ Before performing this job, review all pertinent safety information in the text and discuss safety procedures with your instructor.

Procedures

Test Charging Excited Field (Alternator)

Vehicle (Year/Make/Model)

_____

1. Make tests and complete the following table for output voltage and amperage at the battery.

> **CAUTION** ⚠ Do not perform a loaded idle test.

	Charging Voltage	Charging Amperage	AC Ripple
Idle No Load			
3,000 rpm			
3,000 rpm Loaded to 12 Volts			

2. Test the voltage drop of the charging wire from the alternator back to the battery.
   Voltage drop:

   _____

3. Test the voltage drop of the ground from the alternator to battery ground.
   Voltage drop:

   _____

4. Check the low amperage voltage wire to the regulator.
   Voltage reading:

   _____

Check Key-On Voltage

5. Turn the key on and touch the alternator shaft with a small screwdriver or feeler gauge.
   Magnetic pull present:

   _____

> **NOTE**   If the field winding is receiving power and is not open or shorted, there will be a slight magnetic pull on the screwdriver or gauge. The magnetic pull indicates that the alternator is capable of producing charging power. If there is no magnetic pull, check whether the regulator is receiving power. If the regulator is receiving key-on power, but there is no magnetic pull, then the field winding is open.

 6. Discuss your findings with your instructor.

Instructor's Initials: _____

Name _____

Job Wrap Up

7. Return all tools and materials to the proper storage areas and clean up your work area.

Final Assessment

_____ 1. Two technicians are discussing servicing an alternator. Technician A says that the unit is usually replaced as a whole. Technician B says that some parts can still be ordered to rebuild an alternator. Who is correct?

A. A only.

B. B only.

C. Both A and B.

D. Neither A nor B.

_____ 2. Two technicians are discussing diagnosing an alternator. Technician A says low output at the battery means that the alternator is faulty. Technician B says the wire between the alternator and the battery can cause low charging voltage. Who is correct?

A. A only.

B. B only.

C. Both A and B.

D. Neither A nor B.

_____ 3. Two technicians are discussing intermittent charging faults. Technician A says to remove the alternator and check the drive flange for damage. Technician B says to remove the alternator to properly test the ground. Who is correct?

A. A only.

B. B only.

C. Both A and B.

D. Neither A nor B.

_____ 4. Two technicians are discussing alternator diagnosis. Technician A says that a faulty charging system can shorten the life of the battery. Technician B says a fully charged battery is necessary to test the alternator output. Who is correct?

A. A only.

B. B only.

C. Both A and B.

D. Neither A nor B.

_____ 5. Two technicians are discussing charging system diagnosis. Technician A says the output voltage from the alternator should go up and down with rpm. Technician B says the output voltage should hold steady with rpm change. Who is correct?

A. A only.

B. B only.

C. Both A and B.

D. Neither A nor B.

Final Instructor Approval: _____

Notes

Name _____ Date _____ Class _____

Job 14-5

Testing Charging System Components

Introduction

Having the skills to test individual charging system components is both helpful in diagnosis and particularly helpful when checking new parts before installation. In this job, you will be using an ohmmeter as well as a battery and a test light to test components. An ohmmeter does not use very much current and can cause an incorrect reading. The battery and test light will carry more current and be a better test of the component than an ohmmeter.

Objective

After successfully completing this job, you will be able to test individual charging system components.

Materials and Equipment

To complete this job, you will need the following tools, equipment, and materials:

- Stator from permanent magnet system
- Excited field alternator
- Appropriate service manual or electronic service information
- Fluke 88 or comparable multimeter
- Battery and incandescent or halogen test light

Instructions

Follow the instructions in the service manual or electronic service information to test the components with both an ohmmeter and a battery and test light. The battery and test light are used to test components that are made up of turns of wire, such as stators or field windings.

Read the job procedures, perform the tasks, and answer all questions. As you complete steps, you will be given instructions to either fill in measurements or perform certain tasks. When you reach a sign, show your work to your instructor. Do not continue until you have instructor approval (instructor will initial job sheet).

> **WARNING** ⚠ Before performing this job, review all pertinent safety information in the text and discuss safety procedures with your instructor.

Procedures

Test Stator

1. Perform a static test of five different charging coils with a test light and a battery. Your instructor will provide you with a charging coil, or direct you to obtain one from a core engine. Your test result will either be open (no light) or shorted (bright light).

2. Test the charge coil from wire to wire to test for opens and from each wire to ground for shorts. Test as many coils as you are assigned. Record your results in the chart.

	Coil 1	Coil 2	Coil 3	Coil 4	Coil 5
Result					

🛑 3. Discuss your findings with your instructor.

Instructor's Initials: _____

Remove and Test Stator Core

Vehicle or Engine (Year/Make/Model)

_____

4. Remove all of the charging system components from a shop core engine.

5. Demonstrate to your instructor the testing of the stator core windings using a battery and test light.

🛑 6. Discuss your findings with your instructor.

Instructor's Initials: _____

Test Alternator Windings

7. Disassemble an alternator supplied by your instructor.

8. Using the service manual, perform tests on the internal alternator components with either an ohmmeter or a battery and test light. Record your results by putting an "X" in the appropriate box.

Component	Open	Not Open	Shorted	Not Shorted
Field Winding				
Stator Winding 1				
Stator Winding 2				
Stator Winding 3				

Name _____

Test Alternator Rectifier

9. Test all of the diodes in the rectifier using the diode setting on your multimeter. Test each diode from where the stator wire bolts to the rectifier. Your answer will be whatever the reading is on the meter.

> **NOTE**   Expect the current to flow from the stator to the alternator output and not flow in the opposite direction.

	Stator to Output Post	**Output Post to Stator**
Diode 1		
Diode 2		
Diode 3		

STOP 10. Discuss your findings with your instructor.

Instructor's Initials: _____

Job Wrap Up

11. Return all tools and materials to the proper storage areas and clean up your work area.

Final Assessment

_____ 1. The type of electricity that comes out of a normally operating alternator stator is _____.
   A. high amperage ac
   B. low amperage ac
   C. high amperage dc
   D. low amperage dc

_____ 2. The type of electricity that comes out of the regulator rectifier on a permanent magnet charging system is _____.
   A. high amperage ac
   B. low amperage ac
   C. high amperage dc
   D. low amperage dc

_____ 3. The type of electricity that goes into the regulator on an excited field (alternator) system is _____.
   A. high amperage ac
   B   low amperage ac
   C. high amperage dc
   D. low amperage dc

_____   4. The type of electricity that comes out of the rectifier on an excited field (alternator) system is _____.
A. high amperage ac
B. low amperage ac
C. high amperage dc
D. low amperage dc

_____   5. The type of electricity that goes into an excited field (alternator) system field winding is _____.
A. high amperage ac
B. low amperage ac
C. high amperage dc
D. low amperage dc

Final Instructor Approval: _____

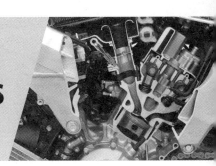

CHAPTER 15

Electrical Accessory Systems

Chapter 15 Quiz

After studying Chapter 15 in the Motorcycles: Fundamentals, Service, Repair textbook, answer the following questions.
For questions 1–11, identify the components of a motorcycle lighting system indicated in the following illustration.

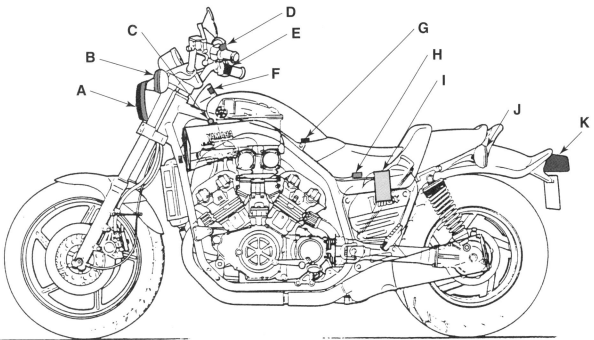

Yamaha Motor Corporation U.S.A.

_____ 1. Main fuse

_____ 2. Main switch

_____ 3. Starter switch

_____ 4. Battery

_____ 5. Headlight

_____ 6. Tail/brake light

_____ 7. "High beam" indicator light

_____ 8. Turn signal

_____ 9. Turn signal

_____ 10. "Lights" (dimmer) switch

_____ 11. Fuse (headlights)

_____ 12. In ac lighting systems, the lighting is powered by the _____.

A. magneto

B. alternator

C. battery

D. Either A or B.

_____ 13. *True or False?* In most ac lighting systems, the headlight comes on when the key is turned to the *on* position without starting the engine.

_____ 14. All of the following statements about halogen bulbs are true, *except*:

A. the glass part should not be handled with bare hands.

B. they provide more light than traditional sealed beam bulbs.

C. they remain cool when the headlight is on.

D. they contain a quartz-glass bulb.

_____ 15. *True or False?* A person should be sitting on the bike while headlights are aimed.

_____ 16. *True or False?* The pass button in a lighting system works only when the headlight is on high beam.

_____ 17. *True or False?* When taillights and brake lights are built into the same assembly and bulb, the brake light is brighter than the taillight.

_____ 18. Compared to incandescent bulbs, LED taillights _____.

A. have more filaments

B. provide brighter lighting

C. consume more power

D. All of the above.

_____ 19. When the front turn signals have two filaments, one filament is used for turn signals and the other is used for _____.

A. brake lights

B. running lights

C. headlights

D. high beams

_____ 20. *True or False?* Troubleshooting lighting systems requires the use of wiring schematics.

_____ 21. Lighting system troubleshooting starts with checking the bulb. If the bulb is good, the next step is to _____.

A. waterproof the bulb assembly

B. unplug the wiring harness and visually check the wiring

C. check for power and ground in the socket and body

D. None of the above.

_____ 22. *True or False?* The brake light switch on the front brake lever of most motorcycles is adjustable.

_____ 23. *True or False?* The oil pressure warning light should be off when the engine is running.

Name _____

_____ 24. The first step in testing the coolant temperature circuit is to _____.

A. measure battery voltage at the ignition switch

B. measure battery voltage at the temperature gauge and temperature sensor

C. bypass the temperature sensor by completing the circuit to ground

D. remove the temperature sensor from the system

_____ 25. The two types of fuel level gauges are the _____-type gauge and the _____-type gauge.

A. return, stop

B. full, empty

C. high, low

D. mechanical, electrical

_____ 26. Some charging systems have a voltage gauge or indicator light, while a few motorcycles use a(n) _____ to allow the rider to monitor the charging system.

_____ 27. Modern motorcycles will not crank if the _____.

A. brake light is on

B. side stand is lowered and the FI light is on

C. transmission is in neutral

D. side stand light is on and the motorcycle is in gear

_____ 28. Hour meters are used mostly on motocross vehicles to calculate the time the meter connects to the _____.

A. camshaft

B. crankshaft

C. charging system

D. ignition system

_____ 29. The horn circuit consists of a horn switch, _____, wires, ignition switch, and horn.

_____ 30. *True or False?* Motorcycle technicians should leave the analysis of radio reception conditions to an authorized communication service center.

_____ 31. Cruise control can be canceled by all of the following rider actions, *except*:

A. accelerating.

B. changing gears.

C. pulling front brake lever.

D. pulling the clutch lever.

_____ 32. A gear or chain drive and a starter _____ are normally used to engage and disengage the starter motor.

_____ 33. In an electric starter system, the starter _____ increase the starter motor's turning force.

A. relays

B. gears

C. switches

D. clutches

_____ 34. *True or False?* An electric starter motor uses electrical energy to magnetically force its armature to turn.

_____ 35. The starter clutch allows the starter motor to spin the _____.

Notes

Name _____ Date _____ Class _____

Job 15-1

Diagnosing Horn Problems

Introduction

The horn is a safety device and the technician must know how to diagnose and repair it. The technician uses wiring diagrams to determine whether there is a relay in the circuit, if it is connected to ground or the positive power supply, and what function the horn switch performs.

Objective

After successfully completing this job, you will be able to diagnose a horn circuit.

Materials and Equipment

To complete this job, you will need the following tools, equipment, and materials:

- Motorcycle or other vehicle
- Appropriate service manual or electronic service information
- Voltmeter (Fluke 88 or comparable multimeter)
- Non-powered test light

Instructions

You will need to print a copy of the wiring diagram that can be highlighted and written on. You will be asked questions based on the wiring diagram and then instructed to make measurements with a voltmeter to confirm what you have decided based on studying the wiring diagram.

Read the job procedures, perform the tasks, and answer all questions. As you complete steps you will be given instructions to either fill in measurements or perform certain tasks. When you reach a 🛑 sign, show your work to your instructor. Do not continue until you have instructor approval (instructor will initial job sheet).

⚠️	Before performing this job, review all pertinent safety information in the text and discuss safety procedures with your instructor.

WARNING

Procedures

Print and Study Wiring Diagram

Vehicle (Year/Make/Model)

_____

1. Locate and print a copy of the wiring diagram for the horn circuit of the vehicle that you are working on. A diagram of just the horn circuit and not the overall wiring diagram is preferred.

2. Study the horn circuit and note the number of horns. Number of horns:

_____

3. Note whether the circuit uses a relay. Yes _____ No _____

   If the circuit does use a relay, what does the horn switch provide to the relay to complete the circuit?

   _____   Battery power

   _____   Ground

4. Locate the fuse providing power to the horn circuit and list other electrical devices powered through the fuse.

   _____

   _____

5. Explain how you can use the information gathered in Steps 2 through 4 to help with horn diagnosis.

   _____

   _____

6. Decide whether the horn has power with the key on and is grounded by the horn switch, or whether it is grounded and powered by the horn switch. Record your findings below.

   _____

STOP 7. Discuss your findings from the wiring diagram with your instructor.

Instructor's Initials: _____

Diagnose Horn Problems on the Vehicle

8. Locate the fuse that protects the horn circuit. Check voltage by leaving the fuse in place and touching both tabs on the back of the fuse with a voltmeter.

   Fuse condition:

   _____   Power on both sides

   _____   Power on only one side

   Based on the reading, the fuse condition is:

   _____   Good

   _____   Blown

9. Unplug one horn connector and install a test light in its place. Press the horn switch. Did the light illuminate? Yes _____ No _____

   Based on the above test, is the horn circuit being supplied with battery power when the horn switch is pressed?

   _____

   _____

Name _____

10. Leave the light attached and measure voltage at the horn connector with the horn switch pressed.

What is the voltage reading on the horn positive connector?

_____

What is the voltage reading on the horn negative connector?

_____

If there were zero volts at the horn positive connector, what should be tested next?

_____

If there was source voltage after the horn positive connector, what should be tested next?

_____

🛑 11. Discuss your findings from the voltage tests with your instructor.

Instructor's Initials: _____

Job Wrap Up

12. Return all tools and materials to the proper storage areas and clean up your work area.

Final Assessment

_____ 1. A circuit that is not working has source voltage on the wire going to the load and on the wire after the load. The load is missing _____.

A. source voltage
B. circuit protection
C. a functioning load
D. a ground path

_____ 2. A circuit that is not working has zero volts on the wire going to the load and on the wire after the load. The load is missing _____.

A. source voltage
B. circuit protection
C. a functioning load
D. a ground path

_____ 3. A circuit that is not working has source voltage on the wire going to the load and zero volts on the wire after the load. The load is missing _____.

A. source voltage
B. circuit protection
C. a functioning load
D. a ground path

_____   4. A fuse is found blown and a replacement fuse blows when the horn switch is pressed. What type of fault will the tech be diagnosing?

    A. High resistance.

    B. Open circuit.

    C. Short to ground.

    D. Faulty switch.

_____   5. Source voltage is measured going into the horn switch and zero volts is measured coming out of the switch when the switch is pressed. Technician A says the horn switch is shorted. Technician B says the horn switch is open. Who is correct?

    A. A only.

    B. B only.

    C. Both A and B.

    D. Neither A nor B.

Final Instructor Approval: _____

Name _____ Date _____ Class _____

Job 15-2

Diagnosing Turn Signals

Introduction

The turn signal circuit is a safety circuit that must work on any motorcycle or other vehicle. Checking the turn signals is standard for a pre-ride walk around. The technician must know how to diagnose this circuit. Wiring diagrams are used to understand the turn signal circuit and the function of the turn signal switch. The service manual or electronic service information is used to diagnose the auto-canceling turn signal system (turns off based on time or distance traveled).

Objective

After successfully completing this job, you will be able to diagnose a turn signal circuit.

Materials and Equipment

To complete this job, you will need the following tools, equipment, and materials:

- Motorcycle or other vehicle
- Appropriate service manual or electronic service information
- Voltmeter (Fluke 88 or comparable multimeter)

Instructions

You will need to print a copy of the wiring diagram that can be highlighted and written on. You will be asked questions based on the wiring diagram and then instructed to make measurements with a voltmeter to confirm what you have determined from the wiring diagram.

Read the job procedures, perform the tasks, and answer all questions. As you complete steps, you will be given instructions to either fill in measurements or perform certain tasks. When you reach a sign, show your work to your instructor. Do not continue until you have instructor approval (instructor will initial job sheet).

> **WARNING** ⚠ Before performing this job, review all pertinent safety information in the text and discuss safety procedures with your instructor.

Procedures

Read Wiring Diagram to Diagnose Problems

Vehicle (Year/Make/Model)

_____

1. Locate and print a copy of the wiring diagram for the turn signal circuit of the vehicle that you are working on. A diagram of just the turn signal circuit and not the overall wiring diagram is preferred.

2. Check the service manual to determine whether this particular vehicle has an automatic canceling turn signal system. Yes _____ No _____

3. Study the turn signal circuit.

   A. Locate the turn signal switch on the diagram. Describe below how the switch provides power to the circuit.

   _____

   _____

   B. Determine whether there is a separate hazard switch. Yes _____ No _____

   C. What would be the cause of the hazard signals working and the turn signals not working?

   _____

   _____

   D. What would be the cause of the turn signals working and the hazard signals not working?

   _____

   _____

4. Locate the fuse providing power for the turn signal and hazard circuit and identify its location below.

   _____

   A. Does the same fuse provide power to another circuit?

   _____

   _____

   B. How can you use this information to help diagnose circuit problems?

   _____

5. Determine whether the turn signal switch has power with the key on or receives power once the switch is operated. Write your answer below.

   _____

6. Determine whether the turn signal bulbs are in series or in parallel. Write your answer below.

   _____

7. Determine from the diagram what could be the problem if only the front turn signals work (what would you be able to determine about the fuse, the flasher relay, and the switch). Write your answers below.

   _____

8. On your diagram, highlight the wires running from power to ground that enable the left turn signals to operate.

STOP 9. Discuss your findings from the wiring diagram with your instructor.

Instructor's Initials: _____

Name _____

Diagnose Turn Signal Problems on Vehicle

Vehicle (Year/Make/Model)

_____

10. Locate the fuse that protects the turn signal circuit, then check voltage by leaving the fuse in place and touching both tabs on the back of the fuse with a voltmeter.

    Fuse condition:

    _____   Power on both sides

    _____   Power on one side only

    Based on the reading, the fuse condition is:

    _____   Good

    _____   Blown

    > **NOTE** When measuring voltage on the turn signal circuit where the flasher is operating, it is sometimes easier to look at the analog portion of the Fluke 88 voltmeter that is just underneath the digital readout.

11. Measure voltage at the easiest place to access a bulb connector.

    Voltage into the turn signal:

    Source voltage flashing: Yes _____ No _____

    Voltage after the turn signal switch:

    _____   Zero volts

    _____   Other voltage

    A. If there were zero volts going to the switch, what should be checked next?

    _____

    B. If there was source voltage after the switch, what should be checked next?

    _____

🛑 12. Discuss your findings from the voltage tests with your instructor.

Instructor's Initials: _____

Job Wrap Up

13. Return all tools and materials to the proper storage areas and clean up your work area.

14. Ask your instructor to check your work and initial this job.

Final Assessment

_____ 1. A turn signal circuit that is not working has source voltage on the wire going to the bulb and on the wire after the load. What is missing?

    A. Source voltage.

    B. Circuit protection.

    C. A functioning load.

    D. A ground path.

_____ 2. A turn signal circuit that is not working has zero volts on the wire going to the bulb and on the wire after the load. What is missing?

    A. Source voltage.

    B. Circuit protection.

    C. A functioning load.

    D. A ground path.

_____ 3. A circuit that is not working has source voltage on the wire going to the bulb and zero volts on the wire after the bulb. What is missing?

    A. Source voltage.

    B. Circuit protection.

    C. A functioning bulb.

    D. A ground path.

_____ 4. The bulbs in a turn signal circuit are illuminated but not flashing. Using your printed wiring diagram, which component is defective?

    A. Hazard switch.

    B. Fuse.

    C. Switch.

    D. Flasher.

_____ 5. Source voltage is measured going into the turn signal switch. Zero volts is measured coming out of the turn signal switch when the switch is operated. Technician A says the turn signal switch may be shorted. Technician B says the turn signal switch may be open. Who is correct?

    A. A only.

    B. B only.

    C. Both A and B.

    D. Neither A nor B.

Final Instructor Approval: _____

Name _____ Date _____ Class _____

Job 15-3

Diagnosing Headlights

Introduction

The headlight circuit is a safety circuit that must work on any motorcycle or other vehicle. Checking the headlight is a standard procedure for a pre-ride walk around. The technician must know how to diagnose the headlight circuit.

Some headlight circuits will include daytime running lights. Some motorcycles need ac power from the stator to energize the headlight relay, therefore the engine must be running before the headlight will light.

Some high beam circuits will have two separate bulbs, while others will have one bulb with two filaments. Some circuits with two filaments will use both filaments for the high beam and other circuits will use one filament for high beam and one filament for low beam with a grounded middle wire.

Objective

After successfully completing this job, you will be able to diagnose a headlight circuit.

Materials and Equipment

To complete this job, you will need the following tools, equipment, and materials:

- Motorcycle or other vehicle
- Appropriate service manual or electronic service information
- Voltmeter (Fluke 88 or comparable multimeter)

Instructions

You will need to print a copy of the wiring diagram that can be highlighted and written on. You will be asked questions based on the wiring diagram and instructed to make measurements with a voltmeter to confirm what you have decided based on studying the wiring diagram.

Read the job procedures, perform the tasks, and answer all questions. As you complete steps, you will be given instructions to either fill in measurements or perform certain tasks. When you reach a sign, show your work to your instructor. Do not continue until you have instructor approval (instructor will initial job sheet).

 WARNING ⚠ Before performing this job, review all pertinent safety information in the text and discuss safety procedures with your instructor.

Procedures

Diagnose Headlights Using a Wiring Diagram

Vehicle (Year/Make/Model)

_____

1. Locate and print a copy of the wiring diagram for the headlight circuit of the vehicle that you are working on. A diagram of just the headlight circuit and not the overall wiring diagram is preferred.

2. Study the headlight circuit and determine the following:

   A. Total number of lights

   _____

   B. Number of separate bulbs

   _____

   C. Number of dual filament bulbs

   _____

   D. Does the circuit use a relay? Yes _____ No _____

   E. If the circuit has a relay, what circuit does the switch connect to the relay?

   _____

3. Determine whether the headlights work with the key on or whether the engine needs to be started. Record findings.

   _____

4. Could you determine this information from the wiring diagram or did you find out from consulting the service manual?

   _____   Wiring diagram

   _____   Service manual

5. Determine which fuse provides power for the headlight circuit and record it here.

   _____

   A. Determine whether the same fuse provides power to another circuit. Record your findings, listing other circuits if used.

   _____

   _____

   B. Explain how this information could be used to help diagnose a problem.

   _____

   _____

6. Determine whether the headlight fuses are powered through the headlight switch. Record your findings, listing the fuses if there are others.

   _____

   _____

Name _____

7. Determine whether the headlight will have power with the key on or if the power comes from the headlight switch. Record your findings here.

_____

_____

8. Determine whether a computer controls the headlights. If so, list the switch inputs to the computer that operates the lights.

_____

_____

_____

🛑 9. Discuss your findings from the wiring diagram with your instructor.

Instructor's Initials: _____

Diagnose Headlights on the Vehicle

10. Locate the fuse that protects the headlight circuit. Check voltage by leaving the fuse in place and touching both tabs on the back of the fuse with a voltmeter.

    Fuse condition:

    _____ Power on both sides

    _____ Power on only one side

    Based on the reading, the fuse condition is:

    _____ Good

    _____ Blown

11. Check the low beams and running lights for proper illumination.

    _____ Illuminated

    _____ Not illuminated

    Describe any lights that are not illuminated:

    _____

    _____

    _____

12. Study the wiring diagram and determine the cause of the running lights working and the headlight not working.

    _____

    _____

    _____

13. Measure the circuit at the closest connector to the bulbs with the circuit on low beams.

Measurement Location	Wire Color	Voltage
Going into the low beam bulb wire		
Going into the high beam bulb wire		
After the headlights on the ground wire		

14. Measure the circuit at the bulbs or closest connector with the circuit on high beams.

Measurement Location	Wire Color	Voltage
Going into the low beam bulb wire		
Going into the high beam bulb wire		
After the headlights on the ground wire		

A. If there were zero volts going to the headlight bulb, what should be tested next?

_____

B. If there was source voltage after the headlight bulb, what should be tested next?

_____

(STOP) 15. Discuss your findings from the wiring diagram with your instructor.

Instructor's Initials: _____

Job Wrap Up

16. Return all tools and materials to the proper storage areas and clean up your work area.

Final Assessment

_____ 1. Source voltage is found on the ground wire after the headlight bulb and the bulb does not work. Where is the fault?

A. Source voltage.

B. Circuit protection.

C. A functioning load.

D. A ground path.

_____ 2. A circuit that is not working has zero volts on the wire going to the load and on the wire after the load. What is missing?

A. Source voltage.

B. Circuit protection.

C. A functioning load.

D. A ground path.

Name _____

_____ 3. A circuit that is not working has source voltage on the wire going to the load and zero volts on the wire after the load. What is missing?

 A. Source voltage.

 B. Circuit protection.

 C. A functioning load.

 D. A ground path.

_____ 4. A fuse is found blown and a replacement fuse blows when the headlight switch is pressed. What type of fault is the most likely cause?

 A. High resistance.

 B. Open circuit.

 C. Short to ground.

 D. Faulty switch.

_____ 5. Source voltage is measured going into the headlight switch and zero volts is measured coming out of the switch when the switch is operated. Technician A says the headlight switch is shorted. Technician B says the headlight switch is open. Who is correct?

 A. A only.

 B. B only.

 C. Both A and B.

 D. Neither A nor B.

Final Instructor Approval: _____

Notes

Name _____ Date _____ Class _____

Job 15-4

Finding Shorts to Ground

Introduction

The motorcycle technician must know how to find shorts to ground. Short locating requires a different strategy than those used to look for other faults. What is missing is a load. The technician must install a load in place of the blown fuse. Once the overloaded circuit is located, the technician can unplug suspect devices or use an inductive amp clamp, or a combination of both methods.

Objective

After successfully completing this job, you will be able to locate shorts to ground.

Materials and Equipment

To complete this job, you will need the following tools, equipment, and materials:

- Vehicle with a short to ground
- Appropriate service manual or electronic service information
- Standard tools
- Sealed beam headlight with fuse adapter
- Voltmeter (Fluke 88 or equivalent multimeter)

Instructions

In this job, you will be locating a short to ground. Shorts can damage vehicles, so use caution and follow instructor directions to create a short. Once a short is created, replace the blown fuse with a sealed beam headlight and associated wires. Use an ammeter to read amperage flow.

Since current is still flowing, this check can be made either by unplugging the shorted component or using an inductive ammeter.

 NOTE You cannot use a voltmeter to find the fault since the available voltage after the headlight bulb will be zero.

Read the job procedures, perform the tasks, and answer all questions. As you complete steps, you will be given instructions to either fill in measurements or perform certain tasks. When you reach a 🛑 sign, show your work to your instructor. Do not continue until you have instructor approval (instructor will initial job sheet).

 WARNING ⚠ Before performing this job, review all pertinent safety information in the text and discuss safety procedures with your instructor.

Procedures

Creating and Locating a Short

 Use all safety precautions and follow instructor directions on creating a short to ground.

1. Find a circuit with multiple connectors and unplug it.

 The turn signal circuit works well to make a short at the rear turning bulb.

2. Using a fuse adapter, connect the sealed beam headlight into the fuse location in place of the fuse. Note which circuit is controlled by the fuse that was replaced.

   _____

3. Record the following voltages:

   A. Voltage entering the bulb:

   _____

   B. Voltage leaving the bulb:

   _____

   C. What is a possible cause if the voltage coming out of the bulb is not zero or the bulb is dim?

   _____

   _____

   _____

4. Test and record the amperage flowing in the circuit after the sealed beam headlight.

   _____

 NOTE Use the above number as a guide to find the short, keeping in mind that there may be other active circuits in different parts of the motorcycle, so you will need to use this number to isolate the wires.

5. Locate the short and record amperage readings:

   A. Amperage flowing in the wire going into the short:

   _____

   B. Amperage flowing in the wire after the short:

   _____

 6. Be prepared to discuss with your instructor the process of finding the short using an ammeter.

Instructor's Initials: _____

Name _____

Unplugging to Isolate Short

> **NOTE**   Leave the sealed beam headlight installed in the fuse holder.

7. Using the wiring diagram for this circuit, find plugs that can be disconnected in this circuit.

8. Unplug the selected connector for this circuit. For example, if you have a short in the turn signal circuit, you can unplug the turn signal flasher. Did the light stay on or turn off?

_____   Stayed on

_____   Turned off

> **NOTE**   If the light stayed on, the short to ground is between the connector and fuse and you have not removed the path to ground. If the light turned off, you have removed the path to ground. Reconnect and move farther into the circuit.

 9. Discuss with your instructor whether or not you need to continue removing connectors and which circuit direction to go based on whether the light is on or off. Your instructor may direct you to go to the job wrap-up section at this time.

Instructor's Initials: _____

Continue to Unplug Connectors

10. After discussing procedures with your instructor, continue to unplug connectors along the circuit until you have found the connector where the light stays on and the next connector where the light goes out. The short to ground is between those two connectors.

11. Write down the location of the short to ground:

_____

 12. Discuss with your instructor the process you took to find the short or any difficulty you had finding the short.

Instructor's Initials: _____

Job Wrap Up

13. Return all tools and materials to the proper storage areas and clean up your work area.

Final Assessment

_____ 1. What causes a short to ground?
- A. Continuity to ground after a load.
- B. Continuity to ground before a load.
- C. Continuity to ground in a load.
- D. Both B and C.

_____ 2. Unplugging connectors when looking for a short removes the _____ path.
- A. load
- B. power
- C. ground
- D. switch

_____ 3. Two technicians are discussing finding shorts. Technician A says that, if the sealed beam does not light, there is no short. Technician B says, if the sealed beam is dim, there is no short. Who is correct?
- A. A only.
- B. B only.
- C. Both A and B.
- D. Neither A nor B.

_____ 4. Two technicians are discussing finding shorts. Technician A says an ammeter is helpful when there are only a few connectors. Technician B says that a low amp ammeter can be used to hook around wires easily when there is no convenient connector. Who is correct?
- A. A only.
- B. B only.
- C. Both A and B.
- D. Neither A nor B.

_____ 5. *True or False?* Shorts to ground can be found using the same procedures used to find shorts to power.

Final Instructor Approval: _____

Name _____ Date _____ Class _____

Job 15-5

Replacing Electrical Components

Introduction

Technicians remove and reinstall bulbs, relays, switches, and other motorcycle electrical components on almost every machine they service. Knowing how to find and use parts-location diagrams and wiring diagrams is imperative for motorcycle technicians who want to become efficient at working on bikes.

This job will allow you to become familiar with methods of replacing motorcycle components.

Objective

After successfully completing this job, you will be able to locate and remove a variety of electrical components from a motorcycle.

Materials and Equipment

To complete this job, you will need the following tools, equipment, and materials:

- Dirt bike
- Sport bike
- Cruiser
- Appropriate service manual or electronic service information
- Hand tools as needed

Instructions

Use the service manual parts-location diagrams and wiring diagrams to locate components. Using the wiring diagram will help narrow your search by showing the color of wires leading to the component.

Read the job procedures, perform the tasks, and answer all questions. As you complete steps, you will be given instructions to either fill in measurements or perform certain tasks. When you reach a sign, show your work to your instructor. Do not continue until you have instructor approval (instructor will initial job sheet).

> **WARNING** ⚠️ Before performing this job, review all pertinent safety information in the textbook and discuss safety procedures with your instructor.

Procedures

Vehicle 1—Dirt Bike

1. Use wiring diagrams and parts-location diagrams to locate the components listed below and fill out the chart with the information requested.

Component	General Location	Number of Wires	Color of Wires
Headlight			
Front Marker Bulbs			
Rear Turn Bulbs			
Horn			
Turn Signal Flasher/Relay			
Starter Relay/High Amp Switch			
Horn Switch			
Turn Signal Fuse			
Ignition Switch			

2. Remove each listed component.

 3. Show your instructor the components you removed and discuss any issues you encountered during the removal process.

Instructor's Initials: _____

Vehicle 2—Sport Bike

4. Use wiring diagrams and parts-location diagrams to locate the components listed below and fill out the chart with the information requested.

Component	General Location	Number of Wires	Color of Wires
Headlight			
Front Marker Bulbs			
Rear Turn Bulbs			
Horn			
Turn Signal Flasher/Relay			
Starter Relay/High Amp Switch			
Horn Switch			
Turn Signal Fuse			
Ignition Switch			

Name _____

   5. Remove each listed component.

 6. Show your instructor the components you removed and discuss any issues you encountered during the removal process.

Instructor's Initials: _____

Vehicle 3—Cruiser

   7. Use wiring diagrams and parts-location diagrams to locate the components listed below and fill out the chart with the information requested.

Component	General Location	Number of Wires	Color of Wires
Headlight			
Front Marker Bulbs			
Rear Turn Bulbs			
Horn			
Turn Signal Flasher/Relay			
Starter Relay/High Amp Switch			
Horn Switch			
Turn Signal Fuse			
Ignition Switch			

   8. Remove each listed component.

 9. Show your instructor the components you removed and discuss any issues you encountered during the removal process.

Instructor's Initials: _____

Job Wrap Up

   10. Reinstall all removed components.

   11. Return all tools and materials to the proper storage areas and clean up your work area.

Final Assessment

_____ 1. The starter relay has a high amperage switch and a(n) _____.
   A. low amperage switch
   B. electromagnet
   C. light bulb
   D. fuse

_____ 2. When halogen bulbs are removed, what must the technician do?
   A. Dispose of the bulb as hazardous waste.
   B. Test the bulb on the bench first.
   C. Not touch the bulb with their bare hands.
   D. Install the bulbs with the lights turned on.

_____ 3. A bulb and socket are found to be corroded. What should the technician do to correct the problem?
   A. Replace the socket and the bulb.
   B. Replace the socket and re-use the bulb.
   C. Clean the socket and re-use the bulb.
   D. Clean the socket and install a new bulb.

_____ 4. When one turn signal bulb is replaced, what other steps should the technician take?
   A. Replace the headlight as well.
   B. Test the remaining bulbs.
   C. Replace the other turn signal bulbs.
   D. Swap the bulbs from front to rear.

_____ 5. The starter high-amperage relay usually contains which of the following additional parts?
   A. Starter.
   B. Main fuse.
   C. Ignition switch.
   D. Turn signal relay.

Final Instructor Approval: _____

Name _____ Date _____ Class _____

Job 15-6

Testing Starters and Starter Circuits

Introduction

Starter diagnosis is an advanced skill requiring knowledge of low and high amperage circuits and how amperage is affected by high resistance and mechanical failure. Starter operation can be affected by high resistance in the engine or starter drive mechanism, or by bad starter cable connections. A bad battery can also affect starter operation.

Diagnosing an inoperative starter can be fairly straightforward. Diagnosing a slow cranking starter takes more knowledge and practice.

Objective

After successfully completing this job, you will be able to test starters and starter circuits.

Materials and Equipment

To complete this job, you will need the following tools, equipment, and materials:

- Starter that is constantly engaged with reduction gears—typical motorcycle starter
- Appropriate service manual or electronic service information
- Fluke 88 or comparable multimeter
- Ammeter capable of high amperage readings or an amp clamp to fit multimeter

Instructions

Consult the service manual for diagnostic procedures. Fill in the charts in this job and think of the relationships between voltage and amperage while the starter is cranking. In this job you will be checking the "big four" of starting system diagnosis:

- Battery open circuit voltage
- Battery loaded voltage
- Starter voltage drop
- Amperage draw

Read the job procedures, perform the tasks, and answer all questions. As you complete steps, you will be given instructions to either fill in measurements or perform certain tasks. When you reach a sign, show your work to your instructor. Do not continue until you have instructor approval (instructor will initial job sheet).

> **WARNING** ⚠️ Before performing this job, review all pertinent safety information in the text and discuss safety procedures with your instructor.

Procedures

Big Four Measurements

1. Measure battery voltage with no electrical loads and record.

2. Disable the ignition to prevent engine starting.

3. Attach the voltage and amperage testing devices.

4. With the ignition disabled, crank the engine and perform the following tests:

> **WARNING** ⚠ Do not crank for more than ten seconds at a time and allow the starter to cool off for two minutes before cranking again.

> **NOTE** ⚙ Make the following measurements (*A*, *B*, and *C*) at the same time to catch intermittent issues that may occur with reduction gears and with faulty one-way clutch mechanisms.

   A. Battery voltage while cranking (volts):

   _____

   B. Voltage drop at starter motor (volts):

   > **NOTE** ⚙ The readings for *A* and *B* should match. If the readings are different, state a possible cause.

   _____

   _____

   _____

   C. Measure the current draw of the starter while cranking (amps):

   _____

5. Remove the spark plugs from the engine.

6. Crank the engine and measure the current draw of the starter while cranking again (amps):

   _____

7. Compare the current draw reading to the previous reading in Step 4. Write a brief explanation of the change in amperage readings.

   _____

   _____

   _____

8. Reinstall the spark plugs.

🛑 9. Discuss your findings with your instructor.

Instructor's Initials: _____

Name _____

Test Control (Relay) Circuit

10. Crank the engine and observe the available voltage at the starter relay coil (volts).

_____

What is a possible cause of low voltage in this circuit?

_____

_____

Measure Voltage Drop on Starter Positive Side

11. Crank the engine while measuring voltage across the connections shown in the chart. Record the measurements.

Voltage Drop Component	Measurement
Battery positive post to positive post on starter	
Battery positive post to battery positive clamp	
Battery positive clamp to positive side of starter relay switch	
Starter relay (solenoid) switch	
Starter relay load side to starter motor	

🛑 12. Discuss your findings with your instructor.

Instructor's Initials: _____

Measure Voltage Drop on Starter Negative (Ground) Side

13. Crank the engine while measuring voltage across the connections shown in the chart. Record the measurements.

Voltage Drop Component	Measurement
Battery negative post to starter housing	
Battery negative clamp to battery negative post	
Battery negative cable	
Battery negative cable bolt on frame to starter housing	

🛑 14. Discuss your findings with your instructor.

Instructor's Initials: _____

Remove and Replace Starter Motor

15. Using service manual instructions, remove the starter motor.

16. Bench test the starter motor for current draw (amps):

_____

CAUTION ⚠	Do not take the starter apart.

17. Remove the starter relay/solenoid.

18. Bench test the starter relay/solenoid using a battery and test light connected through the switch to simulate the starter load.

(STOP) 19. Discuss your findings with your instructor.

Instructor's Initials: _____

20. Reinstall the relay/solenoid on the starter.

21. Reinstall the starter on the engine.

22. Retest the starter for proper operation and make sure the vehicle can be started.

(STOP) 23. Discuss your findings with your instructor.

Instructor's Initials: _____

Job Wrap Up

24. Return all tools and materials to the proper storage areas and clean up your work area.

Final Assessment

_____ 1. The starting system has two electrical circuits. They are the _____ and _____.
A. motor circuit, ignition circuit
B. insulated circuit, power circuit
C. motor circuit, control circuit
D. ground circuit, control circuit

_____ 2. The following big four measurements were made. Choose the best answer based on the readings.

	Measurement
Battery Open Circuit	11.4
Battery Loaded	7.1
Starter Voltage Drop	7.1
Amperage Draw	35

A. Faulty battery.
B. Faulty starter or high engine resistance.
C. Faulty wires.
D. Both A and B.

Name _____

_____ 3. The following big four measurements were made. Choose the best answer based on the readings.

	Measurement
Battery Open Circuit	12.6
Battery Loaded	8.5
Starter Voltage Drop	8.5
Amperage Draw	400

  A. Faulty battery.
  B. Faulty starter or high engine resistance.
  C. Faulty wires.
  D. Defective starter relay.

_____ 4. The following big four measurements were made. Choose the best answer based on the readings.

	Measurement
Battery Open Circuit	12.6
Battery Loaded	10.1
Starter Voltage Drop	7.2
Amperage Draw	95

  A. Faulty battery.
  B. Faulty starter or high engine resistance.
  C. Faulty wires.
  D. Broken starter drive clutch.

_____ 5. When an engine starts, the pinion gear is disconnected from the starter by the _____.
  A. magnetic switch
  B. plunger
  C. one-way clutch
  D. switch return spring

Final Instructor Approval: _____

Notes

Name _____ Date _____ Class _____

Job 15-7

Aiming Headlights

Introduction

Headlight aiming is a common task performed for new vehicle delivery, used vehicle inspection, and after accident repair. There are a wide variety of mechanisms used for aiming headlights.

Objective

After successfully completing this job, you will be able to aim a headlight.

Materials and Equipment

To complete this job, you will need the following tools, equipment, and materials:

- Motorcycle or other vehicle
- Appropriate service manual or electronic service information
- Hand tools as needed

Instructions

Usually there are two adjustments for each bulb, horizontal and vertical. Concentrate on aiming the low beam. Let the high beams fall where they will as there should be no oncoming traffic when the high beams are being used.

Read the job procedures, perform the tasks, and answer all questions. As you complete steps, you will be given instructions to either fill in measurements or perform certain tasks. When you reach a (STOP) sign, show your work to your instructor. Do not continue until you have instructor approval (instructor will initial job sheet).

> **WARNING**  Before performing this job, review all pertinent safety information in the text and discuss safety procedures with your instructor.

Procedures

Aiming Headlights

1. Find the headlight aiming procedure in the service manual and answer the following questions:

   A. What distance should the motorcycle be from the wall you are shining the lights on?

   _____

   B. Should a rider be on the bike when the lights are being aimed?

   _____

   C. Should the bike be held vertical?

   _____

   D. How many inches below or above vertical is the main part of the beam supposed to land?

   _____

2. Using the service manual procedure, adjust the headlights.

 3. Discuss your adjustment with your instructor. Be prepared to show your instructor vertical and horizontal adjustments.

Instructor's Initials: _____

Job Wrap Up

4. Return all tools and materials to the proper storage areas and clean up your work area.

Final Assessment

_____ 1. Two technicians are discussing headlight aiming. Technician A says that the vehicle must be placed a specific distance from the wall to measure the headlight aim. Technician B says that the vehicle must be at a specific height to measure the headlight aim. Who is correct?
   A. A only.
   B. B only.
   C. Both A and B.
   D. Neither A nor B.

_____ 2. Two technicians are discussing headlight aiming. Technician A says to concentrate on aiming the low beams. Technician B says to concentrate on aiming the high beams. Who is correct?
   A. A only.
   B. B only.
   C. Both A and B.
   D. Neither A nor B.

_____ 3. Two technicians are discussing headlight aiming. Technician A says that some motorcycles have bubbles for headlight aim. Technician B says that some motorcycle headlights are nonadjustable. Who is correct?
   A. A only.
   B. B only.
   C. Both A and B.
   D. Neither A nor B.

_____ 4. A headlight does not adjust when the adjusters are moved. Technician A says something in the aiming mechanism is damaged or disconnected. Technician B says this is normal on some motorcycles. Who is correct?
   A. A only.
   B. B only.
   C. Both A and B.
   D. Neither A nor B.

_____ 5. Technician A says proper headlight aiming is performed to improve the vision of the rider. Technician B says proper headlight aiming is performed to improve the vision of oncoming drivers. Who is correct?
   A. A only.
   B. B only.
   C. Both A and B.
   D. Neither A nor B.

Final Instructor Approval: _____

CHAPTER 16

Wheels and Tires

Chapter 16 Quiz

After studying Chapter 16 in the Motorcycles: Fundamentals, Service, Repair textbook, answer the following questions.

_____ 1. The _____ of a wire wheel contains the wheel bearings and inner end of the spokes.

_____ 2. *True or False?* The hub, axle, and motorcycle's weight are supported by the lower spokes.

_____ 3. Which spoke pattern is shown in the following illustration?
  A. Cross-zero pattern.
  B. Cross-one pattern.
  C. Cross-two pattern
  D. Cross-three pattern.

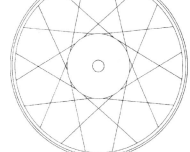

Goodheart-Willcox Publisher

_____ 4. Spokes are two different lengths on the same wheel with a(n) _____ hub.

_____ 5. A(n) _____ wheel is poured into a mold and is all one piece to make it very strong.

_____ 6. A(n) _____ wheel consists of separate parts fastened together.

_____ 7. An axle goes through the wheel _____ and connects the wheel assembly to either the rear swingarm or the front fork.

_____ 8. A(n) _____ is needed between bearings to prevent side loading when the axle is tightened.

_____ 9. *True or False?* In order to check a wheel for binding and for loose wheel bearings, technicians must manipulate the wheel with their hands.

_____ 10. When a spoke is tapped with a spoke wrench, the technician will hear _____ if the spoke is properly adjusted.
  A. a ring
  B. a vibrating tone
  C. a dull tone
  D. no sound

_____ 11. *True or False?* Replacing a dented rim on a wire wheel requires wheel truing.

_____ 12. When lacing a symmetrical wheel, the last step is to _____ the spokes to true the wheel.

_____ 13. Up-and-down movement of the rim is called _____ runout.
    A. lateral
    B. vertical
    C. symmetrical
    D. radial

_____ 14. The three types of motorcycle tires used today are bias-ply, bias-belted, and _____.

_____ 15. Tire size is determined by tire width at its widest point and the rim _____.

_____ 16. A maximum sustained speed limit of 150 mph (240 km/h) is indicated in a tire marking by the _____.
    A. number *150/240*
    B. letter *H*
    C. letter-number combination *H-150*
    D. letter *V*

_____ 17. Overinflation of tires causes _____.
    A. the cord layers to separate
    B. the tread to wear at its center
    C. superior riding comfort
    D. heat due to sidewall bending

_____ 18. To dismount a tire, the technician unscrews and removes the _____ from the valve stem.

_____ 19. When removing a tire, lubricate the rim with a rubber lubricant or _____ in order to aid removal and prevent damage.

_____ 20. *True or False?* Most ATV tires can be removed from either side of the rim.

_____ 21. When a tire is installed, the balance dot should align with the _____.

_____ 22. Before a tube tire is inflated, the valve stem must be _____.

_____ 23. *True or False?* When installing a tubeless tire, the tire should be installed on the rim at a point where the rim shoulder width is narrowest.

_____ 24. Before mounting a tubeless tire on the wheel, the tire bead seat should be lubricated with _____ water or a tire lubricant.

_____ 25. *True or False?* A tubeless tire with 3/8″ of damage should be repaired by a professional tire repair shop.

_____ 26. All of the following statements about using a bubble balancer are true, *except*:
    A. the bubble indicates the light side of the wheel.
    B. the wheel is suspended horizontally.
    C. the wheel is spun rapidly.
    D. lead weights are added until the bubble is centered.

Name _____

_____ 27. *True or False?* Electronic wheel balancers can be used for both static and dynamic balancing.

_____ 28. Which of the following problems can be caused by a bent rim?

    A. Uneven tire wear.

    B. Front wheel wobbling.

    C. Hard steering.

    D. Wheel turns hard.

Notes

Name _____ Date _____ Class _____

Job 16-1

Reading Tire Sidewall Information

Introduction

Selling tires is an everyday operation for a power sports store and all personnel must be able to "talk tires." Identifying the correct tires for vehicles is a critical skill for motorcycle technicians to ensure rider safety and to increase store profitability.

The technician should be able to verify that the machine has the proper tires.

Objective

After successfully completing this job, you will be able to identify motorcycle tires based on sidewall information.

Materials and Equipment

To complete this job, you will need the following tools, equipment, and materials:

- Motorcycles or other vehicles
- Appropriate service manual or electronic service information

Instructions

In this job, you will identify the type and brand of tires on motorcycles or other vehicles and decipher codes found on the tire sidewall.

Read the job procedures, perform the tasks, and answer all questions. As you complete steps, you will be given instructions to either fill in measurements or perform certain tasks. When you reach a 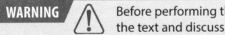 sign, show your work to your instructor. Do not continue until you have instructor approval (instructor will initial job sheet).

| WARNING | ⚠ | Before performing this job, review all pertinent safety information in the text and discuss safety procedures with your instructor. |

Procedures

Tire Identification

Vehicle One (Year/Make/Model)

_____

1. Inspect the tire sidewall(s) and locate the information required to fill out the chart below. Consult the vehicle and tire manufacturer information as necessary.

   Front tire(s):

Brand of Tire	
DOT Date of Construction	
Front or Rear	
Wheel Diameter	
Tread Width	
Aspect Ratio	
Tire Construction	
Load Rating	
Speed Rating	
Tube or Tubeless	
If tube, what type/direction of valve stem	

   Rear tire(s):

Brand of Tire	
DOT Date of Construction	
Front or Rear	
Wheel Diameter	
Tread Width	
Aspect Ratio	
Tire Construction	
Load Rating	
Speed Rating	
Tube or Tubeless	
If tube, what type/direction of valve stem	

2. **STOP** Determine the proper size tires for this vehicle. The information may be on a sticker on the vehicle or in the service manual. Discuss your findings with your instructor.

Instructor's Initials: _____

Name _____

Vehicle Two (Year/Make/Model)

_____

3. Inspect the tire sidewall(s) and locate the information required to fill out the chart below. Consult the vehicle and tire manufacturer information as necessary.

Front tire(s):

Brand of Tire	
DOT Date of Construction	
Front or Rear	
Wheel Diameter	
Tread Width	
Aspect Ratio	
Tire Construction	
Load Rating	
Speed Rating	
Tube or Tubeless	
If tube, what type/direction of valve stem	

Rear tire(s):

Brand of Tire	
DOT Date of Construction	
Front or Rear	
Wheel Diameter	
Tread Width	
Aspect Ratio	
Tire Construction	
Load Rating	
Speed Rating	
Tube or Tubeless	
If tube, what type/direction of valve stem	

4. Determine the proper size tires for this vehicle. The information may be on a sticker on the vehicle or in the service manual. Discuss your findings with your instructor.

Instructor's Initials: _____

Vehicle Three (Year/Make/Model)

5. Inspect the tire sidewall(s) and locate the information required to fill out the chart below. Consult the vehicle and tire manufacturer information as necessary.

Front tire(s):

Brand of Tire	
DOT Date of Construction	
Front or Rear	
Wheel Diameter	
Tread Width	
Aspect Ratio	
Tire Construction	
Load Rating	
Speed Rating	
Tube or Tubeless	
If tube, what type/direction of valve stem	

Rear tire(s):

Brand of Tire	
DOT Date of Construction	
Front or Rear	
Wheel Diameter	
Tread Width	
Aspect Ratio	
Tire Construction	
Load Rating	
Speed Rating	
Tube or Tubeless	
If tube, what type/direction of valve stem	

 6. Determine the proper size tires for this vehicle. The information may be on a sticker on the vehicle or in the service manual. Discuss your findings with your instructor.

Instructor's Initials: _____

Job Wrap Up

7. Return all tools and materials to the proper storage areas and clean up your work area.

Name _____

Final Assessment

_____ 1. A brand-new tire comes with a small circle painted on the sidewall. Technician A says that the circle is to help balance the wheel and tire. Technician B says that the circle indicates a tube tire that does not require balancing. Who is correct?

A. A only.

B. B only.

C. Both A and B.

D. Neither A nor B.

_____ 2. Technician A says to always make sure that a new tire is installed in the proper direction. Technician B says to extend the life of the tire, reverse the installed direction after 10,000 miles. Who is correct?

A. A only.

B. B only.

C. Both A and B.

D. Neither A nor B.

_____ 3. Two technicians are discussing tires. Technician A says different brands of the same size can actually be differently sized. Technician B says different brands of the same size can have different traction patterns. Who is correct?

A. A only.

B. B only.

C. Both A and B.

D. Neither A nor B.

_____ 4. Two technicians are discussing tires. Technician A says that temperature can affect tire pressure. Technician B says that tread wear can affect tire pressure. Who is correct?

A. A only.

B. B only.

C. Both A and B.

D. Neither A nor B.

_____ 5. Two technicians are discussing tires. Technician A says that nitrogen is better than air because it performs better in cold weather. Technician B says that nitrogen is not commonly used in motorcycle tires. Who is correct?

A. A only.

B. B only.

C. Both A and B.

D. Neither A nor B.

Final Instructor Approval: _____

Notes

Name _____ Date _____ Class _____

Job 16-2

Checking Tire Pressure

Introduction
Checking tire pressure is critical before every ride and can drastically change performance of any type of motorcycle. Altitude can impact tire pressure. There are many different types of tire gauges. Tire gauges should be checked often to make sure that they remain accurate.

Objective
After successfully completing this job, you will be able to check tire pressure properly.

Materials and Equipment
To complete this job, you will need the following tools, equipment, and materials:
- Four motorcycles (two street bikes and two dirt bikes)
- Appropriate service manual or electronic service information
- Multiple tire pressure gauges (preferably different types)

Instructions
In this job, you will be checking your tire pressure gauge against other gauges and checking tire pressure in several tires.

As you complete steps, you will be given instructions to either fill in measurements or perform certain tasks. When you reach a (STOP) sign, show your work to your instructor. Do not continue until you have instructor approval (instructor will initial job sheet).

> **WARNING** ⚠ Before performing this job, review all pertinent safety information in the text and discuss safety procedures with your instructor.

Procedures

Test Tire Pressure Gauge

1. Fill in the chart with the results of checking several different gauges.

Gauge	Pressure	Difference from your gauge
Your Gauge		—
Gauge 2		
Gauge 3		
Gauge 4		

Check Tire Air Pressure

2. Check tire pressures of four different vehicles and fill in the charts for each vehicle. Two should be street bikes and two should be dirt bikes.

Vehicle One (Year/Make/Model)

Tire	Actual	Specification	Max. psi
Front			
Rear			

Vehicle Two (Year/Make/Model)

Tire	Actual	Specification	Max. psi
Front			
Rear			

Vehicle Three (Year/Make/Model)

Tire	Actual	Specification	Max. psi
Front			
Rear			

Vehicle Four (Year/Make/Model)

Tire	Actual	Specification	Max. psi
Front			
Rear			

STOP 3. Discuss your findings with your instructor.

Instructor's Initials: _____

Job Wrap Up

4. Return all tools and materials to the proper storage areas and clean up your work area.

Name _____

Final Assessment

_____ 1. Two technicians are discussing tire pressure. Technician A says that low tire pressure can cause excessive tire wear. Technician B says high tire pressure can cause excessive tire wear. Who is correct?

    A. A only.

    B. B only.

    C. Both A and B.

    D. Neither A nor B.

_____ 2. Two technicians are discussing tire pressure. Technician A says that low tire pressure can cause handling problems. Technician B says that high tire pressure can cause handling problems. Who is correct?

    A. A only.

    B. B only.

    C. Both A and B.

    D. Neither A nor B.

_____ 3. Two technicians are discussing tire pressure. Technician A says the proper tire pressure is molded into the sidewall of the tire. Technician B says the maximum tire pressure when loaded is molded into the sidewall of the tire. Who is correct?

    A. A only.

    B. B only.

    C. Both A and B.

    D. Neither A nor B.

_____ 4. Two technicians are discussing tire pressure. Technician A says that some gauges with fluid can compensate for altitude. Technician B says that altitude changes tire pressure only below certain temperatures. Who is correct?

    A. A only.

    B. B only.

    C. Both A and B.

    D. Neither A nor B.

_____ 5. Two technicians are discussing tire pressure. Technician A says that temperature can affect tire pressure. Technician B says to check tires when they are cold before riding. Who is correct?

    A. A only.

    B. B only.

    C. Both A and B.

    D. Neither A nor B.

Final Instructor Approval: _____

Notes

Name _____ Date _____ Class _____

Job 16-3

Using a Tire Machine

Introduction

Tire maintenance is one of the most common motorsports shop tasks. Replacing tires with a tire machine is a mandatory task for a motorcycle technician. There are several tire variations that you will have to deal with, including tires with and without tubes.

Objective

After successfully completing this job, you will be able to remove and replace tires using a tire machine.

Materials and Equipment

To complete this job, you will need the following tools, equipment, and materials:

- Wheel and tire assembly (preferably the first tire serviced should be a solid wheel and tubeless tire)
- Appropriate service manual or electronic service information
- Tire machine

Instructions

In this job, you will be removing and replacing tires on a wheel using a tire machine. Do not use the machine until you receive operating instructions. You will be practicing until you are proficient, not just performing the task one time.

As you complete steps, you will be given instructions to either fill in measurements or perform certain tasks. When you reach a sign, show your work to your instructor. Do not continue until you have instructor approval (instructor will initial job sheet).

| **WARNING** | ⚠ | Before performing this job, review all pertinent safety information in the text and discuss safety procedures with your instructor. |

Procedures

Learning the Machine

1. Find and operate the following levers and controls, checking off as you locate them.

_____   Bead breaker

_____   Table rotator

_____   Rim clamp

_____   Tire pressure and bead setting controls

Removing and Installing Tubeless Tire

2. Remove the tire from the rim, checking off each task listed as it is completed.

CAUTION ⚠	If the tire gets stuck, stop and ask your instructor for help. Tires should never get stuck or tear when done properly.

WARNING ⚠	Keep your hands away from moving parts.

_____ Make sure that you are using the proper PPE.

_____ Remove the valve core.

_____ Break the bead (lubricating the bead as you break it).

_____ Turn the tire and wheel around and break the bead on the other side.

_____ Remove the tire top bead.

_____ Remove the tire bottom bead.

_____ Clean and inspect the wheel (on customer wheels you would replace the valve stem at this point).

_____ Make sure the tire is facing the correct direction.

_____ Lubricate the bead.

_____ Install the bottom bead.

_____ Install the top bead.

_____ Rotate the tire until the balancing dot lines up with the valve.

_____ Remove tire and wheel from machine.

_____ Set the bead using high air pressure.

_____ Install the valve core.

_____ Set the tire pressure to proper pressure.

_____ Clean the assembly of any tire lube and remove any stickers.

3. Repeat the procedures in Step 2 until you are comfortable with the process.

🛑 4. Demonstrate the entire procedure to your instructor.

Instructor's Initials: _____

Name _____

Removing and Installing Tube-type Tire

    5. Check off the task as it is completed.

> **CAUTION** ⚠ If the tire gets stuck, stop and ask your instructor for help. Tires should never get stuck or tear when done properly.

> **WARNING** ⚠ Keep your hands away from moving parts.

_____   Make sure that you are using the proper PPE.

_____   Remove the valve core.

_____   Break the bead (lubricating the bead as you break it).

_____   Turn the tire and wheel around and break the bead on the other side.

_____   Remove the tire top bead.

_____   Remove the tube.

_____   Remove the tire bottom bead.

_____   Clean and inspect the wheel (on a customer wheel you would replace the valve stem at this point).

🛑 > **NOTE** ⚙ At this point, stop and discuss with your instructor the best strategy for installing the tube. Some techs prefer to install one bead first and then feed the tube in. Some techs prefer to install the tube and then fold it over the wheel and work around the tube (similar to working around a tire pressure sensor).

_____   Make sure the tire is facing the correct direction.

_____   Lubricate the bead.

_____   Install the bottom bead.

_____   Install the top bead.

_____   Rotate the tire for balancing dot to line up.

_____   Remove tire and wheel from machine.

_____   Set the bead using high air pressure.

_____   Install the valve core.

_____   Set the tire pressure to proper pressure.

_____   Clean the assembly of any tire lube and remove any stickers.

    6. Repeat the procedures in Step 5 until you are comfortable with the process.

🛑   7. Demonstrate the entire procedure to your instructor.

Instructor's Initials: _____

Job Wrap Up

8. Return all tools and materials to the proper storage areas and clean up your work area.

Final Assessment

_____ 1. Two technicians are discussing tire removal and installation. Technician A says that motorcycle tires are designated front or rear. Technician B says that tires can be used on either the front or rear as long as the size is right. Who is correct?

A. A only.

B. B only.

C. Both A and B.

D. Neither A nor B.

_____ 2. Two technicians are discussing tire removal and installation. Technician A says that breaking the bead before removing the valve core can save time. Technician B says breaking the bead before removing the valve core can be dangerous. Who is correct?

A. A only.

B. B only.

C. Both A and B.

D. Neither A nor B.

_____ 3. Two technicians are discussing tire removal and installation. Technician A says that tire lube is only used on disassembly. Technician B says that tire lube is only used on assembly. Who is correct?

A. A only.

B. B only.

C. Both A and B.

D. Neither A nor B.

_____ 4. Two technicians are discussing tire removal and installation. Technician A says that the drop center of the wheel is used for removing tires. Technician B says that the drop center of the wheel is used for installing tires. Who is correct?

A. A only.

B. B only.

C. Both A and B.

D. Neither A nor B.

_____ 5. Two technicians are discussing tire balancing. Technician A says that lining up the alignment dot with the valve stem means that the tire is balanced. Technician B says lining up the alignment dot with the valve stem will make it easier to balance. Who is correct?

A. A only.

B. B only.

C. Both A and B.

D. Neither A nor B.

Final Instructor Approval: _____

Name _____ Date _____ Class _____

Job 16-4

Changing Dirt Bike Tires with Spoons

Introduction

Replacing dirt bike tires with spoons is a mandatory task for a motorcycle technician. There are several tire replacement variations you will have to master, including a variety of rim locks, different styles of bead savers, and tubeless tires.

Objective

After successfully completing this job, you will be able to remove and replace tires using tire spoons.

Materials and Equipment

To complete this job, you will need the following tools, equipment, and materials:

- Dirt bike wheel and tire
- Appropriate service manual or electronic service information
- Tire stand and spoons

Instructions

In this job, you will be removing and replacing tires on a wheel using tire spoons. Do not attempt this job until you have had a tutorial on spoons and working with dirt bike tires. You will be practicing until you are proficient, not just performing the task one time.

As you complete steps, you will be given instructions to either fill in measurements or perform certain tasks. When you reach a sign, show your work to your instructor. Do not continue until you have instructor approval (instructor will initial job sheet).

> **WARNING** ⚠️ Before performing this job, review all pertinent safety information in the text and discuss safety procedures with your instructor.

Procedures

Removing Tire

1. Remove the tire from the rim, checking off each task listed as it is completed.

> **CAUTION** ⚠ If the tire gets stuck, stop and ask your instructor for help. Tires should never get stuck or tear when done properly.

> **WARNING** ⚠ Keep your hands away from moving parts.

_____ Make sure that you are using the proper PPE.

_____ Remove the valve core.

_____ Loosen the bead locks.

_____ Break the bead, lubricating the bead as you break it.

_____ Turn the tire and wheel around and break the bead on the other side.

_____ Remove the tire top bead.

_____ Remove the tube, if used.

_____ Remove the bead lock.

_____ Remove the tire bottom bead.

_____ Clean and inspect the wheel (on customer wheels you would replace the rim strap at this point).

_____ Lubricate the bead.

_____ Install the bottom bead.

_____ Install the bead lock.

_____ Install the tube, if used.

_____ Install the top bead.

_____ Snug up the bead lock.

_____ Set the bead using high air pressure.

_____ Recheck bead lock and valve stem nut torque.

_____ Install the valve core.

_____ Set the tire pressure to proper pressure.

_____ Clean the assembly of any tire lube and remove any stickers.

2. Repeat the procedures in Step 1 until you are comfortable with the process.

🛑 3. Demonstrate the entire procedure to your instructor.

Instructor's Initials: _____

Name _____

Job Wrap Up

4. Return all tools and materials to the proper storage areas and clean up your work area.

Final Assessment

_____ 1. Two technicians are discussing dirt bike tire removal. Technician A says that you must break the tire bead using a machine. Technician B says you must break the tire bead with your hands to not damage the rim. Who is correct?

A. A only.

B. B only.

C. Both A and B.

D. Neither A nor B.

_____ 2. Two technicians are discussing changing tires. Technician A says that some wheels have two rim locks. Technician B says to install the rim lock after the tube. Who is correct?

A. A only.

B. B only.

C. Both A and B.

D. Neither A nor B.

_____ 3. Two technicians are discussing changing tires. Technician A says to slightly inflate the tube prior to installation. Technician B says to install the tube with no air in it. Who is correct?

A. A only.

B. B only.

C. Both A and B.

D. Neither A nor B.

_____ 4. Two technicians are discussing changing tires. Technician A says that tubes can be repaired for a customer. Technician B says that tubes should only be repaired in an emergency on the trail. Who is correct?

A. A only.

B. B only.

C. Both A and B.

D. Neither A nor B.

_____ 5. Two technicians are discussing changing tires. Technician A says that tubes can be reused with new tires. Technician B says a rim lock can be reused with new tires. Who is correct?

A. A only.

B. B only.

C. Both A and B.

D. Neither A nor B.

Final Instructor Approval: _____

Notes

CHAPTER 17 / Brakes

Chapter 17 Quiz

After studying Chapter 17 in the Motorcycles: Fundamentals, Service, Repair textbook, answer the following questions.

_____ 1. A brake applies _____ to a moving device to slow it down and bring it to a stop.

_____ 2. A(n) _____ brake system is operated by a rod or cable.

_____ 3. In a hydraulic brake system, fluid, pistons, and cylinders provide _____ for brake application.
  A. high pressure
  B. localized heat
  C. friction
  D. mechanical action

_____ 4. *True or False?* A hydraulic brake system is self-adjusting.

For questions 5–12, identify the components of a mechanical brake system shown in the following illustration.

_____ 5. Brake pedal

_____ 6. Drum

_____ 7. Cam arm

_____ 8. Brake operating rod

_____ 9. Return spring

_____ 10. Adjuster

_____ 11. Actuating cam

_____ 12. Torque arm

Goodheart-Willcox Publisher

For questions 13–19, match the name of each component in a hydraulic brake system with the phrase that describes it.

A. Brake lever

B. Master cylinder

C. Brake line

D. Stoplight switch

E. Brake pad

F. Caliper

G. Rotor

_____ 13. Transfers hydraulic pressure.

_____ 14. Friction device.

_____ 15. Clamps around the disc.

_____ 16. Pushes on master cylinder.

_____ 17. Attached to the wheel.

_____ 18. Controls the brake light.

_____ 19. Produces pressure.

_____ 20. In a hydraulic brake system, minimal _____ is maintained between the brake pad and brake disc when pressure is released.

_____ 21. In a drum brake system, one or two _____ cause shoes to expand against the inside of a brake drum.

_____ 22. In a disc brake system, a(n) _____ applies pressure to brake pads to slow or stop rotation of a disc attached to the wheel.

_____ 23. Two types of calipers found in disc brake systems are _____.
   A. leading and trailing
   B. single-piston and double-piston
   C. single-leading and double-leading
   D. linked and nonlinked

_____ 24. Which of the following statements is *true* of rear disc brakes?
   A. Rear disc brakes work differently than front disc brakes.
   B. Rear calipers are larger than front calipers.
   C. Rear calipers have fewer pistons than front calipers.
   D. All of the above.

_____ 25. *True or False?* A DOT 5 brake fluid has a lower boiling point than a DOT 3 brake fluid.

_____ 26. Which of the following statements about brake fluids is *true*?
   A. A DOT 4 system can be filled with DOT 3 brake fluid.
   B. DOT 5.1 fluids can be used in DOT 4 systems.
   C. DOT 5 is compatible with DOT 5.1.
   D. DOT 3 and DOT 4 brake fluids can be mixed.

_____ 27. Brake fluid can be contaminated by dust and by absorption of _____ from the air.

_____ 28. During installation of a drum brake on a front wheel, the _____ should be lubricated with grease.
   A. brake drum
   B. fork legs
   C. axle bolt
   D. axle shaft

Name _____

_____ 29. *True or False?* A technician centers the brake shoes by applying brakes before and during tightening of the axle.

_____ 30. One of the steps in replacing drum brake shoes is to lubricate the _____.
   A. actuating cam
   B. backing plate
   C. drum surface
   D. None of the above.

_____ 31. Forcing all of the air out of a hydraulic brake system is called _____ the brakes.

_____ 32. *True or False?* Air in the brake lines makes the brake lever or pedal feel hard or stiff.

_____ 33. Which of the following should *not* be allowed to contact the brake disc or pads?
   A. Brake fluid.
   B. Grease.
   C. Oil.
   D. All of the above.

_____ 34. The master cylinder piston should be measured with a(n) _____.
   A. telescoping gauge
   B. outside micrometer
   C. machinist's rule
   D. Both A and B.

_____ 35. *True or False?* Brake pads that are worn to the groove or line wear indicator must be replaced.

_____ 36. To remove the piston from a caliper, the technician uses _____.
   A. hydraulic pressure
   B. a special tool
   C. compressed air
   D. Either A or B.

_____ 37. When replacing brake pads, the technician should _____.
   A. replace the brake disc if it is scored
   B. pump the brake handle or pedal a few times
   C. reuse shims and pad springs
   D. Both A and B.

_____ 38. A(n) _____ braking system automatically applies both the front and rear brakes when the rear brakes are applied.

_____ 39. *True or False?* In a linked braking system, applying the foot brake pedal presses the front and rear calipers simultaneously.

For questions 40–49, identify the ABS system components indicated in the following illustration.

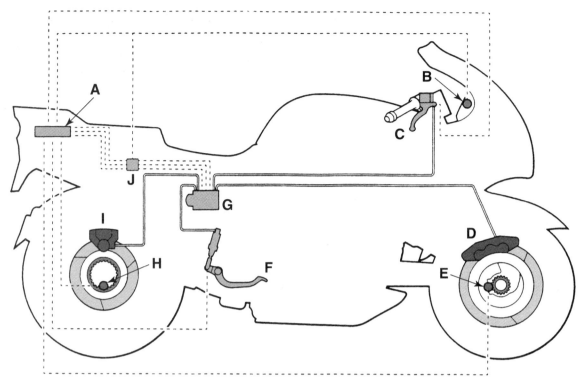

Yamaha Motor Corporation U.S.A.

A. ECM
B. Relay box
C. Brake caliper rear
D. Sensor ring rear

E. Hydraulic unit
F. Brake pedal
G. Sensor ring front
H. Brake caliper front

I. Front brake lever
J. Warning lamp

_____ 40. Relay box

_____ 41. Warning lamp

_____ 42. ECM

_____ 43. Brake pedal

_____ 44. Sensor ring (rear)

_____ 45. Front brake lever

_____ 46. Brake caliper (front)

_____ 47. Brake caliper (rear)

_____ 48. Sensor ring (front)

_____ 49. Hydraulic unit

_____ 50. All of the following statements about anti-lock braking systems are true, *except*:
    A. the hydraulic unit receives control signals from wheel speed sensors.
    B. the ABS warning light illuminates when the bike is first started.
    C. an ABS system reduces wheel lockup.
    D. wheel speed sensors monitor actual wheel speed.

Name _____ Date _____ Class _____

Job 17-1

Testing Brake Fluid

Introduction

Brake fluid must be inspected on a regular basis. Brake fluid absorbs moisture, lowering its boiling point. DOT 3 and 4 brake fluids get darker as they absorb moisture, so the color can be an indication that the fluid needs to be changed. There are several testers available. Some of them are strips that you dip in and out of the fluid and read. Other testers have probes that are dipped into the fluid and held until results are read. Exact procedures in this job are determined by which types of testers are available in the shop.

If, after checking fluid, there is any doubt about its condition, flush the brake system and add new fluid.

Objective

After successfully completing this job, you will be able to test brake fluid.

Materials and Equipment

To complete this job, you will need the following tools, equipment, and materials:
- Motorcycle or other vehicle with hydraulic brakes
- Appropriate service manual or electronic service information
- Brake fluid strips or tester

Instructions

In this job, you will use either brake fluid strips or a brake fluid tester to check the moisture content and boiling temperature of the brake fluid.

Read the job procedures, perform the tasks, and answer all questions. As you complete steps, you will be given instructions to either fill in measurements or perform certain tasks. When you reach a (STOP) sign, show your work to your instructor. Do not continue until you have instructor approval (instructor will initial job sheet).

> **WARNING** ⚠ Before performing this job, review all pertinent safety information in the text and discuss safety procedures with your instructor.

Procedures

Brake Fluid Testing

1. Remove the cover to the front master cylinder. It may be necessary to use an impact screwdriver to remove the screws holding the cover.

> **CAUTION** ⚠ Be careful using an impact screwdriver in this situation as the master cylinder could be damaged by excessive force.

2. Use brake fluid strips or a tester to determine fluid condition. Record your findings in the chart.

	Front Master Cylinder	Rear Master Cylinder
Color of Fluid		
Boiling Temperature		
Color of Test Strip		

🛑 3. Discuss your findings with your instructor.

Instructor's Initials: _____

Job Wrap Up

4. Return all tools and materials to the proper storage areas and clean up your work area.

Final Assessment

_____ 1. *True or False?* Brake fluid gets dark from exposure to air and aluminum.

_____ 2. *True or False?* Brake fluid should be changed when brake pads are changed.

_____ 3. *True or False?* Brake fluid should be changed every two years if not changed with brake pad replacement.

_____ 4. *True or False?* Contaminated brake fluid can cause caliper failure.

_____ 5. *True or False?* DOT 4 is compatible with DOT 5 brake fluid.

Final Instructor Approval: _____

Name _____ Date _____ Class _____

Job 17-2

Testing and Adjusting Brake Light Switches

Introduction

Brake light switch adjustment is critical for safety. Typically, the front brake switch is not adjustable and the rear brake is adjustable. The technician must make sure that the switch is adjusted properly and works without sticking.

Objective

After successfully completing this job, you will be able to test and adjust the brake light switch.

Materials and Equipment

To complete this job, you will need the following tools, equipment, and materials:
- Vehicle with adjustable brake light switch
- Appropriate service manual or electronic service information
- Voltmeter (Fluke 88 or equivalent multimeter)

Instructions

In this job, you will be measuring brake light switch adjustment and voltage output.

Read the job procedures, perform the tasks, and answer all questions. As you complete steps, you will be given instructions to either fill in measurements or perform certain tasks. When you reach a 🛑 sign, show your work to your instructor. Do not continue until you have instructor approval (instructor will initial job sheet).

> ⚠️ **WARNING** Before performing this job, review all pertinent safety information in the text and discuss safety procedures with your instructor.

Procedures

Inspect Brake Switch

Vehicle (Year/Make/Model)

_____

1. Determine whether the front brake switch has an adjustment.

   _____ Adjustable

   _____ Not adjustable

2. Determine whether the rear brake switch has an adjustment.

   _____ Adjustable

   _____ Not adjustable

3. Find the procedure for adjusting the brake light switch in the service manual. List the distance that the brake pedal should move before the brake light turns on.

Circle one: inches/millimeters

_____

4. Adjust the brake light switch until the light is on all the time.

5. Readjust the brake light switch to specification and retest.

(STOP) 6. Have your instructor check your work.

Instructor's Initials: _____

Job Wrap Up

7. Return all tools and materials to the proper storage areas and clean up your work area.

Final Assessment

_____ 1. *True or False?* Brake light switch adjustment is a critical safety adjustment.

_____ 2. *True or False?* Brake light switch adjustment can have an effect on cruise control operation.

_____ 3. *True or False?* The brake light switch can be adjusted to the point that the light never comes on.

_____ 4. Two technicians are testing a brake light switch. It has source voltage on both wires. Technician A says the switch is faulty. Technician B says the switch may be adjusted improperly. Who is correct?

A. A only.

B. B only.

C. Both A and B.

D. Neither A nor B.

_____ 5. Two technicians are testing a brake light switch. There are zero volts on both brake light switch wires. Technician A says the switch is faulty. Technician B says the switch may be improperly adjusted. Who is correct?

A. A only.

B. B only.

C. Both A and B.

D. Neither A nor B.

Final Instructor Approval: _____

Name _____ Date _____ Class _____

Job 17-3

Servicing Drum Brakes

Introduction

Motorcycle drum brakes are mechanically operated by a rod from the rear brake lever to the drum actuator. Hydraulic drum brakes are sometimes used on side-by-sides and larger vehicles. Drum brake service must be performed accurately and properly.

Objective

After successfully completing this job, you will be able to service drum brakes.

Materials and Equipment

To complete this job, you will need the following tools, equipment, and materials:

- Motorcycle with drum brakes
- Appropriate service manual or electronic service information
- Drum diameter measurement tool
- Brake tools as necessary
- Hand tools as necessary
- Anti-seize lubricant

Instructions

In this job, you will be disassembling the drum brakes, lubricating the proper points, re-assembling the brakes, and adjusting the pedal travel. Pay attention to adjustment methods. There are usually two adjustments, one on the pedal and one on the rod. Usually a pointer is installed on the rear mechanism to indicate that the brakes are properly adjusted.

Read the job procedures, perform the tasks, and answer all questions. As you complete steps, you will be given instructions to either fill in measurements or perform certain tasks. When you reach a sign, show your work to your instructor. Do not continue until you have instructor approval (instructor will initial job sheet).

> **WARNING** ⚠ Before performing this job, review all pertinent safety information in the text and discuss safety procedures with your instructor. Protect the vehicle from brake fluid being spilled on painted or sensitive surfaces.

Procedures

Check Brake Adjustment

1. Secure the vehicle with the rear wheel off the ground.

2. Test the operation of the rear brake.

   Does applying the brake pedal lock up the wheel? Yes _____ No _____

3. Measure the distance that the pedal has to move to stop the wheel.

_____ Rear brake pedal distance

_____ Rear brake pedal specification

4. Note how many threads are exposed on the rear adjuster and whether or not more adjustment is available. Record the number of exposed threads.

_____

Remove and Replace Drum Brake Components

5. Remove the rear brake drum and inspect the braking surface condition:

_____ Smooth

_____ Grooves

_____ Overheated

_____ Other damage

If there is damage, consult with your instructor as to what steps to take next.

6. Measure the rear drum diameter using the proper measuring tool.

_____ Drum diameter (in./mm)

_____ Drum diameter specification (in./mm)

Is drum diameter greater than the specified maximum? Yes _____ No _____

If yes, consult with your instructor as to what steps to take next.

7. With the rear drum brakes removed, remove the shoes from the backing plate. Fill in the chart with your assessment of part condition.

> **CAUTION** ⚠ If the vehicle has hydraulic drum brakes, do not remove the wheel cylinder.

Component	Condition	Needs Lubrication? (Yes/No)
Shoes		
Anchor pin		
Pivot pin		
Return springs		

🛑 8. Show your instructor the disassembled brake components. Gain permission to reassemble the brakes. Discuss where and how much lubricant to apply.

Instructor's Initials: _____

Name _____

9. Reassemble the drum brakes and install them on the motorcycle. Check off the steps on the chart as they are performed:

Task	Process	Done
Drum installation	Install all nuts and bolts loosely.	
Adjust rear wheel alignment	Turn rear wheel adjusters.	
Chain or belt tension setting	Turn/move rear wheel adjusters and axle torque.	
Axle cotter pin replacement	Use new pin unless this is a shop unit.	
Drum brake rod adjustment	Turn drum brake rod nut and pedal screw.	
Brake light operation check	Make brake light switch adjustment as necessary.	
Drum fastener tightening	Tighten to specified torque.	
Cleanup	Clean and wipe down vehicle.	

(STOP) 10. Have your instructor check your reassembly and final adjustment.

Instructor's Initials: _____

Job Wrap Up

11. Return all tools and materials to the proper storage areas and clean up your work area.

Final Assessment

_____ 1. Two technicians are discussing drum brakes. Technician A says that drum brakes that are adjusted too tightly will wear out prematurely. Technician B says that drum brakes adjusted too tightly can cause poor gas mileage. Who is correct?

A. A only.

B. B only.

C. Both A and B.

D. Neither A nor B.

_____ 2. Two technicians are discussing drum brakes. Technician A says that loosely adjusted drum brakes are a dangerous safety concern. Technician B says that loosely adjusted drum brakes can cause the motorcycle to have a longer stopping distance. Who is correct?

A. A only.

B. B only.

C. Both A and B.

D. Neither A nor B.

_____ 3. Two technicians are discussing drum brakes. Technician A says that on some vehicles, if the drum is worn too much, the whole wheel will need replacing. Technician B says that a drum with damage to the braking surface will need to be replaced. Who is correct?

A. A only.

B. B only.

C. Both A and B.

D. Neither A nor B.

_____ 4. _True or False?_ Misadjusting the brake light switch can cause the rear brakes to fail.

_____ 5. Two technicians are discussing drum brakes. Technician A says that drum brake shoes wear faster than disc brake pads. Technician B says that drum brake shoes wear more slowly than disc brake pads. Who is correct?

A. A only.

B. B only.

C. Both A and B.

D. Neither A nor B.

Final Instructor Approval: _____

Name _____ Date _____ Class _____

Servicing Disc Brakes

Introduction

Disc brake service is a basic and common service, but it must be done right. Pads and calipers must be properly secured. In order to have a high level of customer satisfaction, all of the components must be secured properly, lubricated, and checked for proper operation.

If there is a customer concern of pulsation, the technician needs to check the wheel bearings and the lateral runout of the wheel and brake disc.

Objective

After successfully completing this job, you will be able to service disc brakes.

Materials and Equipment

To complete this job, you will need the following tools, equipment, and materials:

- Motorcycle with disc brakes
- Appropriate service manual or electronic service information
- Pad measurement tool as needed
- Dial indicator
- Hand tools as needed
- Anti-seize lubricant
- Loctite

Instructions

In this job, you will be checking disc brake components for proper operation and checking for excessive lateral runout. You will also be removing the brake disc and replacing brake pads. Caliper overhaul is not part of this job and will be covered in Job 17-5.

Read the job procedures, perform the tasks, and answer all questions. As you complete steps, you will be given instructions to either fill in measurements or perform certain tasks. When you reach a 🛑 sign, show your work to your instructor. Do not continue until you have instructor approval (instructor will initial job).

> **WARNING** ⚠️ Before performing this job, review all pertinent safety information in the text and discuss safety procedures with your instructor.

Procedures

Check Brake Operation

1. Secure the vehicle with the front wheel off the ground.

2. Apply the front brake lever and check that the front wheel cannot be turned.

   Front brakes apply? Yes _____ No _____

3. Describe how the front brake lever feels when applying the brake (use terms such as solid, spongy, soft, excessive lever travel).

_____

_____

4. Remove the caliper from the motorcycle.

5. Measure the thickness of the brake pads at the thinnest point of each pad.

> **NOTE**   Measure the friction material only, not including the pad backing plate.

_____   Pad thickness smallest measurement (in./mm)

_____   Pad thickness specification (in./mm)

_____   Brake disc thickness (in./mm)

_____   Brake disc thickness specification (usually stamped on disc) (in./mm)

6. Check wheel bearing play by grabbing the wheel at the top and bottom and rocking the wheel gently. Any play in the wheel indicates loose bearings.
   Wheel bearing play? Yes _____ No _____

7. Using a dial indicator, check the wheel for lateral runout to determine whether the wheel is bent.

_____   Wheel lateral runout (in./mm)

_____   Wheel lateral runout specification (in./mm)

_____   Brake disc lateral runout (in./mm)

_____   Brake disc lateral runout specification (in./mm)

8. Remove the brake pads from the caliper(s).

9. Lay out the pads and any shims installed on the pads, pins, and any retainers.

10. If the calipers are floating calipers, remove the calipers and remove the slides from the calipers.

🛑 11. Show your instructor the disassembled components and discuss where and how much lubricant to apply.

Instructor's Initials: _____

Remove Brake Disc

12. Remove the wheel.

13. Mark the location of the brake disc so it can be reinstalled in the same location.

14. Heat the bolts one at a time to loosen the Loctite and remove the bolts.

15. Remove the disc and hub from the wheel.

16. Use a tap to clean out the bolt holes in the wheel. Use a die to remove any residual Loctite on the bolts.

🛑 17. Have your instructor give you permission to reassemble.

Instructor's Initials: _____

Name _____

Reassemble

18. As you reassemble the unit, fill in the chart with torque specs, lubricant type, and check off as you complete the tasks.

Task	Torque Spec	Lubricant	Completed
Brake disc installation			
Axle and nut installation			
Brake caliper installation			
Brake pad and shim installation	—		
Brake bleeding		—	
Fluid top off, surface cleaning	—	—	

 NOTE Make sure that pads fit correctly, all parts move properly, and there is no foreign material on the pads, rotor, caliper housing, or vehicle body.

STOP 19. Have your instructor check your work.

Instructor's Initials: _____

Job Wrap Up

20. Return all tools and materials to the proper storage areas and clean up your work area.

Final Assessment

_____ 1. Two technicians are discussing disc brakes with floating calipers. Technician A says if the brake pad next to the piston is worn thinner than the other pad, the caliper slide is not working. Technician B says if the brake pad on the opposite side from the piston is worn thinner than the other pad, the caliper slide is not working. Who is correct?

   A. A only.

   B. B only.

   C. Both A and B.

   D. Neither A nor B.

_____ 2. Two technicians are discussing disc brakes. Technician A says that if the wheel bearings are loose, the front wheel cannot be checked for lateral runout. Technician B says that a loose wheel bearing can cause brake pulsation. Who is correct?

   A. A only.

   B. B only.

   C. Both A and B.

   D. Neither A nor B.

_____ 3. Two technicians are discussing disc brake reassembly. Technician A says to lubricate the back of the brake pads with anti-seize. Technician B says to lubricate caliper slide bolts with anti-seize. Who is correct?

A. A only.

B. B only.

C. Both A and B.

D. Neither A nor B.

_____ 4. _True or False?_ If replacing a brake disc, brake pads should be replaced at the same time.

_____ 5. Two technicians are discussing disc brake service. Technician A says that brake pads must be replaced when the rotor is replaced. Technician B says that it is not necessary to install new brake pads with a new rotor if the pads are thick enough. Who is correct?

A. A only.

B. B only.

C. Both A and B.

D. Neither A nor B.

Final Instructor Approval: _____

Name _____ Date _____ Class _____

Job 17-5

Overhauling Hydraulic Brake Calipers

Introduction

The caliper gets very hot due to brake operation and is exposed to rain and dirt. Overhauling calipers, therefore, is a normal service procedure. Overhauling includes taking the caliper apart, cleaning and inspecting parts, and reassembling the caliper using the correct lubricant. There are a variety of lubricants and many manufacturers have their own brands. It is important to use the correct lubricants in the correct amounts.

Objective

After successfully completing this job, you will be able to service hydraulic brake calipers.

Materials and Equipment

To complete this job, you will need the following tools, equipment, and materials:

- Vehicle with front and rear hydraulic brake calipers
- Appropriate service manual or electronic service information
- Standard tools
- Torque wrench
- Correct brake fluid and lubricants for caliper overhaul
- Sil-Glyde or equivalent

Instructions

In this job, you will be overhauling the caliper(s) after they are removed from the vehicle. Refer to the service manual for instructions on taking the calipers apart.

 NOTE Some calipers are taken apart in two pieces for piston service, while on others compressed air is needed to remove the piston from the body.

 WARNING If you are using compressed air, make sure you take all the proper precautions.

Read the job procedures, perform the tasks, and answer all questions. As you complete steps, you will be given instructions to either fill in measurements or perform certain tasks. When you reach a 🛑 sign, show your work to your instructor. Do not continue until you have instructor approval (instructor will initial job sheet).

 WARNING Before performing this job, review all pertinent safety information in the text and discuss safety procedures with your instructor. Protect painted or sensitive surfaces from brake fluid spills.

Procedures

Motorcycle Disc Brake and Caliper Service

Vehicle (Year/Make/Model)

_____

How many calipers are on this vehicle?

_____

What type of brake fluid is used on this vehicle?

_____

Hint: The type of brake fluid is found on the master cylinder cover.

⚠ WARNING	Follow precautions and all safety procedures when disassembling calipers. Be sure that you understand how to safely disassemble a caliper with compressed air. Always wear eye protection when using compressed air.

Remove, Disassemble, Reassemble, and Reinstall Caliper

1. Determine the type of caliper.

   _____ Floating

   _____ Fixed

2. Clamp the brake line to the caliper.

⚠ WARNING	Do not clamp the line with pliers that have sharp edges. Use line clamps or a folded soft cloth to protect the brake line. The brake line needs only to be clamped to stop the fluid from leaking. No additional pressure is needed.

3. Referring to service manual procedures, remove the caliper.

4. Measure the thickness of the brake pads and rotor at their thinnest point following the procedure outlined in Job 17-4.

   _____ Pad thickness (in./mm)

   _____ Minimum pad thickness (in./mm)

   _____ Rotor thickness (in./mm)

   _____ Minimum rotor thickness (in./mm)

Name _____

5. Disassemble the caliper according to service manual instructions.

 CAUTION If the caliper piston must be removed with compressed air, demonstrate to your instructor that you understand the necessary precautions.

 NOTE If this is a multi-piston caliper, it is necessary to remove, clean, and reassemble the pistons one at a time. Use small C-clamps to hold in the pistons that have been rebuilt. Reinstall each piston in its original bore.

6. Remove all slide components from the sliding caliper, if used.

7. Inspect all components, including O-rings and rubber boots, for wear, swelling, and contamination. Check sliding surfaces for corrosion and scoring.

8. Remove and clean the bleeder valve and make sure that it flows properly.

 9. Discuss with your instructor the condition of the parts and how to clean them before reassembly.

Instructor's Initials: _____

10. Lubricate all caliper internal parts with brake fluid or approved piston lubricant.

 WARNING Do not use anti-seize or any kind of petroleum-based products. If in doubt, use brake fluid.

11. Show your instructor the assembled caliper prior to installation.

12. Lubricate the caliper slides with Sil-Glyde or equivalent.

13. Lubricate the pads' moving parts with anti-seize. Be neat — the final presentation of your work is important.

 CAUTION Do not get any kind of lubricant on the pad surfaces.

14. Reinstall the caliper on the wheel. Caliper bolt torque (Ft-lbs. N·m):

_____

 NOTE Make sure that the pads fit and are aligned correctly, all parts move properly, and there is no residue of brake fluid or anti-seize on the outside of the calipers or vehicle.

 15. Show the installed caliper to your instructor.

Instructor's Initials: _____

16. Repeat Steps 2 through 15 for all of the disc brakes on the motorcycle.

Instructor's Initials: _____

Bleed Brakes

 NOTE It may be necessary to gravity bleed the brakes first if there is a lot of air in the system.

17. Bleed the brakes, starting with the caliper farthest from the master cylinder. If the service manual has a special order or process for bleeding, follow that process.

 NOTE Certain vehicles are difficult to bleed; the service manual process is designed to bleed the brakes with a minimum of difficulty.

 18. Demonstrate proper hydraulic bleeding to your instructor. Show your instructor the completed vehicle — clean, no brake fluid residue, and all master cylinders filled properly.

Instructor's Initials: _____

Job Wrap Up

19. Return all tools and materials to the proper storage areas and clean up your work area.

Final Assessment

_____ 1. Two technicians are discussing floating caliper overhaul. Technician A says that if the pad next to the piston is much thinner than the other pad, the piston is stuck. Technician B says that if the pad next to the piston is much thinner, the slides are stuck. Who is correct?

A. A only.

B. B only.

C. Both A and B.

D. Neither A nor B.

_____ 2. A floating caliper is being overhauled and the pads have worn at an angle. Technician A says the piston is seized. Technician B says one of the caliper slides is seized. Who is correct?

A. A only.

B. B only.

C. Both A and B.

D. Neither A nor B.

_____ 3. Two technicians are discussing caliper overhaul. Technician A says that a piston with some pitting can be sanded and reinstalled. Technician B says pistons with pitting should have the caliper replaced with a new one. Who is correct?

A. A only.

B. B only.

C. Both A and B.

D. Neither A nor B.

Name _____

_____ 4. One caliper on a dual front disc brake motorcycle is not working properly. Technician A says to overhaul both calipers. Technician B says to overhaul the faulty caliper only. Who is correct?

A. A only.

B. B only.

C. Both A and B.

D. Neither A nor B.

_____ 5. Two technicians are discussing brake lockup. Technician A says that a caliper is locking up. Technician B says that the master cylinder compensating port could be plugged. Who is correct?

A. A only.

B. B only.

C. Both A and B.

D. Neither A nor B.

Final Instructor Approval: _____

Notes

CHAPTER 18 Frame, Chassis, and Suspension Systems

Chapter 18 Quiz

After studying Chapter 18 in the Motorcycles: Fundamentals, Service, Repair textbook, answer the following questions.

_____ 1. The frame provides a non-flexing mount for the engine, suspension, and
_____.

_____ 2. The frame absorbs _____ from the engine.
A. heat
B. sound
C. vibration
D. All of the above.

_____ 3. Most aluminum frame members use _____ tubing.
A. rectangular
B. round
C. square
D. pentagonal

_____ 4. *True or False?* Subframes may be fixed or removable.

_____ 5. On the _____ frame, the engine hangs from the top of the rear of the frame.

_____ 6. The _____ frame is similar to the single cradle frame, but the engine forms the final portion
of the frame structure.
A. delta-box
B. diamond
C. perimeter
D. pentagonal

For questions 7–12, identify the types of frames shown in the following illustrations.

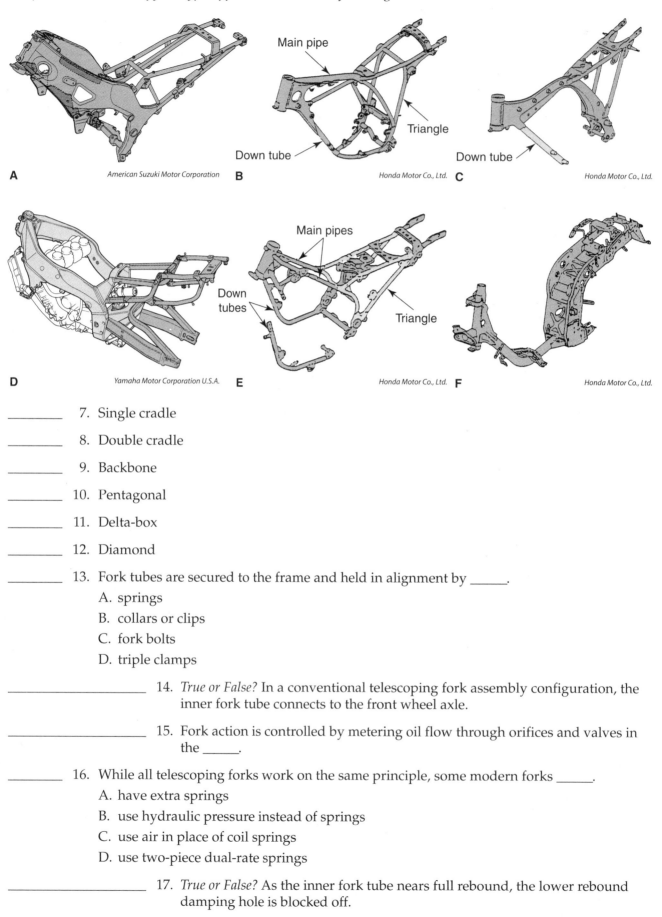

A — American Suzuki Motor Corporation

B — Main pipe / Triangle / Down tube — Honda Motor Co., Ltd.

C — Down tube — Honda Motor Co., Ltd.

D — Yamaha Motor Corporation U.S.A.

E — Main pipes / Down tubes / Triangle — Honda Motor Co., Ltd.

F — Honda Motor Co., Ltd.

_____ 7. Single cradle

_____ 8. Double cradle

_____ 9. Backbone

_____ 10. Pentagonal

_____ 11. Delta-box

_____ 12. Diamond

_____ 13. Fork tubes are secured to the frame and held in alignment by _____.
A. springs
B. collars or clips
C. fork bolts
D. triple clamps

_____ 14. *True or False?* In a conventional telescoping fork assembly configuration, the inner fork tube connects to the front wheel axle.

_____ 15. Fork action is controlled by metering oil flow through orifices and valves in the _____.

_____ 16. While all telescoping forks work on the same principle, some modern forks _____.
A. have extra springs
B. use hydraulic pressure instead of springs
C. use air in place of coil springs
D. use two-piece dual-rate springs

_____ 17. *True or False?* As the inner fork tube nears full rebound, the lower rebound damping hole is blocked off.

Name _____

_____   18. The angle of the forks from true vertical is called _____.

_____   19. The distance on the ground between the centerline of the fork and a vertical line through the axle center is called _____.

_____   20. Steering is given a self-centering effect by _____.
   A. thrust angle
   B. rake
   C. trail
   D. offset

_____   21. Steering oscillation and wobble are reduced by a device called a steering _____.

_____   22. *True or False?* Under ideal conditions, fork oil should be changed every other year.

_____   23. *True or False?* Improper adjustment of steering head bearings will make the motorcycle dangerous to ride.

_____   24. A single-shock rear suspension may have a shock absorber mounted in front of the rear wheel or on one side of the _____.

_____   25. *True or False?* Dual-shock rear suspensions are found only on motorcycles with large-displacement engines.

_____   26. A(n) _____ rear suspension provides ideal damping over a wide range of riding conditions.

_____   27. On shaft drive motorcycles, one leg of the swingarm houses the _____.

_____   28. When checking suspension balance, the technician should check for air pressure buildup in the _____.

_____   29. The tracking of the rear tires in relation to the front tires on a UTV is called _____.
   A. thrust angle
   B. offset
   C. steering angle
   D. trail

_____   30. If the side stand still moves too easily after the pivot bolt has been tightened, the _____ should be replaced.

Notes

Name _____ Date _____ Class _____

Job 18-1

Inspecting Forks

Introduction

There are different categories of fork service. Service can be as simple as changing fork hydraulic fluid and inspecting for leaks, or it can be more complex, such as adjusting compression and preload or changing the spring in the fork. Before performing these procedures, it is important to inspect a fork for damage, height, and fluid leaks.

Objective

After successfully completing this job, you will be able to inspect a motorcycle fork.

Materials and Equipment

To complete this job, you will need the following tools, equipment, and materials:

- At least three motorcycles with fluid-filled forks
- Appropriate service manual or electronic service information

Instructions

In this job, you will be inspecting forks for leaks and determining whether they are installed properly.

Read the job procedures, perform the tasks, and answer all questions. As you complete steps, you will be given instructions to either fill in measurements or perform certain tasks. When you reach a sign, show your work to your instructor. Do not continue until you have instructor approval (instructor will initial job sheet).

> **WARNING** ⚠ Before performing this job, review all pertinent safety information in the text and discuss safety procedures with your instructor.

Procedures

Inspect Fork

> **NOTE** Some fluid on the fork surface is normal. Most service manuals indicate the normal and abnormal amounts of fluid leakage.

1. Inspect vehicles assigned by your instructor for the conditions shown in the charts, then fill in the charts with your findings.

   Vehicle One (Year/Make/Model)

Excessive fluid leakage	
Forks installed at same height	
Fork compression correct	
Hardware guards and seals in good shape	

   Vehicle Two (Year/Make/Model)

Excessive fluid leakage	
Forks installed at same height	
Fork compression correct	
Hardware guards and seals in good shape	

   Vehicle Three (Year/Make/Model)

Excessive fluid leakage	
Forks installed at same height	
Fork compression correct	
Hardware guards and seals in good shape	

 2. Discuss with your instructor your inspection of the three vehicles.

Instructor's Initials: _____

Job Wrap Up

3. Return all tools and materials to the proper storage areas and clean up your work area.

Name _____

Final Assessment

_____ 1. A front fork is leaking fluid. Technician A says both forks should have their seals replaced at the same time. Technician B says that all fork bushings should be replaced at the same time. Who is correct?

A. A only.

B. B only.

C. Both A and B.

D. Neither A nor B.

_____ 2. Technician A says that if fork fluid leaks and goes low, the fluid can aerate and cause serious handling issues. Technician B says that if both forks are leaking equally, there should be no handling complaints. Who is correct?

A. A only.

B. B only.

C. Both A and B.

D. Neither A nor B.

_____ 3. Technician A says that all forks have drain plugs and can be drained without taking the forks off the bike. Technician B says that only some bikes have a drain plug and can be drained while on the bike. Who is correct?

A. A only.

B. B only.

C. Both A and B.

D. Neither A nor B.

_____ 4. Two technicians are discussing front fork service. Technician A says the forks must be clamped so their height is the same. Technician B says that changing where the forks are clamped will also change the trail measurement. Who is correct?

A. A only.

B. B only.

C. Both A and B.

D. Neither A nor B.

_____ 5. Two technicians are discussing fork service. Technician A says that all steering head bearings must be serviced at the same time. Technician B says that steering head bearing service is not required, but is a good idea when servicing the forks. Who is correct?

A. A only.

B. B only.

C. Both A and B.

D. Neither A nor B.

Final Instructor Approval: _____

Notes

Name _____ Date _____ Class _____

Job 18-2

Draining and Filling Fork Fluid

Introduction

Fork fluid service is a basic maintenance service. It is not difficult, but is absolutely critical for motorcycle safety and performance. This job covers draining and filling the fork on and off the motorcycle.

Objective

After successfully completing this job, you will be able to drain and fill a fork on or off a motorcycle.

Materials and Equipment

To complete this job, you will need the following tools, equipment, and materials:

- Motorcycle with forks that have drain plugs
- Motorcycle with forks without drain plugs
- Appropriate service manual or electronic service information
- Fork fluid of the appropriate weight
- Hand tools as needed

Instructions

In this job, you will be changing fork fluid on a motorcycle with drain plugs and removing a fork to drain fluid when there is no drain plug.

Read the job procedures, perform the tasks, and answer all questions. As you complete steps, you will be given instructions to either fill in measurements or perform certain tasks. When you reach a 🛑 sign, show your work to your instructor. Do not continue until you have instructor approval (instructor will initial job sheet).

> **WARNING** ⚠ Before performing this job, review all pertinent safety information in the text and discuss safety procedures with your instructor.

Procedures

Locate Service Information

1. Locate the following information in the service manual:
   A. What type of fork is used?

   _____ Inverted

   _____ Standard

   B. Can fluid be drained without removing the fork?

   Yes_____ No_____

C. What weight fork fluid should be used?

_____

D. How much fluid is needed?

_____

E. What method is used to check fork fluid level?

_____ Volume

_____ Level

_____ Both

F. Are there any external adjustments on this fork (jounce and/or rebound)? If yes, write them below.

_____

_____

NOTE ⚙ Be prepared to discuss external adjustments with your instructor.

Drain the Fluid

2. Secure the vehicle so that you can:
   A. Drain the fluid from the front forks.
   B. Work the fork through its stroke.

3. Place a drain pan under the fork drain plug.

NOTE ⚙ Make sure that the drain pan is empty and clean so that you can inspect the fluid once drained.

CAUTION ⚠ Read the service manual for any specific procedures for draining the fork fluid.

4. Remove the fork caps and springs.

5. Remove the drain plug(s).

6. Drain the fluid by moving the forks smoothly and slowly through their full range. This will remove as much fluid as possible.

7. Reinstall the drain plugs.

🛑 8. Discuss with your instructor the condition of the fluid that has come out of the forks. Your instructor's assessment of fluid condition can be helpful when diagnosing fluid condition in the future.

Instructor's Initials: _____

Name _____

Add Fluid and Bleed Fork

 NOTE Some forks list an amount to be added. Other forks have an amount and then a level that must be adjusted.

9. Remove the fork cap(s).

10. Add fluid through the cap opening.

11. Slowly work the forks through their full stroke to bleed air out of the system.

 CAUTION Do not move the forks too quickly when bleeding the air, as this may trap air bubbles.

12. If the service manual calls for setting the fluid level at this point, use the appropriate tool and set the fluid level.

13. Ensure that the fork cap seals are present and in good condition; then reinstall the fork cap.

 14. Discuss with your instructor your fork drain and fill process.

Instructor's Initials: _____

Drain and Fill Fork Off the Bike

15. Locate the following information:
     A. What type of fork is used?

         _____ Inverted

         _____ Standard

     B. Can fluid be drained without removing the fork?

         Yes_____ No_____

     C. What weight fork fluid should be used?

         _____

     D. How much fluid is needed?

         _____

     E. What method is used to check fork fluid level?

         _____ Volume

         _____ Level

         _____ Both

F. Are there any external adjustments on this fork (jounce and/or rebound)? If yes, write them below.

_____

_____

 NOTE Be prepared to discuss external adjustments with your instructor.

Remove the Fork

16. Raise the vehicle so that the fork can be removed.

17. Consult the service manual for any specific procedures to remove the fork.

 CAUTION Make sure that you record where the forks are mounted in the triple tree.

18. Loosen the fork caps and remove the forks from the triple tree.

19. Remove the fork caps, invert the forks over a clean drain pan, and allow the fluid to drain out.

20. Move the forks smoothly and slowly through their full range to remove as much fluid as possible.

 21. Discuss with your instructor the condition of the fluid that has come out of the forks, the fork spring length, and condition of the forks.

Instructor's Initials: _____

Filling and Bleeding the Fluid

22. Secure the fork in an upright position so that it can be filled and bled.

 NOTE Some forks list an amount to be added. Other forks have an amount and then a level that must be adjusted.

23. Add the fluid and slowly work the forks through their full stroke to bleed the air out of the system.

 CAUTION Do not move the forks too quickly when bleeding the air, as this may trap air bubbles.

24. If the service manual calls for setting the fluid level at this point, use the appropriate tool and set the level.

25. Check that the fork cap seals are present and in good condition; then reinstall the fork caps.

26. Reinstall the forks into the triple tree and make sure you have installed the forks at the same height that they were before removal.

 27. Discuss with your instructor the fork drain and fill process.

Instructor's Initials: _____

Name _____

Job Wrap Up

28. Return all tools and materials to the proper storage areas and clean up your work area.

Final Assessment

_____ 1. Technician A says fork fluid viscosity has a direct effect on spring preload. Technician B says that fork fluid viscosity has a direct effect on damping. Who is correct?
   A. A only.
   B. B only.
   C. Both A and B.
   D. Neither A nor B.

_____ 2. Both forks are bent on a motorcycle from an accident. Technician A says to check the steering head neck and bearings for damage. Technician B says to check the wheel and front axle for runout. Who is correct?
   A. A only.
   B. B only.
   C. Both A and B.
   D. Neither A nor B.

_____ 3. Two technicians are discussing fork damping adjustments. Technician A says that adjusting preload changes compression as well. Technician B says that adjusting rebound will not affect preload settings. Who is correct?
   A. A only.
   B. B only.
   C. Both A and B.
   D. Neither A nor B.

_____ 4. Two technicians are discussing fork service. Technician A says only standard forks have drains. Technician B says inverted forks have drains also. Who is correct?
   A. A only.
   B. B only.
   C. Both A and B.
   D. Neither A nor B.

_____ 5. Two technicians are discussing fork service. Technician A says that the correct weight of fluid has a direct effect on damping. Technician B says that using heavier weight fluid will increase damping. Who is correct?
   A. A only.
   B. B only.
   C. Both A and B.
   D. Neither A nor B.

Final Instructor Approval: _____

Notes

Name _____   Date _____   Class _____

Job 18-3

Replacing Fork Seals

Introduction

Fork seal replacement procedures change with the type of fork. Different forks have different compression and rebound devices, and external gas charges. Some forks are inverted. All of these variables affect the procedures needed to change seals. No exact procedure, therefore, can be given. You must have a service manual for the specific motorcycle.

Objective

After successfully completing this job, you will be able to replace fork seals.

Materials and Equipment

To complete this job, you will need the following tools, equipment, and materials:

- Motorcycle with forks
- Appropriate service manual or electronic service information
- Fork fluid of the appropriate weight
- Fork seal kit
- Hand tools as needed

Instructions

In this job, you will be changing fork seals.

Read the job procedures, perform the tasks, and answer all questions. As you complete steps, you will be given instructions to either fill in measurements or perform certain tasks. When you reach a sign, show your work to your instructor. Do not continue until you have instructor approval (instructor will initial job sheet).

WARNING	⚠	Before performing this job, review all pertinent safety information in the text and discuss safety procedures with your instructor.

Procedures

1. Refer to the service manual and disassemble the fork assembly.

CAUTION	⚠	To avoid damage, use the proper tool to loosen the bolt holding the compression damper valve.

2. Lay the fork parts out on a clean workbench, inspect them, and fill out the chart.

	Condition	Replace or Reuse
Fork bushings		
Inner tube runout		
Fork cap O-rings		

STOP 3. Discuss with your instructor the condition of the forks and components. Ask your instructor about saving the fork fluid, as it may be reused.

Instructor's Initials: _____

4. Reassemble the core and list here parts that would be replaced when servicing forks. Typically, replaced parts would be the fork seals, dust seals, fork cap O-rings, compression valve gasket, and fluid. Other parts may be replaced, depending on the fork design.

1. _____

2. _____

3. _____

4. _____

5. _____

6. _____

7. _____

Filling and Bleeding the Fluid

5. Secure the fork in an upright position so that it can be filled and bled.

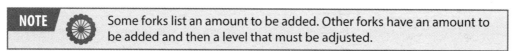 **NOTE** Some forks list an amount to be added. Other forks have an amount to be added and then a level that must be adjusted.

6. Add fluid and slowly work the forks through their full stroke to bleed the air out of the system.

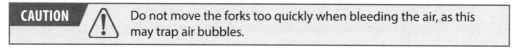 **CAUTION** Do not move the forks too quickly when bleeding the air, as this may trap air bubbles.

7. If the service manual calls for setting the fluid level at this point, use the appropriate tool to set the level.

8. Reinstall the fork caps.

9. Reinstall the fork on the motorcycle.

10. Adjust fork height as necessary.

STOP 11. Discuss with your instructor your fork drain and fill process.

Instructor's Initials: _____

Job Wrap Up

12. Return all tools and materials to the proper storage areas and clean up your work area.

Name _____

Final Assessment

_____ 1. Technician A says that to increase compression, a thicker viscosity fluid can be used. Technician B says that to increase compression, a stiffer spring can be installed. Who is correct?

A. A only.

B. B only.

C. Both A and B.

D. Neither A nor B.

_____ 2. The forks on a motorcycle are bottoming out over bumps. Fluid is new and preload is maxed out. Technician A says that the spring should be replaced with a stiffer spring. Technician B says that the oil should be replaced with a thicker viscosity. Who is correct?

A. A only.

B. B only.

C. Both A and B.

D. Neither A nor B.

_____ 3. Two technicians are discussing fork adjustments. Technician A says that preload should be adjusted before adjusting compression and rebound. Technician B says that compression and rebound should be adjusted before preload. Who is correct?

A. A only.

B. B only.

C. Both A and B.

D. Neither A nor B.

_____ 4. Two technicians are discussing fork service. Technician A says that fork seals can be reused if they are carefully removed. Technician B says fork bushings can be reused if they are in good condition. Who is correct?

A. A only.

B. B only.

C. Both A and B.

D. Neither A nor B.

_____ 5. Two technicians are discussing fork service. Technician A says that used fork oil changes its viscosity over time. Technician B says that used fork oil can be filtered and used again. Who is correct?

A. A only.

B. B only.

C. Both A and B.

D. Neither A nor B.

Final Instructor Approval: _____

Notes

Name _____ Date _____ Class _____

Job 18-4

Adjusting Rear Sag

Introduction

Adjusting ride height is critical to rider safety and handling. Not all suspension systems are adjustable, but more and more suspension systems have fully adjustable suspensions. Rear sag changes with different riders and when a second rider or luggage is added.

A rule of thumb is that sag is about a third of total suspension travel. Adjusting sag is actually adjusting preload. Increasing preload will reduce the sag by stiffening the spring. Decreasing preload will increase the sag by softening the spring.

Objective

After successfully completing this job, you will be able to adjust rear sag on a motorcycle.

Materials and Equipment

To complete this job, you will need the following tools, equipment, and materials:

- Cruiser motorcycle with adjustable preload
- Sport bike with adjustable preload
- Dirt bike with adjustable preload
- Appropriate service manual or electronic service information
- Variety of spanner wrenches and hand tools

Instructions

In this job, you will be adjusting the rear sag on three different motorcycles to observe the variety and similarities in adjustment methods.

Read the job procedures, perform the tasks, and answer all questions. As you complete steps, you will be given instructions to either fill in measurements or perform certain tasks. When you reach a sign, show your work to your instructor. Do not continue until you have instructor approval (instructor will initial job sheet).

> **WARNING** ⚠ Before performing this job, review all pertinent safety information in the text and discuss safety procedures with your instructor.

Procedures

Adjust Rear Ride Height on Cruiser Bike

1. Use the appropriate service manual to find procedures for measuring and adjusting rear ride height and sag.

   _____ Sag specification (in./mm)

   _____ Current unloaded ride height (in./mm)

   _____ Current sag with rider (in./mm)

   _____ Adjustment needed (in./mm)

2. Adjust ride height if possible (refer to the service manual).

   _____ New sag with rider (in./mm)

3. Does this bike have adjustments other than ride height (compression/rebound)?

   Yes _____ No _____ If yes, describe:

   _____

(STOP) 4. Discuss with your instructor the sag adjustment you have just completed.

Instructor's Initials: _____

Rear Ride Height Adjustment on Sport Bike

5. Use the appropriate service manual to find the procedure for measuring and adjusting rear ride height and sag.

   _____ Sag specification (in./mm)

   _____ Current unloaded ride height (in./mm)

   _____ Current sag with rider (in./mm)

   _____ Adjustment needed (in./mm)

6. Adjust ride height if possible (refer to the service manual).

   _____ New sag with rider (in./mm)

7. Does this bike have adjustments other than ride height (compression/rebound)?

   Yes _____ No _____ If yes, describe:

   _____

(STOP) 8. Discuss with your instructor the sag adjustment you have just completed.

Instructor's Initials: _____

Name _____

Rear Ride Height Adjustment on Dirt Bike

9. Use the appropriate service manual to find the procedure for measuring and adjusting rear ride height and sag.

_____   Sag specification (in./mm)

_____   Current unloaded ride height (in./mm)

_____   Current sag with rider (in./mm)

_____   Adjustment needed (in./mm)

10. Adjust ride height if possible (refer to the service manual).

_____   New sag with rider (in./mm)

11. Does this bike have adjustments other than ride height (compression/rebound)?

Yes _____   No _____   If yes, describe:

_____

🛑 12. Discuss with your instructor the sag adjustment you have just completed.

Instructor's Initials: _____

Job Wrap Up

13. Return all tools and materials to the proper storage areas and clean up your work area.

Final Assessment

_____   1. Technician A says that excessive sag will have an effect on handling. Technician B says that excessive sag will have an effect on braking distance. Who is correct?
   A. A only.
   B. B only.
   C. Both A and B.
   D. Neither A nor B.

_____   2. Two technicians are discussing rear sag on a dirt bike. Technician A says that the rear sag adjustment will also affect trail. Technician B says that the rear sag adjustment will also affect compression. Who is correct?
   A. A only.
   B. B only.
   C. Both A and B.
   D. Neither A nor B.

_____ 3. Two technicians are discussing rear sag adjustment. Technician A says that tightening preload will decrease sag and raise the rider on the bike. Technician B says that tightening preload will make the spring stiffer. Who is correct?

A. A only.

B. B only.

C. Both A and B.

D. Neither A nor B.

_____ 4. Two technicians are discussing rear sag adjustment. Technician A says that if the rider is going on a long trip, rear sag adjustment should be made with the bike fully loaded. Technician B says sag adjustment is only about the rider and not the gear or a second rider. Who is correct?

A. A only.

B. B only.

C. Both A and B.

D. Neither A nor B.

_____ 5. Two technicians are discussing rear sag. Technician A says that adjusting sag is basically the same process no matter the bike. Technician B says that if the sag cannot be adjusted within the correct range, the spring needs to be replaced. Who is correct?

A. A only.

B. B only.

C. Both A and B.

D. Neither A nor B.

Final Instructor Approval: _____

Name _____ Date _____ Class _____

Job 18-5

Checking Motorcycle Alignment

Introduction

Motorcycle alignment is checked to ensure proper installation of parts and to diagnose possible damage to suspension components and frames. To check alignment, the tires must be in good condition and inflated properly. Alignment procedures consist of using the width of the tires and a length of string to make sure that the front and rear wheels are in line.

Objective

After successfully completing this job, you will be able to check alignment on a street motorcycle.

Materials and Equipment

To complete this job, you will need the following tools, equipment, and materials:

- Street motorcycle
- Appropriate service manual or electronic service information
- String and other measuring tools as needed

Instructions

In this job, you will be checking front and rear wheel alignment. To do this you will attach a long string around the back of the rear tire, run both ends of the string to the front, and measure how far the tires are from the string.

Read the job procedures, perform the tasks, and answer all questions. As you complete steps, you will be given instructions to either fill in measurements or perform certain tasks. When you reach a sign, show your work to your instructor. Do not continue until you have instructor approval (instructor will initial job sheet).

 WARNING ⚠ Before performing this job, review all pertinent safety information in the text and discuss safety procedures with your instructor.

Procedures

Checking Alignment

1. Inspect swing arm bushings, front forks and other steering/suspension components for obvious bending or other damage.

   Damage found? Yes _____ No _____ If yes, consult with your instructor as to whether to continue with this procedure.

2. Set tire pressure to the manufacturer's recommended pressure.

3. Find and record the tire width.

   > **NOTE** Tire width in mm is found on the tire sidewall (e.g., on a tire marked 205/80R 18, 205 is the width of the tire).

Width of Rear Tire	Width of Front Tire

4. Set the front wheel in the straight-ahead position.

5. Tape the middle of a long string to the rear tire and extend both ends of the string forward past the front tire.

   > **NOTE** You will need to attach the string fairly low to clear the other motorcycle parts.

6. Secure the string to a solid point in front of the front tire. Any stationary object, such as a board, will work.

7. Measure how far apart the two sides of string are in three places:

   A. _____ Just in front of the rear tire

   B. _____ Behind the front tire

   C. _____ In front of the front tire

8. Adjust the string until all three measurements are the same (e.g., if 205 mm is the width of the tire, both sides of the string should be 205 mm apart at all three measurement spots).

9. Measure how far away the string is from the front and rear of the front tire on both sides of the tire.

> **NOTE** If the measurements are the same, the wheels are aligned. If the measurements are different, check the frame, fork, swing arm, or other parts for damage or looseness.

Name _____

10. Record the readings from Steps 7 and 9 in the chart.

Location	Measurement
Width of rear tire	
Width of front tire	
Difference between width of both tires divided by two	
From front of front tire on the left edge to the string on the left side	
From rear of front tire on left edge to the string on the left side	
From the front of the front tire on the right edge to the string on the right side	
From rear of front tire on left edge to the string on the left side	

11. Are the four measurements from the front string the same? Yes _____ No _____
    If no, what could be the problem?

    _____

    _____

(STOP) 12. Discuss with your instructor the measurements you have made.

Instructor's Initials: _____

Job Wrap Up

13. Return all tools and materials to the proper storage areas and clean up your work area.

Final Assessment

_____ 1. *True or False?* Wheel alignment is checked to confirm that the vehicle has not been damaged and the frame is straight.

_____ 2. *True or False?* Wheel alignment is checked to confirm that the vehicle suspension is in good condition.

_____ 3. *True or False?* Wheel alignment is checked whenever the motorcycle is brought in for other service.

_____ 4. *True or False?* Wheel alignment will be affected by rider height and weight.

_____ 5. *True or False?* Wheel alignment could be off when new tires are installed.

Final Instructor Approval: _____

Notes

Name _____   Date _____   Class _____

Job 18-6

Checking ATV/UTV (Quad and Side-by-Side) Alignment

Introduction

Checking alignment on ATVs and UTVs, often called quads and side-by-sides, is critical to the safety issues of handling and tire wear. Checking alignment can be done with a variety of tools. The goal of alignment is to make sure the wheels on an axle are headed straight and parallel with each other.

Prior to checking alignment, it is very important to find any steering or suspension component damage. This type of damage is common with off-road vehicles. Alignment is fine tuning, not a way to compensate for damage.

Objective

After successfully completing this job, you will be able to perform an alignment on ATVs and UTVs.

Materials and Equipment

To complete this job, you will need the following tools, equipment, and materials:

- ATV or UTV (quad or side-by-side vehicle)
- Appropriate service manual or electronic service information
- Measuring tools

Instructions

In this job, you will be checking wheel alignment on ATVs and UTVs. You will be measuring from center to center of the front tires, both in the front of the tire and the rear of the tire, and determining the difference. This is often referred to as checking toe. Measurements should be even from side to side, and the tie rods on each side should be the same length.

Read the job procedures, perform the tasks, and answer all questions. As you complete steps, you will be given instructions to either fill in measurements or perform certain tasks. When you reach a sign, show your work to your instructor. Do not continue until you have instructor approval (instructor will initial job sheet).

> **WARNING** ⚠ Before performing this job, review all pertinent safety information in the text and discuss safety procedures with your instructor.

Procedures

Check Steering and Suspension Parts

1. Refer to the service manual for alignment specifications and procedures.

2. Inspect the following parts and fill in the chart. Refer to the service manual for information on how to check each component or ask your instructor.

> **NOTE** Sometimes you will need to unload (remove tension from) some suspension parts to check certain components. Consult the service manual for details.

Component	Specification	Actual
Tire pressure		
Wheel bearings		
Tie rods		
Suspension links		

STOP 3. Discuss with your instructor the measurements you have made.

Instructor's Initials: _____

Make Measurements and Perform Alignment

4. Fill in the chart with measurements taken according to service manual procedures.

	Measurement	Spec
Left front tie rod length		
Right front tie rod length		
Distance from front center of left tire to front center of the right tire		
Distance from rear center of left tire to rear center of the right tire		

_____ Center to center difference (in./mm)

_____ Adjustment(s) needed (in./mm)

5. After studying the results of the above measurements, make alignment adjustments as necessary. Adjustment(s) made:

_____

STOP 6. Discuss with your instructor the measurements you have made and be prepared to show the corrected measurements.

Instructor's Initials: _____

Name _____

Job Wrap Up

   7. Return all tools and materials to the proper storage areas and clean up your work area.

Final Assessment

_____ 1. *True or False?* Wheel alignment should be made only on vehicles with undamaged suspension/steering parts and tires that are in good condition.

_____ 2. *True or False?* Wheel alignment is checked with the vehicle tires inflated properly.

_____ 3. *True or False?* Wheel alignment is checked as part of most services.

_____ 4. *True or False?* Wheel alignment will be affected by rider height and weight.

_____ 5. *True or False?* Most ATVs and UTVs have adjustable camber.

Final Instructor Approval: _____

Notes

Name _____ Date _____ Class _____

Job 18-7

Servicing a Steering Neck

Introduction

Steering neck service is absolutely critical and must be done correctly. Steering neck service includes checking the steering neck for vertical fork play, checking bearing fall away (sometimes called preload), cleaning and lubricating bearings, and resetting vertical play and fall away. You must locate and use service manual specifications for checking fall away, since specs vary with different motorcycles.

Objective

After successfully completing this job, you will be able to service motorcycle steering necks.

Materials and Equipment

To complete this job, you will need the following tools, equipment, and materials:

- Motorcycle
- Appropriate service manual or electronic service information
- Spanner wrenches and hand tools as needed

Instructions

In this job, you will be checking, removing, cleaning, and reassembling steering neck bearings.

Read the job procedures, perform the tasks, and answer all questions. As you complete steps, you will be given instructions to either fill in measurements or perform certain tasks. When you reach a sign, show your work to your instructor. Do not continue until you have instructor approval (instructor will initial job sheet).

 WARNING ⚠ Before performing this job, review all pertinent safety information in the text and discuss safety procedures with your instructor.

Procedures

Inspect Vehicle Fork Play

1. Secure the motorcycle with the front wheel off the ground.

2. Straddle the front wheel and pull up on the lower front forks in order to feel for any vertical (up and down) play in the steering neck bearing.

   A. Steering neck bearing vertical play felt:

   _____

   B. Steering neck bearing vertical play specification (if listed):

   _____

   C. Is the vertical play:

   _____ Correct

   _____ Too loose

   _____ Too tight

3. Use the service manual procedure to test fall away (preload).

4. Determine whether the fall away meets specs.

   A. Fall away specification:

   _____

   B. Is the fall away:

   _____ Correct

   _____ Too loose

   _____ Too tight

(STOP) 5. Discuss with your instructor the inspection results.

Instructor's Initials: _____

Disassemble Steering Neck

6. Use the service manual procedure to remove the steering neck bearings.

   > **NOTE** The lower steering neck bearing will stay with the steering neck. A special tool is needed to remove it. For this job, leave the bearing on the steering neck.

7. Arrange parts so that the set of forks is removed, the handlebars are laid to one side, and the steering neck parts are laid out in order.

(STOP) 8. Discuss bearing cleaning with your instructor (most service information calls for a high flash cleaner like brake cleaner).

Instructor's Initials: _____

Name _____

Service and Reinstall Bearings

9. Clean the bearings according to your instructor's directions.

10. Pack the bearings according to your instructor's directions. Your shop may have different tools for packing bearings, but most technicians use hand packing to make sure grease gets into all the bearing rollers.

11. Use service manual procedures to reinstall the bearings in the fork.

12. Set the preload (on most motorcycles the lower nut is used for adjusting preload and the top nut is used for locking the adjustment).

  CAUTION Setting preload takes a sense of feel. The bearings must move smoothly with no play.

 13. Discuss with your instructor the preload setting procedure.

Instructor's Initials: _____

Assemble Steering Neck

14. Use the service manual to reassemble the motorcycle steering neck.

15. Retest vertical movement and fall away.

 NOTE This step is the final fall away test. If fall away is too slow or does not move far enough, repeat Step 12 to loosen the preload. If the fall away is too quick or moves too soon, repeat Step 12 to increase the preload.

 16. Discuss with your instructor the final adjustment and assembly of the motorcycle.

Instructor's Initials: _____

Job Wrap Up

17. Return all tools and materials to the proper storage areas and clean up your work area.

Final Assessment

_____ 1. *True or False?* Steering neck bearing service is done only when the bearings are damaged.

_____ 2. *True or False?* Some steering neck bearings can be greased without being removed.

_____ 3. *True or False?* When replacing steering neck bearings, the bearing race must also be replaced.

_____ 4. *True or False?* Fall away is the final test for preload on an assembled fork.

_____ 5. *True or False?* If the steering is shaking while the motorcycle is being driven, the bearings need to be serviced.

Final Instructor Approval: _____

Notes

CHAPTER 19 Power Transmission Systems

Chapter 19 Quiz

After studying Chapter 19 in the Motorcycles: Fundamentals, Service, Repair textbook, answer the following questions.

_____ 1. A primary drive transfers engine power from the crankshaft through the clutch to the _____ assembly.

_____ 2. The two main types of primary drives are gear drives and _____ drives.

_____ 3. The _____ connects the engine power to the transmission.

_____ 4. The most common type of manual clutch is the _____ clutch.
   A. dry
   B. single-plate
   C. one-way
   D. multi-plate

_____ 5. The primary drive chain or gear turns the clutch _____.

_____ 6. The driven plates in a multi-plate clutch are locked to the clutch _____.

_____ 7. *True or False?* Most multi-plate clutches are wet clutches.

For questions 8–15, the following illustration shows power flow through an engaged clutch. Identify the components indicated.

_____ 8. Clutch drive plates

_____ 9. Crankshaft

_____ 10. Clutch basket

_____ 11. Primary drive gear or sprocket

_____ 12. Transmission main shaft

_____ 13. Primary gears or chain

_____ 14. Clutch inner hub

_____ 15. Clutch driven plates

Goodheart-Willcox Publisher

_____ 16. Clutch springs apply pressure to the _____ plate.

_____ 17. The two main types of clutch springs are coil springs and _____ springs.

_____ 18. The one-way clutch system prevents a loss of _____ if multiple downshifts are made.

_____ 19. The _____ shaft of a transmission has a countershaft sprocket mounted on its outer end.

_____ 20. All of the following statements about multi-speed transmission are true, *except*:

A. the gears are in constant mesh.

B. the largest gear on the input shaft is low gear.

C. sliding gears are moved by shifting forks.

D. only one pair of gears transfers power when a speed is selected.

_____ 21. When the rider's foot moves the gearshift lever, the _____ slide the gears sideways.

A. shift forks and shift return spring

B. shift drum and shift forks

C. shift drum and locator plate

D. shift forks and shift shaft

_____ 22. All of the following are shift drum location methods, *except*:

A. shouldered crankcase halves encasing the drum.

B. a shouldered bolt engaged in a slot on the drum.

C. cam grooves cut into the drum.

D. a flat plate engaged in a slot on the drum.

_____ 23. *True or False?* A dual-range transmission has an auxiliary transmission.

_____ 24. Many ATVs and UTVs have a(n) _____ gear that applies power directly to the output shaft through a third layshaft.

_____ 25. *True or False?* Continuously variable transmissions are a type of manual transmission.

_____ 26. *True or False?* CVT transmissions allow for a variable drive ratio according to engine speed and load.

Name _____

For questions 27–37, identify the CVT components indicated in the following illustration.

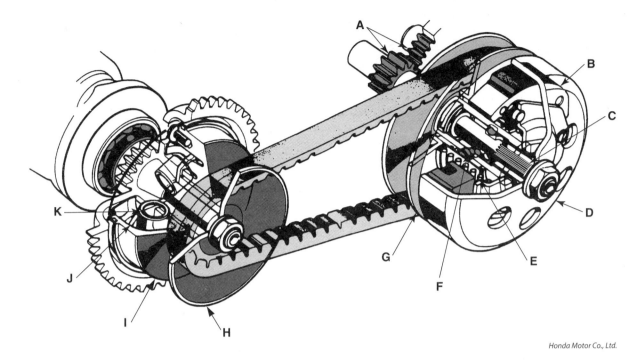

Honda Motor Co., Ltd.

_____ 27. Clutch outer

_____ 28. Ramp plate

_____ 29. Movable drive face

_____ 30. Driveshaft

_____ 31. Movable driven face

_____ 32. Clutch weight

_____ 33. Driven face spring

_____ 34. Weight roller

_____ 35. Drive face

_____ 36. Guide pin and roller

_____ 37. Reduction gears

_____ 38. Final drive ratio is the relationship of rear wheel speed to _____ speed.

_____ 39. *True or False?* In a chain drive, the front drive sprocket drives the wheel.

For questions 40–46, identify the parts of the roller chain shown in the following illustration.

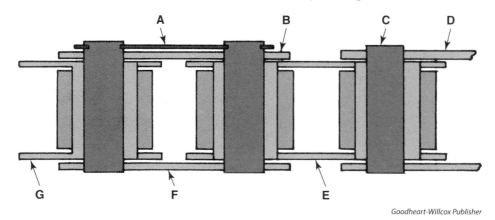

Goodheart-Willcox Publisher

_____ 40. Roller link

_____ 41. Removable side plate

_____ 42. Roller link

_____ 43. Pin link

_____ 44. Master link clip

_____ 45. Master link

_____ 46. Pin

_____ 47. On _____ chains, rings between the side plates of the pin and roller links keep dirt and moisture out and seal in lubrication.
   A. X-ring and O-ring
   B. O-ring and endless
   C. X-ring and solid-ring
   D. solid impregnated

_____ 48. A belt drive requires _____.
   A. frequent lubrication
   B. more maintenance than a chain drive
   C. careful tension adjustment
   D. All of the above.

_____ 49. On a shaft drive, a(n) _____ may be placed in the driveline to provide smooth starts and stops.

_____ 50. *True or False?* For a chain drive, final drive ratio is determined by dividing the number of rear sprocket teeth by the number of front sprocket teeth.

_____ 51. *True or False?* If a larger front sprocket is installed in a chain drive, top speed will be decreased.

_____ 52. *True or False?* To change final drive ratio for a shaft drive, the ring and pinion gears must be replaced.

_____ 53. A kick-start mechanism connects the kick-start lever to the engine _____.

Name _____ Date _____ Class _____

_____ 54. All of the following statements about a non-primary kick-starting system are true, *except*:

   A. this system is found in most kick-starting street motorcycles.

   B. the transmission must be in neutral to start the engine.

   C. the clutch must be disengaged to start the engine.

   D. the system uses the primary drive's clutch outer hub.

For questions 55–62, identify the components of the electric starting system shown in the following illustration.

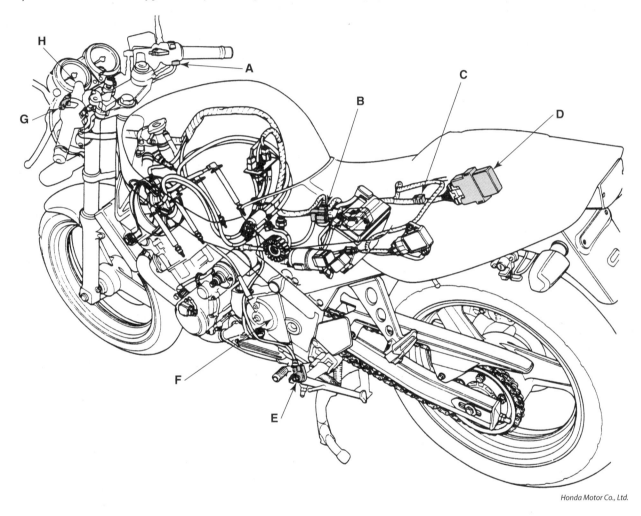

Honda Motor Co., Ltd.

_____ 55. Spark unit

_____ 56. Neutral switch

_____ 57. Clutch switch diode

_____ 58. Starter switch

_____ 59. Side stand switch

_____ 60. Starter relay switch

_____ 61. Clutch switch

_____ 62. Side stand indicator light

Notes

Name _____ Date _____ Class _____

Job 19-1

Testing Clutch and Transmission Operation

Introduction

To diagnose clutch and transmission concerns, the motorcycle must be driven. In the school environment, this is difficult without a dynamometer (dyno). The first half of this job consists of testing shifting, which can be done without a dyno. If your shop has a dyno, you can use it to complete this job.

To successfully perform this job, you must understand what is going on inside of the clutch and transmission. You will be testing for operation and noise in both the clutch system and the transmission.

Objective

After successfully completing this job, you will be able to test a transmission and clutch for proper operation.

Materials and Equipment

To complete this job, you will need the following tools, equipment, and materials:

- Motorcycle with manual clutch and transmission
- Appropriate service manual or electronic service information
- Hand tools as needed
- Dynamometer, if available

Instructions

In this job, you will be checking for clutch free play, clutch operation, clutch noises, transmission shifting, and transmission noises.

Read the job procedures, perform the tasks, and answer all questions. As you complete steps, you will be given instructions to either fill in measurements or perform certain tasks. When you reach a 🛑 sign, show your work to your instructor. Do not continue until you have instructor approval (instructor will initial job sheet).

> **WARNING** ⚠ Before performing this job, review all pertinent safety information in the text and discuss safety procedures with your instructor.

Procedures

Test Shifting with Engine Not Running

1. Operate the clutch and note the free play.

   _____ Clutch free play observed

   _____ Clutch free play specification

   Is free play correct? Yes _____ No _____

   Does the clutch move smoothly? Yes _____ No _____

2. Shift the transmission through all gears and note shift quality on the chart.

> **NOTE** You may have to rock the vehicle forward and backward to get it to shift through the gears. If the transmission will not shift through all gears, check the service manual and discuss the problem with your instructor. On some transmissions, the shafts must be rotating in order to shift.

Gear	Proper Shift	Shift Hard	Cannot Shift
1			
2			
3			
4			
5			
6			

STOP 3. Discuss with your instructor the results of this test. Also, discuss the proper procedure for starting the vehicle to complete this job.

Instructor's Initials: _____

Test Shifting with Engine Running

4. Make sure that the engine is prepared to run. Check all motorcycle fluids and tire pressures.

5. Start the engine, perform the following shift procedures, and fill out the chart.

Situation	Proper Operation	Hard Lever Movement or Other Problem	Abnormal Noises
Neutral clutch lever out			
Neutral clutch lever in			
1st gear clutch lever in			
Shift 1st to 2nd			
Shift 2nd to 3rd			
Shift 3rd to 4th			
Shift 4th to 5th			
Shift 5th to 6th			

6. Safely shift the transmission back to neutral.

7. Turn off the engine.

STOP 8. Discuss your findings so far with your instructor.

Instructor's Initials: _____

Name _____

Test Shifting on Dynamometer

WARNING ⚠	You must have approval from the instructor before using dyno.

9. Place the motorcycle on the dyno and secure it according to instructions.

10. Start the engine.

11. Perform the following shift procedures and fill out the chart.

NOTE	Some dyno instructions do not call for downshifting. Instead, pull the clutch lever in, shift to neutral, and let the transmission and dyno wind down.

Situation	Proper Operation	Hard Lever Movement or Other Problem	Abnormal Noises
Neutral clutch lever out			
Neutral clutch lever in			
1st gear clutch lever in			
Shift 1st to 2nd			
Shift 2nd to 3rd			
Shift 3rd to 4th			
Shift 4th to 5th			
Shift 5th to 6th			

12. Turn off the engine and remove the motorcycle from the dyno.

 13. Discuss your findings with your instructor.

Instructor's Initials: _____

Job Wrap Up

14. Return all tools and materials to the proper storage areas and clean up your work area.

Final Assessment

_____   1. *True or False?* Motorcycle transmissions should shift with the engine off.

_____   2. *True or False?* When the clutch lever is out, the clutch is engaged.

_____   3. A transmission will shift up into the first three gears but not into 4th gear. The problem is most likely in the _____.

    A. transmission

    B. clutch

    C. clutch cable

    D. None of the above.

_____   4. *True or False?* Transmissions are easier to shift when the engine is cold than when the engine is warm.

_____   5. A transmission is difficult to shift into any gear at any speed. The problem is most likely in the _____.

    A. transmission

    B. clutch

    C. clutch cable

    D. None of the above.

Final Instructor Approval: _____

CHAPTER 20

Engine Disassembly

Chapter 20 Quiz

After studying Chapter 20 in the Motorcycles: Fundamentals, Service, Repair textbook, answer the following questions.

_____ 1. When preparing for engine removal, the technician should have an engine _____ or an engine box ready to support the engine's weight.

_____ 2. *True or False?* A tiny particle of dirt can ruin an engine bearing.

_____ 3. *True or False?* Using an engine _____ with a pressure washer or steam cleaner makes cleaning easier.

_____ 4. *True or False?* Drive chain areas should be cleaned with a high-pressure spray.

_____ 5. *True or False?* Engine removal is usually necessary for transmission repair.

_____ 6. The service manual tells the technician which cables, linkages, and electrical wires must be _____.

    A. cleaned

    B. disconnected

    C. insulated

    D. All of the above.

_____ 7. *True or False?* Dry sump lubrication systems must be drained and disconnected before the engine is removed.

_____ 8. What type of connector is shown in the following image?

    A. Forked connector.

    B. Male-female connector.

    C. Plug-in connector.

    D. Eyelet connector.

Mihancea Petru/Shutterstock.com

_____ 9. Removal of the fuel _____ is usually required to obtain clearance for the engine.

_____ 10. Carburetors are attached to the engine by a spigot, _____, or flange.

_____ 11. When a chain final drive is disconnected, the chain should be _____.
   A. inspected
   B. lubricated
   C. cleaned
   D. All of the above.

_____ 12. At least _____ people should work together to remove an engine.

_____ 13. _____ should be placed on wires to identify them, because part damage could result if wires are crossed during reassembly.

_____ 14. To organize fasteners, it is a good idea to make a(n) _____ board of bolt and screw locations.

_____ 15. When the engine is disassembled, it should be separated into which of the following groups?
   A. Top end, left side, right side, and bottom end.
   B. Top end, left side, right side, bottom end, and transmission.
   C. Cylinder, primary drive, crankcase, and transmission.
   D. None of the above.

_____ 16. All of the following parts may be encountered on the left or right side of the engine, *except*:
   A. reed valve.
   B. magneto.
   C. cam gears and chains.
   D. kick-start mechanism.

_____ 17. To prevent movement and rotation of engine parts, tools called engine _____ are used during disassembly.

_____ 18. Types of special pullers include bolt pullers, double-threaded pullers, slide hammer pullers, _____ pullers, and blind bearing pullers.

_____ 19. Methods used to heat parts include a propane torch, _____, hot plate, or oven.

_____ 20. When heating parts, the technician should do all of the following, *except*:
   A. continually move the torch.
   B. heat the whole crankcase when removing crankcase bearings.
   C. heat parts to at least 365° (185°C).
   D. wear insulated gloves when handling heated parts.

Name _____ Date _____ Class _____

Job 20-1

Removing an Engine

Introduction

The process of removing an engine can vary widely depending on the type of vehicle that you are working on. Dirt bike engines can be fairly easy to remove, as they have minimal wiring harnesses and fairly good access. Cruisers have good access, but the engine is big and heavy and an engine jack is needed. Sport bikes may present a challenge depending on the style of frame, since the engine may need to be removed from the bottom. Side-by-sides (UTVs), which are becoming more common, can present their own challenges as most shops do not have four-post lifts to raise the vehicle.

The following hints can make the engine removal process easier:

- Protect all painted surfaces, including the frame.
- Determine whether the wire harness will stay with the vehicle or remain attached.
- Label all connectors on the wiring harness, including unused ones.
- Whenever possible, remove hoses from one end only. Label the hose and the connection from which it was removed.
- Reinstall all frame bolts back in the frame holes.
- Take pictures of the assembled engine and use the wire/hose/cable routing diagrams to aid in reassembly.
- Drain all fluids, but expect components to have some fluid left inside.
- Clean up spills immediately.

Objective

After successfully completing this job, you will be able to remove an engine from a vehicle.

Materials and Equipment

To complete this job, you will need the following tools, equipment, and materials:

- Vehicle
- Appropriate service manual or electronic service information
- Hand and power tools as needed
- Tape and pen for marking components
- Camera if desired

Instructions

In this job, you will be removing an engine from a vehicle. Depending on your instructor's directions, you will also be reinstalling the engine or continuing with other engine tasks. Check with your instructor to see if you will be reusing any fluids. Make sure you have secured the vehicle properly to compensate for engine removal. If necessary, make sure that the frame can be lifted.

Read the job procedures, perform the tasks, and answer all questions. As you complete steps, you will be given instructions to either fill in measurements or perform certain tasks. When you reach a sign, show your work to your instructor. Do not continue until you have instructor approval (instructor will initial job sheet).

> **WARNING** Before performing this job, review all pertinent safety information in the text and discuss safety procedures with your instructor.

Procedures

Removing Engine

> **CAUTION** This project is often assigned as a team. If multiple people are working on the task, make sure that one step is completed before going on to the next one. When multiple people are removing different parts, confusion often occurs during reassembly.

> **NOTE** As you perform the tasks outlined, mark them as completed in the chart.

Vehicle (Year/Make/Model)

_____

1. Locate the appropriate service manual and read the entire engine removal section.

2. Remove the battery. Label the battery with the customer name or bike repair number.

3. Drain the coolant.

4. Drain the oil.

5. Remove all plastics or trim, then remove the fuel tank. Store all pieces where they will not be damaged. Drain fuel out of the tank.

6. Remove the exhaust components. Store the components where they will not be damaged.

7. Remove and label wiring, hoses, and cables and any other parts that could be damaged during engine removal.

8. Tape, or otherwise protect, any part of the frame that could be damaged during engine removal.

9. Set up a space for the engine once it is removed.

Name _____

Task	Completed
Locate service manual and read engine removal section	
Remove battery, label battery if necessary	
Drain coolant	
Drain oil	
Remove and store plastics, trim, and the fuel tank	
Remove and store exhaust	
Remove and label hoses, wiring, cables, and other parts as necessary	
Protect frame as necessary	
Set up a space for the removed engine	

 10. Show your instructor that the engine is prepared for removal.

Instructor's Initials: _____

    11. Attach a suitable lifting device to the engine.

    12. Remove the fasteners holding the engine to the frame.

    13. Remove the engine using the lifting device.

    14. Secure the engine in a stand or jig so that it can be disassembled.

    15. Clean up any spills and place pans and/or absorbent towels to catch any leaking fluids.

    16. Repair any stripped threads on frame or exhaust.

 17. Discuss with your instructor whether you will be replacing this engine or completing other engine tasks with the engine removed.

Instructor's Initials: _____

Job Wrap Up

    18. Return all tools and materials to the proper storage areas and clean up your work area.

Final Assessment

_____ 1. Two technicians are discussing replacing an engine. Technician A says to use all new fluids. Technician B says to use a new oil filter, spark plugs, and air filter. Who is correct?

  A. A only.

  B. B only.

  C. Both A and B.

  D. Neither A nor B.

_____ 2. Two technicians are discussing removing an engine. Technician A says to keep all old parts until repairs are complete. Technician B says to throw away used parts as you take them off the vehicle. Who is correct?

  A. A only.

  B. B only.

  C. Both A and B.

  D. Neither A nor B.

_____ 3. Two technicians are discussing wiring harnesses while removing an engine. Technician A says that all connectors should be labeled. Technician B says that only connectors that could fit multiple places or look like others should be labeled. Who is correct?

  A. A only.

  B. B only.

  C. Both A and B.

  D. Neither A nor B.

_____ 4. _True or False?_ Air filters should be replaced or cleaned and oiled with a new engine.

_____ 5. _True or False?_ Engine removal can cause damage to electronic components if they are not removed or moved out of the way.

Final Instructor Approval: _____

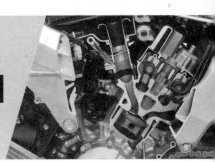

CHAPTER 21
Two-Stroke Engine Overhaul

Chapter 21 Quiz

After studying Chapter 21 in the Motorcycles: Fundamentals, Service, Repair textbook, answer the following questions.

_____ 1. Compared to a four-stroke engine, a two-stroke engine _____.

    A. has lower temperatures

    B. requires service and repair less often

    C. uses oil that is diluted with air and fuel

    D. All of the above.

_____ 2. Cylinder scoring appears as _____.

    A. scratches or grooves on the surface

    B. discoloration on the bottom

    C. rust or corrosion

    D. material built up on the surface

_____ 3. *True or False?* To determine cylinder condition, the cylinder should be measured at two or three points.

_____ 4. Piston galling can be caused by excessive _____.

    A. lubrication

    B. heat

    C. rust

    D. All of the above.

_____ 5. Piston skirt diameter is measured with a(n) _____.

    A. feeler gauge

    B. outside micrometer

    C. dial bore gauge

    D. Either B or C.

_____ 6. *True or False?* Piston ring end gap is measured with a feeler gauge.

_____ 7. Ring free gap is measured with a(n) _____.

_____ 8. A ridge at the top of a cylinder indicates _____.

    A. cylinder taper

    B. cylinder out-of-roundness

    C. cylinder galling

    D. incorrect piston-to-cylinder clearance

_____ 9. Cylinder out-of-roundness is caused by _____.

    A. excessive ring end gap

    B. insufficient ring side clearance

    C. piston thrust

    D. excessive piston-to-cylinder clearance

_____ 10. Piston-to-cylinder clearance is equal to cylinder bore diameter minus _____ diameter.

_____ 11. Engine decarbonizing is usually done by soaking the component in decarbonizing solvent, scraping, wire brushing, and _____ cleaning.

_____ 12. After deglazing, the last step in cleaning is to wipe the cylinder with a clean cloth soaked in _____ until the cloth is clean.

    A. solvent

    B. white grease

    C. detergent

    D. oil

_____ 13. _True or False?_ If the cylinder is within specs and the piston is worn undersize, ring replacement alone is sufficient.

_____ 14. After honing or deglazing, a technician must _____ the edges of the ports inside the cylinder.

_____ 15. If the connecting rod tip is excessive, there is excessive wear in the _____.

    A. wrist pin bearing

    B. thrust washers

    C. big end bearing

    D. oil pump housing

_____ 16. Connecting rod side play is measured with _____.

    A. a dial indicator

    B. an outside micrometer

    C. feeler gauges

    D. a vernier caliper

_____ 17. The technician should check main bearings for _____ play and radial play.

_____ 18. Crankshaft alignment after reassembly is checked with a truing stand and two _____.

_____ 19. _True or False?_ Dial indicators move in opposite directions when crankshaft axles are misaligned vertically.

_____ 20. _True or False?_ Excessive blowby caused by normal wear can lead to piston overheating.

_____ 21. The most common cause of two-stroke engine damage is _____.

    A. overheating

    B. improperly mixed fuel

    C. lack of lubrication

    D. improper repair procedures

Name _____   Date _____   Class _____

_____   22. An incorrect spark plug heat range or incorrect ignition _____ can cause overheating.

_____   23. *True or False?* Detonation occurs when an overheated surface in the combustion chamber ignites the air-fuel mixture before the spark plug fires.

_____   24. Excessive compression ratio and _____ are causes of detonation.
   A. an overly rich air-fuel mixture
   B. low octane fuel
   C. a high spark plug heat range
   D. lubrication failure

_____   25. Damage caused by the fuel system often appears to have been caused by the _____.
   A. lubrication system
   B. ignition system
   C. cooling system
   D. starting system

_____   26. All of the following statements are true of cold seizure, *except*:
   A. damage is caused by operating the engine without proper warm-up.
   B. the cylinder expands faster than the piston.
   C. it is more likely on liquid-cooled cast-iron sleeved cylinders.
   D. scoring marks are present on the pistons.

_____   27. *True or False?* During engine assembly, all-purpose grease can be used on seals.

_____   28. After each installation of a rotating component, the technician should check for _____ to ensure free movement.

_____   29. If there is no gasket, machined surfaces must be sealed with a(n) _____-based sealant or an approved liquid gasket.

_____   30. Piston rings must be properly installed in grooves and _____ on locating pins.

_____   31. A crankcase pressure test is performed with the piston _____.
   A. at BDC
   B. at TDC
   C. between the transfer ports
   D. 10 mm from TDC

_____   32. Prior to attempting to start a newly overhauled engine, the technician should _____.
   A. clean the sediment bowl
   B. service the air filter
   C. fill the transmission with lubricant
   D. All of the above.

Notes

Name _____ Date _____ Class _____

Job 21-1

Pressure Testing Two-Stroke Engines

Introduction

Two-stroke engines must be sealed at the top and bottom so that the engine will run properly and to reduce wear. Keeping a two-stroke engine sealed properly keeps out unwanted dirt and keeps in needed compressed air.

Objective

After successfully completing this job, you will be able to pressure test a two-stroke engine.

Materials and Equipment

To complete this job, you will need the following tools, equipment, and materials:

- Vehicle with two-stroke engine or a core two-stroke engine
- Appropriate service manual or electronic service information
- Hand tools as needed
- Two-stroke pressure tester

Instructions

In this job, you will be pressure testing a two-stroke engine. You will need to remove the carburetor and muffler and plug openings. Access to the crank seals on both sides of the engine helps to properly check for leaks. Different pressure testing kits have different adapters to apply pressure through the intake and exhaust ports.

Read the job procedures, perform the tasks, and answer all questions. As you complete steps, you will be given instructions to either fill in measurements or perform certain tasks. When you reach a sign, show your work to your instructor. Do not continue until you have instructor approval (instructor will initial job sheet).

 WARNING ⚠ Before performing this job, review all pertinent safety information in the text and discuss safety procedures with your instructor.

Procedures

Pressure Test Engine

 CAUTION   This project is often assigned as a team. If multiple people are working on the task, make sure that one step is completed before going on to the next one. When multiple people are performing different tasks, confusion often occurs.

Vehicle (Year/Make/Model)

_____

1. Locate the proper service manual or pressure tester manual.
2. Read the entire process for pressure testing the engine.
3. Remove the carburetor and plug the intake port.
4. Remove the exhaust and plug the exhaust port.

 NOTE   Steps 5 and 6 may vary depending on engine design.

5. Remove the right side cover to expose the crank seal.
6. Remove the stator/left side cover to expose the crank seal.
7. Move the piston to bottom dead center (BDC).
8. Install the pressure tester.
9. Operate the pressure tester to obtain the specified range.

 NOTE   The usual range is 6 psi for six minutes, with a maximum of 10 psi.

Does pressure hold for the minimum time? Yes _____ No _____ If no, consult your instructor.

 10. Show your instructor the properly prepared engine with the pressure tester installed.

Instructor's Initials: _____

11. Obtain the proper solution for spraying the engine to look for leaks.
12. Use the pressure tester to raise pressure to the specified range.
13. Spray the following engine parts and look for air leakage as indicated by bubbles.

 NOTE   Continue the test for six minutes, making double and triple checks.

Name _____

Task	Result	Repeat	Repeat
Exhaust and intake plugs			
Head gasket			
Reed valve housing			
Left side crank seal			
Right side crank seal			
Housing (casting defects and/or cracks)			

STOP 14. Discuss the results with your instructor, and be prepared to point out any leaks.

Instructor's Initials: _____

Job Wrap Up

15. Return all tools and materials to the proper storage areas and clean up your work area.

Final Assessment

_____ 1. Two technicians are discussing two-stroke pressure testing. Technician A says that pressure leaks can cause hard starting. Technician B says that pressure leaks can cause a no-start condition. Who is correct?

A. A only.

B. B only.

C. Both A and B.

D. Neither A nor B.

_____ 2. Two technicians are two-stroke pressure testing. Technician A says that if one crank seal is leaking, both should be replaced. Technician B says that once one leak is found and repaired, the engine will need to be tested again. Who is correct?

A. A only.

B. B only.

C. Both A and B.

D. Neither A nor B.

_____ 3. Two technicians are discussing two-stroke pressure testing. Technician A says that a right side crank seal leak can cause rich running. Technician B says that a head gasket leak can cause rich running. Who is correct?

A. A only.

B. B only.

C. Both A and B.

D. Neither A nor B.

_____   4. *True or False?* Leaks that are exposed to atmospheric pressure will cause the engine to run lean.

_____   5. *True or False?* Running lean can cause overheating.

Final Instructor Approval: _____

Name _____ Date _____ Class _____

Job 21-2

Servicing Two-Stroke Engine Top End

Introduction

While disassembling the top end, you will make some measurements to determine whether or not further repair will be required. Understanding the proper measurements of the top end is critical to know whether the pieces can be used again or must be replaced. For example, if the cylinder is to be bored, then you know that you will be replacing the piston, rings, wrist pin, and bearings. The top end components will be reinstalled in Job 21-4. Using the proper tools is critical. The wrong tools can cause damage to threads and engine components.

Objective

After successfully completing this job, you will be able to service the top end of a two-stroke engine.

Materials and Equipment

To complete this job, you will need the following tools, equipment, and materials:

- Vehicle with two-stroke engine or a core two-stroke engine
- Appropriate service manual or electronic service information
- Hand tools and other tools as necessary
- Micrometer, feeler gauge set, and cylinder bore gauge

Instructions

In this job, you will be removing the parts of a two-stroke engine top end. Before beginning, determine whether there is a performance complaint or if it is a standard maintenance procedure. You will need to measure the piston and cylinder using the service manual procedure. If there is obvious wear and scoring, a decision of whether to bore or replace the cylinder will be made. This is also a good time to service the carburetor and repack the exhaust, which were covered in earlier jobs.

Read the job procedures, perform the tasks, and answer all questions. As you complete steps, you will be given instructions to either fill in measurements or perform certain tasks. When you reach a sign, show your work to your instructor. Do not continue until you have instructor approval (instructor will initial job sheet).

> **WARNING** ⚠ Before performing this job, review all pertinent safety information in the text and discuss safety procedures with your instructor.

Procedures

<table>
<tr><td>

CAUTION</td><td>This project is often assigned to a team. If multiple people are working on the task, make sure that one step is completed before going on to the next one. When multiple people are removing different parts, confusion often occurs during reassembly.</td></tr>
</table>

Vehicle (Year/Make/Model)

_____

Disassemble Top End

1. Determine whether the engine is being serviced because of a customer complaint or as part of regular maintenance.

   _____

   If there was a specific complaint, write the complaint in the space below.

   _____

   _____

   _____

2. Locate the service manual and read the entire section on removing the top end components.

<table>
<tr><td>

NOTE</td><td>While performing Steps 3 through 9, write your observations in the chart.</td></tr>
</table>

3. Remove the cylinder head.

4. Hold the cylinder in place and turn the crankshaft to observe the piston going up and down. Note any defects.

   _____

   _____

5. Remove the cylinder.

6. Feel the wrist pin bearing for play.

7. Remove the piston.

8. Pull the connecting rod up and down and check for play.

9. Check the side play of the connecting rod thrust washers with feeler gauges.

Task	Completed	Observations/Readings
Locate and read service manual		
Remove the cylinder head		
Hold cylinder in place and observe piston going up and down		
Remove cylinder		

(Continued)

Name _____

Task	Completed	Observations/Readings
Feel the wrist pin bearing		
Remove piston		
Pull connecting rod up and down to check for play		
Check the side play of the connecting rod thrust washers		

 10. Show your instructor your results as entered in the chart and discuss the measurements that must still be made.

> **NOTE** Certain types of damage are severe enough that it is obvious that the part must be replaced without further inspection. If the cylinder crosshatching looks good and clearances are in spec, the top end may just need deglazing and re-ringing.

Instructor's Initials: _____

Inspect Top End Components

11. Make the following inspections and/or measurements and record your findings in the chart.

> **NOTE** You will find inspection parameters and specifications in the service manual. If a measurement is not listed in the manual, the part should still be inspected.

Task	Measurement	Spec	Reading
Piston scoring or other damage	—	—	
Piston diameter			
Piston out of round			
Cylinder scoring	—	—	
Cylinder diameter			
Cylinder out-of-round			
Wrist pin bearing diameter			
Wrist pin wear	—	—	
Wrist pin diameter			
Ring end gap			
Piston-to-cylinder clearance			
Cylinder head warpage			
Cylinder warpage at head mating surface			

12. Discuss the results with your instructor. Be prepared to discuss what your decisions on parts replacement would be based on part condition and measurements.

Instructor's Initials: _____

Honing a Cylinder

13. Discuss with your instructor whether you will be using the cylinder in this job for honing.

14. Obtain the proper hone for the cylinder.

> **NOTE** The hone size decision is based on the service manual specifications and the piston and cylinder diameter readings in the chart you have filled out.

> **CAUTION** ⚠ Make sure that you have had a demonstration on how to hone a cylinder.

15. Hone the cylinder to the proper finish (all glazing removed) and answer the following:

A. _____ Cylinder diameter

B. _____ Piston-to-cylinder clearance

C. _____ Amount of material removed

D. _____ Crosshatch angle

16. Wash the cylinder in soap and water and then lightly coat it with two-stroke engine oil.

 17. Discuss the results with your instructor. Be prepared to show the cylinder crosshatching pattern and final cylinder measurements.

Instructor's Initials: _____

Chamfering the Port Openings

> **NOTE** You may be performing chamfering on core engines or on the outside edges of the engine to practice using the tool prior to chamfering customer engines.

18. Discuss with your instructor methods of chamfering ports inside the cylinder.

> **NOTE** Chamfering is used to remove sharp edges from the transfer ports inside the cylinder to make rings last longer. It takes experience to remove the proper amount of material.

19. Follow your instructor's directions to chamfer cylinder port openings.

 20. Discuss the chamfering results with your instructor. Be prepared to discuss whatever challenges you had chamfering the ports.

Instructor's Initials: _____

Name _____

Job Wrap Up

21. Return all tools and materials to the proper storage areas and clean up your work area.

22. Ask your instructor to check your work and initial this job sheet.

Final Assessment

_____   1. You are testing the side play of the connecting rod. If play is excessive, what component must be replaced?
   A. Connecting rod.
   B. Crankshaft.
   C. Crankshaft side spacers.
   D. Wrist pin bearing.

_____   2. Two technicians are discussing two-stroke top end service when the cylinder is out-of-round but the piston is not. Technician A says to bore the cylinder and replace the piston. Technician B says to bore the cylinder and reuse the piston. Who is correct?
   A. A only.
   B. B only.
   C. Both A and B.
   D. Neither A nor B.

_____   3. Two technicians are discussing two-stroke top end service where cylinder-to-piston clearance is correct but scratching is excessive. Technician A says the cylinder will need to be bored or replaced and the piston replaced. Technician B says that the scratching is normal and the cylinder can be reused. Who is correct?
   A. A only.
   B. B only.
   C. Both A and B.
   D. Neither A nor B.

_____   4. *True or False?* New two-stroke pistons are sold with a new wrist pin bearing, wrist pin, and clips.

_____   5. *True or False?* If cylinder scratches are too deep to be bored out, the cylinder must be replaced.

Final Instructor Approval: _____

Notes

Name _____   Date _____   Class _____

Job 21-3

Servicing Two-Stroke Engine Bottom End

Introduction

You must understand the proper measurements of the bottom end to determine whether components should be used again or replaced. Taking accurate measurements is critical to making these decisions. The installation of new bearings and gaskets takes practice to avoid damaging parts.

Objective

After successfully completing this job, you will be able to service the bottom end of a two-stroke engine.

Materials and Equipment

To complete this job, you will need the following tools, equipment, and materials:

- Vehicle with two-stroke engine or a core two-stroke engine
- Appropriate service manual or electronic service information
- Hand tools as needed
- Case splitter
- Micrometer, feeler gauge set, and cylinder bore gauge

Instructions

In this job, you will be disassembling the bottom end of a two-stroke engine, removing the crankshaft from the engine, and pressing out the case bearings. (Pressing apart crankshafts is covered in Job 21-5.)

Read the job procedures, perform the tasks, and answer all questions. As you complete steps, you will be given instructions to either fill in measurements or perform certain tasks. When you reach a 🛑 sign, show your work to your instructor. Do not continue until you have instructor approval (instructor will initial job sheet).

> **WARNING** ⚠ Before performing this job, review all pertinent safety information in the text and discuss safety procedures with your instructor.

Procedures

Disassemble Bottom End

 CAUTION   This project is often assigned as a team. If multiple people are working on the task, make sure that one step is completed before going on to the next one. When multiple people are removing different parts, confusion often occurs during reassembly.

Vehicle (Year/Make/Model)

_____

1. Locate the service manual and read the entire procedure for removing the bottom end components.

2. Remove the top end components as covered in Job 21-2. Lay them to the side on a clean workbench.

3. Use a feeler gauge set to check the connecting rod side play.

4. Remove the stator and generator components as necessary.

5. Remove the shift mechanism(s).

6. Remove the clutch and place clutch components in order on a clean workbench.

7. Remove any oil injection pump components (make notes and take pictures of routing).

 8. Discuss with your instructor how to separate the cases using a case splitter.

Instructor's Initials: _____

Disassemble Bottom End

9. Remove all the screws and/or bolts holding the case halves together.

10. Separate the case halves with a case splitter.

11. Using a press and the proper adapters, remove the crankshaft from the case assembly.

Inspect Bottom End Components

12. Inspect all bearings.

 NOTE   You will find inspection procedures and specifications in the service manual. If a particular measurement is not listed in the manual, the part should still be inspected.

13. Inspect any bushings.

14. Check crankshaft runout.

　　A. _____   Crankshaft runout

　　B._____   Runout specification

 15. Discuss the inspection results with your instructor. Be prepared to discuss what your decisions on parts replacement would be based on part condition and measurements.

Instructor's Initials: _____

Name _____

Press Out Bearings

16. Consult the service manual for the proper bearing pressing procedure.

17. Press out the bearings from both side case assemblies.

18. Clean both case halves.

19. Check and restore the threads of all fasteners used to assemble both case halves and top end.

 20. Discuss the results with your instructor. Be prepared to discuss installation of new bearings.

Instructor's Initials: _____

Press in New Bearings

 CAUTION The performance of Steps 21 and 22 varies depending on the type of engine. To avoid bearing damage, consult the service manual before proceeding.

21. If any bearings need to be pressed in after heating the case, press them in now.

22. If any bearings need to be pressed in after being chilled, press them in once the case has cooled off (if it was heated to install bearings in Step 21).

23. Describe the process needed for bearing installation:

_____

_____

24. Lubricate the crankshaft and press it into the first half of the engine as outlined in the service manual.

 25. At this point the case halves will need to be reassembled. Discuss with your instructor the details of case reassembly.

Instructor's Initials: _____

Press Case Halves Together

26. Install new gasket(s) according to service manual instructions.

27. Press the case halves together.

 CAUTION When pressing, make sure that you support and press on the proper bearing races to avoid pressing through the rolling elements.

 NOTE Consult the service manual to determine whether locking agent should be applied to the case screws.

_____ Locking agent, if used

28. Install the case bolts and/or screws and tighten them to the proper torque.

_____ Case bolt torque (ft./lbs. N·M)

29. Check that the crankshaft rotates. If it does not rotate, the case must be disassembled to locate the problem.

Install Remaining Bottom End Components

30. Using the service manual, reinstall the shifter linkage and clutch assembly.

31. Reassemble the stator and generator rotor (make sure to properly lock the gears to hold the crankshaft while torquing the rotor bolt). After performing Steps 30 and 31, make sure that the crankshaft still turns freely.

_____ Rotor bolt torque

32. Install any remaining covers and other parts.

  The top end components will be reinstalled as part of Job 21-4. If Job 21-4 will not be performed immediately, place the top end components in a secure area and cover them with shop towels.

 33. Discuss the final engine bottom end assembly with your instructor.

Instructor's Initials: _____

Job Wrap Up

34. Return all tools and materials to the proper storage areas and clean up your work area.

Final Assessment

_____ 1. When testing the side play of the connecting rod, the play is excessive. What component must be replaced?

    A. Connecting rod.

    B. Crankshaft.

    C. Crankshaft side spacers.

    D. Wrist pin bearing.

_____ 2. Two technicians are discussing two-stroke engine bottom end service. Technician A says that bearings can be reused after being pressed out. Technician B says any bearing that is pressed out should be replaced. Who is correct?

    A. A only.

    B. B only.

    C. Both A and B.

    D. Neither A nor B.

_____ 3. Two technicians are discussing two-stroke bottom end service. Technician A says that ThreeBond adhesive can be used in place of a gasket. Technician B says that ThreeBond adhesive can be used in addition to a gasket if the case half condition is suspect. Who is correct?

    A. A only.

    B. B only.

    C. Both A and B.

    D. Neither A nor B.

_____ 4. _True or False?_ Two-stroke engine crankshafts should be replaced with every bottom end service.

_____ 5. _True or False?_ New crankshafts should be checked for runout.

Final Instructor Approval: _____

Name _____ Date _____ Class _____

Job 21-4

Reassembling Two-Stroke Engines

NOTE	This job is the final job of the two-stroke engine rebuilding process begun in Jobs 21-2 and 21-3.

Introduction

This job is meant to follow Job 21-2, Servicing Two-Stroke Engine Top End, and Job 21-3, Servicing Two-Stroke Engine Bottom End. In this job, you will be reinstalling the engine top end onto the bottom end.

Objective

After successfully completing this job, you will be able to reassemble a two-stroke engine.

Materials and Equipment

To complete this job, you will need the following tools, equipment, and materials:

- Two-stroke engine
- Appropriate service manual or electronic service information
- Hand tools as needed
- Torque wrench

Instructions

In this job, you will reassemble the top end parts onto the assembled bottom end. Be sure to lubricate places with proper oil where indicated. Clean and dry gasket sealing surfaces. If not done in earlier jobs, all fastener threads should be tapped and cleaned for ease of reassembly and proper torque.

Read the job procedures, perform the tasks, and answer all questions. As you complete steps, you will be given instructions to either fill in measurements or perform certain tasks. When you reach a **STOP** sign, show your work to your instructor. Do not continue until you have instructor approval (instructor will initial job sheet).

WARNING ⚠	Before performing this job, review all pertinent safety information in the text and discuss safety procedures with your instructor.

Procedures

Consult the service manual for each step. As you perform each task, check it off in the chart.

Vehicle (Year/Make/Model)

_____

Install Rings, Piston, and Cylinder

1. Install the rings on the piston.

> **CAUTION**    Pay close attention to ring position and ring end location.

2. Install one clip into the piston.
3. Lubricate and install the wrist pin bearing.
4. Install the piston and wrist pin and install the remaining clip.
5. Clean the case base gasket surface.
6. Install the base gasket on the case.
7. Lubricate the cylinder and install it over the piston, using any ring compressor or other special tools as necessary.
8. Torque the cylinder fasteners, if applicable.
9. Install the head gasket.
10. Install and align the power valve mechanisms, if necessary.

Task	Completed	Type of Lube	Torque
Locate service manual and read the top end installation section		—	—
Install the rings in proper locations			—
Install one clip into piston			—
Lubricate and install wrist pin bearing			—
Install piston and wrist pin			—
Install remaining clip			—
Clean base gasket surface		—	—
Install base gasket		—	—
Lubricate cylinder and install, torque if applicable			
Install head gasket		—	—
Install and align power valve mechanisms			

🛑 11. Discuss with your instructor the installation so far, prior to final cylinder head installation and torque.

Instructor's Initials: _____

Name _____

Install Cylinder Head

12. Place the cylinder head gasket on the cylinder.

13. Install the cylinder head and torque the cylinder head bolts to the proper specification. Cylinder head bolt torque:

    _____

14. Install pressure testing equipment and inspect the seals and gaskets for leaks. (Refer to Job 21-1 for procedures.)

    _____ Pressure applied

    _____ Time applied

    Any leaks? Yes _____ No _____ If yes, where?

    _____

>   Sometimes core engines used for this purpose will have leaks. Since the engine will not be installed in a vehicle, leaks are acceptable, but you should be able to locate the leaks.

 15. Discuss the results with your instructor and discuss any final assembly of exterior components.

Instructor's Initials: _____

Job Wrap Up

16. Return all tools and materials to the proper storage areas and clean up your work area.

Final Assessment

_____ 1. Two technicians are discussing leak testing a reassembled two-stroke engine. Technician A says that some air leaking during the pressure test is normal until an engine is broken in. Technician B says that no air should leak if the repairs were done correctly. Who is correct?

   A. A only.

   B. B only.

   C. Both A and B.

   D. Neither A nor B.

_____ 2. Two technicians are discussing two-stroke engine break-in. Technician A says that a properly rebuilt engine can be driven normally right away. Technician B says there should be a break-in period to properly set the rings. Who is correct?

   A. A only.

   B. B only.

   C. Both A and B.

   D. Neither A nor B.

_____   3. Two technicians are discussing two-stroke engine break-in. Technician A says that some manufacturers recommend using a fuel-oil mixture during initial start-up, even if the engine has an oil injection system. Technician B says that the oil injection system should be primed prior to start-up. Who is correct?

   A. A only.

   B. B only.

   C. Both A and B.

   D. Neither A nor B.

_____   4. *True or False?* Two-stroke engines with oil injection should be run without oil to burn off the oil from assembly at initial start-up.

_____   5. *True or False?* Two-stroke engines that are liquid cooled should have the cooling system pressure tested prior to start-up.

Final Instructor Approval: _____

Name _____   Date _____   Class _____

Job 21-5

Pressing Crankshafts and Servicing Components

Introduction

This job is concerned with pressing crankshafts apart and replacing thrust washers and bearings. There are fewer two-stroke engines in service than previously, so this procedure is becoming less common. Some shops find it more economical to install a new crankshaft rather than rebuilding the old one, but some manufacturers and regional shops continue to press crankshafts. The process requires the proper press jig and adapters.

Objective

After successfully completing this job, you will be able to press crankshafts and service components.

Materials and Equipment

To complete this job, you will need the following tools, equipment, and materials:

- Two-stroke multipiece crankshaft
- Appropriate service manual or electronic service information
- Press jig for pressing crankshaft
- Dial indicator set up for checking crank runout
- Micrometer

Instructions

In this job, you will press a crankshaft to replace thrust washers and crankshaft big end bearings. As part of this process, you will inspect washers and bearings and check crankshaft runout.

Read the job procedures, perform the tasks, and answer all questions. As you complete steps, you will be given instructions to either fill in measurements or perform certain tasks. When you reach a 🛑 sign, show your work to your instructor. Do not continue until you have instructor approval (instructor will initial job sheet).

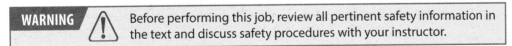

WARNING ⚠ Before performing this job, review all pertinent safety information in the text and discuss safety procedures with your instructor.

Procedures

Consult the service manual procedures for any specifics to your engine. Then fill out the chart as you perform the following steps.

 WARNING A press can cause severe injury. Use caution when pressing. Make sure that you know which part of the bearings should be supported and pressed. Do not allow the force of the press to be transferred through the ball or needle bearings.

Press Crankshaft Apart

1. Remove any bearings and drive sprockets from the crankshaft.
2. Mark the flywheel(s) to aid reassembly.
3. Check connecting rod width.

 NOTE Step 3 is explained in detail later in this job. Your instructor may want you to perform this step at this time.

4. Set up the press jig and the proper adapters for the next steps.
5. Press the crankpin from one flywheel.
6. Remove the thrust washers, bearing, and connecting rod from the crankshaft.
7. Press the crankpin from the other flywheel.
8. Inspect flywheels and connecting rod for damage.

Task	Completed
Remove bearings and drive sprockets from the crankshaft	
Mark flywheels for reassembly	
Check connecting rod width	
Press crankpin out of one flywheel	
Remove thrust washers, bearing, and connecting rod	
Press crankpin out of other flywheel	
Inspect flywheels and connecting rod for damage	

(STOP)   9. Discuss the process, results, and any special procedures needed with your instructor.

Instructor's Initials: _____

Press Crankshaft Together

Using the service manual and advice from your instructor, reassemble the crankshaft using the press jig and adapters. Fill out the chart as you perform the following steps.

10. Using the press jig and proper adapters, press the crankpin into the first flywheel.
11. Install the thrust washers, bearings, and connecting rod on the crankshaft.
12. Using the proper adapters, press the second flywheel onto the crank pin.

Name _____ Date _____ Class _____

13. Check for smooth connecting rod movement.

Task	Completed
Press crankpin into first flywheel	
Install thrust washers, bearings, and connecting rod	
Press second flywheel onto crankpin	
Check smooth connecting rod operation	

Check Connecting Rod Width and Alignment

> **NOTE**   In an actual service situation, connecting rod width and alignment are checked before crankshaft disassembly and after reassembly.

14. Obtain a micrometer capable of reading connecting rod width.

15. Check connecting rod width in four places around the crankshaft and record.

Location	Width	Difference
One		—
Two		
Three		
Four		

16. Determine from the chart whether the flywheel width and alignment are correct.

Width correct? Yes _____ No _____

Alignment correct? Yes _____ No _____

17. Discuss the above readings with your instructor and discuss the process of correcting misalignment.

18. Correct the flywheel width and alignment as necessary.
Briefly describe the method used.

_____

_____

19. Recheck the flywheel width and alignment and record.

Location	Width	Difference
One		—
Two		
Three		
Four		

20. Check thrust washer clearance.

_____ Side clearance

_____ Specification

A. Is side clearance within specs? Yes _____ No _____
B. If the side clearance is excessive, press the flywheels closer together and recheck the width.
C. If the side clearance is too small, press the flywheels farther apart and recheck the width.

(STOP) 21. Discuss the procedure and its results with your instructor and receive approval to move ahead to checking runout. (Make sure that the diameter and thrust washer clearance is correct prior to checking and fixing runout.)

Instructor's Initials: _____

Check Runout

22. Set up two dial indicators as shown in the Figure 21-5.1.

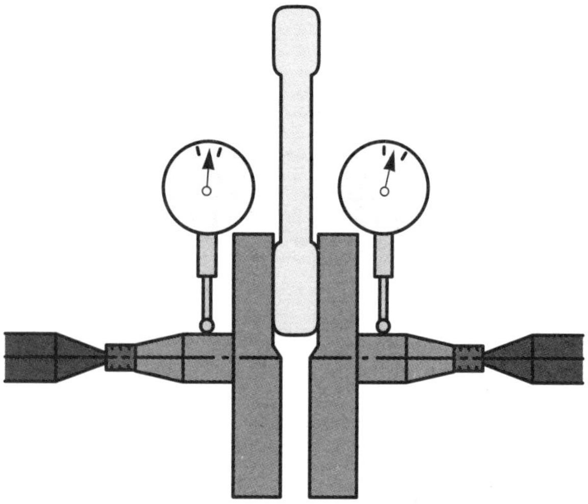

Bombardier Ltd.

Figure 21-5.1.

23. Measure the current runout on both dial indicators.

_____ Runout

_____ Specification

_____ Runout

_____ Specification

Is the runout within specs? Yes _____ No _____

24. Discuss with your instructor how to repair any runout issues. If there were no issues, ask your instructor whether Step 25 should be performed.

Name _____

25. Repeat width, runout, and thrust washer measurements and fill out the chart.

Task	Measurement	Spec
Width		
Runout		
Thrust washer clearance		

26. Press the bearings back onto the crankshaft.

(STOP) 27. Discuss the results with your instructor.

Instructor's Initials: _____

Job Wrap Up

28. Return all tools and materials to the proper storage areas and clean up your work area.

Final Assessment

_____ 1. Two technicians are discussing two-stroke crankshafts. Technician A says that thrust washers and big end bearings can be reused if they are within specifications. Technician B says that, if the crankshaft is being pressed apart, always use new thrust washers and bearings. Who is correct?

A. A only.

B. B only.

C. Both A and B.

D. Neither A nor B.

_____ 2. Two technicians are discussing engine break-in. Technician A says that break-in is most important for the rings and cylinder. Technician B says break-in is most important for the lower end bearings. Who is correct?

A. A only.

B. B only.

C. Both A and B.

D. Neither A nor B.

_____ 3. Two technicians are discussing two-stroke crankshafts. Technician A says that runout is more important than the flywheels being parallel. Technician B says runout will not be correct unless the flywheels are parallel. Who is correct?

A. A only.

B. B only.

C. Both A and B.

D. Neither A nor B.

_____ 4. *True or False?* Two-stroke crankshafts have to be taken apart at regular hourly intervals.

_____ 5. *True or False?* Two-stroke crankshafts are only taken apart when the bearing and/or thrust washers and connecting rod need replacing.

Final Instructor Approval: _____

Notes

CHAPTER
22

Four-Stroke Engine Overhaul

Chapter 22 Quiz

After studying Chapter 22 in the Motorcycles: Fundamentals, Service, Repair textbook, answer the following questions.

_____ 1. The _____ end of a four-stroke engine includes the camshafts, valves, cylinders, and pistons.

_____ 2. *True or False?* Any variation in cam lobe height indicates wear.

_____ 3. A camshaft is checked for straightness with a _____.

    A. micrometer

    B. dial indicator

    C. vernier caliper

    D. feeler gauge

_____ 4. Camshaft journal-to-bearing clearance can be measured with _____.

    A. feeler gauges

    B. a dial indicator

    C. Plastigage

    D. All of the above.

_____ 5. Prior to inspecting camshafts, followers, and rocker arms the technician should clean the parts with clean _____ and dry them with compressed air.

_____ 6. Which of the following statements about push rods is *true*?

    A. The ends should be checked for wear or damage.

    B. If the rod is bent, it should be replaced.

    C. A dial indicator is used to check for bends.

    D. All of the above.

_____ 7. The _____ is most commonly driven with a chain and sprockets.

_____ 8. Most chain drives require a(n) _____ and one or two chain guides.

_____ 9. Valve springs are checked for free height with _____.

    A. a micrometer

    B. feeler gauges

    C. calipers

    D. Plastigage

_____ 10. Damage to collars, retainers, and keepers can be caused by _____ failure and excessive engine speeds.

_____ 11. Before valve-to-guide clearance, the valve stem is cleaned with solvent to remove gum and _____.

_____ 12. Checking for cylinder head warpage is done with a _____ and _____.

A. micrometer, vise

B. dial indicator, V-blocks

C. vernier caliper, clamps

D. straightedge, feeler gauge

_____ 13. If too much material is removed when a cylinder is resurfaced, _____ timing will be altered and compression will be increased.

_____ 14. Important considerations for valve seat re-cutting are valve seat concentricity, valve seat surface finish, valve seat _____, and valve seat-to-valve contact.

_____ 15. Valve seat concentricity means that the valve seat _____.

A. touches the center of the valve face

B. is a uniform width and an equal distance around the valve guide bore

C. has a finish that is smooth and even to permit good sealing

D. is wide enough to prevent overheating but not wide enough to trap carbon

_____ 16. _True or False?_ A valve cutter pilot should fit loosely in the valve guide in order to center the cutter.

_____ 17. All of the following statements about re-cutting valve seats are true, _except_:

A. light, even pressure should be used to cut a valve seat.

B. a 45° cutter is used to adjust valve seat width and position.

C. seat width is measured with a dial caliper.

D. re-cutting valve seats requires cutters or stones of different angles.

_____ 18. Valve spring height is adjusted with _____.

A. shims

B. spacers

C. an adjusting screw

D. All of the above.

_____ 19. _True or False?_ Progressively wound valve springs are installed with the tighter coils towards the top collar.

_____ 20. After the cylinder head is reassembled, it should be wrapped in _____ or put in a sealed box to prevent contamination.

_____ 21. _True or False?_ To measure a cylinder for wear, six measurements should be made.

_____ 22. _True or False?_ Piston skirt diameter is measured perpendicular to the piston pin.

_____ 23. _True or False?_ If ring end gap is too small, the ring must be replaced.

_____ 24. Piston ring end gap and ring-to-groove clearance is measured with a _____.

A. micrometer

B. vernier caliper

C. feeler gauge

D. depth gauge

Name _____

_____ 25. If new piston rings are installed in a reconditioned cylinder, the piston ring _____ should be checked after cylinder deglazing.

_____ 26. Roller bearings and needle bearings should be checked for _____ play.

_____ 27. *True or False?* Oil pumps should be inspected and measured even if lubrication problems are not evident.

_____ 28. *True or False?* A thin oil film on connecting rod roller bearings makes wear easier to detect.

_____ 29. *True or False?* Crankshaft journals that are within specs and have a smooth surface can be polished and reused.

_____ 30. Major crankshaft reconditioning involves grinding rod or main journals and fitting _____ bearings.

_____ 31. When bearings and rod journals are excessively worn, the connecting rod's big end may become _____-shaped.

_____ 32. All of the following are guidelines for plain bearing installation, *except*:
A. gloves should be worn when handling the bearing surface.
B. Plastigage is used to determine bearing clearance.
C. crankshaft and bearing shells are lubricated prior to installation.
D. bearing shells must be fully seated before installation.

_____ 33. *True or False?* If engine components are not lubricated during assembly, immediate damage can result when the engine is run for the first time.

_____ 34. Which of the following statements about piston ring installation is *true*?
A. The oil ring is installed last.
B. Markings on top of the ring aid in installation.
C. The scraper ring is placed in the top groove.
D. All of the above.

_____ 35. Cam timing determines _____ movement in relation to piston movement.

_____ 36. On engines with rocker arm adjusters, valves are adjusted _____.
A. by replacing shims of different thickness
B. by loosening a locknut and adjusting a screw
C. after checking clearance with a feeler gauge
D. Both B and C.

_____ 37. *True or False?* During engine break-in, the engine should be allowed to idle for a long period of time.

Notes

Name _____ Date _____ Class _____

Job 22-1

Testing Four-Stroke Compression

Introduction

Compression testing is vital to determining the condition of a four-stroke engine. Poorly running engines should be compression tested. Tuning an engine that has weak compression in one or more cylinders is impossible. Compression issues must be resolved first.

Valve clearance has a direct correlation to compression. The sooner the intake valve can close on the compression stroke, the longer the piston has to compress the air-fuel charge. If engine dry compression is slightly low and the valve clearance can be adjusted, adjust the valves. If the compression is still low after the valve clearance is adjusted, the technician can perform other tests. A wet compression test can determine whether low compression is caused by the rings or valves. Leak down and smoke tests will identify the source of a leak. All of these tests are performed in this job.

Objective

After successfully completing this job, you will be able to make a compression test.

Materials and Equipment

To complete this job, you will need the following tools, equipment, and materials:

- Multiple-cylinder four-stroke engine (four-cylinder preferred)
- Appropriate service manual or electronic service information
- Compression tester
- Leak down tester
- Smoke machine, if available
- Hand tools as needed

Instructions

In this job, you will be making dry compression tests, wet compression tests, and leak down tests. If equipment is available, you will also make a smoke test. It is important to understand that your diagnosis may end at any point depending on the severity of the damage.

Read the job procedures, perform the tasks, and answer all questions. As you complete steps, you will be given instructions to either fill in measurements or perform certain tasks. When you reach a sign, show your work to your instructor. Do not continue until you have instructor approval (instructor will initial job sheet).

> **WARNING** ⚠️ Before performing this job, review all pertinent safety information in the text and discuss safety procedures with your instructor.

Procedures

Make Dry Compression Test

1. Locate and record the compression specifications for the engine being tested.

   _____ Specifications

2. If the engine is operable, start and warm up the engine.

> **NOTE** If the engine is cold, expect compression readings slightly lower than specifications.

3. Remove all engine spark plugs.

4. Ensure that the battery can crank the engine.

5. Set throttle to the fully open position.

6. Install compression tester in a spark plug opening.

7. Crank the engine through at least four compression strokes. (Four is the recommended minimum, after which the compression reading should stabilize.)

8. Repeat the compression checking procedure on all cylinders and fill in the chart.

	Cylinder 1	Cylinder 2	Cylinder 3	Cylinder 4
Dry compression				

Check Valve Clearance

9. Check the valve clearances, compare them against specifications, and fill in the chart.

Cylinder	1 In	1 Ex	2 In	2 Ex	3 In	3 Ex	4 In	4 Ex
Clearance								
Specification								
Difference								

 10. Discuss your initial compression readings and valve clearance. Ask your instructor whether you should adjust the clearance at this time.

Instructor's Initials: _____

Make Wet Compression Test

The wet compression test determines how well the rings seal. If a cylinder with low compression shows a significant compression rise when oil is added, the rings are not sealing. A wet compression test is normally done only if dry compression is low.

11. Squirt enough oil in one cylinder to seal the rings (usually a teaspoon or less is enough).

12. Crank the engine to distribute the oil in the cylinder.

13. Install the compression tester and check compression as in Step 7.

Name _____

14. Repeat Steps 11, 12, and 13 on all cylinders and record.

	Cylinder 1	Cylinder 2	Cylinder 3	Cylinder 4
Wet Compression				

(STOP) 15. Discuss the meaning of the readings with your instructor.

Instructor's Initials: _____

Make Leak Down Test

16. Place the piston at TDC (top dead center) compression (both valves closed).

17. Ensure that there is no pressure on the air regulator.

18. Remove the oil filler cap, air filter, breather hose, and radiator cap.

19. Screw the air pressure adapter into one spark plug opening and attach a shop air hose.

20. Apply the specified pressure to the cylinder, ensuring that pressure does not push the piston down in the cylinder.

21. Observe the gauge until the pressure stabilizes.

22. Listen for air escaping at the oil filler cap, air filter, breather hose, and/or radiator cap.

23. Repeat Steps 19, 20, 21, and 22 for all cylinders and record.

	Cylinder 1	Cylinder 2	Cylinder 3	Cylinder 4
Percent of Leakage				
Air Leaking From				

(STOP) 24. Discuss your findings with your instructor.

Instructor's Initials: _____

Make Smoke Leak Test

25. If a smoke machine is available, perform Steps 19, 20, 21, and 22 for all cylinders and record readings.

	Cylinder 1	Cylinder 2	Cylinder 3	Cylinder 4
Smoke Leaking From				

26. Reinstall the spark plugs and any other parts that were removed.

(STOP) 27. Discuss your findings with your instructor.

Instructor's Initials: _____

Job Wrap Up

28. Return all tools and materials to the proper storage areas and clean up your work area.

Final Assessment

_____ 1. Two technicians are discussing compression readings. Technician A says all readings should be within 10% of each other. Technician B says that all readings should be exactly the same, if possible. Who is correct?

   A. A only.

   B. B only.

   C. Both A and B.

   D. Neither A nor B.

_____ 2. Two technicians are discussing compression testing. Technician A says if all cylinders are low, the technician should use another compression tester to confirm. Technician B says if all measurements are low, the technician should make sure that the throttle is open and the battery fully charged. Who is correct?

   A. A only.

   B. B only.

   C. Both A and B.

   D. Neither A nor B.

_____ 3. Two technicians are discussing leak down testing. Technician A says that some air leaking past the rings is normal. Technician B says air leaking out of the oil filler cap is caused by intake valve leaks. Who is correct?

   A. A only.

   B. B only.

   C. Both A and B.

   D. Neither A nor B.

_____ 4. *True or False?* Smoke leaking from the exhaust could happen if the exhaust valve is bent or the engine is on the wrong stroke.

_____ 5. *True or False?* Air bubbles in the radiator can be caused by a cracked cylinder head.

Final Instructor Approval: _____

Name _____ Date _____ Class _____

Job 22-2

Understanding Mechanical Timing

Introduction

The technician must understand mechanical timing to adjust valves.

Many engines have a timing chain and a tensioner that make timing the crankshaft and camshaft a straightforward procedure. Some engines are more complex, such as V-type engines, which have one timing chain per bank. Each bank has to be timed with the engine in a certain position.

When adjusting timing, a solid understanding of what the valves should be doing in relation to the pistons will help you identify if the engine is timed incorrectly.

Objective

After successfully completing this job, you will be able to set mechanical timing on a four-stroke engine.

Materials and Equipment

To complete this job, you will need the following tools, equipment, and materials:

- At least three four-stroke engines (can be core engines)
- Appropriate service manual or electronic service information
- Hand tools as needed

Instructions

In this job, you will check the mechanical timing of a four-stroke engine, then remove and reinstall the engine's timing components in order to recheck timing.

Read the job procedures, perform the tasks, and answer all questions. As you complete steps, you will be given instructions to either fill in measurements or perform certain tasks. When you reach a sign, show your work to your instructor. Do not continue until you have instructor approval (instructor will initial job sheet).

> **WARNING** ⚠ Before performing this job, review all pertinent safety information in the text and discuss safety procedures with your instructor.

Procedures

Perform Mechanical Timing on Engine #1

Vehicle or engine (Year/Make/Model)

_____

1. Check that the mechanical timing is correct. (If it is not correct, discuss the problem with your instructor.)

2. Describe the type of valve train and components used on this engine.

_____

_____

3. Using the service manual, identify and explain the marks and directions used for setting the timing at TDC (top dead center) of the compression stroke.

_____

_____

4. Check and record the valve clearance here:

Cylinder	#1	#2	#3	#4
Intake				
Exhaust				

5. Remove the timing chain just enough so that you will have to retime the engine. Do not take the entire engine apart.

6. Determine whether the engine has a compression release mechanism. Yes _____ No _____

🛑 7. Show your instructor the removed camshaft and, if used, demonstrate how the compression release works. (Hint: It should push on the exhaust valve at low rpm and recede when rpm increases.)

Instructor's Initials: _____

8. Reassemble the engine.

9. Time the engine according to the service manual.

10. Turn the engine over by hand and follow the valve opening and closing sequences.

🛑 11. Show your instructor the properly timed engine and demonstrate the four strokes of the engine, including valve operation.

Instructor's Initials: _____

Name _____

Perform Mechanical Timing on Engine #2

Vehicle or engine (Year/Make/Model)

_____

12. Check that the mechanical timing is correct. If it is not correct, discuss the problem with your instructor.

13. Describe the type of valve train and components used on this engine.

_____

_____

14. Using the service manual, identify and explain the marks and directions used for setting the timing at TDC of the compression stroke.

_____

_____

15. Check and record the valve clearance here:

Cylinder	#1	#2	#3	#4
Intake				
Exhaust				

16. Remove the timing chain just enough so that you will have to retime the engine. Do not take the entire engine apart.

17. Determine whether the engine has a compression release mechanism. Yes _____ No _____

STOP 18. Show your instructor the removed camshaft and, if used, demonstrate how the compression release works. (Hint: It should push on the exhaust valve at low rpm and recede when rpm increases.)

Instructor's Initials: _____

19. Reassemble the engine.

20. Time the engine according to the service manual.

21. Turn the engine over by hand and follow the valve opening and closing sequences.

STOP 22. Show your instructor the properly timed engine and demonstrate the four strokes of the engine, including valve operation.

Instructor's Initials: _____

Perform Mechanical Timing on Engine #3

Vehicle or engine (Year/Make/Model)

_____

23. Check that the mechanical timing is correct. If it is not correct, discuss the problem with your instructor.

24. Describe the type of valve train and components used on this engine.

_____

_____

25. Using the service manual, identify and explain the marks and directions used for setting the timing at TDC of the compression stroke.

_____

_____

26. Check and record the valve clearance here.

Cylinder	#1	#2	#3	#4
Intake				
Exhaust				

27. Remove the timing chain just enough so that you will have to retime the engine. Do not take the entire engine apart.

28. Determine whether the engine has a compression release mechanism. Yes _____ No _____

🛑 29. Show your instructor the removed camshaft and, if used, demonstrate how the compression release works. (Hint: It should push on the exhaust valve at low rpm and recede when rpm increases.)

Instructor's Initials: _____

30. Reassemble the engine.

31. Time the engine according to the service manual.

32. Turn the engine over by hand and follow the valve opening and closing sequences.

🛑 33. Show your instructor the properly timed engine and demonstrate the four strokes of the engine, including valve operation.

Instructor's Initials: _____

Job Wrap Up

34. Return all tools and materials to the proper storage areas and clean up your work area.

Name _____

Final Assessment

_____ 1. Between which two strokes does valve overlap occur?

A. Intake and compression.

B. Compression and power.

C. Power and exhaust.

D. Exhaust and intake.

_____ 2. With no valve overlap, which stroke does the intake valve open on?

A. Intake.

B. Compression.

C. Power.

D. Exhaust.

_____ 3. With no valve overlap, which stroke does the intake valve close on?

A. Intake.

B. Compression.

C. Power.

D. Exhaust.

_____ 4. With no valve overlap, which stroke does the exhaust valve open on?

A. Intake.

B. Compression.

C. Power.

D. Exhaust.

_____ 5. With no valve overlap, which stroke does the exhaust valve close on?

A. Intake.

B. Compression.

C. Power.

D. Exhaust.

_____ 6. With valve overlap, which stroke does the intake valve open on?

A. Intake.

B. Compression.

C. Power.

D. Exhaust.

_____ 7. With valve overlap, which stroke does the intake valve close on?

A. Intake.

B. Compression.

C. Power.

D. Exhaust.

_____ 8. With valve overlap, which stroke does the exhaust valve open on?

A. Intake.

B. Compression.

C. Power.

D. Exhaust.

_____ 9. With valve overlap, which stroke does the exhaust valve close on?

A. Intake.

B. Compression.

C. Power.

D. Exhaust.

_____ 10. During which stroke does a compression release mechanism work?

A. Intake.

B. Compression.

C. Power.

D. Exhaust.

Final Instructor Approval: _____

Name _____ Date _____ Class _____

Job 22-3

Adjusting Screw and Nut Valve Trains

Introduction

Valve clearance adjustment is a core skill that all technicians must be able to perform. Valve checking is part of regular maintenance, engine rebuilds, and engine diagnosis. Valve clearance (sometimes called valve lash) is the space between the camshaft and the valve tip. This clearance will be measured in different places with different valve train configurations.

This job covers screw- and nut-type valve adjusters. The technician must develop a sense of feel to adjust valves.

Objective

After successfully completing this job, you will be able to check and adjust valve clearance.

Materials and Equipment

To complete this job, you will need the following tools, equipment, and materials:

- Vehicle engine (four-cylinder engine preferred) with screw and nut valve adjusters
- Appropriate service manual or electronic service information
- Feeler gauges
- Compression tester
- Hand tools as needed

Instructions

In this job, you will be adjusting screw and nut valves. In the first part of the job, you will be testing compression while adjusting valves to learn the relationship between valve adjustment and compression.

Read the job procedures, perform the tasks, and answer all questions. As you complete steps, you will be given instructions to either fill in measurements or perform certain tasks. When you reach a sign, show your work to your instructor. Do not continue until you have instructor approval (instructor will initial job sheet).

> **WARNING** ⚠ Before performing this job, review all pertinent safety information in the text and discuss safety procedures with your instructor.

Procedures

Record Present Valve Adjustment

Vehicle (Year/Make/Model)

_____

1. Find the proper service manual and read the process for adjusting valves on this vehicle.

> **NOTE** Use the service manual for all procedures, since engine configuration can be different and certain procedures can vary from engine to engine.

2. Check that the mechanical timing is correct and record the marks used for checking timing.

_____

_____

3. Set the engine at top dead center on the compression stroke.

> **NOTE** If the valve cover is removed, the last valve to close would be the intake valve.

4. Determine whether the engine has a compression release mechanism. Yes _____ No _____

> **NOTE** If the engine has a compression release mechanism, you may see the exhaust valve "bump" as it opens slightly.

5. Check and record valve clearance.

	Left Intake Valve	Right Intake Valve	Left Exhaust Valve	Right Exhaust Valve
Cylinder 1				
Cylinder 2				
Cylinder 3				
Cylinder 4				
Specification				

6. Circle any measurements that are out of specification.

 7. Discuss your findings with your instructor.

Instructor's Initials: _____

Name _____

Adjust Valve Clearance

    8. Adjust valve clearance so that the exhaust valves are in the middle of the specification range. General procedures:

        A. Loosen the locknut at the valve to be adjusted.

        B. Insert the proper thickness feeler gauge between the valve tip and rocker arm.

        C. Turn the adjusting screw until the feeler gauge slips between the rocker arm and tip with a slight drag.

        D. While holding the adjusting screw, tighten the locknut.

        E. Recheck clearance after tightening the locknut.

        F. Repeat Steps A through E on all valves needing adjustment.

   9. Discuss your findings with your instructor.

Instructor's Initials: _____

Determine Valve Clearance Effect on Compression

    10. Adjust one cylinder's intake valve until there is no clearance.

    11. Test compression for the cylinder.

      _____ Compression reading

    12. Adjust the same cylinder's intake valve clearance to the high side of spec (as loose as spec will allow).

    13. Test the compression for that cylinder.

      _____ Compression reading

    14. Reset valve adjustment so that the valve is within specifications.

   15. Discuss your findings with your instructor. Be prepared to discuss valve adjustment in relation to compression.

Instructor's Initials: _____

Job Wrap Up

    16. Return all tools and materials to the proper storage areas and clean up your work area.

Final Assessment

_____ 1. How many revolutions does the camshaft turn during two revolutions of the crankshaft?
   A. One.
   B. Two.
   C. Three.
   D. Four.

_____ 2. What effect does increasing valve clearance have on compression?
   A. Compression stays the same.
   B. Compression goes down.
   C. Compression goes up.
   D. Compression is divided in half.

_____ 3. On what stroke does the intake valve close?
   A. Intake.
   B. Compression.
   C. Power.
   D. Exhaust.

_____ 4. On what stroke does the exhaust valve open?
   A. Intake.
   B. Compression.
   C. Power.
   D. Exhaust.

_____ 5. What is valve overlap?
   A. When both intake valves are open at the same time.
   B. When the intake valves hit the piston.
   C. When the intake and exhaust valves are open at the same time.
   D. When the exhaust valves are open at the same time.

Final Instructor Approval: _____

Name _____ Date _____ Class _____

Job 22-4

Adjusting Shim-Type Valve Trains

Introduction

On some engines, valves are adjusted by replacing the original shims with shims that are thinner or thicker. Valve adjustment, or at least valve clearance checking, is done as part of regular maintenance, during engine rebuilds, and for diagnosis.

Objective

After successfully completing this job, you will be able to check and adjust valve clearance on an engine with shim-type valve adjusters.

Materials and Equipment

To complete this job, you will need the following tools, equipment, and materials:

- Engine (four-cylinder preferred) with shim-type valve adjusters
- Appropriate service manual or electronic service information
- Feeler gauges
- Shim kit
- Hand tools as needed

Instructions

In this job, you will be adjusting shim-type valves. Once you decide on a measurement, you should always check the next clearance measurement (up or down) to make sure that you have chosen correctly. You will then remove the shims and measure them accurately. Even though shims are stamped with their measurements, sometimes that can change or the measurement can be worn off.

Once you have made the measurements and decisions on new shims, you will compare your results to a shim chart in the service manual. In this way you will understand the process and be able to make measurements without a shim chart.

Read the job procedures, perform the tasks, and answer all questions. As you complete steps, you will be given instructions to either fill in measurements or perform certain tasks. When you reach a sign, show your work to your instructor. Do not continue until you have instructor approval (instructor will initial job sheet).

WARNING ⚠️ Before performing this job, review all pertinent safety information in the text and discuss safety procedures with your instructor.

Procedures

Check Valve Clearance

Vehicle (Year/Make/Model)

_____

1. Find the correct service manual and read the process for adjusting valves.

   > **NOTE** ⚙ Always consult the service manual. Engine configuration and procedures can vary from engine to engine.

2. Check that the mechanical timing is correct and record the marks used for checking timing.

   _____

   _____

3. Set the engine at top dead center on the compression stroke.

4. Determine whether the engine has a compression release mechanism. Yes _____ No _____

   > **NOTE** ⚙ If the engine has a compression release mechanism, you may see the exhaust valve "bump" as it opens slightly.

5. Check and record intake valve clearance.

	Left Intake Valve Clearance	Correction Needed	Shim Size	New Shim Size
Cylinder 1				
Cylinder 2				
Cylinder 3				
Cylinder 4				
Specification				

	Right Intake Valve Clearance	Correction Needed	Shim Size	New Shim Size
Cylinder 1				
Cylinder 2				
Cylinder 3				
Cylinder 4				
Specification				

🛑 6. Discuss your intake valve clearance findings with your instructor.

Instructor's Initials: _____

Name _____

7. Check and record the exhaust valve clearance.

	Left Exhaust Valve Clearance	Correction Needed	Shim Size	New Shim Size
Cylinder 1				
Cylinder 2				
Cylinder 3				
Cylinder 4				
Specification				

	Right Exhaust Valve Clearance	Correction Needed	Shim Size	New Shim Size
Cylinder 1				
Cylinder 2				
Cylinder 3				
Cylinder 4				
Specification				

 8. Discuss your exhaust valve clearance findings with your instructor.

Instructor's Initials: _____

Check Shim Chart

9. Locate the shim chart in the service manual and determine whether you have chosen the same size shim as the chart indicates.

 10. Discuss your findings with your instructor.

Instructor's Initials: _____

Adjust Clearance

11. Obtain a shim kit from your instructor.

12. Install the shims as outlined in the service manual.

> **NOTE** It is usually not necessary to install the timing chain to check valve clearance with the new shims.

13. Record the final valve clearance.

	Left Intake	Right Intake	Left Exhaust	Right Exhaust
Cylinder 1				
Cylinder 2				
Cylinder 3				
Cylinder 4				
Specification				

(STOP) 14. Discuss your findings with your instructor.

Instructor's Initials: _____

Job Wrap Up

15. Return all tools and materials to the proper storage areas and clean up your work area.

Final Assessment

_____ 1. The purpose of the compression release is to _____.
    A. make deceleration easier by acting as an exhaust brake
    B. make going uphill easier by acting as a torque multiplier
    C. cool the cylinder under high rpm situations
    D. make cranking the engine easier during starting

_____ 2. Which valve opens on which stroke for compression release?
    A. Exhaust on exhaust.
    B. Exhaust on compression.
    C. Intake on compression.
    D. Any stroke, depending on engine rpm.

3. Do the needed math to figure out what shim needs to be used to correct the valve adjustment (keep in mind that shims are available only in 0.05 mm increments).
Current clearance= 0.19 mm   Desired clearance= 0.08 mm   Current shim= 3.60 mm

_____ Shim needed (mm)

4. Do the needed math to figure out what shim needs to be used to correct the valve adjustment (keep in mind that shims are available only in 0.002" increments).
Current clearance= 0.004"   Desired clearance= 0.007"   Current clearance= 0.004"

_____ Shim needed (in.)

5. Do the needed math to figure out what shim needs to be used to correct the valve adjustment (keep in mind that shims are available only in increments of 0.002").
Current clearance= 0.011"   Desired clearance= 0.008"   Current shim= 0.219"

_____ Shim needed (in.)

Final Instructor Approval: _____

Name _____ Date _____ Class _____

Job 22-5

Setting Clearance with Adjustable Push Rods

Introduction

Some engines may be manufactured with adjustable push rods and hydraulic lifters or adjustable push rods may be installed as an aftermarket option. Not all push rods are adjustable. Some engines have solid push rods and adjustable rocker arms. Some engines, typically older models, have adjustable push rods and solid lifters. Valves usually do not need adjustment when hydraulic lifters or lash adjusters are used. There is, however, a method of increasing performance by adjusting the push rod.

Objective

After successfully completing this job, you will be able to adjust push rods on engines with hydraulic lifters.

Materials and Equipment

To complete this job, you will need the following tools, equipment, and materials:

- Engine (two-cylinder preferred) with hydraulic lifters and adjustable push rods
- Appropriate service manual or electronic service information
- Hand tools as needed

Instructions

In this job, you will be adjusting push rods. To adjust push rods, you must understand how hydraulic lifters operate. You will be adjusting the push rod to take up about one-half of the travel allowed by the hydraulic lifter.

Read the job procedures, perform the tasks, and answer all questions. As you complete steps, you will be given instructions to either fill in measurements or perform certain tasks. When you reach a sign, show your work to your instructor. Do not continue until you have instructor approval (instructor will initial job sheet).

> **WARNING** ⚠ Before performing this job, review all pertinent safety information in the text and discuss safety procedures with your instructor.

Procedures

Find the Base Circle

Vehicle (Year/Make/Model)

_____

1. Find the appropriate service manual and read the process for finding TDC (top dead center) on the compression stroke.

> **NOTE** The most efficient method of finding TDC is to:
> A. Raise the rear tire.
> B. Put the transmission in a high gear like fourth or fifth.
> C. Remove the spark plug(s) to make engine turning easier.
> D. Use the rear wheel to rotate the engine until both push rods rotate easily.

Adjust Clearance on Cylinder #1

2. Remove push rod covers.

> **CAUTION** ⚠ Be careful not to damage the push rod O-rings and gaskets.

3. Ensure the free movement of both push rods. This ensures that the camshaft lobe is on the base circle (lobes not pushing on the hydraulic lifter).

4. Loosen the adjuster lock nut.

5. Turn the adjuster nut while counting the flats (nut sides) as you turn. Six flats equal one full rotation of the nut.

_____   Number of flats to bottom

> **CAUTION** ⚠ Do not force the adjuster. When it stops turning, it has reached the bottom.

6. Now turn the adjuster back one-half the number of flats. This provides extra valve lift.

> **NOTE** If installing a replacement push rod kit, follow the kit instructions as to the specific number of flats to turn back.

> **CAUTION** ⚠ When you complete Step 6, you will not be able to turn the push rod. Do not turn the engine until the lifter bleeds down and you can rotate the push rod.

7. Repeat Steps 4, 5, and 6 for the exhaust valve on the same cylinder.

8. Allow enough time for the lifter to bleed down and then make sure that both push rods turn.

9. Tighten the push rod locknuts.

Name _____

 10. Discuss the adjustment process with your instructor before turning the engine to place the next cylinder on TDC. Demonstrate that the push rods rotate and then demonstrate how to find the base circle of the camshaft for the next cylinder.

Instructor's Initials: _____

Adjust Clearance on Cylinder #2

11. Remove push rod cover(s) if not already done.

> **CAUTION** Be careful not to damage the push rod O-rings and gaskets.

12. Ensure the free movement of both push rods. This ensures that the camshaft lobe is on the base circle (lobes not pushing on the hydraulic lifter).

13. Loosen the adjuster lock nut.

14. Turn the adjuster nut while counting the flats (nut sides) as you turn. Six flats equal one full rotation of the nut.

_____ Number of flats to bottom

> **CAUTION** Do not force the adjuster. When it stops turning, it has reached the bottom.

15. Turn the adjuster back one-half the number of flats. This provides extra valve lift.

> **NOTE** If installing a replacement push rod kit, follow the kit instructions as to the specific number of flats to turn back.

> **CAUTION** When you complete Step 15, you will not be able to turn the push rod. Do not turn the engine until the lifter bleeds down and you can rotate the push rod.

16. Repeat Steps 13, 14, and 15 for the exhaust valve on the same cylinder.

17. Allow enough time for the lifter to bleed down and then make sure that both push rods turn.

18. Tighten the push rod locknuts.

 19. Discuss the adjustment process with your instructor before turning the engine to place the next cylinder on TDC. Demonstrate that the push rods rotate and then demonstrate how to find the base circle of the camshaft for the next cylinder.

Instructor's Initials: _____

Job Wrap Up

20. Reinstall the valve covers if not already done.

21. Return all tools and materials to the proper storage areas and clean up your work area.

Final Assessment

_____ 1. Push rod engines are also called _____ engines.
  A. OHV
  B. OHC
  C. DOHC
  D. V-twin

_____ 2. Hydraulic lifters allow for zero valve clearance in order to _____.
  A. increase performance
  B. reduce maintenance
  C. have quieter operation
  D. Both B and C.

_____ 3. Adjusting push rods in the manner done in this job will increase which of the following engine parameters?
  A. Piston stroke.
  B. Valve lift.
  C. Valve opening duration.
  D. Cylinder bore.

_____ 4. _True or False?_ All push rods with hydraulic lifters are adjustable.

_____ 5. _True or False?_ Adjusting push rods is a method of compensating for a bent push rod.

Final Instructor Approval: _____

Name _____ Date _____ Class _____

Job 22-6

Disassembling Overhead Camshaft Four-Stroke Engines

Introduction

The motorcycle technician must be able to disassemble an engine, check various parts, and make decisions about replacing parts. Engines are taken apart for service or to make performance upgrades. In this job, the engine is simply being disassembled.

There are many variations on the four-stroke engine. This job is a generic procedure that can be applied to any overhead camshaft four-stroke engine.

Objective

After successfully completing this job, the student will be able to disassemble overhead camshaft four-stroke engines.

Materials and Equipment

To complete this job, you will need the following tools, equipment, and materials:

- Overhead camshaft four-stroke engine (can be core engine)
- Appropriate service manual or electronic service information
- Hand tools as needed
- Clean workbench and large area for laying out parts
- Appropriate cleaning supplies for coolant and oil spills

Instructions

In this job, you will be disassembling an overhead camshaft four-stroke engine and laying out parts in an organized fashion. You will also be using appropriate cleaning supplies to clean up coolant and oil spills. (The engine will contain some oil and coolant, even after the engine has been drained.)

Read the job procedures, perform the tasks, and answer all questions. As you complete steps, you will be given instructions to either fill in measurements or perform certain tasks. When you reach a sign, show your work to your instructor. Do not continue until you have instructor approval (instructor will initial job sheet).

> **WARNING** ⚠ Before performing this job, review all pertinent safety information in the text and discuss safety procedures with your instructor.

Procedures

 CAUTION This project is often assigned as a team. If multiple people are working on the task, make sure that one step is completed before going on to the next one. When multiple people are removing different parts, it is important to organize and lay out parts correctly to avoid confusion during reassembly. Fill out the charts provided as the engine is disassembled.

Describe the engine being disassembled:

_____

_____

_____

 NOTE For this job, it is assumed that the carburetor/injectors and intake manifold have previously been removed.

Remove Top End Components

1. Locate the appropriate service manual and read the entire process for removing the top end components.
2. Drain the engine oil and coolant.
3. Remove the valve cover.
4. Confirm that timing is correct and make note of timing marks.
5. Check the valve adjustment and record.
6. Remove or disconnect the timing chain from the camshaft as applicable.
7. Remove the camshaft.

 NOTE If the engine uses shim-type valve adjustment, set the shims aside in order. If the engine has hydraulic lifters or clearance adjusters, set them aside in order.

Task	Completed	Part Condition (if Applicable)
Read procedure in service manual		
Drain fluids		
Remove valve cover		
Confirm timing is correct; note timing marks		
Check the valve adjustment and record		
Release timing chain tensioner and remove or disconnect timing chain from camshaft		
Remove camshaft		
Set aside shims and hydraulic lifters or clearance adjusters in order		

Name _____

 8. Discuss with your instructor the disassembly process so far and the next steps to take.

Instructor's Initials: _____

Remove Cylinder Head

9. Break loose and remove all studs and bolts holding the cylinder head.

10. Remove the cylinder head.

11. If cylinders are separate from the bottom end, remove them and lay them aside in order.

12. If engine has thrust washers on the sides of the connecting rod, measure connecting rod side play. Record any that are out of specification.

13. Remove the clutch. Place the parts aside in order.

14. Remove the shift mechanism, if applicable.

15. Remove the water pump, if applicable.

16. Check crankshaft end play.

> **NOTE** Sometimes there is no specification for end play.

Task	Completed	Part Condition (if Applicable)
Remove all fasteners holding the cylinder head		
Remove cylinder head		
Remove cylinders, if applicable		
Measure the side play of connecting rods if thrust washers used at rods		
Remove clutch		
Remove shift mechanism		
Remove water pump		
Check crankshaft end play, if possible		

 17. Discuss disassembly and parts organization so far. Discuss whether this is a vertically or horizontally split crankcase and the process for separating the two halves.

Instructor's Initials: _____

Split Crankcase and Remove Parts

18. Remove the fasteners holding the halves together (use the service manual to find any bolts hidden under components).

19. Using a case splitter if necessary, separate the two halves of the case.

> **CAUTION** ⚠ Separate the halves carefully and take pictures if possible.

20. Remove any transmission components necessary.

21. If necessary, use a press to remove the crankshaft from the case. Make sure to store any thrust washers or other washers in their proper location.

22. Remove the timing chain tensioner and remove or disconnect the timing chain from the camshaft.

Task	Completed	Part Condition (if Applicable)
Remove all fasteners holding the halves		
Separate the case halves (using a case splitter, if necessary)		
Remove transmission components as necessary		
Remove crankshaft from case		
Remove or disconnect timing chain from the camshaft		

> **NOTE** At this point the engine should be fully disassembled.

 23. Discuss the disassembly with your instructor.

Instructor's Initials: _____

Job Wrap Up

24. Return all tools and materials to the proper storage areas and clean up your work area.

Final Assessment

_____ 1. *True or False?* Pistons should be able to move from side to side on the connecting rod.

_____ 2. *True or False?* Connecting rods should be able to move from side to side on the crankshaft.

_____ 3. *True or False?* The rocker arms should be able to move from side to side on the rocker arm shaft.

_____ 4. *True or False?* The piston should move smoothly on the wrist pin.

_____ 5. *True or False?* The piston rings should not be able to move freely in the ring lands.

Final Instructor Approval: _____

Name _____ Date _____ Class _____

Job 22-7

Disassembling Overhead Valve Four-Stroke Engines

Introduction

An engine can be taken apart for many reasons, including repairs and adding high performance equipment.

There are many variations on the four-stroke engine. This job covers disassembling an overhead valve four-stroke engine, sometimes called a push rod engine.

Objective

After successfully completing this job, the student will be able to disassemble an overhead valve four-stroke engine.

Materials and Equipment

To complete this job, you will need the following tools, equipment, and materials:

- Overhead valve four-stroke engine (can be core engine)
- Appropriate service manual or electronic service information
- Hand tools as needed
- Clean workbench
- Large area for laying out and organizing parts
- Cleaning supplies appropriate for cleaning coolant and oil spills

Instructions

In this job, you will be disassembling an overhead valve four-stroke engine and laying out the parts in an organized fashion. You will need appropriate cleaning supplies to clean up coolant and oil spills as the engine is disassembled. The engine will have oil and coolant in it, even after being drained.

Read the job procedures, perform the tasks, and answer all questions. As you complete steps, you will be given instructions to either fill in measurements or perform certain tasks. When you reach a sign, show your work to your instructor. Do not continue until you have instructor approval (instructor will initial job sheet).

 Before performing this job, review all pertinent safety information in the text and discuss safety procedures with your instructor.

Procedures

CAUTION This project is often assigned as a team. If multiple people are working on the task, make sure that one step is completed before going on to the next one. When multiple people are removing different parts, confusion can occur during reassembly. Fill out the charts provided as the engine is disassembled.

Describe the engine being disassembled:

_____

_____

_____

NOTE For this job, it is assumed that the carburetor/injectors and intake manifold have previously been removed.

Disassemble Top End Components

1. Locate the appropriate service manual and read the entire process for removing the top end components.
2. Drain the oil and coolant.
3. Remove the valve cover and cam timing cover and ensure that the mechanical timing marks line up.
4. Remove the push rod covers to expose the push rods.
5. Practice locating the base circle of the camshaft for each cylinder by finding top dead center and making the push rods rotate smoothly.
6. Remove rocker arms, push rods, and rocker covers on both cylinders.
7. Remove the lifters and store in order.
8. Remove the cam plate(s) and camshafts.

Task	Completed	Part Condition (if Applicable)
Read the service manual process for removing the top end components		
Drain fluids		
Remove the valve cover and cam timing cover		
Ensure the mechanical timing marks line up		
Remove the push rod covers to expose the push rods		
Practice finding top dead center for each cylinder		
Remove the rocker arms, push rods, and rocker covers		
Remove lifters		
Remove cam plate and camshafts		

9. Discuss with your instructor the disassembly process so far and the next steps to take.

Instructor's Initials: _____

Name _____

Disassemble Cylinders and Measure Play

10. Remove the cylinders, if applicable.

11. Measure the side play of the connecting rods if the engine has thrust washers on the sides of the connecting rod. Record any that are out of specification.

12. Check for crankshaft end play.

> **NOTE** Sometimes there is no end play specification.

Task	Completed	Part Condition (if Applicable)
Remove cylinders		
Measure side play of connecting rods		
Check crankshaft end play if a spec is given		

 13. Discuss disassembly and parts organization so far, and the next steps to take.

Instructor's Initials: _____

Split Crankcase Halves

14. Remove all fasteners holding case halves together. (Use the service manual to find bolts hidden under components.)

15. Separate the two halves of the case, using a case splitter if necessary.

> **NOTE** Split the case carefully and take pictures if desired.

16. Remove any transmission components as necessary.

17. If necessary, use a press to remove the crankshaft from the case.

> **NOTE** Store any thrust washers or other washers in their proper location.

18. Release the timing chain tensioner and remove or disconnect the timing chain from the camshaft.

Task	Completed	Part Condition (if Applicable)
Remove fasteners holding case halves together		
Separate case halves		
Remove transmission components as necessary		
Remove crankshaft from case		
Remove or disconnect timing chain from camshaft		

🛑 19. Discuss the disassembly results with your instructor. The engine should be fully disassembled.

Instructor's Initials: _____

Job Wrap Up

20. Return all tools and materials to the proper storage areas and clean up your work area.

Final Assessment

_____ 1. Two technicians are discussing engine teardown. Technician A says not to worry about mechanical timing, just take the engine apart. Technician B says determining whether the engine timing is off or the chain is stretched will help to diagnose other issues. Who is correct?

A. A only.

B. B only.

C. Both A and B.

D. Neither A nor B.

_____ 2. Two technicians are discussing push rod engines. Technician A says that camshaft bearing failure can cause the timing chain to jump. Technician B says that camshaft chain tensioner failure can cause the timing chain to jump. Who is correct?

A. A only.

B. B only.

C. Both A and B.

D. Neither A nor B.

_____ 3. Two technicians are discussing engine oil burning. Technician A says that if an engine is burning oil, it will also have low compression. Technician B says that if an engine is burning oil, it will also have excessive blowby. Who is correct?

A. A only.

B. B only.

C. Both A and B.

D. Neither A nor B.

_____ 4. *True or False?* Low oil pressure can cause engine knocking.

_____ 5. *True or False?* High oil pressure can cause oil leaks.

Final Instructor Approval: _____

Name _____   Date _____   Class _____

Job 22-8

Measuring Four-Stroke Engine Components

Introduction

Measuring engine components is a critical step in correctly repairing an engine. Some very important steps must be taken to ensure correct repairs. For instance, a cylinder may look good due to a lack of scoring, but may have excessive cylinder-to-piston clearance. If the clearance is not noticed, the repaired engine can make noise and have excessive blowby.

　　This job does not cover checking every possible engine part. To check parts such as oil pumps, water pumps, push rods, and rocker arms, consult the service manual and your instructor.

Objective

After successfully completing this job, the student will be able to measure components of a four-stroke engine.

Materials and Equipment

To complete this job, you will need the following tools, equipment, and materials:

- Disassembled four-stroke engine
- Appropriate service manual or electronic service information
- Valve removal tools as necessary
- Micrometers, vernier caliper, dial indicator, straightedge, feeler gauges, and cylinder bore gauge
- Plastigage
- Hand tools as needed

Instructions

In this job, you will be measuring components of a four-stroke engine. Measuring takes practice and you may need to make measurements several times until you are comfortable using the measuring tools. Measurements must be made while keeping the tools perpendicular or parallel to the working surface. Do not make measurements at angles to flat surfaces, since this will result in incorrect measurements and false conclusions.

　　Read the job procedures, perform the tasks, and answer all questions. As you complete steps, you will be given instructions to either fill in measurements or perform certain tasks. When you reach a sign, show your work to your instructor. Do not continue until you have instructor approval (instructor will initial job sheet).

> **WARNING** ⚠ Before performing this job, review all pertinent safety information in the text and discuss safety procedures with your instructor.

Procedures

Check Cylinder Head and Valve Condition

1. Remove the valves from the cylinder head using the correct tools.

> **CAUTION** ⚠️ Keep the parts from each valve together and in the proper location so they can go back in the same place. It is important that parts go back where they came from.

2. Determine from the service manual the type of metal used in the valves.

> **NOTE** 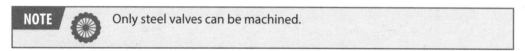 Only steel valves can be machined.

3. Inspect the valve seat contact areas and fill in the chart for:
   A. Excessive grooving
   B. Pitting (especially on exhaust valves)
   C. Margins that are too thin

Record your findings in the chart by placing the matching letter in the column.

	1	2	3	4	5	6	7	8
Intake								
Exhaust								

Check Valve-to-Valve Guide Play

Record the readings in Steps 4 and 5 in the chart.

4. Make sure valves are not bent by checking for runout with a dial indicator.

5. Measure the difference between the valve guide and the valve stem to determine whether the guide and/or valve needs replacement. There are two methods:
   A. Measure the valve when inserted in the guide and subtract the difference. A common method is to install the valve in the guide and check wobble with a dial indicator.
   B. Measure valve stem thickness in three locations, then measure the internal width of its corresponding guide, and subtract the difference. Some service manuals may not give the difference as a specification, but only list the valve thickness or guide diameter.

Intake Valve

	Runout	Valve Stem	Guide	Difference	Specification
Top	—				
Middle					
Bottom	—				

Name _____

Exhaust Valve

	Runout	Valve Stem	Guide	Difference	Specification
Top	—				
Middle					
Bottom	—				

Cylinder Head Warpage

6. Measure cylinder head warpage with a straightedge and feeler gauges.

_____ Maximum warpage

_____ Warpage specification

Measure Cam Lobe Height

7. Use a micrometer to measure maximum cam lobe height on each lobe and record heights below.

Lobe	1	2	3	4
Intake				
Exhaust				

Check Camshaft

8. Measure the camshaft for runout and journal diameter and check for wear and discoloring. Note information on the chart.

	Runout Measured	Runout Specification	Journal Diameter	Wear or Discoloring?
Intake				
Exhaust				

 9. Discuss your measurements so far with your instructor.

Be prepared to discuss the following:

- Magna fluxing.
- Valve lapping.
- Replacing valve stem seals.

Get the instructor's permission to reassemble your cylinder head.

Instructor's Initials: _____

Measure Actual Top Dead Center (TDC)

10. Measure the actual piston TDC of the piston with a dial indicator and compare it to the factory timing mark. Check the box that corresponds to the actual timing mark of the engine.

Before TDC	Correct	After TDC

Measure Crankshaft End Play

11. Measure crankshaft end play by installing a dial indicator on the end of the crankshaft and prying the crankshaft back and forth in the engine. Record the end play.

_____ Crankshaft end play

_____ Crankshaft end play specification

Measure Crankshaft Side Clearance (Split Engines with Cylinders Removed)

12. Use feeler gauges to check the clearance on either side of the connecting rod and record results.

	Side Clearance	Specification
Cylinder 1		
Cylinder 2		

If side clearance is incorrect, what component needs to be replaced?

_____

Measure Connecting Rod Vertical Play (Rod Bearing Play)

13. Measure rod bearing play with a dial indicator installed against the top of the connecting rod at the wrist pin hole.

	Vertical Play	Specification
Cylinder 1		
Cylinder 2		

Name _____

Measure Cylinder Out-of-Round and Taper

14. Measure the cylinder for out-of-round and taper as shown in **Figure 22-8.1** using a cylinder bore tool. Fill out the chart.

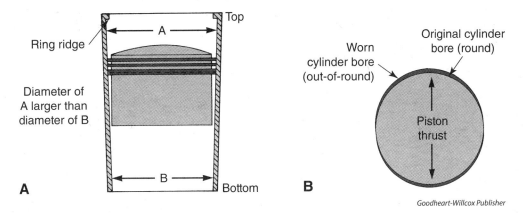

Goodheart-Willcox Publisher

Figure 22-8.1. Cylinder wear. A—Cylinder taper and ridge results from normal wear. A ridge is formed at the end of piston ring travel. The cylinder also becomes larger at the top because there is less lubrication at the top of the cylinder. B—Cylinder out-of-roundness is caused by the piston's thrust.

	Top A	Top B	Out-of-Round (Difference)	Specification
Cylinder 1				
Cylinder 2				

	Top A	Bottom A	Taper (Difference)	Top B	Bottom B	Taper (Difference)	Specification
Cylinder 1							
Cylinder 2							

Check Ring End Gap

15. Measure ring end gap using a feeler gauge as shown in **Figure 22-8.2**. This measurement is used to determine whether the original rings are worn or (with new rings) whether the cylinder is worn.

Goodheart-Willcox Publisher

Figure 22-8.2. Before the end gap can be measured, the ring must be installed squarely in the cylinder. After slipping the ring into the cylinder, use the piston to push the ring a little farther into the cylinder. This will ensure the ring is square in the cylinder. The end gap can then be accurately measured with a feeler gauge.

Ring End Gap A	Specification
Ring End Gap B	**Specification**

Name _____

Measure Ring-to-Groove Clearance

16. Measure ring-to-groove clearance using a feeler gauge as shown in **Figure 22-8.3**. Use a new ring to make the measurment. This measurement will help determine if the piston ring lands are excessively worn.

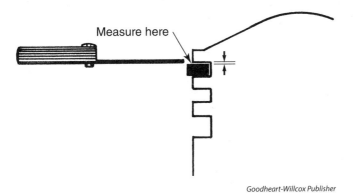

Goodheart-Willcox Publisher

Figure 22-8.3. Ring-to-groove clearance is measured with a feeler gauge. The largest gauge that fits between the ring and groove shows the ring-to-groove clearance.

Ring #1-to-Groove Clearance	Specification
Ring #2-to-Groove Clearance	**Specification**

Measure Piston-to-Bore Clearance

17. Install the piston in the cylinder bore.

18. Use a feeler gauge to determine the clearance between the piston and the bore (cylinder wall).

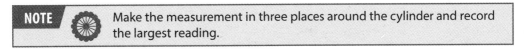

NOTE Make the measurement in three places around the cylinder and record the largest reading.

	Piston-to-Bore Clearance	Specification
Cylinder 1		
Cylinder 2		

Connecting Rod Oil Clearance

19. To make the oil clearance measurement on split bearing connecting rods, perform the following steps:

    A. Place a strip of Plastigage on the connecting rod journal.

    B. Install and tighten the bearing and bearing cap.

    C. Remove the bearing and bearing cap.

    D. Compare the width of the flattened Plastigage with the chart on the Plastigage package.

    _____ Oil clearance

20. If you have an assembled crankshaft, make the following measurements of the crankshaft and assembled parts.

	Cylinder 1	Cylinder 2	Cylinder 3	Cylinder 4
Crank Pin Bearing Wear				
Thrust Washer Side Play				
Crankshaft Runout				

21. Use **Figure 22-8.4** to see the setup for the following measurements to determine if the crankshaft would need to be disassembled and/or replaced.

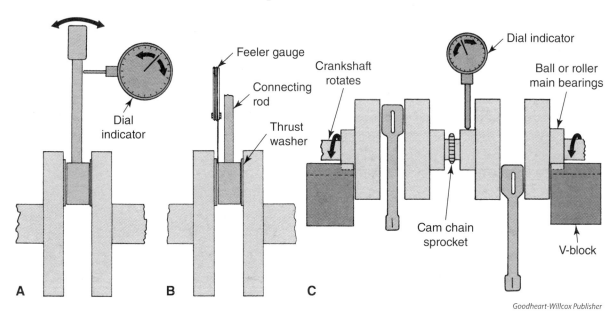

Goodheart-Willcox Publisher

Figure 22-8.4. Measuring an assembled crankshaft. A—Measurement of rod tip determines crankpin bearing and rod big end wear. B—A feeler gauge inserted between the connecting rod and thrust washer measures side play. C—Measurement of crankshaft deflection is accomplished by supporting the crankshaft by its outside ball or roller main bearings. Measure the runout in the center main bearings while rotating the crankshaft.

A. _____ Side play

B. _____ Deflection

C. _____ Runout

STOP 22. Discuss the measurements with your instructor. Be prepared to discuss what parts would need to be replaced or machined. Discuss any measurements that the service manual calls for that are not included in this job.

Instructor's Initials: _____

Name _____

Job Wrap Up

23. Return all tools and materials to the proper storage areas and clean up your work area.

Final Assessment

_____ 1. Two technicians are discussing piston measurements. Technician A says that some out-of-round is normal. Technician B says some taper is normal. Who is correct?

A. A only.

B. B only.

C. Both A and B.

D. Neither A nor B.

_____ 2. Two technicians are discussing engine wear. Technician A says that most cylinder wear is on the thrust surfaces. Technician B says the lack of crosshatching is an indication of cylinder wear. Who is correct?

A. A only.

B. B only.

C. Both A and B.

D. Neither A nor B.

_____ 3. Two technicians are discussing engine oil burning. Technician A says that an engine can burn oil through worn valve guides. Technician B says an engine can burn oil through excessive ring gap. Who is correct?

A. A only.

B. B only.

C. Both A and B.

D. Neither A nor B.

_____ 4. Two technicians are discussing crankshafts. Technician A says, if the journal surfaces look smooth, they can be reused. Technician B says crankshaft journals must be perfectly round with no taper. Who is correct?

A. A only.

B. B only.

C. Both A and B.

D. Neither A nor B.

_____ 5. Two technicians are discussing boring an engine. Technician A says that new pistons will be needed. Technician B says that the same pistons can be used with larger rings. Who is correct?

A. A only.

B. B only.

C. Both A and B.

D. Neither A nor B.

Final Instructor Approval: _____

Notes

Name _____ Date _____ Class _____

Job 22-9

Reassembling Four-Stroke Engines

Introduction

This job involves many procedures that must be accomplished in order to properly reassemble a four-stroke engine. The job begins with cylinder honing and valve lapping.

Honing is done after a cylinder has been bored or to remove glazing from a used cylinder. Honing must be done when new rings are used with an existing cylinder. Valve lapping is done to help seal valves. There are arguments for and against valve lapping.

Objective

After successfully completing this job, you will be able to reassemble a four-stroke engine.

Materials and Equipment

To complete this job, you will need the following tools, equipment, and materials:

- Disassembled four-stroke engine (can be core engine)
- Appropriate service manual or electronic service information
- Cylinder hone
- Valve lapping tool
- Honing and lapping compounds
- Hand tools as needed
- Torque wrench
- Lubricating oil and assembly lube as needed
- Sealant as needed

Instructions

In this job, you will reassemble the engine top end back onto the bottom end. Pay attention to parts that need to be lubricated with oil and surfaces that need to be kept clean for gasket sealing. All of the threads should be tapped and cleaned for ease of reassembly and accurate torquing.

Read the job procedures, perform the tasks, and answer all questions. As you complete steps, you will be given instructions to either fill in measurements or perform certain tasks. When you reach a sign, show your work to your instructor. Do not continue until you have instructor approval (instructor will initial job sheet).

> **WARNING** ⚠ Before performing this job, review all pertinent safety information in the text and discuss safety procedures with your instructor.

Procedures

Consult the service manual and discuss the different cylinder honing and valve lapping options with your instructor. Perform each task and check it off as you complete.

Engine (Year/Make/Model)

_____

1. Hone all cylinders according to procedures outlined by the service manual and your instructor.

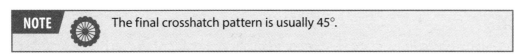

> **NOTE**   The final crosshatch pattern is usually 45°.

2. Lap all valves according to procedures outlined by the service manual and your instructor.

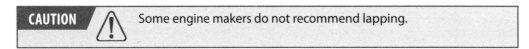

> **CAUTION**   Some engine makers do not recommend lapping.

3. Tap out any bolt holes not already tapped.

4. Clean all parts and make sure that all gasket material has been removed.

Task	Completed	Type of Lube	Torque, if Applicable
Hone cylinders			
Lap valves			
Tap bolt holes			
Clean parts			

 5. Discuss with your instructor the installation procedure so far.

Instructor's Initials: _____

6. Install the crankshaft.

7. Install the balance shafts.

8. Install the transmission if necessary.

9. Install the case halves.

10. Install the pistons on the connecting rods.

11. Install the base gaskets (if used) and install the cylinders over the pistons.

12. Install the head gasket.

Task	Completed	Type of Lube or Sealer	Torque, if Applicable
Install crankshaft			
Install balance shafts			
Install transmission			
Install case halves			

(Continued)

Name _____

Task	Completed	Type of Lube or Sealer	Torque, if Applicable
Install pistons onto connecting rods			
Install cylinder and base gasket			
Install head gasket			

🛑 13. Discuss with your instructor the installation procedure so far.

Instructor's Initials: _____

Cylinder Head Installation

14. Install the valves in the cylinder head(s).

15. Install the cylinder head(s) onto the cylinder(s).

16. Install the camshaft and compression release mechanism, if used.

17. Install the push rods, camshaft, and/or other valve train components as necessary.

18. Adjust the valve clearance.

19. Install the timing chain and tensioner.

20. Install the generator, starter gears, and other electrical components as necessary.

21. Install the clutch and shift mechanisms.

Task	Completed	Type of Lube or Sealer	Torque, if Applicable
Install valves into cylinder head			
Install cylinder head onto cylinder			
Install camshaft and compression release mechanism			
Install valve train components			
Adjust valve clearance			
Install timing chain and tensioner			
Install generator, starter gears, and all other electrical components			
Install clutch and shift mechanisms			

🛑 22. Show your instructor the assembled and properly timed engine and accessory components. Discuss any problems that you had during reassembly.

Instructor's Initials: _____   _____

Job Wrap Up

23. Install engine covers.

24. Return all tools and materials to the proper storage areas and clean up your work area.

Final Assessment

_____ 1. Two technicians are discussing engine reassembly. Technician A says that assembly lube should be used on piston rings. Technician B says that engine oil should be used on piston rings. Who is correct?

    A. A only.

    B. B only.

    C. Both A and B.

    D. Neither A nor B.

_____ 2. Two technicians are discussing engine break-in. Technician A says that the oil should be changed at a sooner than normal interval after break-in. Technician B says that for the first 500 miles, engine rpm should be varied but not rise too high. Who is correct?

    A. A only.

    B. B only.

    C. Both A and B.

    D. Neither A nor B.

_____ 3. Two technicians are discussing engine assembly. Technician A says that, if the head bolt torque specification calls for an extra 90° turn, then torque to yield (TTY) bolts are being used. Technician B says that it is best practice to always replace used TTY bolts. Who is correct?

    A. A only.

    B. B only.

    C. Both A and B.

    D. Neither A nor B.

_____ 4. Two technicians are discussing gasket installation. Technician A says some paper gaskets need silicone bond to help them seal. Technician B says paper gaskets should never be used with silicone bond. Who is correct?

    A. A only.

    B. B only.

    C. Both A and B.

    D. Neither A nor B.

_____ 5. Two technicians are discussing torquing bolts. Technician A says to always use the torque specification and a torque wrench in all cases. Technician B says that on some applications like a rubber gasket, the technician needs a good sense of feel to properly tighten fasteners. Who is correct?

    A. A only.

    B. B only.

    C. Both A and B.

    D. Neither A nor B.

Final Instructor Approval: _____

| CHAPTER | **Power Transmission** |
| 23 | **Overhaul** |

Chapter 23 Quiz

After studying Chapter 23 in the Motorcycles: Fundamentals, Service, Repair textbook, answer the following questions.

_____ 1. A primary chain drive assembly that has been properly maintained usually requires only
_____.
   A. chain replacement
   B. sprocket replacement
   C. sprocket repair
   D. inspection of the chain tensioner

_____ 2. *True or False?* An internal primary chain drive has a shorter service life than an external primary chain drive.

_____ 3. When a clutch cable is too _____, the pressure plate may partially release, causing the clutch discs to slip and wear under heavy loads.
   A. long
   B. loose
   C. tight
   D. worn

_____ 4. *True or False?* Clutch engagement at high engine rpm is a cause of clutch wear.

_____ 5. The clutch basket and bearing wears in the basket fingers, basket cushion, basket center bearing or bushing, and center bearing _____.

_____ 6. All of the following statements about clutch plates are true, *except*:
   A. a friction plate is the same thing as a drive plate.
   B. a driven plate is also called a plain plate.
   C. driven plates are subject to warpage.
   D. friction plates engage with the hub.

_____ 7. *True or False?* Worn clutch drive plates are a common cause of clutch slippage.

_____ 8. To determine the condition of clutch springs, the spring free height, squareness, and spring _____ are measured.

_____ 9. A primary kick-start system directly engages the clutch _____.

_____ 10. The rear unit of a CVT contains all of the following components, *except*:

    A. centrifugal clutch.

    B. rollers.

    C. movable driven face.

    D. guide pins.

_____ 11. When inspecting a variator, the technician should measure the inner _____ diameter for wear.

_____ 12. *True or False?* A drive belt should be taken off the driven and drive pulleys before the driven pulley and clutch assembly are removed.

_____ 13. *True or False?* When reassembling a clutch, the lock washer should be assembled with the concave side in.

_____ 14. *True or False?* When the transmission is locked up, one gear ratio is a false neutral.

_____ 15. Before disassembling the transmission for service or repair, the technician should check the _____ mechanism operation.

_____ 16. Worn gear engagement dogs can cause _____.

    A. binding of the shift mechanism

    B. jumping out of gear

    C. a locked up transmission

    D. None of the above.

_____ 17. Shift fork-to-groove clearance is measured with a(n) _____ gauge.

_____ 18. In a cassette-type transmission, the transmission and cover assembly are inserted into the _____ cavity.

_____ 19. When the transmission is being assembled, _____ compound should be used on all fasteners.

_____ 20. *True or False?* The most common method of chain adjustment is to move the rear wheel and axle.

_____ 21. *True or False?* In order to be adjusted, a chain must be lubricated.

_____ 22. Belt tension is checked with a special tool that applies _____ to the belt.

_____ 23. Ring and pinion _____ is measured by holding the ring gear and measuring pinion gear movement with a dial indicator.

_____ 24. A low oil level can cause _____.

    A. excessive noise in the side gear

    B. excessive noise in the final drive

    C. an oil leak at the final gear case

    D. All of the above.

Name _____ Date _____ Class _____

Job 23-1

Adjusting Clutch Cables

Introduction

Clutch cable adjustment is critical for proper clutch and transmission operation. The technician needs to know how to make proper clutch adjustments and be able to recognize problems that can arise from such clutch cable problems as improper adjustment, stretching, and wear.

Objective

After successfully completing this job, you will be able to adjust a clutch cable.

Materials and Equipment

To complete this job, you will need the following tools, equipment, and materials:

- Vehicle with clutch cable
- Appropriate service manual or electronic service information
- Hand tools as needed
- Cable lube and lubricating tool

Instructions

In this job, you will be adjusting a clutch cable and identifying the effect that a misadjusted cable has on vehicle operation.

   Read the job procedures, perform the tasks, and answer all questions. As you complete steps, you will be given instructions to either fill in measurements or perform certain tasks. When you reach a sign, show your work to your instructor. Do not continue until you have instructor approval (instructor will initial job sheet).

WARNING	Before performing this job, review all pertinent safety information in the text and discuss safety procedures with your instructor.

Procedures

Adjust Clutch Cable

CAUTION /!\	For learning purposes, the student should first operate a motorcycle with a properly adjusted cable to note the feel of a normally adjusted clutch. Operating a motorcycle with a misadjusted clutch can damage the transmission and the clutch.

1. Secure the vehicle properly for service.

2. Locate the clutch cable adjustment procedure and specifications in the service manual.

3. Inspect the cable for any damage:

   _____ Kinked cable

   _____ Frayed cable

   _____ Melted or worn through sheathing

   Other damage or wear:

   _____

   _____

   Explain:

   _____

   _____

4. Check the cable free play.

   _____ Free play specification

   _____ Observed free play

   Is free play within specifications? Yes _____ No _____

5. Adjust cable until there is no free play and check cable operation. Type of adjuster mechanism:

   _____

6. Pull the clutch lever to disengage the clutch, put the transmission in low gear, operate the clutch, and observe the following:

   Was it easy to get into gear? Yes _____ No _____

   Did the clutch engage at the proper point? Yes _____ No _____

   Did the cable feel tighter or looser than before adjustment?

   _____ Tighter

   _____ Looser

7. Adjust the cable until there is too much free play and feel the cable operation.

8. Pull the clutch lever to disengage the clutch, put the transmission in gear, operate the clutch, and observe the following:

   Was it easy to get into gear? Yes _____ No _____

   Did the clutch engage at the proper point? Yes _____ No _____

   Did the cable feel tighter or looser than before adjustment?

   _____ Tighter

   _____ Looser

9. Following service manual instructions, remove the entire cable.

Name _____

10. Determine cable condition.

Does the cable slide smoothly? Yes _____ No _____

Is the cable bent at either end? Yes _____ No _____

Is the cable frayed at either end? Yes _____ No _____

Is any of the retaining hardware damaged? Yes _____ No _____ If yes, explain:

_____

_____

_____

STOP 11. Show the removed cable to your instructor.

Instructor's Initials: _____

12. Obtain cable lubricant and a lubricating tool and properly lubricate the cable.

13. Reinstall the cable and adjust for proper free play.
Does the cable slide smoothly? Yes _____ No _____
Is the cable bent at either end? Yes _____ No _____
Is the cable frayed at either end? Yes _____ No _____
Is any of the retaining hardware damaged? Yes _____ No _____ If yes, explain:

_____

_____   _____

STOP 14. Demonstrate proper clutch cable installation and adjustment to your instructor, including:

_____ Proper procedure and final operation of system

_____ No fluid spills or excess fluid on fasteners

_____ Fasteners tight

Instructor's Initials: _____

Job Wrap Up

15. Return all tools and materials to the proper storage areas and clean up your work area.

Final Assessment

_____ 1. A clutch on a motorcycle is slipping (rpms go very high between shifts and it takes a few seconds for the gears to engage). Technician A says the clutch cable may not have enough free play. Technician B says the clutch cable may be worn. Who is correct?

   A. A only.

   B. B only.

   C. Both A and B.

   D. Neither A nor B.

_____ 2. Technician A says that if the clutch lever is adjusted too loosely (too much free play), the gears could grind from the clutch not being disengaged all the way. Technician B says that if the clutch is adjusted too tightly (not enough free play), the clutch could slip all the time. Who is correct?

   A. A only.

   B. B only.

   C. Both A and B.

   D. Neither A nor B.

_____ 3. Technician A says that a clutch cable can be lubricated while still on the motorcycle. Technician B says that the clutch cable must be removed for proper lubrication. Who is correct?

   A. A only.

   B. B only.

   C. Both A and B.

   D. Neither A nor B.

_____ 4. Two technicians are discussing gear grinding when shifting into gears. Technician A says this can be caused by a stretched clutch cable. Technician B says this can be caused by a clutch cable with too much free play. Who is correct?

   A. A only.

   B. B only.

   C. Both A and B.

   D. Neither A nor B.

_____ 5. Two technicians are discussing lubricating a clutch cable. Technician A says that any spray lubricant can be used, including rust penetrant or silicone spray. Technician B says to use a specialized clutch cable lubricant only. Who is correct?

   A. A only.

   B. B only.

   C. Both A and B.

   D. Neither A nor B.

Final Instructor Approval: _____

Name _____ Date _____ Class _____

Job 23-2

Adjusting Clutch Push Rods

Introduction
Proper clutch push rod adjustment is critical to the performance and safe riding of a motorcycle. Push rod adjustment must be performed in the proper order and accurately. Not all motorcycles have clutch push rods and not all push rods are adjustable.

Objective
After successfully completing this job, you will be able to adjust a clutch push rod.

Materials and Equipment
To complete this job, you will need the following tools, equipment, and materials:
- Vehicle or core engine with adjustable clutch push rod
- Appropriate service manual or electronic service information
- Hand tools as needed, to include various sizes of box end wrenches

Instructions
In this job, you will be adjusting a clutch push rod. The push rod connects the clutch cable actuator and clutch, passing through the engine. Use the service manual to familiarize yourself with push rod adjustment and any special tools or procedures needed prior to performing the task.

Read the job procedures, perform the tasks, and answer all questions. As you complete steps, you will be given instructions to either fill in measurements or perform certain tasks. When you reach a sign, show your work to your instructor. Do not continue until you have instructor approval (instructor will initial job sheet).

> **WARNING** ⚠ Before performing this job, review all pertinent safety information in the text and discuss safety procedures with your instructor.

Procedures

Clutch Push Rod Adjustment

1. Secure the vehicle or engine properly for service.

2. Drain the engine if necessary.

> **NOTE** The push rod is likely above the oil level and the oil may not need to be drained.

3. If you are performing this adjustment on the vehicle, first measure the clutch lever free play.

_____ Free play

_____ Free play specification

4. Using the service manual, follow procedures to loosen the lock mechanism and perform the following adjustments:

   A. Adjust the push rod too tightly and check clutch operation. What effect did this adjustment have on clutch operation?

   _____

   _____

   B. Adjust the push rod too loosely and check clutch operation. What effect did this adjustment have on clutch operation?

   _____

   _____

   _____

5. Discuss push rod adjustment with your instructor.

Instructor's Initials: _____

6. Demonstrate the proper adjustment of the clutch push rod to your instructor, including:

   _____ all fasteners checked for stretching.

   _____ all gasket surfaces cleaned for proper reassembly.

   _____ all fasteners tightened and torqued properly.

   _____ all fluids refilled properly.

Instructor's Initials: _____

Job Wrap Up

7. Return all tools and materials to the proper storage areas and clean up your work area.

Final Assessment

_____ 1. Adjusting a push rod too loosely will cause which of the following?
   A. Clutch will slip.
   B. Clutch will not engage completely.
   C. Clutch will not disengage completely.
   D. Transmission will jump out of gear.

_____ 2. Adjusting a push rod too tightly will cause which of the following?
   A. Clutch will slip.
   B. Clutch will not engage completely.
   C. Gears will grind when shifting.
   D. Both A and B.

Name _____

_____   3. If a clutch push rod is bent, it can cause the _____.
           A. transmission to bind up when shifting
           B. clutch to slip
           C. clutch to not fully engage
           D. All of the above.

4. Why should the push rod adjuster be backed off slightly after bottoming out?

_____

_____

5. If a customer is having a new clutch and cable installed, should the push rod also be replaced?

Yes _____ No _____ Why?

_____

_____

_____

Final Instructor Approval: _____

Notes

Name _____ Date _____ Class _____

Job 23-3

Servicing Multi-Plate Wet Clutches

Introduction

The clutch connects the engine to the transmission and is a major component of the motorcycle powertrain. Clutches are removed and inspected for normal maintenance, diagnostic reasons, and when engine or transmission work is being performed. It is vital that a technician perform clutch service correctly.

Objective

After successfully completing this job, you will be able to service a multi-plate wet clutch.

Materials and Equipment

To complete this job, you will need the following tools, equipment, and materials:

- Vehicle or core engine with multi-plate wet clutch
- Appropriate service manual or electronic service information
- Hand tools as necessary
- Flywheel holding tool
- T-square
- Impact wrench
- Torque wrench
- Vernier caliper or micrometer
- Clutch oil

Instructions

In this job, you will be servicing and inspecting a multi-plate wet clutch and related parts. You will be removing the various parts of the clutch, measuring and reinstalling parts, torquing parts to the correct values, and providing proper lubrication.

Read the job procedures, perform the tasks, and answer all questions. As you complete steps, you will be given instructions to either fill in measurements or perform certain tasks. When you reach a sign, show your work to your instructor. Do not continue until you have instructor approval (instructor will initial job sheet).

> **WARNING** ⚠ Before performing this job, review all pertinent safety information in the text and discuss safety procedures with your instructor.

Procedures

> **WARNING** ⚠ Follow all safety precautions. Secure components safely in a vise when necessary. Take precautions with spring-loaded components.

Clean parts as they are removed and keep parts organized. Assume that an engine contains oil and be prepared to clean up any spills immediately.

Inspect and Remove Clutch

1. Find the service manual for the engine and transmission and determine whether the clutch mechanism is installed correctly.

   Yes _____ No _____ If no, describe:

   _____

   _____

2. Remove the clutch cover (assume there may be oil in the assembly). Describe the clutch release mechanism.

   _____

   _____

   _____

3. Remove the clutch assembly using a flywheel holding tool or lock the crankshaft to the clutch drum.

   > **NOTE** ⚙ Using an impact wrench usually makes holding the flywheel unnecessary.

   > **WARNING** ⚠ The clutch assembly is usually spring-loaded. Take all precautions needed when disassembling a part under spring tension.

   > **NOTE** ⚙ Make sure you keep the components in order and facing the same direction.

Instructor's Initials: _____

4. Take friction disc measurements using a vernier caliper. Fill in the following chart.

Friction Disc	Thickness	Specification
1		
2		
3		
4		

Name _____

5. Inspect plate condition and use a feeler gauge to check for warpage. Fill in the following chart.

Metal Plate	Condition (scored, overheated, other damage)	Warpage	Specification
1			
2			
3			
4			

6. Use a ruler or T-square to measure spring height and warping and fill in the chart.

Spring	Height	Specification
1		
2		
3		
4		
5		
6		

 7. Explain the measurements and any other findings you have with your instructor.

Instructor's Initials: _____

Inspect Clutch Basket and Hub

8. Inspect the clutch basket (sometimes referred to as the clutch inner or clutch drive) by following service manual instructions. Look for finger wear or fracture damage, broken torsional springs, or other items called out by the service manual.

Basket condition:

_____

9. Inspect the clutch hub and related bearings and washers by following service manual instructions. Look for any damage or overheating.

Hub condition:

_____

 10. Review your inspection results with your instructor.

Instructor's Initials: _____

11. Reinstall the clutch components on the engine using the proper procedure as outlined in the service information.

 When the hub is reinstalled on the input shaft of the transmission, a new lock washer should be used.

> **NOTE** During reassembly, pay special attention to the following:
> - All gasket surfaces cleaned before reassembly
> - Clutch plates lubricated properly
> - Clutch hub and basket move smoothly
> - All washers in correct position and facing correct direction
> - All fasteners torqued properly
> - Fully assembled clutch engaged and spring(s) holding the clutch plates and discs tightly together

(STOP) 12. Have your instructor inspect the assembled clutch.

Instructor's Initials: _____

Job Wrap Up

13. Reinstall the clutch cover and add the proper oil if the vehicle will be returned to service.

14. Return all tools and materials to the proper storage areas and clean up your work area.

Final Assessment

1. How often should the clutch discs be replaced?

_____

_____

2. How often should the clutch cable be replaced?

_____

_____

_____

3. What is the difference between a wet clutch and a dry clutch?

_____

_____

4. If a technician finds only one clutch spring to be too short, what should be done to correct the problem?

_____

_____

5. Clutch friction discs are within thickness specification, but the metal plates show signs of bluing and the basket has excessive grooves. Should the technician replace the friction discs also? Explain why or why not.

_____

_____

_____

Final Instructor Approval: _____

Name _____ Date _____ Class _____

Job 23-4

Inspecting Transmissions

Introduction

In this job, you take apart and inspect a motorcycle transmission. Motorcycle transmissions are simple and similar from manufacturer to manufacturer, an advantage for a technician working in a multiline shop. Transmission failures fall into three common categories: shifting issues, noises, and leaks.

Transmissions are often serviced when engines are overhauled, since most motorcycle transmissions and engines are housed in the same case. Familiarization and comfort with working on transmissions is a must for the motorcycle technician.

Objective

After successfully completing this job, you will be able to inspect a transmission.

Materials and Equipment

To complete this job, you will need the following tools, equipment, and materials:

- Motorcycle or core engine with transmission (horizontal split engines are good for this exercise, but not necessary)
- Appropriate service manual or electronic service information
- Hand tools as needed
- Measuring tools as needed

Instructions

For this job, you will be given a transmission to disassemble. Prior to beginning disassembly, you will shift the transmission through all gears.

Read the job procedures, perform the tasks, and answer all questions. As you complete steps, you will be given instructions to either fill in measurements or perform certain tasks. When you reach a sign, show your work to your instructor. Do not continue until you have instructor approval (instructor will initial job sheet).

> **WARNING** ⚠ Before performing this job, review all pertinent safety information in the text and discuss safety procedures with your instructor.

Procedures

Check Shifting with Transmission Assembled

1. Shift the transmission through all gears and answer the following questions:

   A. Does the transmission shift? Yes _____ No _____ If no, explain:

   _____

   _____

   B. How many gears can be accessed? (Hint: It helps to rotate the output shaft while shifting.)

   _____

   C. Does the neutral switch work? (Use a battery, wiring, and a bulb to check operation.)

   _____

🛑 2. Discuss any shifting problems with your instructor prior to disassembly.

Instructor's Initials: _____

Check Internal Transmission Shifting

3. Remove the clutch and shift mechanisms in an orderly fashion (sometimes the clutch assembly can stay in one piece as it is removed).

4. Use the instructions in the service manual to split the case.

5. Before removing shafts from the case, answer the following questions:

   A. How many shafts are used in the transmission?

   _____

   B. How many gears does the transmission have?

   _____

   C. What are the names of the shafts?

   _____

   _____

   D. Are the shafts bolted or splined to the clutch hub or output shaft?

   _____

6. Move the transmission clutch hub with the transmission in neutral.
   List specifically what gears are moving in the transmission:

   _____

   _____

7. Turn the transmission with the output shaft or chain drive with the transmission in neutral and while holding the clutch hub still. List specifically what gears are moving in the transmission:

   _____

   _____

Name _____

STOP 8. Discuss with your instructor why knowing what is turning can help diagnose noises.

Instructor's Initials: _____

Inspect Shafts

> **CAUTION** ⚠ Be aware of bearings that may fall out during disassembly. Refer to the service manual for specific instructions.

9. Remove all shafts.

10. Disassemble each shaft one at a time — do not take apart both shafts at the same time.

> **CAUTION** ⚠ Note the snap ring installation. Snap rings are positioned in specific ways and may have different thicknesses to control lateral thrust.

11. Describe the condition of the gears.

_____

_____

12. Describe the condition of the gear dogs and dog holes.

_____

_____

STOP 13. Discuss with your instructor any damage found and the location of snap rings.

Instructor's Initials: _____

14. Reassemble and lubricate the shaft.

15. Repeat Steps 10, 11, and 12 on the other transmission shaft(s).

16. Note any damage to the other shaft components.

_____

_____

STOP 17. Discuss with your instructor any shaft damage found and the location of snap rings.

Instructor's Initials: _____

18. Install each shaft in the case.

19. Roll each shaft in the case. Does the shaft roll smoothly with no drag?

Yes _____ No _____ If no, explain:

_____

_____

20. Spin the input shaft while shifting through each gear. Observe the power flow.

> **NOTE** ⚙ If the transmission gets stuck in two gears at once, it will not turn.

Inspect Shift Fork and Drum

21. Use a micrometer to measure the thickness of the shift forks (this is often the only specification given in the service manual).

22. Measure shift fork-to-slider gear clearance using a feeler gauge between shift fork and groove on the slider gears.

23. Record the information gathered in Steps 21 and 22 in the chart.

Shift Fork	Thickness	Specification	Clearance	Specification
1				
2				
3				

24. Insert the shift fork nub into the shift drum and make sure that it moves smoothly through the drum. Repeat the process for all shift forks.

25. Note any damage to the star wheel at the end of the drum. Damage? Yes _____ No _____

 26. Discuss the shifting mechanisms and overall transmission operation with your instructor and gain permission to reassemble the transmission.

Instructor's Initials: _____

Reassemble Transmission

27. Reassemble the transmission using the proper lubricant.

 NOTE Ask your instructor if you should use sealer on a core engine. This is a good time to practice using a bond sealer on case halves.

28. Torque fasteners carefully and occasionally turn the shafts as they are reassembled into the case. Make sure all components operate smoothly after reassembly.

 29. Before installing the clutch, show your instructor that you can shift the transmission through all of its gears. Gain permission to reassemble the clutch and engine as necessary.

Instructor's Initials: _____

Job Wrap Up

30. Return all tools and materials to the proper storage areas and clean up your work area.

Name _____

Final Assessment

_____ 1. Two technicians are discussing a transmission noise that is present at idle with the clutch engaged and the transmission in neutral. The noise goes away at idle with the clutch disengaged and the transmission in first gear. Technician A says that the noise is caused by a transmission gear or bearing. Technician B says that the noise could be caused by the clutch hub bushing or bearing. Who is correct?

A. A only.

B. B only.

C. Both A and B.

D. Neither A nor B.

_____ 2. Two technicians are discussing a transmission noise heard at idle with the clutch disengaged and the transmission in first gear. No noise is heard at idle with the clutch engaged and the transmission in neutral. Technician A says the noise is caused by a transmission gear or bearing. Technician B says the noise could be caused by the clutch hub bushing or bearing. Who is correct?

A. A only.

B. B only.

C. Both A and B.

D. Neither A nor B.

_____ 3. Two technicians are discussing a transmission that will not downshift from second to first, but works well in all other gears. Technician A says the clutch cable adjustment should be checked. Technician B says the shifter drum and forks should be checked. Who is correct?

A. A only.

B. B only.

C. Both A and B.

D. Neither A nor B.

_____ 4. Two technicians are discussing a transmission that shifts into all gears except third gear. Technician A says the gear dogs may have broken off third gear. Technician B says the shift fork may have broken. Who is correct?

A. A only.

B. B only.

C. Both A and B.

D. Neither A nor B.

_____ 5. Two technicians are discussing resealing an engine after transmission work. Technician A says to use a brand-new tube of bond as old bond doesn't work as well. Technician B says to make sure you use just enough bond to see the edge of the bond once the fasteners are installed. Who is correct?

A. A only.

B. B only.

C. Both A and B.

D. Neither A nor B.

Final Instructor Approval: _____

Notes

Name _____ Date _____ Class _____

Job 23-5

Servicing Drive Chains

Introduction

Servicing drive chains is a common task for a motorcycle technician. The technician must know how to check for a stretched chain and how to properly service a chain. Proper service is critical to drive chain life.

It is important to note that motorcycle owners often service their own chains and may be highly sensitive to an improperly serviced chain.

Objective

After successfully completing this job, you will be able to service motorcycle drive chains.

Materials and Equipment

To complete this job, you will need the following tools, equipment, and materials:
- Motorcycle with chain drive or core chain
- Appropriate service manual or electronic service information
- Hand tools as needed
- Chain breaker
- Yardstick or similar measuring tool (preferably metric)
- Chain cleaner and brush
- Appropriate chain lubricant

Instructions

In this job, you will be checking chain condition for binding, stretching, and alignment. You will also service the chain and adjust tension and rear wheel alignment.

Read the job procedures, perform the tasks, and answer all questions. As you complete steps, you will be given instructions to either fill in measurements or perform certain tasks. When you reach a sign, show your work to your instructor. Do not continue until you have instructor approval (instructor will initial job sheet).

> **WARNING** ⚠️ Before performing this job, review all pertinent safety information in the text and discuss safety procedures with your instructor.

Procedures

Refer to the service manual for all procedures. Every motorcycle requires specific procedures and tests.

Service Chain

1. Inspect the chain and record your findings in the chart.

	Chain Size	Number of Links	Front Sprocket Teeth	Rear Sprocket Teeth
Installed Chain				
Stock Chain				

2. Determine whether the chain is a stock or aftermarket model.

   _____ Stock

   _____ Aftermarket

3. Check the chain by trying to pull it away from the rear sprocket.

   Does the chain pull away from the rear sprocket? Yes _____ No _____

4. Locate the procedure for measuring chain length (stretching) and the correct number of links for the particular motorcycle.

	Length	Specification
Number of Chain Links		

5. Determine the following things about the chain:

   A. Does the chain have a master link? Yes _____ No _____

   B. Is the master link installed correctly (open end should face toward the back of the bike with the link on top)? Yes _____ No _____

   C. Is this an O-ring chain? Yes _____ No _____

   D. Does the chain show signs of rust or corrosion? Yes _____ No _____

6. Check chain deflection by rotating the chain and using a gloved hand to feel the links for binding. Is deflection the same each time? Yes _____ No _____

   If deflection was different in various spots, what would that indicate?

   _____

   _____

	Current Deflection	Specification
Chain Deflection		

Name _____

Inspect Sprockets

7. Inspect the front and rear sprockets for bent/broken teeth. Problems present?

   Yes _____ No _____

8. Inspect for excessive tooth wear.

Clean and Lubricate Chain and Sprockets

9. Use chain cleaner and a brush to clean the chain (the chain should be warm if possible).

10. Lubricate the chain while turning the wheel slowly.

> **CAUTION** ⚠ Use the proper chain lubricant.

Adjust and Align Rear Wheel

11. Following instructions in the service manual, check and align the rear wheel. (This was covered in Chapter 18, Job 5.) Make sure the rear wheel is aligned perfectly, not just close.

12. Using the procedure outlined in the service manual, adjust the chain to obtain proper free play.

 13. Have your instructor inspect your work. Be prepared to show chain stretching and adjustment measurements and procedures.

Instructor's Initials: _____

Remove Link

14. Remove a link from a chain using a chain breaker.

> **NOTE** ⚙ This is a necessary task. New chains are usually sold with extra links which must be removed. It is helpful to grind off the end of the pin prior to pressing the pin out of the chain.

 15. Discuss replacing new chains with your instructor and show your removed link.

Instructor's Initials: _____

Job Wrap Up

16. Return all tools and materials to the proper storage areas and clean up your work area.

Final Assessment

_____   1. Two technicians are discussing chain service. Technician A says that a stretched chain is a safety concern. Technician B says that a stretched chain can shorten the life of the sprockets. Who is correct?

   A. A only.

   B. B only.

   C. Both A and B.

   D. Neither A nor B.

_____   2. Two technicians are discussing chain service. Technician A says the O-rings keep out dirt. Technician B says the O-rings keep in lube. Who is correct?

   A. A only.

   B. B only.

   C. Both A and B.

   D. Neither A nor B.

_____   3. Two technicians are discussing chain service. Technician A says that if the chain free play is correct, then the alignment will be correct. Technician B says that if the alignment is correct, then the chain free play will be correct. Who is correct?

   A. A only.

   B. B only.

   C. Both A and B.

   D. Neither A nor B.

_____   4. Two technicians are discussing chain free play and alignment adjustments. Technician A says to adjust chain free play first. Technician B says to adjust alignment first. Who is correct?

   A. A only.

   B. B only.

   C. Both A and B.

   D. Neither A nor B.

_____   5. Two technicians are discussing chain service. Technician A says that dirt bikes usually have different free play specifications than street bikes. Technician B says that dirt bikes usually have different sprocket ratios than street bikes. Who is correct?

   A. A only.

   B. B only.

   C. Both A and B.

   D. Neither A nor B.

Final Instructor Approval: _____

Name _____ Date _____ Class _____

Job 23-6

Servicing Belt Drives

Introduction

The motorcycle technician must know how to inspect, adjust, and replace drive belts and pulleys.

A belt must be replaced if it has any damage or shows signs of wear. Belt replacement is recommended at certain service intervals to avoid failure. Not only can belt failure result in a rider being stranded, it can also cause a serious safety concern.

While pulleys last longer than belts, they must be inspected and/or replaced when the belt is changed.

Objective

After successfully completing this job, you will be able to service motorcycle belt drives.

Materials and Equipment

To complete this job, you will need the following tools, equipment, and materials:

- Motorcycle or core with belt drive
- Appropriate service manual or electronic service information
- Hand tools as needed
- Belt tension gauge
- Straightedge

Instructions

In this job, you will be checking a drive belt for proper tension and signs of wear. Then you will remove and replace the belt, inspect the pulleys, and adjust the rear wheel tension and alignment.

Read the job procedures, perform the tasks, and answer all questions. As you complete steps, you will be given instructions to either fill in measurements or perform certain tasks. When you reach a sign, show your work to your instructor. Do not continue until you have instructor approval (instructor will initial job sheet).

> **WARNING** ⚠️ Before performing this job, review all pertinent safety information in the text and discuss safety procedures with your instructor.

Procedures

Consult the service manual for all procedures. Specific tests and procedures will need to be done, and the service manual will assist the technician.

Inspect Drive Belt

Vehicle (Year/Make/Model)

_____

1. Find the recommended drive belt replacement interval in the service manual.

   _____ Interval

2. Find the drive belt condition checklist in the service manual (some vehicles have allowable belt defect tolerances).

3. Determine whether the drive belt shows any signs of damage or wear (rotate the belt all the way around).

   _____ Damage

   _____ No damage

   If there is damage, explain.

   _____

4. Inspect both pulleys for damage or wear.

   > **NOTE** Some pulleys have a light chrome coating that will flake off and damage the belt.

   Do either of the pulleys show signs of damage or wear? Yes _____ No _____ If yes, explain.

   _____

Remove Drive Belt

5. Remove the drive belt according to service manual procedures.

   > **WARNING** Properly support the bike during this procedure.

6. Show your instructor the removed belt and discuss replacement.

Instructor's Initials: _____

Name _____

Install Drive Belt

7. Install and tension the new drive belt according to service manual procedures.

> **CAUTION** ⚠ Use a new cotter pin when required. Use the service manual tensioning specification.

8. Check belt and pulley alignment using a straightedge. Is alignment satisfactory?

   Yes _____ No _____ If no, consult your instructor.

🛑 9. Show your instructor the properly tensioned and aligned drive belt and discuss the final belt tension and wheel alignment procedures.

   Instructor's Initials: _____

Job Wrap Up

10. Return all tools and materials to the proper storage areas and clean up your work area.

Final Assessment

_____ 1. Two technicians are discussing drive belt service. Technician A says that, if a belt is not tensioned properly, it can affect acceleration. Technician B says that, if a belt is not tensioned properly, it can affect deceleration. Who is correct?
   A. A only.
   B. B only.
   C. Both A and B.
   D. Neither A nor B.

_____ 2. Two technicians are discussing drive belt service. Technician A says letters on the belt are usually installed so that you can read them. Technician B says to turn the belt around at 20k miles for longer life. Who is correct?
   A. A only.
   B. B only.
   C. Both A and B.
   D. Neither A nor B.

_____ 3. Two technicians are discussing belt service. Technician A says that if the belt tension is correct, then the alignment will be correct. Technician B says that if the alignment is correct, then the belt tension will be correct. Who is correct?
   A. A only.
   B. B only.
   C. Both A and B.
   D. Neither A nor B.

4. Two technicians are discussing belt service. Technician A says to adjust belt tension first. Technician B says to adjust alignment first. Who is correct?

A. A only.

B. B only.

C. Both A and B.

D. Neither A nor B.

5. Two technicians are discussing belt service. Technician A says that different brands and models have different belt tension specifications. Technician B says all belts are tensioned the same. Who is correct?

A. A only.

B. B only.

C. Both A and B.

D. Neither A nor B.

Final Instructor Approval: _____

Name _____ Date _____ Class _____

Job 23-7

Inspecting Shaft Drives

Introduction

Shaft drives on motorcycles are generally maintenance-free, other than inspecting for leaks and changing final drive gear oil. The shaft drive and final drive bevel gear set can last the life of the motorcycle. If there is a failure, the entire unit is usually replaced. The technician should understand, however, that many of the tasks in this job will be the result of warranty service and non-warranty noise or vibration complaints.

Objective

After successfully completing this job, you will be able to inspect a shaft drive and final drive.

Materials and Equipment

To complete this job, you will need the following tools, equipment, and materials:

- Motorcycle with shaft drive
- Appropriate service manual or electronic service information
- Hand tools as necessary
- Dial indicator, dial torque-o-meter
- Gear marking compound
- Torque wrench

Instructions

In this job, you will be checking runout of several items to make sure they are not the cause of vibration. You will also be rolling and checking a pattern on the final drive gear. Although this procedure is not a common exercise in the modern motorcycle shop, it can help the technician find the cause of a noise complaint.

Read the job procedures, perform the tasks, and answer all questions. As you complete steps, you will be given instructions to either fill in measurements or perform certain tasks. When you reach a  sign, show your work to your instructor. Do not continue until you have instructor approval (instructor will initial job sheet).

WARNING ⚠️ Before performing this job, review all pertinent safety information in the text and discuss safety procedures with your instructor.

Procedures

Use the service manual for all procedures, since there are specific tests and procedures that need to be done. The service manual will greatly assist the technician in safely and efficiently removing the rear wheel and drive shaft from the motorcycle.

Check Wheel Lateral and Radial Runout on Vehicle

1. With the wheel installed on the motorcycle, use a dial indicator to measure rear wheel lateral and radial runout and record.

	Measurement	Specification
Rear Wheel Lateral Runout		
Rear Wheel Radial Runout		

Remove Rear Wheel

2. Make sure that the front wheel is mounted solidly on the lift and that the motorcycle is secured.

3. Remove the rear wheel according to service manual procedures.

Check Rear Axle Runout

4. Install a set of V-blocks and a dial indicator at the rear wheel. Remember to zero the dial indicator.

5. Measure the rear axle runout and record.

	Measurement	Specification
Rear Axle Runout		

Remove Driveshaft

6. Using the service manual, remove the driveshaft from the motorcycle.

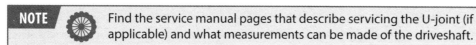
NOTE Find the service manual pages that describe servicing the U-joint (if applicable) and what measurements can be made of the driveshaft.

 7. Discuss the measurements made so far and the possible driveshaft inspections that can be made.

Instructor's Initials: _____

8. Reinstall the driveshaft.

Inspect Final Drive

9. Using a dial indicator, check backlash at the ring gear hub splines (splines that connect to rear wheel) and record.

10. Using a precision dial torque-o-meter, check total preload and record.

Name _____

	Measurement	Specification
Backlash		
Total Preload		

11. Remove the final drive gear case cover bolts and remove the cover.

12. Inspect the ring gear teeth for wear.

13. Inspect the bearings for wear.

14. Inspect the seals for leaks or other damage.

15. Use the service manual procedure and gear marking compound to check the gear tooth pattern. A general procedure is given:

    A. Use the service manual to properly torque the final gear case cover.

    B. Coat the ring and pinion gears with marking compound.

    C. Rotate the pinion gear one turn in each direction while applying slight drag on the ring gear hub splines.

    D. Remove the final gear case cover bolts and inspect the gear tooth pattern on both the drive side and coast side.

	Heel	Toe	Bottom	Top
Drive Side Pattern				
Coast Side Pattern				

    E. From the pattern, determine whether the ring and pinion are properly adjusted. (Some service manuals do not have good pictures of the possible patterns and corrections.) Record your findings on the chart.

 16. Discuss the contact pattern with your instructor.

Instructor's Initials: _____

17. Reassemble the final gear case.

18. Replace the rear wheel.

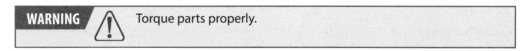

WARNING ⚠ Torque parts properly.

 19. Have your instructor inspect the vehicle and confirm the amount of oil used in the final gear housing.

Instructor's Initials: _____

Job Wrap Up

20. Return all tools and materials to the proper storage areas and clean up your work area.

Final Assessment

_____ 1. Technician A says that excessive lateral runout could be caused by loose rear wheel bearings. Technician B says that excessive lateral runout could be caused by a bent rear axle. Who is correct?

    A. A only.

    B. B only.

    C. Both A and B.

    D. Neither A nor B.

_____ 2. What effect will over-torquing the pinion nut have on total preload?.

    A. It will cause total preload to be higher than the factory specification.

    B. It will cause total preload to be lower than the factory specification.

    C. It would have no effect on total preload.

    D. None of the above. The pinion nut cannot be over-torqued.

_____ 3. Two technicians are discussing torque on the final gear case cover. Technician A says that improper torque will cause improper backlash. Technician B says that improper torque will cause improper ring gear runout. Who is correct?

    A. A only.

    B. B only.

    C. Both A and B.

    D. Neither A nor B.

_____ 4. Two technicians are discussing final gear drives. Technician A says that excessive backlash can cause noise. Technician B says that excessive backlash can cause premature gear failure. Who is correct?

    A. A only.

    B. B only.

    C. Both A and B.

    D. Neither A nor B.

_____ 5. Two technicians are discussing gear ratios. Technician A says that changing from a 4:1 ratio to a 3.8:1 ratio would cause the torque to decrease and the top speed to increase. Technician B says that the torque will increase with no effect on top speed. Who is correct?

    A. A only.

    B. B only.

    C. Both A and B.

    D. Neither A nor B.

Final Instructor Approval: _____

CHAPTER
24

Tune-Up and Periodic Maintenance

Chapter 24 Quiz

After studying Chapter 24 in the Motorcycles: Fundamentals, Service, Repair textbook, answer the following questions.

_____ 1. A(n) _____ is a procedure that returns an engine to peak operating efficiency.

_____ 2. *True or False?* Before performing a tune-up, a complete vehicle inspection should be performed.

_____ 3. If a vehicle owner does not authorize the repair of an unsafe condition, the owner must sign a(n) _____ statement to release the shop from potential liability.

_____ 4. At the beginning of a tune-up or periodic maintenance, the technician should check the ECM for stored _____ codes.

_____ 5. In most cases, an air filter is removed by opening the _____ and removing the old filter.

_____ 6. Before removing and replacing a fuel filter, the technician shuts off the fuel _____ and relieves fuel system pressure.

_____ 7. *True or False?* When distilled water has been added to a battery, the battery should be charged after the specific gravity is checked.

_____ 8. On liquid-cooled engines, the coolant's concentration should be checked with a _____.
   A. refractometer
   B. hydrometer
   C. specific gravity test
   D. Either A or B.

_____ 9. *True or False?* After changing the oil and filter, the throttle cables should be lubricated.

_____ 10. On ATVs and UTVs, tire inflation includes checking the _____ of each wheel and tire combination.

_____ 11. All of the following statements about spark plug replacement are true, *except*:
   A. a spark plug socket, extension, and ratchet are used to remove the plugs.
   B. spark plug replacement is the primary reason for a tune-up.
   C. a spark plug should be started with a torque wrench and then tightened by hand.
   D. after removal, the spark plug tip should be checked for damage or fouling.

_____ 12. A compression test determines how much power each _____ can produce based on compression pressure.

_____ 13. *True or False?* A compression test should be done if a vehicle lacks power during acceleration.

_____ 14. Before testing an electric start model, the technician should _____.
  A. ground all spark plug wires
  B. turn on the engine stop switch
  C. close the throttle valve
  D. All of the above.

_____ 15. A wet compression test involves placing about a(n) _____ of clean engine oil in the cylinders with low compression.

_____ 16. _True or False?_ A leak-down test is a less accurate diagnostic tool than a compression test.

_____ 17. During a cylinder leak-down test, the technician listens at the intake or airbox, _____, and crankcase breather outlet for escaping air.

_____ 18. _True or False?_ Intake and exhaust removal is required to perform two-stroke crankcase pressure testing.

_____ 19. Two-stroke crankcase pressure testing requires _____.
  A. the piston to be positioned at BDC
  B. the crankcase to be pressurized to 6 psi (41 kPa)
  C. using a soap and water solution to find leaks
  D. All of the above.

_____ 20. Contact point gap is adjusted either with a(n) _____ or with a dwell meter.

_____ 21. On engines without timing marks, a(n) _____ is usually needed to measure piston position.

_____ 22. When dynamic ignition timing is performed, _____.
  A. the engine is not running
  B. an ohmmeter is used
  C. a timing light is triggered by ignition operation
  D. a buzz box indicates when contact points begin to open

_____ 23. _True or False?_ Air gap adjustment may be needed on an electronic ignition.

_____ 24. When valve clearance is too _____, valves can overheat.

_____ 25. _True or False?_ Screw valve adjustment requires the cylinder to be brought to BDC.

_____ 26. _True or False?_ On an adjustable push rod engine, the push rod is adjusted until resistance is felt and the push rod can no longer be rotated.

_____ 27. _True or False?_ Carburetor synchronization is affected by valve clearance.

_____ 28. Recommended idle speed adjustments range from about _____ rpm to _____ rpm.

_____ 29. Vehicle storage preparation procedures include all of the following, _except_:
  A. lubricate drive chains.
  B. cover the machine with sheet plastic.
  C. inflate tires to recommended air pressure.
  D. drain the fuel tank and carburetor float bowls.

_____ 30. _True or False?_ Before the unit is returned to service after storage, nuts and bolts should be checked to ensure that they are tight.

Name _____ Date _____ Class _____

Job 24-1

Inspecting Motorcycles

Introduction

Rider safety and dealership reputation depend on accurate motorcycle inspections. The technician must be able to inspect the vehicle quickly and thoroughly and make recommendations to the owner or sales department based on what is needed. Inspections of new and used vehicles lie at the heart of a service department and are tasks that are done all of the time by technicians. Filling out paperwork properly and completely is absolutely critical to the smooth operation of a motorcycle shop.

In this job, you will need a local dealership inspection sheet actually used to perform inspections.

Objective

After successfully completing this job, you will be able to inspect a motorcycle.

Materials and Equipment

To complete this job, you will need the following tools, equipment, and materials:

- Motorcycle
- Appropriate service manual or electronic service information
- Inspection sheet acquired from local motorcycle dealership

Instructions

In this job, you will be using a local motorcycle dealership inspection sheet to inspect a motorcycle.

Read the job procedures, perform the tasks, and answer all questions. As you complete steps, you will be given instructions to either fill in measurements or perform certain tasks. When you reach a sign, show your work to your instructor. Do not continue until you have instructor approval (instructor will initial job sheet).

 WARNING Before performing this job, review all pertinent safety information in the text and discuss safety procedures with your instructor.

Procedures

Vehicle (Year/Make/Model)

_____

Inspection sheet acquired from:

_____

1. Determine whether the frame of the motorcycle is bent. Yes _____ No _____

   Does the inspection sheet have a place to indicate a bent frame? Yes _____ No _____

   > **CAUTION** ⚠️ In most states you cannot continue work on a vehicle if the frame is bent.

2. Fill out the inspection sheet completely.

3. List the services that you would recommend. Start with customer concerns, then safety-related recommendations, then regular maintenance recommendations.

   Customer concerns:

   _____

   _____

   _____

   _____

   Safety-related recommendations:

   _____

   _____

   _____

   _____

   Regular maintenance recommendations:

   _____

   _____

   _____

   _____

   Is there a place to indicate item condition using a red, yellow, or green system (or a similar system)?

   Yes _____ No _____

   Is there a place to indicate the DOT age of the tires? Yes _____ No _____

Name _____

STOP 4. Discuss the inspection sheet with your instructor and whether the sheet had a way to list all concerns.

Instructor's Initials: _____

Job Wrap Up

5. Return all tools and materials to the proper storage areas and clean up your work area.

6. Attach the completed inspection sheet to this job.

Final Assessment

_____ 1. Two technicians are discussing a used vehicle inspection. Technician A says that the tires must be less than ten years old. Technician B says that the tires must not have any age cracks. Who is correct?

A. A only.

B. B only.

C. Both A and B.

D. Neither A nor B.

_____ 2. Two technicians are discussing a used vehicle inspection. Technician A says that a compression test is mandatory to gauge valve condition. Technician B says that if the bike runs, that is good enough for a used vehicle inspection. Who is correct?

A. A only.

B. B only.

C. Both A and B.

D. Neither A nor B.

_____ 3. Two technicians are discussing used vehicle inspections. Technician A says that any out-of-specification adjustments should be corrected. Technician B says that needed adjustments should simply be noted and sold as recommended services. Who is correct?

A. A only.

B. B only.

C. Both A and B.

D. Neither A nor B.

_____ 4. Two technicians are discussing used vehicle inspections. Technician A says that an oil change is usually part of the inspection. Technician B says to always make sure that fluids are full before starting the bike. Who is correct?

A. A only.

B. B only.

C. Both A and B.

D. Neither A nor B.

_____ 5. Two technicians are discussing used vehicle inspections. Technician A says that the condition of plastics and seats is not important. Technician B says to check whether the vehicle has been in an accident, if possible. Who is correct?

   A. A only.

   B. B only.

   C. Both A and B.

   D. Neither A nor B.

Final Instructor Approval: _____